Genderscapes

Genderscapes
Revisioning Natural Resource Management

◆

SUMI KRISHNA

zubaan

ZUBAAN
an imprint of Kali for Women
128 B Shahpur Jat, 1st floor
NEW DELHI 110 049
Email: contact@zubaanbooks.com
Website: www.zubaanbooks.com

First published by Zubaan 2009
First paperback edition 2014
Copyright © Sumi Krishna 2008

10 9 8 7 6 5 4 3 2

ISBN 978 93 83074 75 4

Zubaan is an independent feminist publishing house based in New Delhi with a strong academic and general list. It was set up as an imprint of India's first feminist publishing house, Kali for Women, and carries forward Kali's tradition of publishing world quality books to high editorial and production standards. *Zubaan* means tongue, voice, language, speech in Hindustani. Zubaan is a non-profit publisher, working in the areas of the humanities, social sciences, as well as in fiction, general non-fiction, and books for children and young adults under its Young Zubaan imprint.

Typeset at Tulika Print Communication Services, 35A/1, Shahpur Jat, New Delhi 110 049
Printed at Raj Press, R-3 Inderpuri, New Delhi 110 012

In memory of K.P.S. Chauhan

Contents

GENDERSCAPES

APPENDIX I SIGNPOSTS: ESSAYS

APPENDIX II: KEYWORDS

Acknowledgements

Writing is a solitary activity but the process or research and subsequent publication involves a vast collective effort of professional colleagues, friends and family. A formal acknowledgement is a rather inadequate recognition of this. It is especially difficult to express the extent of my indebtedness to my father K. Sridharan, my late husband Krishna Chauhan, and our son Sandeep Krishna for their love, support and encouragement that has always been there for me in abundant measure. The vicissitudes of feminist publishing and my own preoccupation with other work, which always seemed more urgent, resulted in a rather long hiatus between completing the manuscript and seeing it in print. Krishna followed its course with deep interest and some impatience but passed away just as the MS was finally being typeset. I dedicate this book to his memory and indeed to the struggles of all pro-feminist men.

Over many years of independent work in the field and in the academy, I have interacted with development practitioners, activists and researchers, students and scholars, accumulating debts to individuals and institutions, too numerous to name. I do, however, wish to thank Mina Swaminathan, the Uttara Devi Centre for Gender and Development and field staff of the M.S. Swaminathan Research Foundation (MSSRF), Chennai, for the interactions and workshops that gave me the space to pursue my ideas; the faculty and staff of the Centre for Women's Development Studies (CWDS), New Delhi; my colleagues and friends in the Indian Association for Women's Studies (IAWS); the Centre for Interdisciplinary Studies in Environment and Development (CISED), Bangalore; the Centre for Education and Documentation (CED), Bangalore; participants of the informal e-group 'jivika' for livelihood and gender equity; and especially all the contributors to my edited volumes for long conversations and stimulating exchanges.

Here, I would also like to identify the background to each of the chapters (with more details in chapter 1 and in the notes to specific chapters). Some elements of the discussion in chapters 3 and 10 have evolved from earlier versions in sections of my Introduction to *Livelihoods and Gender: Equity in Community Resource Management* (Sage: 2004). Chapter 4 draws partly upon my experience, thanks to Prof. C.R. Babu, on the guest faculty of the University of Delhi's Master of Science course in Environmental Biology, and on interactions with field scientists from different organizations. Earlier versions were presented in March 2004 at a conference on 'Women in Science: The Glass Ceiling' organized by the National Institute of Science, Technology and Development, New Delhi, and in informal talks at the Centre for Science and Environment, New Delhi, and Alochana, Pune. Chapter 5 is based on an unpublished study that I undertook in 2003 in collaboration with R. Indira of Mysore University and Jayand H. Derekar, which was inspired and supported by Devaki Jain, Bangalore. Some sections of Chapter 6 draw upon studies done for MSSRF, Chennai, which were covered in my overview 'Gender and Biodiversity Management' in *Gender Dimensions in Biodiversity Management* (Konark: 1998) and in an unpublished paper 'Involving Women, Ignoring Gender' (1999). Much of the research in Chapter 7 was done under the Uttara Devi visiting Fellowship, 2004, and first presented as a keynote paper at a seminar at the regional center of the Indian Council of Agricultural Research in Umiyam, Meghalaya. A considerably shortened version appeared in the *Economic and Political Weekly* Vol XL No 25. Part of one section of Chapter 8 takes forward work done as an external collaborator with CWDS, published as a chapter in *Shifting Sands*

(Stree: 2000) and revisited in my monograph *Globalization, Livelihoods and People's Development Choices* (Hivos: 2004). An earlier version of one section of Chapter 9 was presented in 2003 at a seminar on participatory governance organized by the Singamma Sreenivasan Foundation, Bangalore, and UNDP, Delhi. Most of the 'Signpost' essays and notes have appeared earlier; their sources are given at the end of the Singposts section; every effort has been made to seek the relevant permissions for reprinting.

And finally, I owe thanks to Urvashi Butalia for nudging me into academic publishing many decades ago, and to her and everyone at Zubaan for being so much more than just publishers!

SUMI KRISHNA
Bangalore, September 2008

INTRODUCTION

1

The Personal, Political and Professional

> I began to have an idea of my life, not as slow shaping of achievement to fit my preconceived purposes, but as the gradual discovery and growth of a purpose which I did not know.
>
> —Joanna Field.[1]

LOOKING BACK THROUGH A GENDERED LENS

The management of natural resources has for long been viewed only through developmental and technocratic lenses. This has been challenged by sections of both the environmental and women's movements, though not necessarily for the same reasons, or indeed together. In the early 1970s, when I first became involved in the field of rural development, 'women and the environment' was an emerging area of concern within the broader developmental arena. It was recognized that issues related to the conservation, use and sustainability of natural resources were inseparable from the conflict of interests between different groups of people and that economic development had a differential impact on women and men. At that time, however, the tendency was to see women as a homogenous category and as victims of environmental degradation. Interventions were simply aimed at alleviating women's drudgery or using women's labour in environment-development programmes. The dimension of gendered power relations within families, communities, traditional and new institutions was missing in research, policy and programme activities.

Following sustained pressure from the the nineteen eighties saw the emergence of women's studies centres being established both as autonomous organizations and within a few Indian universities. 'Gender studies' evolved later and has moved beyond this base although one critique of it has been that it is more academic than women's studies and that it lacks the political thrust of the global women's movement. In the Indian subcontinent, this critique is possibly less relevant because gender studies has been largely unfettered by academia. The disciplinary initiative has remained with activists, independent researchers and autonomous action-research groups whose core strengths derive from an engagement with women's lived experience in specific contexts. Gender studies has been relatively non-hierarchical, with an immense diversity of practitioners many of whom do not have either institutional affiliations or formal qualifications as 'gender specialists'. While gender studies has largely drawn upon the concepts and ideas of European and American socialist-feminist approaches, it is not a simple western transplant into Indian soil and is perhaps characterized by greater ideological inclusiveness. Its exponential growth as a new area of knowledge has been possible because of its porous boundaries and eclectic encroachment upon other disciplines, owing allegiance to none. This makes for more creativity, and to my mind greater professional relevance.

Many diverse aspects of human life and livelihoods have been enlightened by gender studies, and the interface with Natural Resource Management (NRM) is a particularly exciting area of research and action. Yet, it was only after the mid-1980s that the need for 'integrating' a gendered perspective began to gain wider recognition in environment-development policy and programmes. In the nearly three decades since then, theory and praxis have grown swiftly with new concepts, methods and tools facilitating the blurring of lines between research and action, scholarship and application.

Over the years my own work has been both reflective of and related to the trends in a wider professional and political arena. For the women's movement in India, the mid-1970s marked something of a watershed. *Towards Equality*, the ground-breaking 1974 Report of the Committee on the Status of Women in India, convincingly showed that the Indian State had not fulfilled the Constitutional commitment to gender equality. This and the UN's International Year for Women, 1975, provided the impetus for a more extensive academic, media and policy focus on the condition and position of women. The Indian Council of Agricultural Research marked the year by a special issue of its journal *Indian Farming* on women in agriculture. I was invited to contribute an article on Chhatera, a village in Haryana state with which I had been associated for some years. 'our Village Chhatera' was a fortnightly column started in 1969 by *The Hindustan Times* (a daily newspaper published in New Delhi), to open a window on rural India. This was a pioneering effort at a time when such writing was entirely unknown in the English language press. I began my research for the article by analysing more than 150 reports (including my own) in the village series, and I soon realized how easily, even with the best of intentions, rural women's work could be rendered invisible. As I wrote then (see 'Signpost' S1), 'My instinct told me women were there, so did my observation. You could see them bringing in fodder for the cattle, cutting grass or tough stalks of *jowar* [sorghum], carrying these loads over slippery field bunds. Yet this was a role that rarely got reported, a role that all the men and women in our team had perhaps deemed not even worth reporting.' Indeed, even *Towards Equality* had not paid much attention to village women's natural resource-related responsibilities, such as collecting fuel for the family hearth and fodder for cattle.

At the time of the United Nations Conference on the Human Environment at Stockholm in 1972, environmental and natural resource concerns were widely perceived as elitist and irrelevant for a poor 'developing' country like India. This began to change with the Chipko movement in the western Himalayan region of Garhwal, (now part of Uttarakhand state). In the early 1970s, small groups of hill women and men had protested against the Forest Department allowing non-local contractors to fell trees for industrial and commercial purposes, even as local cooperatives were refused permission to extract even small timber for local village needs, such as for agricultural implements. One woman declared that she would rather embrace the trees 'as a mother hugs her child to her breast to save it from the tiger's wrath' than let outside contractors have access to them. This gave the movement its creed of non-violent protest and the name Chipko, which in Hindi means to cling to or hug, a rough translation of the Garhwali word *angwaltha* to embrace. In early 1975, when I visited the area and wrote about the struggle, it was still little known outside the region although it had been reported in the local Hindi press and mentioned in scientific gatherings. For many, including myself, the Chipko struggles altered the parameters of environmental concern by forcing our attention to the natural resource base of development. Subsequently, Chipko was to be celebrated somewhat simplistically as an environmental icon and as a quintessentially women's movement, obscuring the complexities of the region's economic history and the prevailing male-dominated structure of social relations, which shaped both the manner and the course of the protest. It is all too easy to romanticize the role of women in environmental activism (see S3), as has happened with Chipko, but women (even Chipko women) are not a homogenous group and their environmentalism does not necessarily impact on their position in the household and community.

In later years, environmentalists began to highlight issues related to community control and management of natural resources, especially forest-based resources, but women's concerns were generally seen as a subset of problems specific to agriculture, forests, energy, water and so on. During 1980-81, I travelled extensively through interior forest areas across the country, including northeastern India and what are now the states of Jharkhand and Chhatisgarh in central India, researching 'forest-people' issues. My articles about the conflicts between forest dwellers and the State over development, forestry and wildlife conservation in central India were swiftly published, widely circulated internationally and drew the attention of the Planning Commission of India. Despite this interest, it was difficult to generate concern for the adivasi women who gathered and sold tussar silk cocoons in the village *haats* (local markets) of Jharkhand and were being regularly exploited by non-adivasi middlemen (see S2). More than one editor told me that such a story was not 'sexy' enough, journalistic shorthand for lacking readership interest.

Soon thereafter, I joined the International Institute for Environment and Development, London, and was involved with habitat-related issues, specifically water, sanitation and health in what we then called the 'Third World' (Asia, Africa and Latin America). There was much international concern about poor rural women who had to fetch water from distant sources and admiration of local women's initiatives in community health care. At one high-powered meeting in western Europe early in the World Water and Sanitation Decade (1981-90), I was conspicuous as the only 'Third World' woman present. But when I tried to raise the issue of rural sanitation as a gender concern, I was told curtly that in Europe it was impolite to discuss such matters in public! International agencies were only interested in the 'picturesque' problems, fed by visual images of long lines of 'Third World' women carrying headloads of firewood or pots of water. Moreover, development practitioners, environmentalists and the media, who were apparently 'pro-women', were resistant to acknowledging the patriarchal exploitation and subordination of women. As I wrote later (see S5), 'Viewing women as environmental victims is a comfortable position for middle class, city-based, male environmentalists. (It is also a comfortable position for middle class urban female environmentalists.) Championing the cause of poor rural women does not affect the patriarchal pattern of their lives, because the women in their own households do not have to perform tasks such as fetching water or gathering fodder and fuelwood. So too, seeing 'Third World' women as victims of developmental and environmental stress, makes it easier for Western environmentalists to advocate gender equality, without examining their own biases too deeply.'

It was not till the late 1980s that a critical perspective on women's environmental concerns was advanced. Among the early studies was the research of Walter Fernandes and Geetha Menon (1987) on forest issues in central India, and the work of Bina Agarwal (1988) on wood stoves. Their material strand of analysis was, however, quickly overtaken by a different perspective that emerged when India's first feminist publishing house, Kali for Women, published Vandana Shiva's *Staying Alive* in 1988, followed by *Ecofeminism* (co-authored with Maria Mies) in 1992. Ecofeminist views had been advocated in the subcontinent earlier by Chhaya Datar and others but Shiva's sharper articulation and Kali's professional promotion of the work gave these views a much higher profile. Drawing upon the deep ecology and the radical feminist movements, ecofeminism vaults over many sectors, concentrating on what are seen as underlying and cross-cutting issues. Despite its singular contribution in viewing women as environmental managers, ecofeminism is politically conservative, veering towards a deterministic and rather essentialist approach to women's nature and women's relationship with nature. Shiva's view of Asian women's diverse interactions with their local environments and natural resources has been critiqued as idealized and remote from the complex realities on the ground by many researchers including Bina Agarwal (1992), Govind Kelkar and Dev Nathan in *Gender and Tribe* (1992, also published by Kali), myself in reviews of the book (see S4) and later in *Environmental Politics: People's Lives and Development Choices* (1996), and by others. This critique, however, does not seem to have made much impression on scientists and technocrats. That one can be concerned about the gender dimensions of natural resource management, and yet distance oneself from ecofeminist ideas, is a distinction that continues to require explanation and elucidation in the NRM field.

Since the early 1990s, other difficulties have come to the fore: the need to establish linkages between the changes taking place in macro-economic policies and local-level impacts on the natural environment and on women. In 1994-95, in collaboration with the Centre for Women's Development Studies in Delhi, I undertook a preliminary study of the impact of India's structural adjustment programme on women and the environment. I started by trying to understand the linkages between poverty, environmental stress and basic needs, and attempted to extend the conceptualization of women's household work to their roles in conservation. I felt that it was necessary to bring the community into the scope of gendered analysis because it is the interaction of households in the community that establishes access and use of available natural resources; at the same time the tendency to romantizise the gender egalitarianism of traditional societies needed to be resisted. I also argued that there were lessons to be drawn from the downside of the Green Revolution in assessing the environmental and social costs of the impact of international trade and biotechnology on agro-biodiversity and on the position of women. (Krishna 2000)

In the course of reviewing literature for that study, I saw that the hiatus between disciplines was very striking. On the one hand, historical and gender studies in South Asia had largely neglected ecological issues (apart from some activist-research on the gender bias in Joint Forest Management (JFM) and a few sociological studies on women and water/wasteland management). On the other hand, social ecology and conservation science had grown swiftly but gender was almost entirely ignored. Indeed, the technology and science of natural resources are deeply gender resistant. Within academic institutions, there have been very few efforts to overcome the disciplinary divide apart from a small initiative is the University of Delhi's post-graduate M.Sc. Environmental Biology course for life-science students. This pioneering course includes a modest social science component, drawing upon the disciplines of sociology, socio-cultural anthropology, economics and law. Serving on the guest faculty, my task was to introduce students to the social and gender aspects of conservation and development. During the years (1996-2001) that I was involved with this course it became increasingly apparent that our educational system, which streams 16-year-old students into science immediately after secondary school, provides little mental training to deal with the relevant social science concepts and issues. It often seemed to me that these bright post-graduate students of science had to catch up with more than two decades of social debate, unlearning firmly ingrained attitudes, methods of analysis and modes of communication.

Also in the 1990s, with the UN Convention on Biodiversity (CBD) providing the impetus, new approaches to conservation and sustainable resource management were being explored at the level of both policy and programme implementation. In 1997, the M.S. Swaminathan Research Foundation (MSSRF), Chennai, with the Food and Agricultural Organisation (FAO) in Bangkok, took the lead in field studies and reviews of the gender dimensions of biological and agro-biological diversity. As an independent adviser, I co-ordinated a team of MSSRF researchers in the first of such studies that covered several Indian states (Swaminathan ed. 1998). During this and a subsequent review of studies on gender and biodiversity in the South Asian region, it was evident that the concept of gender was inadequately understood and fuzzily implemented in conservation and agro-biodiversity policy and programmes, resulting in using women's knowledge and skills in an instrumental way, it was for this reason that my synthesis report was titled 'Involving Women, Ignoring Gender', (Krishna 1999). This was further substantiated in a study of gender relations in the rice farming systems of north-eastern India that I undertook in late 2004 (Krishna 2005b).

For some six years from 1997, I was also involved both formally and informally in helping MSSRF scientists and social scientists find ways to incorporate gender concerns in their work in field sites. These projects, in ecologically and culturally varied locations in southern and eastern India, were related to natural resource conservation and sustainable livelihoods for the poor. Equitable access to benefits was a critical aspect of the work. This is, of course, much easier proclaimed than achieved, and I was plunged into the difficult process of 'mainstreaming' social and gender concerns when I was invited to design and facilitate what eventually became a series of workshops for project staff. The interaction with these professionals, almost all of them young men, has been particularly valuable. Nudging others to interrogate the processes of socialization and the social constructions that have shaped their identities, perceptions and professional knowledge bases, requires a considerable degree of self-reflection as well and this helped me to a more nuanced understanding of how gender operates at the level of individuals, institutional structures, policies and project interventions in the field.

Since the early 1980s, community participation and management have been the proclaimed (although not implemented) central tenets of resource management. In the 1990s, the focus shifted to community rights, which were given legitimacy both by the

international Convention on Biological Diversity and the Constitutional changes in India that furthered political decentralization
through the rural panchayats and the urban local bodies (the 73rd
and 74th amendments). Many scientists and practitioners acknowledge that community rights need to be recognized in the management of watersheds, forests, biodiversity and other natural resources, but they are reluctant, sometimes even hostile, to opening up the community in terms of class, caste, gender and age.
My concern has been that the new and emerging environmental
rights, as in wasteland and watershed development, cannot be
separated from the gender and caste biases in old rights to land
and equal wages and that not recognizing this is to further male
domination in resource management. I attempted to address this,
in collaboration with CWDS, at the Indian Association for
Women's Studies (IAWS) Conference on 'Women's Perspectives
on Public Policy' (Hyderabad: January 2000). The sub-theme on
gender and community rights in NRM drew very rich, diverse
and nuanced contributions and eventually resulted in the edited
publication, *Livelihood and Gender: Equity in Community Resource
Management* (2004). In the Introduction to this work, I put forward the concept of a 'genderscape' as a way of envisioning, interpreting and representing the complex and dynamic inter-linkages
between gender and natural resources. The collection reflected
the complexities of the issue and pointed to the disturbing conclusion that, despite remarkable gains, the struggle against the
subordination of women is a continuing process.

The interactions that led to putting together *Livelihood and
Gender* was especially satisfying because this 'project' was entirely
unfunded and was sustained only by the commitment of all those
concerned. In a market-oriented age, when all transactions are
monetised, this is a small indication that some idealism, joint
endeavour and voluntary effort can produce results. One offshoot
of this has been the setting up of an electronic list serve, called
jivika, concerned with natural resource-based livelihoods and gender equity. The exchanges on this e-group, with members from
South Asia and beyond, have taken forward the discussions on
many of the issues in *Livelihood and Gender* and opened up new
areas of concern and enquiry.

The issue of resource rights is at the heart of the globalization debate. In 2004, I revisited some of the questions with which I had been concerned, the linkages between natural resource policies at the macro level and people's lives in micro contexts, questions of democratization, decentralization and entitlements, and ways to keep women's subordination in focus within these larger frameworks. These concerns were also reflected in a monograph *Globalisation and People's Development Choices*, undertaken for Hivos (Humanist Institute for Co-operation with Developing Countries). This report drew on my earlier work and on current dialogues on livelihoods and the natural resource environment. A wide spectrum of people's struggles and civil society action have attempted to forge alliances against the forces of economic globalization. Even as these efforts continue, it is difficult to envisage how contradictions between the various struggles themselves, and between them, political parties and the State will play out. The question of what citizenship actually means for poor, marginalized women (whose survival with dignity is linked to natural resource-based livelihood rights) drew me once again to the forum of the Indian Association for Women's Studies (IAWS), coordinating a sub-theme on citizenship, livelihoods, work and natural resource rights at the IAWS Conference on 'Sovereignty, Citizenship and Gender' (Goa: May 2005). The exchanges among activists, development practitioners, students and academics with varied disciplinary backgrounds and conflicting ideologies, have been particularly stimulating (see Krishna (ed) 2007).

During the last few years, I have also had the opportunity to interact (formally and otherwise) with a range of different organizations in southern India working with rural women towards gender equity and political participation. Many of these efforts are directed specifically and primarily at empowerment: challenging gender stereotypes, enhancing women's self-esteem, articulating women's voices, seeking political spaces and so on. At a personal level, some of the rural women's groups have an inspirational impact reminiscent of the early years of the Chipko struggle. The philosophical and feminist underpinning of many of those working with poor women is that enhanced livelihood options and economic strengths will come in the wake of collective socio-political education and empowerment. This is in contrast both to Chipko's early livelihood focus and the approach of many formal institutions/organizations, which prioritize natural resource-based livelihood interventions and take for granted that empowerment will then follow. Since the year 2000, with the new national policy focus on Self Help Groups, SHGs have proliferated across the country, riding piggy-back upon the empowering effects of women's collectivity and hoping that micro-credit will expand livelihood options. The experience in southern India in particular has been that regardless of the livelihood effect, the very action of coming together in a public forum has an almost 'magical' impact on enhancing women's *dhairiam* (courage) and self esteem. The challenge, however, continues to be how to develop and strengthen the linkages between organizational interventions that empower and technical interventions that seek to advance livelihoods.

Over the years, it also became clear to me that methodology for the field could not be developed without taking the conceptual debates forward, and that 'doing gender' in the field could not be dissociated from the internalizing of a gender perspective within organizations and by individuals. Mainstreaming gender in a project does not simply mean shoving in another piece in an NRM jigsaw. Mainstreaming is not necessarily empowering unless the course of the mainstream of development and resource management is itself re-aligned. Moreover, gender concerns need to be both intuitively perceived and rationally analysed. The methodological issue of using the 'master's tools' to 'dismantle the master's house' has also remained a nagging question. This is not simply a matter of how to (or even whether to) meld conventional and participatory tools, qualitative and quantitative information, but also involves questions of how 'we' represent 'them', how we deal with relations between the researcher and the researched and with the often-messy interfaces of the personal, political and professional in our lives. (see S9)

All of these varied interactions and collective experiences are reflected in this book. While it is framed by my own personal interests and political positions, these have themselves been shaped by the wider political and professional milieu in which I have lived and worked over the last thirty five years. I did not plan to specialize in 'gender and environment development'; it was rather, as in the epigram at the start of this Introduction, a 'gradual discovery and growth of a purpose', which grew out of an involvement with social and environmental issues from a young age. Disciplinary boundaries have also not seemed 'real' to me. Perhaps, this was because I moved out of a formal academic position very early; or perhaps it was due to (or despite!) my early immersion in two different arenas of biology and literature. Nor have I been comfortable with distinctions between scholarship, project interventions and advocacy, all of which seem to me necessary aspects of one's life and work. Researching and documenting the oppressive power relations that underlie patterns of social and gender inequity requires an empathetic engagement with the 'noise and chaos' of people's lives as they are lived; so too attempts to intervene, or struggles against inequitable resource use, require the analytical insights and understanding gained from reflective scholarship.

Environmental Politics

Genderscapes is conceptually linked to my earlier work *Environmental Politics: People's Lives and Development Choices* (1996) and it may be useful, therefore, to briefly sketch some aspects of that work. Starting from the position that human beings are a part of nature, the above study analysed some key aspects of the debate on the direction and content of environmentalism in India. Three broad environmental approaches were identified—popular, managerial and progressive—depending mainly on different characterizations of the environmental crisis. These approaches were then related to some of the unresolved conflicts between people, technology and resources. The study went on to highlight a pervasive tendency to symbolism and rhetorical flourishes, on the one hand, and the neglect of social structures, processes, and intermediate levels of technology and decision-making, on the other. In conclusion, and with particular reference to India, four areas of concern were delineated. First, that environmental approaches are limited because environmentalists share ideological roots with the very paradigms that are sought to be changed. Second, that environmentalists are little concerned with the establishment of de-

centralized institutions. Third, that the people's rights and capacities to determine for themselves the course of change have
been largely overlooked. And fourth, that environmentalists have
little idea about how to generate a mass base of the necessary
shared values. Thus, I wrote (Krishna 1996: 269): 'At present,
environmentalism does not seem to offer an alternative strategy
for human development. Perhaps, it is environmentalism that we
need to redirect. Maybe the real question is about evolving a new
environmental perspective.' *Genderscapes* takes forward the concern for an alternative environmental perspective through a more
explicit focus on the crosscurrents of gender and NRM.

Environmental Politics discussed the gendered role of tradition, caste and community; touched upon women's access to resources and markets, and their power to make decisions; it also
critiqued theories of the biological basis of all social behaviour, the
relation between caste divisions and ecological sustainability, and
the homogeneity of local communities. I have held that the ideology that sees biology as the essential determinant of social divisions is contrary to the evidence and makes for dangerously divi-
sive politics. If humane qualities of nurturance and caring for nature are seen as being rooted in women's reproductive capacities,
as is advocated by a wide spectrum of environmental approaches,
the problematic corollary is that men are incapable of such knowledge and nurturance. I have also argued against the position that
the caste-based Indian social order has been exclusively shaped by
adaptive responses to ecological niches rather than by socio-economic and political factors. Such a position cannot explain the
social and gender oppressiveness of caste, and the family and kinship system with which caste has been so intimately intertwined.
This is evident in constructions of masculinity and femininity,
and in the traditional norms that have sought to control the sexuality, mobility and independent agency of many sections of Indian women. And further, I have also held that the picturesquely
seductive image of India's unchanging, self-contained village communities is naive and ahistorical. This imagined landscape, which
was shaped in colonial times by foreign anthropologists and Indian nationalists, now serves as a powerful symbol for eco-activ-
ists. The seeming environmental equilibrium of pre-colonial In-

dia, based on the social harmony of traditional communities, obscures processes of change that were already underway as also the oppression of powerless and subordinate groups within them, including women. Changes in people's lifestyles and occupations over time may entail losses but that does not mean that women should be locked into traditional systems of resource use that are maintained through their drudgery and subordination.

Framed by these positions, *Genderscapes* seeks to understand the persistence of gender bias in the management of natural resources despite seemingly greater recognition for gender equity at the academic, policy and project levels. Three major trends during the last decade lend urgency to this task: First, the swift spread and penetration of global economic and information networks into every area of activity from resource management to gender relations, telescoping the time available for systematically suppressed groups to respond. Second, the fragmentation of peoples' rights as new areas of concern in the natural resource field are being demarcated and legislated upon through international agreements, national law, and new institutions, submerging gender concerns, reinforcing or even creating new gender-biases. Third, the increasingly utilitarian approach to 'integrating' some gender parameters into natural resource policy, programmes and projects side-by-side with an unwillingness to explicitly consider the power relations of gender in social analysis and project implementation. All of this also raises methodological, and I believe significant ethical, issues about the questions that need to be researched and the kinds of methods used.

ABOUT THIS BOOK

In many parts of India today poor people are engaged in protracted struggles to safeguard their local natural resources against the onslaught of the state and corporate interests. Activists ask whether, in such tortuous times as these, gender matters. While sharing and supporting the concerns of these struggles, I believe that gender-power issues cannot be postponed to a future when other campaigns have been won. My purpose in this book is to enhance understanding of why gender-bias persists in NRM, despite policies and programme interventions that appear to be geared towards women's concerns. My concern is not with any particular natural resource but with the linkages between socialized attitudes, disciplinary knowledge, policy approaches and institutional practice.

Among those engaged in action-research, as also professionals stepping across disciplinary boundaries, there is clearly a need for mapping the ground that needs to be traversed. This book is a response to this felt need. My intention was not to write an academic treatise or a manual on gender and NRM but to elucidate concepts and approaches, highlight certain issues, chart possible routes for graduate students, young professionals and field workers, particularly young scientists, who are working in NRM programmes and want to incorporate a socially sensitive gender perspective in their work and their lives. There are many gender training manuals and toolkits which are used mechanically, tables are filled in, checklists ticked off. This does not help young professionals to internalize a gender perspective, grapple with concepts and issues at different levels, and develop approaches, methods and tools that are appropriate to their own specific contexts. What seems to be necessary is a deeper process of exposure, interaction, reading and reflection. My endeavour in this book is to contribute to such a process, starting with this introductory chapter where I have traced my own personal, professional and political path. The book overall is about issues that have concerned me for many years.

It consists of three 'divisions': the main text (made up of ten chapters); a set of accompanying 'Signposts'; and a glossary of 'Keywords'. The chapters are structured in four interlinked (and somewhat overlapping) parts, which I have called: Wordscapes, Workscapes, Actionscapes and Genderscapes. The postfix 'scapes' is used to reflect the many-layered spread and dynamic complexity of concepts and terms of discourse (that is, *words*), ethnographic accounts of women's life-worlds (their *work*), and research, policy and programme interventions (*actions* that elucidate or have an impact upon livelihoods).

'Wordscapes' consists of three chapters which are concerned with ways of talking and seeing. Chapter 2 on gender-power relations clears the ground for those who are new to gender studies by introducing some necessary concepts and terms, and also discusses the contentious issue of how differences between the sexes are socially perceived. Chapter 3 deals with the gender implications of different developmental perspectives and approaches to women in the environmental domain; in the Indian context, I have categorized these as Conventional, Celebratory and Gendered. Chapter 4 concentrates on the neglected area of gender bias embedded in the language, imagery and theories of the natural and life science disciplines; it suggests that this influences practices and needs to be recognized and resisted.

The three chapters that comprise 'Workscapes' are mainly 'notes from the field' that attempt to depict aspects of the 'reality' of women's lives on the ground. Chapter 5 draws upon a collaborative study in which I, along with a small team,[2] explored the caring practices of women forest-dwellers in the Western Ghats. By listening to the 'voices' of the women themselves, the study represents and articulates women's roles in nurturing their families and the natural environment. This shows that women's caring practices are located in a socio-cultural and political context, and by implication refutes the ecofeminist thesis of women being intrinsically caring and having a natural spiritual link to nature. Chapter 6 is based on my own work and that of other researchers[3] in documenting the gender dimensions of biodiversity management. This shows that there is no simple division of roles by sex and that some acclaimed community conservation practices are deeply sexist. Chapter 7 is the outcome of an intensive field study of gender relations in the rice farming communities of north-eastern India, where I suggest that there is a 'gendered price' that women are paying for the rich agro-biodiversity and food production systems in the region.

The two chapters in 'Actionscapes' cover a wide range. Chapters 8 views 'gender mainstreaming' from the macro to the micro levels, from the policy environment to project implementation. Taking contemporary forest and watershed management programmes as examples, the attempt is to show how modern resource management continues to follow conventional approaches to women and to use women as instruments of conservation, although under the guise of empowerment. The chapter also discusses innovative NGO interventions in NRM, which show the potential and limitations of different kinds of facilitation in changing gender-iniquitous processes. Chapter 9 brings two different threads together: the first section analyses learnings from selected research studies that have 'opened up' the community and the household; the second section outlines a variety of participatory and /or gendered research methods. The chapter emphasizes the need to bend conventional research processes and search for more inclusive methods and tools that bridge the distance between the researcher and the researched.

This leads to 'Genderscapes' which contains chapter 10. The chapter starts with a brief recapitulation of the ground traversed thus far, which points to the need to go beyond the addition of a 'woman' component in existing programmes so as to change the ways in which we live, talk, observe, think, plan and act. This leads first to the question of addressing gender ideologies, women's resistance and negotiation, the appropriation of their dissent and the role of 'sisterhood' in reclaiming women's rightful spaces. The chapter develops the concept of *genderscapes* as more richly layered and nuanced than gender analyses and encompassing greater complexity. Genderscapes enable us to find a way around the methodological problem of understanding and representing the linkages between word, work and action, the ideological and material features that make up the entirety of women's selves, their lives and livelihoods. Revisioning natural resource management requires transformations at many different levels (from reorienting public policy to redefining research methodologies). This cannot be done without addressing the gender ideologies of both traditional and modern institutions and altering our frame of vision, from the standpoint of the marginalized.

The main text is followed by a set of essays that I have called 'Signposts'. These are like extended 'footnotes' to some of the themes that run through the chapters. Most of the Signposts are extracts or updated and edited versions of essays that I have published earlier but which are scattered in different publications. (The Signpost essays are cross-referenced here and in the following chapters as S1, S2 etc.).

The Signposts are followed by Keywords, which includes an

interpretive glossary of more than a hundred words. Understanding keywords is an essential entry point into any area of knowledge and praxis. For instance, in this book, I have generally treated
the terms 'tribal' and 'adivasi' as interchangeable, which reflects
current usage in many sections of activist and academic work. But
we do need to be aware that each term also has its own history and
contemporary implications. Many problems arise because the same
words mean different things to people trained in different disciplines or with different ideologies. Several threads run through
the glossary; readers may start with any keyword and follow the
cross-references (shown in SMALL CAPITALS) to a cluster of words in
the thread. I hope this will help readers discern that words evolve
and are encrusted with 'meanings'. The Keywords are intended to
be browsed through, following the cross-references in a kind of
'wordscape'.

Books (like people) tend to have a life of their own. This is so
even in the process of research and writing, and even more so,
once a book is published. This 'life' may take a book in directions
that are sometimes surprisingly unlike that intended by its author. My intention in this book was not to provide a comprehensive analysis of NRM, to set out a blueprint or an agenda, but to
indicate a path towards developing a different gendered vision.
Research and writing are not a substitute for action but may be
tools for those working towards socio-political change. So, for my
part, I would like *Genderscapes* to be read as an impetus to reflection, thinking in new directions, and innovatively revisioning natural resource management.

NOTES

[1] Joanna Field is the pseudonym of the early 20th century British psychologist
Marion Milner. The epigram is from *A Life of One's Own*, London: Virago,
1986 (republished).

[2] The team comprised of myself, R. Indira (Department of Sociology, University of Mysore) and Jayanand H. Derekar (Community Researcher, Deriya
village, supported by Deuaki Jaiu).

[3] Including Vineeta Hoon, L. Vedavalli, N. Anil Kumar, S.D. Sharma, Smita
Tripathy, Pratima Gurung and Hemal S. Kanvinde, M.S. Swaminathan Research Foundation, Chennai.

WORDSCAPES

2

Clearing the Ground: Gender-Power Relations

'I can climb a coconut tree, but will my husband clean my child? Never.'
—Woman farmer, Konkan, western Maharashtra.[1]

In order to understand the universe of gender we need to comprehend its language, to 'read' the elements of which it is composed. All organized discussions around a theme involve the use of terminology, a set of special words that express specific concepts (see Keywords). Words such as 'work' and 'power' in physics, or 'development' in biology and psychology, have been taken from common usage but bear defined meanings that express particular concepts within the respective disciplines. The assigned meanings of such terms have become established over a long historical period and are not now disputed. These terms help to shorten the path of discussion and to take it forward. Changing social situations and perspectives provide the impetus for the adoption of new terms that in turn may shape the way we perceive and understand situations. The first section of this chapter is concerned with what we mean by gender, by gender relations (which are relations of power) and gender ideology. The next section outlines theories of male domination, forms of patriarchy; and the interlinkages between gender and tribe/caste. The third section deals with the contentious issue of biological sex differences, and the final section sums up the different aspects of gender roles and relations.

WHAT GENDER IS—AND WHAT IT IS NOT

Concepts, Terms and Theories

The English language word 'gender' (like *ling* in Hindi) was formerly a linguistic and grammatical term used as a sex category. Economists treat gender as a variable. For example, Amartya Sen (1990) has said, 'the importance of gender as a crucial parameter in social and economic analysis is complementary to, rather than competitive with, the variables of class, ownership, incomes and family status.' Since the 1970s, however, social anthropologists and feminists have appropriated the word gender to denote something more than a sex category or socio-economic variable. As Sandra Harding (1986: 17) points out, 'Once we begin to theorize gender—to define gender as an analytical category within which humans think about and organize their social activity rather than as a natural consequence of sex difference, or even merely as a social variable assigned to individual people in different ways from culture to culture—we begin to appreciate the extent to which gender meanings have suffused our belief systems and institutions.' This broader meaning of gender encompasses those differences in the behaviour, role and status of women and men, which are determined by society and culture and not by a person's biological sex. Most Indian languages do not have a single word translation of gender, but it is possible to express the socio-cultural concept of gender briefly in a phrase, or by creating new meanings for existing words. For example, some women's groups in Karnataka are using the Kannada word *lingatva* (derived from the Sanskrit word for sexuality) to denote the feminist concept of gender.

Many find the present conceptualization of gender difficult to understand. They just don't get it, rather like people who cannot see the figures hidden in stereoscopic pictures until they are told what to look for in the apparent maze of patterns and colours. It may, therefore, help to summarize briefly what gender is *not*. First, the term gender is not simply a grammatical category although linguists use the word gender in English to distinguish between what they call feminine and masculine forms of words in a language (*stree-ling/ pu-ling* in Hindi for feminine/ masculine gender). Second, gender is not simply another word for 'women' although this inaccurate usage is widely prevalent. Third, the term gender does not refer to any concepts that can be equated with anatomical sex. Indeed, we can speak of more than two genders; in some views there are three, five or even seven different gender categories. Fourth, gender is not a fixed entity but may be viewed as a process by which one acquires certain characteristics, interests and needs and undertakes certain roles and responsibilities.

Social expectations shape the roles, responsibilities and needs of both women and men in accordance with ideas of what a typical woman or man should be and do. Such gender stereotypes may be encountered everywhere. For example, my computer's dated Thesaurus provides stereotypical synonyms for both masculinity and femininity—virility, potency, muscularity and toughness are equated with masculinity, while gentleness, softness, sensitivity and kindness are equated with femininity. Similarly, the phrase 'the fair sex', which is commonly used by the media to refer to women, reflects a particular gender biased stereotype. Yet, we know that both sexes may have varying shades of complexion; and that neither darkness nor fairness of skin is indicative of femininity or masculinity. So too, character traits such as gentleness or toughness are not bound to either sex. Because gender is a dynamic, socially constructed process a person born female may acquire characteristics of behaviour, roles and functions that society associates more with masculinity than femininity and vice-versa. Viewed in this way, gender is not something that is given but something that is performed.

Our ideas about a particular gender are moulded by socially and historically shifting contexts, in ways similar to the shaping of our ideas about 'age'. Childhood, youth, adulthood, and old age are categories signifying demographic age groups. Yet, what we consider 'old age' has changed during one generation as life expectancies have risen. 'Childhood' and 'youth' have similarly expanded, particularly among better-off sections of the population. Terms such as 'mental age' and 'legal age' have specific meanings. In the case of some specially challenged persons, the mental age may not have kept pace with biological age. The law may also arbitrarily define age groups. For instance, under Indian criminal law, the term 'juvenile' used to refer to a particular age group of males between boyhood and adulthood, but no equivalent group was defined for females (Krishna 1996c). Thus, many aspects of age are social rather than biological constructs. So too with gender. However, while we qualify the noun 'age' with adjectives like 'mental' or 'biological' to produce a range of meanings related to age, the word gender gives us a separate term that moves beyond a biologically bounded sex category to encompass a dynamic process of social relations.

Gender Relations

Gender relations, like age, caste, race or class relations, are hierarchical in the common-sense use of the word hierarchy to denote different strata or levels of power. This should be distinguished from the technical use of the term hierarchy in scientific classification, where it is used to denote a two-way scale with one element in the scale subsuming or/and being part of another as, for example, in the taxonomic hierarchy of kingdom, phyla, genus, species. Gender relations are dynamic and involve a special kind of power. The common-sense use of the word power usually refers to the power exercised by government, dominant social classes, or an employer. This is not the kind of power to which we are referring. Gender relations are power relations involving conflict, resistance and bargaining between the more and the less powerful. This is an example of the kind of power relations that have been conceptualized by the modern European philosopher Michel Foucault who defined power as being present in all kinds of human relationships (see Foucault 1984). In a relation of power one person tries to control the way another behaves and this can happen at different levels and in different ways. It need not, for instance, involve verbal communication. Following Foucault, gender-power relations may be seen as a form of control, as active and mobile, not fixed and permanent. Gender relations are contested and negotiated, involving bargaining between the less powerful and the more powerful. Such negotiation for power is also a form of politics. It is easy to recognize the politics of government and affairs of State but more difficult to recognize the politics of gender relations.

Gender-power relations are often mistakenly seen as being

only between spouses, husband and wife, but these can be of many kinds involving different processes of conflict, resistance and negotiation. Usually, the balance of power in gender relations favours men and boys over women and girls but this may not always be so. For example, an older woman entrepreneur who has young boys in her employment is likely to be the more powerful due to her age and position of authority. It is also possible that in a family of say four siblings, three brothers and a sister, the girl may have the more favoured gender status, be more indulged. Gender relations are also discernable in the balance of power between individuals of the same sex at different stages in their lifecycles. For example, in many Indian communities the relations between father and son, or mother-in-law and daughter-in-law are gender-power relations, involving social concepts of masculinity and femininity, of what it means to be a man or a woman at a certain stage in their lives. Gender relations are not just a matter between two individuals but are a way by which social groups exercise political control over the organization of society and people's roles in it. Gender relations do not operate in isolation of other social structures and processes. In any given situation, class, caste, age etc. operate together with gender, strengthening or lessening gender biases.

Different forms of hierarchy and male domination exist in societies across the world. Many hill-dwelling and tribal groups are stratified but are relatively egalitarian, especially regarding the sharing of common resources among the families in a village, clan or group of kin. This is in contrast to plains-dwelling peasant and caste societies, which are characterized by hierarchies based on the control of productive resources, knowledge, and labour. Hierarchies may also involve ritual status, such as that of the Hindu castes, and relations based on concepts of purity and impurity as between the high status brahmans and low status dalits (whose ritual status is that of 'untouchables'). The social relations of caste are very closely intertwined with economic relations. The concept of class refers to unequal economic relations as between wealthy landlords (who control productive economic assets) and poor landless labour or small/marginal peasants. Social status and material wealth tend to feed into each other, and because of the merging of social and economic power, there is considerable parallelism in caste and class hierarchies in India.

Indeed, all hierarchies reflect relations of power. Open violence and subtle, hidden coercion may be involved in maintaining hierarchical relations. Gender hierarchies (like those of class and caste) reflect relations of power maintained through force, fear and inducement. Both class and caste hierarchies seek to maintain themselves by controlling women's labour, their access to ritual knowledge and their sexuality. Among brahman and other 'upper caste' groups, women's subordination is characterized by loss of control over resources, right to property, and freedom of movement. Indeed, the subordination of women is itself a means of reinforcing material and social power between groups.

GENDER IDEOLOGIES

The gender ideology that is prevalent in a particular social group circumscribes the behaviour and actions of women and men and underpins the relations between them. The term patriarchy is commonly used to refer to a gender ideology that is characterized by male domination of institutions, i.e. with a male head ruling the society/ community/ tribe and family; by patrilineal descent, tracing descent through the male line; and by low female status. Patriarchy affects women variously at different stages of their lives; unmarried girls, wives and mothers experience patriarchy in different ways. The forms of male domination vary in different societies. For instance, a community such as the matrilineal Muslims of the Lakshadweep islands, traces descent through the female line but are male dominated in most other respects. The tribal Khasis and Garos of Meghalaya are also matrilineal but customary practices do not give women any role in public decision-making. Dalit women who, along with the men of their community experience subordination in wider society, are themselves oppressed in other ways by dalit men. Because of the different forms of male domination, some prefer to recognize different gender ideologies, of which patriarchy is one. Others feel that the concept of patriarchy has wide applicability and that it is more accurate to speak of patriarchies in the plural to indicate that there are different forms of patriarchy rather than one universal patriarchy.

Theories of Male Domination

There are various views on the question of how male domination arose. It is difficult to be absolutely certain about the processes by which women were forced into subordinate roles and positions in the pre-historical and early historical periods, and whether and how they negotiated or resisted the division of their societies into hierarchical gender-specific domains and spaces. We do know that the oppression, exploitation and violence associated with such division have particular social histories. As Vina Mazumdar and Kumud Sharma (1990: 185-86) have pointed out, 'The search for the origins of women's subordination has led many to examine the historical context of sexual inequality and the relationship between the sexual division of labour and women's subordination.' However, the 'important issue is not at what point of human history the sexual division of labour emerged; the issue is how unequal relationships between men and women have been historically generated.'

Special skills in the use of different kinds of 'tools' are necessary to find and interpret the clues or sources, so as to construct a picture of the social and environmental contexts that existed hundreds of thousands of years ago (See also Omvedt 1990: 35-37). Archaeological sources include material objects, tools, weapons, cave paintings, ritual artefacts and so on but interpreting the function and meaning of these objects requires caution. Folklore provides narrative clues like the oral stories people tell about their origins and history through legend and song, which in later periods were written down. Oral stories are often constructions of how some sections of people want their lives to be viewed and may not always be how people actually lived. Therefore, 'counter-stories' reflecting different points of view also need to be considered. Literary sources include inscriptions and texts which may have been preserved by a small elite group of literate people. In India much of this literature is derived from brahmanical Hinduism or the religious traditions of Buddhism and Jainism. These texts generally reflect the interests of the men who created them and are not always an accurate picture of all sections of society, so there is need to go beyond these to search for the 'sub-texts' (alternative texts) that reflect the views of disadvantaged groups of people.

Anthropological sources consist of ethnographic studies, such as studies of contemporary adivasi/ tribal and forest-dwelling groups. Such ethnography provides valuable insights into current processes of changing gender relations. Present characteristics, however, cannot necessarily be taken as indicators or vestiges of societies that may have existed thousands of years ago because the enveloping circumstances have changed so greatly.

Of the many theories about how gender differentiation and male domination emerged in human societies, the most influential is the conventional Marxist position on the sexual division of labour, set out by Engels in *The Origin of the Family, Private Property and the State* (1884). Drawing upon the natural history and anthropological knowledge available in his time, Engels provided a historical materialist theory of epochal stages of social evolution. He viewed the relations between the sexes in pre-agricultural societies as balanced and gender-egalitarian with a 'natural' division of labour based on men's productive and women's reproductive activities, which were related to outer and inner social spaces. In a much-cited passage, he said:

> Division of labour between men and women was a pure and simple outgrowth of nature: it existed only between the sexes. The men went to war, hunted, fished, provided the raw material for food and the tools necessary for these pursuits. The women cared for the house, and prepared food and clothing, they cooked, weaved and sewed. Each was the master in his or her own field of activity; the men in the forest, the women in the house. Each owned the tools he or she made and used; the men, the weapons and the hunting tackle, the women the household goods and utensils. (Engels [1884] 1972: 14)

Engels believed that in a household, such as he had sketched, production relations were 'communistic', that is, the household was made up of several families and whatever they produced was considered 'common property' to be commonly used. He argued that reproduction (producing and nurturing children) was initially the more significant activity giving women a greater control over their own sexuality and a higher status than men. Later, as settled agriculture and herding emerged, surpluses developed and were controlled by men. Men first established their ownership

and control over women's labour power and then over their reproductive power, i.e. both the 'means of production' in the public
sphere and the family in the private sphere. It is this that led to
the 'world historic defeat of the female sex.' Thus, patriarchy
emerged from men's struggle to subordinate women's labour. At
the same time conflicts arose between different sections of men
over these means of production and the State evolved to manage
these conflicts. This view gives primacy to economic exploitation
and its associated violence.

Aspects of Engels' theory—the 'natural' sexual division of
labour and the related dichotomy between public and private
worlds—have had wide and lasting influence. A hundred years
after Engels, Marxist anthropologist Eleanor Leacock (1977; 1981:
134-36) contended that in foraging bands, women and men had
control over their own spheres 'women were autonomous in egalitarian societies—that is, they held decision-making power over
their own lives and activities to the same extent that men did over
theirs', that they were 'separate but equal'. This balanced non-
hierarchichal state was upset, in her view, only when capitalism
brought about a shift from production for use to production for
exchange. This view has been critiqued by radical feminists and
others who question whether men's control of women's productive
labour *preceded* their control of women's sexuality and reproductive labour.

Engels' approach has been critiqued both from within Marxism and from other perspectives. In a socialist rethinking of the
Marxist approach, the German ecofeminist Maria Mies argues that
reproduction cannot be separated from production, that child-
bearing is a form of engagement with nature, and that the sexual
division of labour is a necessary consequence of this interaction,
arising out of 'qualitatively different' male and female bodies (Mies
1988: 73). This position is also taken by Indian environmentalist
Vandana Shiva who combines ecofeminism with some Gandhian
ideas (see Chapter 3 and S4). Govind Kelkar and Dev Nathan
(1991) distance themselves from the ecofeminism of Mies and
Shiva, to present a more nuanced Marxist analysis based on ethnography among the Jharkhand tribes of central India. They hold
that the social division of labour creates two genders, men and

women, but that this is not neutral, natural or biological. Draw-ing upon *The German Ideology* (another work of Engels co-authored with Marx), they point out that even a 'primitive division of labour' inevitably involves a relation of dominance between different spheres of activity and also the unequal distribution of labour and its prod-ucts. In their view, the woman may have had some degree of au-tonomy within the dominated (domestic) sphere, which is lost when man takes 'command in the home also'. They recognize that the division of labour may occur in many fields, not just the eco-nomic, and that the loss of women's ritual status may precede changes in production relations.

More comprehensive critiques of Engels' approach question the broad sweep of such meta-narratives to understand all of hu-man history categorized into epochal stages and prefer context-specific explanations. A wide spectrum of feminists have argued that the sexual division of labour in human societies is not univer-sal, natural and biological, and that the sharp demarcation be-tween the worlds of home and work, may be characteristic of cer-tain middle class societies at particular times in history but does not hold for poor rural women in many parts of the world. This is apparent, for instance, in many of the traditional crafts of India, such as weaving and pottery in which production is family-based and carried out within the household (see S8). It is also debatable whether foraging (i.e. 'hunting-gathering') societies were indeed marked by a sexual division of labour. Theories of a women-domi-nated 'matriarchal stage' of society, a kind of precursor to patriar-chy, have also been disputed.

An alternative approach to the creation and evolution of male domination is that of feminist historian Gerder Lerner, who deals with some 2,500 years of Middle Eastern civilization in *The Cre-ation of Patriarchy* (1979). Lerner gives primacy to the social ex-change of women among kin groups. This is an idea taken from the French anthropologist Levi-Strauss who viewed kinship as a cultural or socio-cultural construct, involving the relationships built through alliances of marriage, rather than a purely biologi-cal or 'blood' relationship of descent. In the structural approach of Levi-Strauss (1956/ 71: 356), womankind were 'treated as a commodity submitted to transactions between male operators'

and, according to him, the 'rules of the game would remain unchanged should it be decided to consider the men as being exchanged by women's groups.' In Lerner's approach, however, this
exchange is not neutral. Using Engels' categorization of reproductive labour, and following another French anthropologist Claude
Meillasoux (1981), she sees the exchange of women between kin
groups as a system by which men gained control of women's reproductive labour: '. . .the first appropriation of private property
consists of the appropriation of the labour of women as reproduc-
ers.' Lerner's historical analysis of the erosion of women's position
and the creation of patriarchy suggests that this served as the model
for slavery by giving humans the idea that one group of people
could be subordinate to another. This leads to the position that
patriarchal forces and state violence actually *preceded* the rise of
class and capitalist accumulation, reversing the conventional Marxist view. Even as Lerner provided an approach that countered the
influence of Engels' century-old theory, she emphasized the linkages of gender with class, arguing that 'throughout the millennia
of pre-industrial society, whatever subordination women experienced must be described and analysed within the context of the
oppression of the males of their group' (Lerner 1979: 170-71).

Many have tried to blend the insights of different approaches.
One of the earliest to do so was Juliet Mitchell (*Women: The Longest Revolution*, 1966) who argued that women's subordination was
neither exclusively due to men's control of work relations nor to
reproductive relations, but was the outcome of a historical process
of change in four interdependent structures—production, reproduction, sex and socialization of children—all of which created a
complex unity located in the kinship system. In the case of contemporary western society this was the nuclear family. Rejecting
the 'predominantly economist' approach of Marxism which stressed
woman's 'simple subordination to the institutions of private property', she later drew upon insights from psychoanalytical theory
to understand how the 'unconscious' shapes gender identity and
thus contributes to women's social oppression (*Psychoanalysis and
Feminism* 1974). Combining Marxian ideas with those of Levi-
Strauss and Freud, Mitchell argues that patriarchy is defined by
the 'controlled exchange of women' and that this is interlinked

with class conflict. In her view, it 'is not only in the ideology of their roles as mothers and procreators but above all in the very psychology of femininity that women bear witness to the patriarchal definition of human society.' Mitchell further says that women's liberation from oppression has to be through 'political struggle.'

The relationship between women, nature and culture was approached differently by Nancy Chodorow (1978). Rejecting Freudian explanations of instinctive drives and using a branch of psychoanalysis called 'object relations theory', Chodorow (1978: 164) emphasized childhood processes of socialization: 'In spite of the approximately close ties between women's capacities for childbearing and lactation on the one hand and their responsibilities for child care on the other, and in spite of the probable prehistoric convenience (and perhaps survival necessity) of a sexual division of labour in which women mothered, biology and instinct do not provide adequate explanations for how women came to mother.' She argues instead that mothering is reproduced. In her view, because of the sexual division of labour, women are encouraged to 'mother' their offspring and such female parenting influences the psychological development of girls and boys differently. Boys strive to distance themselves from their mothers to achieve an autonomous masculine gender identity, and so they reject the empathetic and nurturing parts of themselves. Girls identify with their mothers and internalize the caring qualities. Women's mothering reproduces the psychological capacity for mothering in girls but not in boys. These psychological differences become culturally fixed. Chodrow sees the social consequence of men's distancing themselves from women as resulting in their domination of women. Thus, gender socialization leads to male domination and inequality. Chodrow's conceptualisation of a 'basic feminine sense of self' that is connected to the world and a 'basic masculine sense of self' that is separate and has rigid ego boundaries, has been criticised because it veers towards essentialism and a false universalism.

Most theories of male domination have been influenced by the question of whether the relations of production or reproduction are the more significant as sites of women's oppression, or whether both work in parallel. Reproduction has also been interpreted more broadly to include, besides child-bearing, a wide range of nurturing work, rearing, caring and domestic tasks. In yet another set of approaches this is not the relevant issue at all. Instead, masculinity and femininity are seen as shaped by the construction of heterosexuality. Adrienne Rich (1976), who is perhaps the most widely known of this group, argues that men derive their power over women through heterosexuality, and its political, economic and cultural propaganda. In this view, it is coercive heterosexuality that imposes norms of femininity and masculinity which devalue women in many different ways. Therefore, for Rich, the issue is not gender inequality, or male domination of culture, or even taboos against homosexuality, 'but the enforcement of heterosexuality for women as a means of assuring male right of physical, economical and emotional access.' In India, such arguments have been taken up by a small group of activists who prefer the term 'hetronormality' as a way of going beyond the term hetrosexuality to deal with the entire range of binary oppositions, which are centred around the duality of female and male. In other words, one cannot challenge male domination of women without challenging the hetronormal socialization processes and practices that have shaped society.

'Brahmanical' and Other Patriarchies

Although the rise of patriarchy in ancient Indian civilization has as yet been little studied, it is generally assumed that the Aryan peoples had adopted certain patriarchal practices by the time they came to India, but that it was not till later Vedic times that the patriarchal features of society became more firmly established. In modern India, theories of male domination have been put forward in the context of political struggles against brahmanical Hinduism, notably by Jyotiba Phule (1826–1890) in Maharashtra and E.V. Ramaswamy Periyar (1879–1973) in Tamil Nadu, both of whom linked the subordination of the lower caste shudra with the subordination of women. Periyar went further than any other male or female politician of his time (or indeed since) to question conventional norms of femininity and masculinity, locating the emergence of male domination within the social and religious structures of society (see Geetha and Rajadurai 1998, Geetha 2002).

With resonances to Engels, he argued that private property and men's control of women's labour led to their control of women's sexuality in the family. Male domination was thus based on the pillars of political and religious authority, control of property and reproduction. For women, marriage and the ideals of chastity and motherhood (to produce male heirs) were a form of bondage, akin to 'shudrahood': 'Just as how Brahminism (sic.) condemns a very large portion of the working population to shudrahood, so it has condemned women to the servitude of marriage. . . . To the extent that a woman lives up to the norms of a chaste and ideal wife, to that extent she accepts and revels in her slavery'. (*Viduthalai* 28.6.73 cited in Geetha 2002: 90).

From a feminist perspective and building on Gerder Lerner's thesis, Uma Chakravarti (1999, 2003) has put forward the concept of 'brahaminical patriarchy' to describe the particular form of caste-linked male domination that arose in ancient India and continues to persist. She argues that the evolution of brahmanical ideology in the middle of the 1st century BC, involved the establishment of high ritual status for upper caste men and the subordination of women through seclusion in the home, the concept of *pativrata* (husband worship), forbidding widow remarriage and controlling women's sexuality. As prescribed in the *Manusmriti*, woman's *dharma* lay in serving her husband as god, and she had no independent existence, material or religious rights. Feminists have drawn attention to the *Manusmriti*'s prescription: 'A virtuous wife should constantly serve her husband like a god, even if he behaves badly, freely indulges his lust, and is devoid of any good qualities. Apart (from their husbands), women cannot sacrifice or undertake a vow or fast; it is because a wife obeys her husband that she is exalted in heaven'. It is suggested that high caste women accepted their subordinate position in the family in a kind of bargain that gained for them their superior caste status. Gail Omvedt (1990, 2000) takes this line of argument further to suggest that a graded subordination of women was in the interest of the state as enunciated by Kautilya in the *Arthashastra*. Lower caste (bahujan/ dalit) women were allowed greater independence in order to increase the population by begetting sons and to maximise production through labour. Therefore, the ban on widow remarriage, for instance, did not apply to bahujan/dalit women who were indeed expected to be 'available' to men.

While men's control of women's sexuality was (and is) central to brahmanical ideology, there was also resistance to this, which is reflected, for instance, in women's folk culture (see Ramaswamy 1997; Raheja (ed.) 2003). During the *bhakti* movement, some women also broke away from male domination in the religious sphere, asserting their independent right to approach their chosen gods. Chakravarti (1999: 317-318) points out that in south India, pre-Sanskritic Tamil cults were extended to create a personalised devotion:

> Through *bhakti*, women also retrieved some of the ground they had lost in the brahmanical order (because of pollution taboos, for example) and in the brahmanical social order, because of their circumscribed role within the household. In *bhakti*, they found the space to break through both these barriers; it enabled women to recite the lord's name even during menstruation and it enabled women to deny the bonds of marriage itself. The *bhaktin* used her devotion as an armour and god as her supporter in her resistance against the priest and the husband.

In their work on the socio-cultural groups of Jharkhand (cited above), Govind Kelkar and Dev Nathan (1991: 34) comment that among present-day Jharkhand tribals, the relations of production and exchange within the family are not balanced or equal and that these relations vary from tribe to tribe. Women have a greater political and management role in the foraging tribes, such as the Birhor, than they do in the agriculturist tribes, such as the Kurukh (or Oraon), Munda, Ho and Santal, which are closer to the patriarchal way of life. The process of women's subordination is initiated in the settled agriculturist tribes and 'perfected' in caste society. They further point out that 'The absence of any seclusion of women in the tribal situation, the free mixing of adolescents of both sexes, the choice of women and men with regard to their marriage partners, the ease of divorce, the practice of widow remarriage—all come under severe attack in the period of formation of caste society.' Indeed, as they say, caste Hindu society looks down upon these practices as signs of 'backwardness'.

Further, Kelkar and Nathan (ibid.) argue that patriarchal caste society is characterized by the evolution of taboos against women using the plough, denying them usufructuary land rights, the phenomenon of witch-hunting and the refusal to involve women in both social rituals and the political system. Some women continue to control the income from gathering and selling forest produce, but men generally control the cash income from agriculture. In agriculturist tribes where the women have retained control over the income from forest-based gathering, patriarchy is not 'full-blown'. This is indicated by the sex ratio, which is favourable to women, reflecting the absence of systematic discrimination against females. Yet, recent trends also show that the favourable sex ratio is declining; so this may mean that changes are occurring and that discrimination is growing. Among those groups such as the Kherwar who have been 'de-tribalised' to a greater extent than others, women's role in marketing has become limited. At the same time, the Kherwar women have been subjected to other non-tribal social practices of patriarchal caste society, including child marriages arranged without the girl's consent. The spread of patriarchy and caste domination, and the formation of class society advances the decline in women's status. The adivasi/tribal woman's loss of control over land and the income from forest resources is related to this wider process. Not only do women lose access to natural resources but their ritual and social status is also eroded.

Elsewhere in India too researchers have noted that changes in gender roles and status occur in the transition from foraging to settled agriculture, communal to individual ownership and tribal belief systems and practices to Hinduism or Christianity. An extensive study of six tribal groups of north eastern India (Fernandes and Barbora 2002) shows that while women in tribal societies had more rights than women in caste societies, they were not equal to men. Today, various forces of modernization have transferred all power to men but women continue to bear the customary responsibility for household provisoning with little control over the necessary resources (see also Krishna 1998 b and c, 2002 and 2004). Another study of three socio-cultural groups in the Nilgiri hills, Tamil Nadu (Thamizoli 1997: 61), compares two tribal groups, the forest-dwelling food-gathering Irula and the pastoralist Toda, and a caste Hindu agriculturist group, the Badaga. The study shows that 'with the increasing complexity of social formation there seems to be a clear assertion of patriarchal values.'

As with the patriarchal peasant communities, among herders and fishers too customary taboos exclude women from certain kinds of resource access and knowledge. A study of community institutions in coastal Kerala, by Arundhuti Roy Choudhury (2004) notes that concepts of purity and impurity are used by fishing communities to keep women from going out to sea. The popular perception is that women are 'impure' (because they menstruate) and will contaminate the sea. Such concepts of pollution serve to curtail women's hold over critical productive resources and to control women's sexuality when the men are away. Yet, these barriers of the mind are not an obstacle to women's work in nurturing their families and the community and carrying out other tasks such as preparing the nets and marketing the harvested fish.

As Chakravarti (2003: 38) has pointed out, in the Indian subcontinent 'there is a fundamental relationship' between a particular social formation and the form of patriarchy that has evolved within that formation. She says:

> As we explore different regions and different time periods, we can see that an evolved caste-based patriarchy is very different from tribal patriarchies. While it is important to study the complexities of patriarchal formations, it is useful to note that dominant arrangements, such as those that the brahmanical model of patriarchy came to evolve, have also influenced the patriarchies in the contiguous social formation. Tribal patriarchies, of which there are many variants, have both co-existed and been reshaped by the dominant model of patriarchy in India, just as the caste system has evolved as a product of different and uneven social systems over the centuries.

Both external gender-power relations and those internal to a group shape the way in which differences between women and men are viewed. Dalit women activists and others on their behalf (see Rao (ed.) 2003) have called attention to the specificity of the dalit women's three-fold subjugation as poor dalits (by class), as women (by patriarchy) and as dalit-women (by caste). Patriarchy and casteism contribute to the oppression of dalit women but also operate within dalit groups. Yet, as Gabrielle Dietrich (1992/

2003: 78) has pointed out, it is also important to get away from perceptions of victimization to look at how dalit women's labour and culture (along with that of the men) have contributed to village ecology and the 'production of life'. The social relations of caste and gender are interlinked and also related to the gendering of the body and conceptualizations of the biological characteristics of women and men, to which I now turn.

FALLACIES OF BIOLOGICAL SEX DIFFERENCE

During the last quarter century, the groundswell of debates and analyses, arising from ethnic and feminist movements in particular, has uncovered the fallacies of the socalled fundamental biological 'truths' about race, ethnicity and gender. Simone de Beauvoir's pioneering book *The Second Sex* (English translation 1953) was hugely influential in distinguishing between sex and gender; providing the socialist feminists' credo: 'One is not born, but rather becomes a woman'. Beauvoir argued that women's maternal and social functions were interdependent, women were victims of menstruation and maternity but could be liberated through a rejection of their biology. It is society that sets up the male as the positive norm against which woman, the 'other' is judged, a norm which is internalized by women themselves. This was later countered by radical feminists and ecofeminists who argued that women should reclaim their natural biological role as mothers (Merchant 1983). Since the mid-1980s, there has been increasing concern that both biological determinism and social determinism are limited and that ways must be found to open up a 'dialogue' (Mellor 1997).

The recorded literature on biological sex differences, and their functional and social expressions is vast. Quasi-scientific attention to women's anatomical, physiological and psychological characteristics has had a long and often prurient history resulting in many naive notions about women's size, strength, brains, hormones, and intuition. These notions underpin women's socially ascribed roles in physical and emotional nurturing, environmental maintenance and food production. There is a pervasive and deeply internalized belief that women lack the physique and

strength for work that requires physical effort, energy and endurance. It is said that women do not climb trees, row boats, wield
the bow to hunt, use the axe to chop wood, or the spade to work
the land, and that they do not handle the plough—because all
these tasks need upper body strength that women do not have.
Yet, many women do find this strength: some in crisis situations,
others in day-to-day life. The overwhelming evidence from field-
work in different regions of South Asia is that women actually
bear greater physical loads than men do as in transporting fuelwood
or fodder, and that they often do so in precarious conditions. A
recent study from the Santal Parganas in Jharkhand notes: 'The
couple spent several hours cutting the wood, arranging and bun-
dling the long pieces. The woman then took the *heavier* bundle on
her head, and the man the lighter one on his shoulder. The logic
of this is that on a steep slope it is difficult to maintain one's
balance with a shoulder load, and men are unable to carry the
wood on their heads.' (Rao 2004: 261) What is defined as 'hard',
however, is determined by who does it. This is so in plains areas as
well. Transplanting rice consists of pulling the saplings out of the
soil and then putting them into the ground. In Tamil Nadu where
men do the pulling, this is considered hard work, but in Kerala
where women pull, it is said to be easy work! (Mencher 1993)
The point is that 'regardless of energy output, when a task is
performed by men alone, it is always described as *hard work*, requiring strength, and when it is done by women it is simply taken
for granted' (ibid: 114). Since hard work translates into wage rates,
differential wage rates for women and men are justified on the
basis that women are not doing the hard jobs, even if they may be
working jointly with men, or for longer hours.

Athletic and Cognitive Abilities

There is also convincing evidence that women's biology (their
anatomy/physiology) is not the constraint that it is made out to
be (Gould 1980, 1983; Birke 1992). Female and male physiques
may define the outer limits of performance in any physical activity, but within those extremes both women and men develop
strength, flexibility and stamina through exercise: that is, through

training and practice. Muscle mass, for example, is developed by the extent of stress to which the muscle is put, and that depends on socio-cultural attitudes, occupations and lifestyles, which are themselves determined by a person's class, caste and gender. It is frequently remarked about world class women athletes, such as tennis players, javelin throwers, pole vaulters, weight lifters, triple jumpers (who must hop-step-and-jump in one continuous movement) that they have bodies 'built like men'. The converse also holds. Margaret Mead (1949: 175) said, 'If we knew no other people than the Balinese we would never guess that men were so made that they could develop heavy muscles.' She pointed out that the arms of the Balinese men 'are almost as free of heavy muscle as those of the women, yet the potentiality for the development of heavy muscle is there, when Balinese work as dock-coolies . . . their muscles develop and harden. But in their own villages they prefer to carry rather than lift, and to summon many hands to every task.'

Studies of the comparative rates of change in Olympic-level records have noted that the steep initial improvement in men's athletic events has been followed in more recent years by a flattening curve (See Fausto-Sterling 1985, revised 1992). Women's records are falling faster than men's but do not seem to be reaching a plateau yet, though no doubt rates of improvement will eventually slow down. An obvious reason is that women's athletics has been around for a much shorter span of years. Not till 1984, for instance, did women run the Olympic marathon. Because women's bodies have a greater distribution of fat they may have the advantage of greater buoyancy in long-distance swimming. The fat reserves would also increase endurance in events like marathon running where it is conceivable that women may outrun men. It has been convincingly argued, however, that the bio-mechanics of male and female bodies determines only the outer limits of possible achievement not the performance of average women and men among whom there is great variability. The reason for the rapid gains of world class women athletes are the sexist attitudes that prevailed earlier and the gender biases by which many socio-cultural groups barred women's participation in sports. The improving curves in women's Olympic records reflect the gender inequities of the recent past and cannot be related to women's biology.

Many socio-cultural groups in the past and in the present practise some form of direct or indirect restraint on women's bodies. Generations of Chinese women had their feet mutilated, because of the tradition of binding them to prevent growth and enhance their supposed beauty and sexual attractiveness. Generations of women in some parts of India have had their ear-lobes mutilated by the weight of ornaments that they are expected to wear. Young Apatani women in north-eastern India are only now giving up the practice, which was mandatory for their mothers, of wearing large buttons embedded in each nostril to signify a woman's married status. The effect of sexist practices on individual bodies, male or female, is clear. Its social repercussions are more difficult to discern. 'In general women have been prevented from developing their capacities for physical speed and strength, and the effects of this prohibition can be seen simply by looking at women's bodies, particularly their upper bodies . . . in the past, social norms have limited the way in which women fulfilled their genetic potential, so that we have no idea of the extent of that potential.' (Jagger 1992: 84) So, it may be surmised that while women may seem to lack upper body strength, the reason they generally do not undertake activities, such as ploughing, is not a simple matter of physical capacity but varied social constraints that determine their biological constitution and the work they do—sanctions against women using an instrument to till the field, or the belief that those who menstruate will pollute the earth. These constraints may be overcome in certain circumstances and in pockets of Karnataka, Tamil Nadu and Kerala women do use the plough.

As in world athletics, a steep improvement curve can presently be observed in the scholastic achievements of Indian school girls. This is shown in the secondary and higher-secondary school-leaving examinations; in many states girls are now doing better than boys. This spurt in school-level academic gains is a reflection of earlier inequality, and rooted in societal constraints rather than in the girls' intrinsic mental abilities. No one now talks about girls' brains. Yet, as a teenager in the early-1960s, I remember sharp debates about the smaller size of women's brains as com-

pared to men's and, therefore, their unsuitability for intellectual
and scholarly pursuits. There were also more subterranean notions that 'overworking' the brain would affect our procreative
abilities. Such socially constructed fears were passed on by one
generation of women to the next, from mothers to daughters. In
Europe, women's entry into universities was resisted on these very
sorts of grounds, provoking the writer Virginia Woolf (1928; republished 1965: 76) to assert: 'Lock up your libraries if you like,
but there is no gate, no lock, no bolt that you can set upon the
freedom of my mind'. As Kaplan and Rogers (1990) have argued,
in discussing the differences between the sexes, the biological and
social contexts are lumped together, and biological explanations
for sex differences subsume sociological explanations.

An example of such lumping is in the realm of inherent differences in cognitive abilities. It is argued that the mathematical and
spatial ability of boys has a biological basis in male brains, which
gives them the advantage over girls. Fausto-Sterling (1985) has
shown that the differences in spatial abilities are not related to the
different features of female and male brains, but rather to the
cultural conditioning that restricts the autonomy and physical
mobility of girls as compared to boys. And further that null results that show no sex-based differences are not documented or
published. The outcome is that differences get magnified in the
public mind and colour thinking. Bleier (1984: 103) cites a report that referred to the supposed sexual difference in aptitudes
and proposed that the 'best way to help girls is to accept it and go
from there.' Such studies that link behaviour to biology ignore
many social variables such as the girls' past experiences, their anxi-
ety about the task, and the interaction between tester and tested
(Kaplan and Rogers 1990: 206-7). There are few longitudinal
analyses. Instead, a single one-time study gets swiftly generalized
and becomes a quantitative measure of ability.

This is paralleled in our context of NRM by the widespread
notion that poor rural and tribal women can measure only small
quantities, handle small amounts of produce or money. In a *haat*
(local market) in central India where tribal women were selling
small piles of dry spices and herbs collected from the forest, I was
told by project staff that tribal women are *naturally* good at this,

that men take over when larger quantities are involved because they are physically and mentally capable of handling bigger amounts. This was seen as a *natural* division of labour because of a *natural* difference in mental capabilities. The patriarchal sub-text, the underlying gender ideology here, was not recognized. I do not know of any studies on this but, if there were such a study, it might well confirm a sex-linked inherent difference in cognitive ability and aptitudes which results in the different marketing abilities of tribal men and women! As Kaplan and Rogers (1990: 217) point out: 'We organize our perception of people into socially constructed categories, and frequently operate on simple dichotomous choices such as black-white, rich-poor, young-old, male-female. It is not correct to force biology, and brain function in particular, into these culturally constructed polarities.'

Hormones and Emotions

A more insidious argument used to bolster gender-bias is based on the difference between the estrogens and androgens (chiefly testosterone). In the popular perception the so-called female and male hormones are sex-differentiated and discrete; female hormones are linked to women's 'moods' and behaviour, which may be negatively perceived. On the contrary, however, the so-called sex hormones are not 'uniquely' male or female. Indeed, it is well-known that:

> Both sexes secrete both types of hormone; what differs is the ratio of estrogen to androgen in the two sexes. Hormones (gonadotropins) from the pituitary—a small gland at the base of the brain—regulate hormonal release from both ovary and testis, which are then carried to other regions. The presence of both androgens and estrogens (as well as other hormones) seems to be required in both sexes to achieve sexual maturity, and both types of hormone are produced not merely by the ovary and the testis but also by the adrenal cortex in both sexes. Furthermore, the two kinds of hormone are chemically closely related and can even be interconverted by enzymes present in the body. (Rose et. al. 1984: 151)

Even the 'pregnancy hormone' progesterone (which is involved in the development of female sexual organs and associated with the menstrual cycle) is not exclusive to females. Progesterone is present in males at levels comparable to the pre-ovulatory phase of the menstrual cycle, and can also be a chemical precursor to testosterone (Rose et al. ibid.). Estrogen also continues to be released from the adrenal glands of post-menopausal women whose ovaries have ceased to function. The diversity of human behaviour, therefore, cannot be linked one-to-one to male and female hormones (see Bleier 1984: 80-90; Fausto-Sterling 2000).

Indeed, there is a considerable degree of 'hormonal overlap' between the sexes due to the complex interactions of genetic and environmental factors, resulting in varied physical types and behaviours. What is socially-perceived as acceptable, 'normal', behaviour in a man or a woman is socially-defined within parameters of gender, age, class, culture etc. The pioneering educationist Ivan Illich (1977) showed how industrial societies defined normality as a universal standard, and were then able to attack deviations from that standard. 'The question of what is normal biology and what is normal behaviour has to be seen in a wider context. The concept of normality is linked to the construct of a male-female dichotomy' (Kaplan and Rogers 1990: 218-219). In the dichotomous view, men's domination of social structures is seen as validated by male hormones, and conversely female hormones are seen as making women instinctively domesticated, caring and nurturing. So, anger, irritation, and aggression, for example, are supposed to be normal for men because of male hormones. But not for women whose anger gets named 'hysteria'. When emotions and behaviour are slotted into what is acceptable for males or females, dual norms prevail.

The counterpart of deterministic negative linkages between women's biology and behaviour are the positive linkages that are sought to be established by essentialist approaches. Such approaches equate the fact of child-bearing with the 'instinct' for mothering, and the ideology of mother-care with concern for nature. As will be discussed in the next chapter, the ecofeminist approach projects an intuitive linkage between women and nature, and locates biological reproduction and nurturing at the core of women's existence (Mies and Shiva 1993; Chakma 1994). Yet, there is no evidence to show that intuition and empathy come from inborn maternal instincts and not from rich experience. Consider this psychological explanation of women's so-called natural intuition (Helen Deutsch cited in Montagu (revised) 1999: 177): 'Woman's understanding of other people's minds, her intuition, is the result of an unconscious process through which the subjective experience of another person is made one's own by association and thus is immediately understood. . . . Since the whole process is very rapid, its second phase, that is, the intellectual elaboration is barely perceived—everything seems to take place in the incongruous and affective element because the conscious ingredient does not come to the fore.' Furthermore,

> . . . The ability to do this will naturally depend on one's sympathy and love for a spiritual affinity with the other person; and the extent of this spiritual affinity for which the German language has the term *einfhulung* (sometimes translated as empathy) depends on the richness of one's own emotional experiences, which underlie the 'inner perception' or the ability to understand one's own feelings and psychological relations and, by analogy, those of others. (ibid.)

Men too are capable of sympathy and love for others, of drawing upon rich emotional experiences and insights into their own feelings and those of others. Women's intuition and nurturing, and men's aggression, are not qualities intrinsic to either sex but are learned through the experiences of life. The gendering of life experiences, perceptions and behaviour are inter-related. Indeed, it has been argued (Rubin 1975: 80) that 'from the standpoint of nature, men and women are closer to each other than either to it or to anyone else. . . . The idea that women and men are two mutually exclusive categories must arise out of something other than a non-existent "natural" opposition . . . exclusive gender identity is the suppression of natural similarities.' There are very few absolute sex differences, and unless there is complete social egalitarianism we cannot really tell what these differences are, for as Fausto-Sterling (1994: 270) points out: 'bodies, minds and cultures interact in such complex and profound ways that we cannot strip them down and compare them separately. Only as the separate culture of men and women become more alike, a spectre that horrifies many, will we be able to assess the possibility of unalterable sex differences.'

Among the first to question women's natural instinct for nurturing was Margaret Mead (1935: 286), who said: 'We have assumed that because it is convenient for a mother to wish to care for her child, this is a trait with which women have been more generously endowed by a carefully teleological process of evolution. We have assumed that because men have hunted, an activity requiring enterprise, bravery and initiative they have been endowed with these useful attributes as part of their sex temperament.' This was disputed by some who doubted Mead's evidence from the field. Others like the psychologist Viola Klein (whose *The Feminine Character*, 1945, preceded de Beauvoir's *The Second Sex*) argued that certain situations if repeated over many generations would result in developing definite psychological characteristics. Klein advocated a more comprehensive view that would include both her own historical approach and the cultural patterns identified by Mead. As Rose, Lewontin and Kamin (1984: 10) have suggested: 'There is no mystical and unbridgeable gulf between the forces that shape human society and those that shape the societies of other organisms; biology is indeed relevant to the human condition, although the form and extent of its relevance is far less obvious than the pretensions of biological determinism imply.' It is pertinent that they also reject the 'antithesis', which 'is a type of cultural determinism' because 'the cultural determinists identify narrow (and exclusive) casual chains in society which are in their own way reductionist as well.' The point is that humanity 'cannot be cut adrift from its own biology', even as it resists being 'enchanted by it.'

IMPLICATIONS OF GENDER IDEOLOGIES

We can now turn to some of the implications of gender-role differentiation and gender relations in society. Gender specific roles are assigned by society and assumed by the different gender groups; these vary by age, caste, class, place and time. The gender roles of women and men require different kinds of knowledge, skills, energy and time, and are differently viewed and valued by the community. As we will see in Chapter 6, gender roles and resource management behaviour are context-specific and diverse. For instance, women are well known for their skill as seed conservers. In varied locations across the country, the tasks of seed selection, cleaning and preservation are done entirely by women. This is as true of the swidden (shifting, slash and burn) rice farmers of the north-eastern Himalaya in Arunachal Pradesh as of the settled millet cultivators in the low hills of the Eastern Ghats in Tamil Nadu. Yet, there are also many places where women are not permitted to touch seeds of food crops that are considered to be 'sacred'. The Kuruchiya, a tribal people of Wayanad in northern Kerala, do not allow women of menstruating age to handle rice seeds because the women's touch is believed to be polluting. This is in keeping with brahmanical Hindu beliefs and is an indication that the tribal Kuruchiya's social practices are in the process of transformation towards brahmanical Hinduism and brahmanical patriarchy.

Male and female physique and physiology, and the ecological/environmental settings in which people live and work, all have a part in shaping what people do and are expected to do, but socially-determined gender relations are the more crucial here. The extent and ease of women's mobility in a society is often an effective indicator of the kind of patriarchy that operates in that society. Mobility involves both physical and socio-cultural factors. By physical factors we do not mean just the paths, roads and modes of transportation, but also how women's bodies have been trained and developed from girlhood to undertake physical activities (for instance, whether or not they climb trees, mentioned in the epigram at the start of this chapter). Socio-cultural factors are the customs and beliefs that regulate women's movements and the societal conditions that create the conditions in which women can move about freely. Women in tribal societies and poor dalit women who work outside the home to contribute to the household income generally enjoy greater freedom of movement than urban upper class and upper caste women. Changes in existing patterns of mobility may be brought about by changes in a person's occupational circumstances.

The gender relations that determine household responsibilities may become even more sharply etched in calamitous situations, when people are displaced because of developments taking place in their areas, the building of dams or mining, or in times of natural disasters, drought, flood, earthquakes, cyclones. Both information and decision-making at times of disaster are gendered (see below). But disaster relief in the short term and rehabilitation in the long term are rarely shaped by an understanding of the gender-power and caste relations of the affected communities. Sometimes, natural calamities and migration may also alter customary gender norms. For example, several decades ago many families from the Sunderbans region of West Bengal migrated to the coastal villages of Orissa. However, even when they settled in the same place the gender norms for the two socio-cultural groups were different. The Bengali women routinely move out of their homesteads and villages unlike the Oriya women who remained mainly confined to their homes. Yet, during the devastating drought in 2000 (following the super cyclone that hit Orissa in 1999) Oriya women too took on work outside their homes in the absence of their men (Prafulla Misra 2000 personal communication).

Gendered Sources of Information and Decision-making in Natural Disasters

It is only in very recent years that the gendered underpinnings in natural disaster situations have begun to draw some attention. Exactly a year after the super cyclone of 1999 struck the Orissa coast, I visited one of the villages that had been devastated.[2] There was a superstitious belief that the cyclone would strike again. The darkening skies, rising winds, heavy rain and continuous cyclone warnings led to near panic as villagers tried to cope with the prospect of a repeat disaster. We returned the next day when the threat of another cyclone had somewhat receded. In small, facilitated groups, the poor peasant women spoke of the gendered sources of information on disasters, and the process of decision-making during the current threat and during the super cyclone the year before. They said that normally it was the men who switched on the transistor radios in their homes, and so it was the men who had first heard the cyclone warnings the previous day as also during the super cyclone of 1999. On that earlier occasion, when the nearest radio station located in Cuttack town had collapsed and gone off the air, only one woman had known how to switch channels to tune-in to the broadcast from Dhaka in Bangladesh. The women said that after the earlier catastrophe, the men had also begun to rely on local Oriya newspapers. Most of the women in the village were illiterate but they also had a new source of information: their school-going children, whose source was their school teacher. Although the government was putting out standard cyclone warnings, mentioning the level of risk, these numbers meant nothing to the women. The warnings had caused panic. Hearing the warnings, young children also feared going to school; more than one child told us 'if we have to die, we would rather die close to our parents.'

The women's primary concern in the present situation (when they apprehended another cyclone) was providing food for the family. The main precaution they had taken after the warnings had been broadcast on the previous day was to cook food for two days in readiness for any eventuality. The men were busy collecting provisions and were trying to ensure adequate water supply in case the village was marooned. Some women said they should call a meeting of the Self Help Group (SHG), which had recently been formed as a savings-cum-credit group, to decide collectively on what they should do. But this meeting did not materialize. Very few women were concerned that the village had no tall trees, which they could climb to take shelter. When the super cyclone had struck in 1999, they said the men had taken all the decisions on routes and modes of escape. The women simply followed. It was also the men who decided on what was to be saved and carried away. The men's main concern was always the safety of their children whereas the women were mainly bothered about saving and carrying kitchen utensils. The men objected to this prioritization but many women felt that cooking vessels were the most important things to be saved. This is not surprising because utensils are the only asset that poor women own and essential to women's ability to fulfil what they see as their primary role of feeding their families. Moreover, while relief agencies may supply raw emergency rations, it was feared that they might not supply cooking utensils. The women also told us that although both men and women shared the tasks of rehabilitation, the women did suffer more because they generally had less food to eat.

It is not possible to generalize from the spontaneous responses of a small group of women in any one village. But the accumulation of such micro-level information in media reports, NGO documents and research studies in South Asia provides a basis for understanding the gendered dimension of disasters, whether cyclones, floods, drought or the more recent tsunami in South and South East Asia (see for example Enarson 2001, OSMDA 2002, Mishra et. al. 2004, Ariyabandu and Wickramasinghe 2005, Murthy et. al. 2005). Immediate survival in a disaster depends on a complex cluster of behavioural patterns that have been inscribed onto the bodies and minds of girls, boys, women and men through socio-cultural processes over a long historical period. During the super cyclone in Orissa in 1999 and in the tsunami that struck southern India in December 2004, observers noted that many more women than men died. Among the reasons put forward were factors related to women's bodily and physical abilities, not having the strength to cling to stationary objects, wearing cumbersome clothes etc. Some reports have also claimed that women and girls did not know how to swim or to climb trees. I am, however, in some doubt whether women indeed did not know how to swim and climb or whether they were hampered by their clothes and social norms, even in times of emergency. There have been suggestions that because of women's deep social conditioning on covering their bodies, they would not tear away their clothes and if their clothes were inadvertently torn, they would rather die than try to escape to safety clad immodestly.

Contrary to the general impression that natural disasters are levelling and that they do not differentiate between groups of people, the impact of disasters and people's experience of them is clearly linked to prior economic and socio-political conditions. People who live on the edge of poverty are already vulnerable and may not have the capacity to cope with the intensification of hazards or the power to wrest resources in the aftermath of a disaster. As Enarson (2001: 1) points out:

Persistent poverty and economic insecurity, the gendered division of domestic labour, reproductive and health differences, exposure to violence, disparate educational and social opportunities, and secondary political status combine to put women at high risk, particularly those who support households alone, the aged and disabled, and women marginalized by caste or religion. Their long-term recovery from the compound effects of these disasters will certainly be complicated by this context.

Poor people who live in hazardous and vulnerable situations do not have the capacity to absorb shocks. Floods and drought affect family survival as a whole, but when the loss of livelihoods forces men to migrate, the pressure increases on all those who are left behind, girls and women of all ages, young boys and elderly men.

In sum, gender ideologies affect every aspect of our lives: the physical-spatial, socio-economic and socio-political. By physical-spatial we mean those features that refer to the body, presumed differences in female and male physiques, the physical spaces through which women and men move, the different manner in which their bodies are expected to move through these spaces and so on. The socio economic factor refers to the historical evolution of gender differences, gendered patterns in social relations and institutions, work, knowledge and technology. The socio-political refers to the cohesion brought about by formal and informal institutions whose norms regulate male and female knowledge, attitudes and practices. Socio-political factors are enmeshed with both the physical-spatial and the socio-economic. That women do not move out alone beyond a certain distance, or at night, is a physical-spatial factor. But socio-political reasons determine how their movements are circumscribed and why they cannot move freely and safely. That women do not own land in many Indian communities is a socio-economic factor; why they do not own land involves socio-political factors.

Several material, cultural and symbolic threads are interwoven in the ideologies that shape unequal gender relations in different social groups and institutions such as the family, household, kin, society, market and government. Gender bias is also embedded in individual minds. Objective conditions and subjective perceptions together create the lifeworlds in which women and men relate to each other, live and work. We can reach a shared understanding of gender relations by summarising those aspects of gender that are common to most gender ideologies (see also Harding 1995: 298-302; Cockburn 1981). Gender relations are specific to particular contexts and diverse; they are changing and dynamic; hierarchical; and intermeshed with other social processes and categories like class and caste. Furthermore, gender relations can be seen as involving physical-spatial, socio-economic and socio-political dimensions; and as being embedded both in social institutions and in human minds. Most importantly, gender relations are oppositional, involving conflicts of power; and following from that, are negotiable. This cluster of characteristics makes for great complexity.

NOTES

[1] Translated from Marathi and cited by Meghana Kelkar, posting on e-group: jivika, 25 Feb. 2005. Sharing her experience of talking to men and women farmers in the Konkan tracts, she wrote: 'All men were supportive when we talked about women getting access to skills that were seen to be 'male', as a part of equity arguments. One of the men farmers, however, was concerned about increase in work load for women, in case they start learning non-traditional skills. When I argued that the other part of the story was men sharing work that is traditionally seen to be 'female', this brought immediate silence. One woman quipped, "I can climb a coconut tree, but will my husband clean my child? Never!" This illustrates the extent to which the ideas about femininities and masculinities are constructed, tightly held and negotiable in different cultures.'

[2] I am indebted to Prafulla Misra, the field staff of MSSRF, Kendrapara, Orissa, and the people of the coastal villages for sharing their experiences with me.

3

Gender Perspectives and Approaches

'What is your problem? In Indian law 'he' always includes 'she'. Men are free to share their rights with their wives. Why do you want women to have *separate* rights?'

—Male conservation scientist [1]

In the previous chapter I tried to build a conceptual picture of gender-power relations. This chapter moves on to examine varied perspectives in three broad and interlinked areas: the production of knowledge and technology; the process of planned development; and approaches to women and the environment. The first section sketches major perspectives on the production of knowledge, the positivist and interpretive positions, and the feminist standpoint. This provides the backdrop to the discussion on the various phases, since Independence, of the planning and practice of development. The third section discusses different approaches to women and environment-development and in the fourth section, I suggest a three-fold typology in the Indian context: conventional, celebratory and gendered. This gendered approach to technology is touched upon briefly, bringing the discussion back to approaches to knowledge production.

THE PRODUCTION OF KNOWLEDGE
AND TECHNOLOGY

The field of NRM falls broadly within the domain of the modern technocrat who expects to bring scientific understanding, specific technologies and management practices to bear on the conservation, use and development of land, soil, water, forests, biodiversity, agriculture etc. In order to understand how and why gender is submerged in the theory and practice of NRM, we need to look at its epistemology, or the process by which knowledge is produced. Each of us brings an accumulation of disciplinary training, experience, knowledge and skills to the issues and problems that concern us, or that we choose to research. This shapes our approach to the problems, the methods that we adopt to deal with them, and also the technologies and research tools that we develop. The research design or the framework within which we locate our questions is also determined by our different outlooks, our worldviews or philosophies, and by theories about how the world works, and how the relationships among the world's people work. Such worldviews are so embedded in thought and action that we are often unaware of them, rather like very young children who learn to speak a language fluently without being conscious of the structure of the language.

Different knowledge systems are related to distinct philosophic approaches. One or the other approach, or strands of different approaches, may be implicitly reflected in our work, actions and writing. The first task of researchers and fieldworkers then is to become aware that all knowledge is situated in a particular context. The creative combination of different methodologies may help to enhance our understanding of the richness and complexity of a particular social situation. Yet, we should also be aware that divergent approaches and methodologies (that is the concepts, methods and tools) may also lead to ambiguities and contradictions in policies and actions.

Historically, modern science evolved in the West in the 18th century, in what is called the period of Enlightenment. The Enlightenment took forward the earlier Renaissance temper of enquiry and humanism and attempted to reconcile the observation of nature with reason. This was a counterpoint to the supra-natural and purely spiritual approaches to understanding the material world. Since the European Renaissance, science has been seen as an alternative to rigid religious authority. But in course of time, science itself has acquired an authoritative voice and fairly inflexible conceptions of what is 'scientific'. The voice of scientific authority now has a very powerful hold on society, and determines what questions are considered worth researching and how these are to be researched. There are many different scientific approaches but most have a positivist core that affects how the linkages between cause and effect are viewed. Briefly, it can be said that positivists seek a predictable regularity of cause and effect, most easily demonstrable in mathematics and the physical sciences and considered by them to be applicable to all natural sciences. The reliance on causal regularity leads to the position that, given the same broad initial conditions, there can be but one solution, one path, and one explanation for most problems. In this approach, the ideal researcher is presumed to be detached, disengaged, and value-neutral. The partiality to predictable causal regularity has had a strong influence on both the biological and social sciences.

Positivist social science assumes that the methods of the natural sciences can be applied to the social sciences, and emphasizes observation, direct experience, and quantitative measurement. This is problematic even for natural sciences like ecology (because of the difficulty of duplicating living systems in experimental conditions) and even more so for most social sciences. Within the NRM field the positivist social science approach has had a huge impact on methodologies. The emphasis in positivist social science, such as some strands of environmental economics, is on quantifiable rather than qualitative factors, on what is measurable rather than comparable. Such an approach tends to treat groups of people as collections of atomistic individuals and 'facts' as only that which can be measured and quantified. In India, today, the practice of NRM whether by government departments, autonomous agencies, universities or even many non-government institutions/ organizations has a strong overlay of both positivist science and positivist social science. This is strikingly apparent, for instance, in Environmental Impact Assessments (EIA) that are now mandatory under Indian environmental law for all large projects that involve changes in land-use and displacement of people. Apart from other problems with the EIA, the positivist approach tends to disregard or underestimate the non-quantifiable ecological, social and human costs. The growing opposition to this by scholars, practitioners and activists has as yet had limited impact on NRM practice.

An alternative to the positivist approach to knowledge production is the social construction approach. Both in theory and practice, there is a very basic divergence between the social constructionist and positivist approaches. Positivists see 'reality' as being discovered rather than created or constructed. In contrast, social constructionists see 'realities' as being created by how we choose to seek and interpret the evidence, which is context-specific, i.e. having historical and location-specificity. In this view, science is also a socially situated construction of reality. This does not mean that nothing is real or that the real is ignored but that different processes of socialization produce different perspectives (See Unger 1990). Because our perspectives are so deeply shaped by gender ideologies, the approach of social construction is especially valuable in understanding and challenging gender bias. Simone de Beauvoir's affirmation in *The Second Sex* (1949) that we are not born women but *become* women is a central tenet of the social construction approach.

The deep fissure between social-constructionist and positivist approaches to knowledge creation is also reflected in conceptualizations of technology and technological advances. Positivist approaches view technology as value-neutral, as having a kind of independent evolution and existence that impacts on society. Social-constructionist approaches critique the positivist approaches for their technological determinism. Instead they view technology and society as intertwined, with social relations playing a significant part in shaping technology, even as technology impacts on social relations. Gender relations are among the societal relations involved in shaping technological change and we will return to this issue at the end of the chapter.

Feminist Standpoints

Feminist approaches to knowledge creation hold that gender influences how we conceptualize and validate knowledge. Feminist anthropologists, sociologists, historians, philosophers, psychologists, biologists and others have shown that the socially constructed conceptualization of knowledge and the methodologies of both science and social science have disadvantaged women in numerous ways. Women and their interests have been rendered invisible by being excluded from research; by ungrounded theories of women's inferiority; by the rejection of different ways of knowing; and by academic practices that reinforce social and gender hierarchies. Those who share a broadly feminist and progressive approach to epistemology agree that gender relations and gendered knowledge are socially constructed but among them two different strands of emphasis may be discerned. These have come to be called a social relations and a materialist perspective, depending on whether they give greater importance to social or material (that is, economic) factors. At present, the social relations perspective has proved to be the more influential.

Central to feminist epistemology is the concept of a situated knower: what one knows, experiences and observes depends on where one is—one's standpoint. 'Situated knowledge' reflects the experience and perspective of the person who is located in a particular situation. This does not mean that there are multiple perspectives and, therefore, that nothing can really be known or that there is no objective reality. It does mean that oppression is both an individual and social experience. It also means that every researcher starts from a particularly situated social and political position that may be shared by others. As Sandra Harding (1991) and others have suggested, a feminist standpoint is not the articulation of women's experience in itself but the insights and theories about nature and social relations that are produced by such a perspective. There is a certain tension in such a position. Harding (1991: 269) notes: 'On the one hand, we should be able to decide the validity of a knowledge claim apart from who speaks it; this is the desirable legacy from the conventional view. . . . On the other hand, it *does* make a difference who says what and when.'

DEVELOPMENT AND WOMEN

During the late 1950s and early '60s, the prevailing theory of development in India and most other low-income countries was overwhelmingly positivist and patriarchal, seeking to bring about technological changes that would transform the economy and the lives of people. The social and human aspects of development were neglected and the emphasis was on technical interventions. Given this context, it is not surprising that early development strategies did not recognize women's work and contribution to the household economy. It was only after the mid-1970s that the invisibility of women's productive work began to be highlighted by the women's movement and academic research. Esther Boserup's *Women's Role in Economic Development* (1970) argued that all societies have developed a division of labour based on sex; that this division is not natural but socio-culturally determined; what is considered a male task or a female task varies from place to place; that economic development has a differential impact on women and men, and that the impact on women is adverse. Boserup's book was particularly influential despite reservations that she did not critique development as such. During the same period, the United Nations Conference on the Human Environment (Stockholm: 1972) provided an impetus to environmental movements in many parts of the world. A few years later in India, the Chipko struggles in the Garhwal Himalaya (Uttarakhand state) highlighted the integral relationship between people's livelihood activities and the local natural resource base.

It took several more years, however, for policy makers and academics to recognize women's productive roles, especially in non-agricultural natural resource-based activities. As mentioned earlier, the gender dimensions of use, access, control and development of natural resources were not considered even by *Towards Equality*, the pioneering Report of the Committee on the Status of Indian Women (ICSSR 1974). Many early studies such as Nici Nelson's review of South Asian literature, *Why has Development Ignored Rural Women?* (1979), Barbara Rogers' *The Domestication of Women: Discrimination in Developing Societies* (1980) and somewhat later studies by Indian researchers focussed attention on agriculture and economic development. But there were very few who drew out the linkages between women's subordination and their roles in NRM.

As the UN Decade for women drew to a close in 1984, a group of feminists from nations in the South came together in Bangalore, India, to form DAWN, Development Alternatives for Women in a New Era. They set out their views in a document titled, *Development, Crises and Alternative Visions: Third World Women's Perspectives* (Sen and Grown 1987). Critiquing three decades of development, they highlighted the linkages between four global crises, famine, debt, militarism and fundamentalism, and the impact of this on poor women. During the same period, other streams of activism and research with roots in the environmental movement concentrated on women's natural resource responsibilities, for example what was seen as the 'women's need' for fuel and forest products. Later a few researchers began to look more specifically at the gender dimensions of particular natural resources such as forests, wastelands, and biodiversity. During the 1990s, the climate of increased awareness, organization and articulation of women's rights, on the one hand, and the new economic policies of globalization, on the other, led to attempts to link the streams of economic development and NRM through a gendered approach. (See Krishna 2000: 175-177, Sharma 2000)

Implications for gender equity

Different approaches to rural development, since Independence, have had varied implications for gender equity. Four overlapping periods from the 1950s to the present are delineated in Table 3.1. Generalizing for India as a whole can only give a very rough picture of particular phases, but it is possible to do so because till recently the national planning process was rigorously centralized, and the country was painted with the same broad developmental brush strokes that required specific modes of response from village communities. Even as the chronology of changing economic policies and administrative thrusts have different gender implications, all the gender outcomes (listed in the last column of the Table) continue to be visible concurrently in NRM programmes and projects, today.

Despite the social reform movements of the pre-Independence

years and the strong participation of women in the freedom struggles, the earliest phase of planning was rather in keeping with the Russian proverb that says: 'I thought I saw two people coming down the road, but when I looked again, I saw it was only a man and his wife.' Two mutually supportive approaches characterized this period. The home science approach was adopted by the Community Development (CD) programme and was directly influenced by the middle class American 'home economics' model, which emphasized women's domestic and nurturing roles and their responsibility for family health and nutrition within the precincts of the home. This fed into the welfare approach which treated women as an adjunct to husbands or fathers, often lumping them together with the 'handicapped' and other 'weaker sections' all of whom were patronisingly seen as victims requiring rescue and 'upliftment' through welfare measures. The welfare approach had a strongly stereotyped middle-class bias: women's productive roles were treated as supplemental to those of the male 'heads of households'; the neediest groups of women were left out, and women's work in subsistence dairying, fisheries, or sericulture was not recognized (Sujaya 1995: 17). This kind of welfare approach to 'suitable' trades and occupations is particularly difficult to shake off. Even in the late 1990s many watershed development projects were continuing to focus on 'making women good housewives' (Datar and Prakash 2001).

In the phase starting in the mid-1960s, the technological breakthrough in agriculture that came to be known as the Green Revolution changed rural life in many parts of the country. The Green Revolution strategy concentrated on states that were already agriculturally and industrially dynamic, notably Punjab, and this aggravated regional imbalances. There were structural changes as small and marginal farming families could not afford the required inputs and had to abandon cultivation for agricultural labour. Most important from a gendered perspective is that the women's customary economic role was marginalized, even among those who gained higher incomes through improved productivity. Without ownership of land and assets, constrained by sexual mores that restricted mobility, lacking education and training in the new skills, women in the Green Revolution areas lost their power to make decisions about household grain requirements, marketing and expenditure (see also S1). Their displacement from productive work and marketing altered gender relations, and women's status and authority within the home. It is now feared that a similar process may be underway with changes in agricultural strategies under the liberalised economic policies.

Social and cultural change cannot be treated separately from economic and political developments. The third phase portrayed in Table 3.1 is of particular interest. In the late 1970s, anti-Congress party coalition governments had emerged in some states. At the Centre, India's first non-Congress party coalition came to power in the elections of 1977 (following the end of the internal Emergency), with a proclaimed commitment to political and administrative decentralization. Since the mid-1970s, the widespread marginalization of oppressed sections of society had stirred a tide of people's struggles. By the early 1980s, various movements for people's rights had emerged: for civil, democratic, human and environmental rights; for the rights of adivasis and dalits; and not least, for the rights of women. These new social groupings, outside the formal party system, were scattered and sometimes contradictory but they constituted 'a rich seam of political experience' (Sathyamurthy 1996: 458). The increased awareness and articulation of women's rights during the 1980s needs to be viewed within this larger context. Such articulation forced some shifts in the emphasis of government and non-government interventions from welfare to providing information and managerial skills to women.

By the 1990s (the start of the fourth phase in Table 3.1) economic liberalization and the thrust towards market-oriented policies and globalization had begun to transform the ground. Even as these developments were swiftly eroding local natural resources, at another level, political and administrative decentralization continued. Most notable was the passing of the 1992 Constitution (73rd Amendment) Act, and the Panchayats (Extension to the Scheduled Areas) Act, 1996, which extended the 73rd Amendment to tribal areas (listed in Schedule V of the Constitution) that had not been covered earlier. (The 1996 Act does not apply to parts of north-eastern India that are in Schedule

VI or to states in the region that are covered by special constitutional arrangements.) The 73rd Amendment provides for a three-tier administrative structure, administrative and financial powers and a historic one-third representation for women in the elected village panchayats. It is of considerable significance for NRM because it provides the legal base for democratic control of local resources and for women's representation. The current policy climate also seems to favour participatory decision-making for a range of interventions from self-help for micro-credit and local management of water resources to participatory processes and techniques of seed exchange and plant breeding. In all of this women's involvement is being sought. Yet, there is considerable debate over whether this does indeed empower women and other subordinated groups, or renders them even more vulnerable to the penetration of global capital through the exploitation of their knowledge, skills and labour.

Current NRM programmes face the challenge of meshing environmental, economic and gender concerns. Let us suppose a programme to conserve the genetic resource of millets, which are dry-land subsistence crops, sets up linkages to metropolitan or export markets, this may well improve local incomes. Yet, because women are mainly responsible for cultivating the millet crops, this improvement in incomes could be at the cost of increasing women's labour. Further, as the scale of the millet production increases, this could also mean that (because of pre-existing patriarchal practices) it is the men who market the produce and control the income. This could then lead to altering women's status in the family. Therefore, the higher economic returns have to be weighed against the possible marginalization of women and the impact on gender relations in the community. So methods must be devised to deal with this. In contrast to interventions that simply increase women's labour, some recent international and national-level programmes for bringing women into the development process have focused on tapping women's energies, knowledge and skills to increase what is seen as the overall economic efficiency. This is in keeping with the global economic and market thrust. It is generally assumed that such an instrumental approach will somehow 'empower' women even if empowerment is not specifically addressed. As NRM is closely allied to the prevalent directions in development practice, it is also affected by these instrumentalist trends. (see S5)

We can conclude this section, by noting that the options before women have been limited in all the phases of development since Independence—through invisibility and marginalization, a welfare or instrumental approach. Typical welfare approaches (as reflected in the epigram above) do not feel the necessity for recognizing women as autonomous human beings in their own right. All of these dimensions can also be traced in the currently prevailing approaches to women and the environment.

APPROACHES TO WOMEN AND ENVIRONMENT

Feminist approaches to women and the environment comprise many diverse strands (Krishna 1995, 1997, 2000). Briefly, the politically liberal Women-Environment-Development (WED) approaches of the international agencies emphasize women's knowledge and skills, but tend to treat women's labour and time instrumentally as the means to increase the effectiveness of resource management. More radical ecofeminist strands highlight women's centrality to resource management and their nurturing and sustaining roles. Other strands draw upon materialist and social relations perspectives to stress the social construction of gender. The political lines between these various feminisms are somewhat blurred in the Indian context but three broad strands may be distinguished. I have called these Conventional, Celebratory and Gendered approaches. (Krishna 1997; 2001; 2004). In this section these various approaches are discussed.

Women-Environment-Development

In the 1970s, international development policy and research emphasized women's unequal share of the benefits of development. The new emphasis on 'integrating' women into the development process was politically liberal and focused on a more equal distribution of benefits in order to improve the efficiency and sustainability of development interventions. Women in Development WID, has led to a spurt in activities geared to income-generation for women so as to alleviate their dependence on male heads of households. The approach, however, has not been particularly concerned with the underlying structures and processes by which women are disadvantaged as compared to men in development policy and programmes. It was extended into the environmental field in the 1980s and came to be known as the Women-Environment-Development (WED) approach. The significance of WED is that it brought women into focus in the environmental field; the difficulty was that this focus valorized what comes 'naturally' to women (see also Jackson 1993).

For many of the anthropologists and development practitioners whose work laid the framework for the WID-WED approach, the concept of equality in biological separateness (derived directly or indirectly from Engels, see Chapter 1) has had a seductive appeal. Social anthropologist Lucy Mair, in an introductory text that is widely read in India and elsewhere, comments (1965, revised 1972):

> The biological division of humans into male and female is the basis for the most elementary social classification everywhere. In every society the division of roles between the sexes results from the fact that women bear and suckle children, and so are tied to the domestic scene for much of their lives. In those societies where the economy is one of *subsistence production*— where, that is, people get their food and other needs by their own labour from their immediate environment—a large share of the work of agriculture falls to women. Sometimes it is entirely their responsibility; in other places men do the heavy work of clearing the ground of grass before planting.

Mair acknowledges that in some societies men and women share agricultural work at all stages, but she also goes on to say that 'Men's tasks are those that call for extra physical strength and agility and that take them away from home—warfare, hunting, herding cattle, sea-fishing, canoe trading.' Noting that the tasks of governance and jural authority are men's, she remarks:

> In the division of roles between the sexes much of the work that falls to men is not manual labour. It consists in a good deal of talking, and since the place for talking can be chosen for its amenities, the talkers may sit in the shade while the toilers stand or walk in the sun. Hence the stereotyped picture of the African or Melanesian male idling while his womenfolk

work. It must be remembered that the tasks of maintaining social order and the right relation with the supernatural guardians of society are just as important for social life as the provision of food, even if they are less physically exhausting.

According to Mair's rather contradictory and ambiguous reasoning, women are tied to their homes because of their children but bear the major responsibility for food provisioning and do most of the agricultural labour out in the fields under the sun. Men's tasks are physically strenuous but men do not undertake much manual labour. If men seem to be idling, she tells us that they are actually maintaining the social and religious order through conversation. We will return to some of these issues (e.g. men's strength, agility and hunting prowess) in Chapter 4, but here it is necessary to note that such flawed socio-anthroplological reasoning fed directly into the politically conservative WID/ WED approach.

Drawing on the early writings of cognitive anthropologist Roy D'Andrade (1970: 15-49), the United Nations Development Programme (UNDP 1980: 6-7) claimed: 'The original basis of all sexual division of labour is undoubtedly men's and women's different role in human reproduction.' And further that this was reflected in the surviving subsistence economies characterized by inside and outside work spaces. In this view, women were responsible for gathering, production and processing food, fetching water and fuel, and local petty trade, all tasks that could be performed near the home. Men went hunting and fishing far from home, cleared the ground for shifting cultivation, were responsible for long distance trade and ensured the security of the community. Children were socialized into these masculine and feminine roles. Like Mair's account (above) the UNDP review too acknowledged that despite the sexual division of labour many activities were not related to physical differences, and furthermore in 'small communities or relatively self-contained households' men and women 'occasionally assisted' in each other's tasks. In this approach, the division of roles, which is seen as natural and functional, becomes rigid only with the stratification of society, cutting across and varying with class.

From a feminist standpoint, the problem with such an

approach is that the division of labour in society is seen as rooted in the division of roles in human sexual reproduction based on very limited and often biased anthropological records. This is narrowly situated knowledge. Moreover, the distinction drawn between the 'natural' and the biological or physical is ambiguous, because the natural is also located in the biological. This confusion is at the core of the WED approach, and has permeated NRM policy and programmes. The WID/WED approaches have been assimilated into Indian development and NRM policy and programmes, and today NRM projects continue to be imbued with the 1980s thesis that the division of labour in the surviving subsistence economies lies in male and female reproductive roles, with women being responsible for the so-called light and easy tasks that can be performed near the home (gathering, production and processing food, fetching water and fuel) while men are the strong hunters and fishers who travel afar.

Ecofeminisms

Even as international development agencies were shuffling between WAD and WID/WED, the more radical ecofeminist approach, which emerged in the 1970s, quickly gained prominence. Ecofeminism gathered into itself the accumulated dissatisfactions of the time, against modern science and technology, western imperialism, industrial development, and male domination of social and political life. Ecofeminism has been less interested in explaining the sexual division of female and male roles as in celebrating this difference. For instance, an early work (Davis: *The First Sex*, 1971: 335-36) stated: 'Man is the enemy of nature: to kill, to root up, to level off, to pollute, to destroy are his instinctive reactions.' Woman, on the other hand, 'is the ally of nature, and her instinct is to tend, to nurture, to encourage healthy growth, and to preserve ecological balance. She is the natural leader of society and civilization, and the usurpation of her primeval authority by man has resulted in uncoordinated chaos.' This had immense influence and inspired a cluster of radical approaches, many of which drew sustenance from poetry and mythology, 'earth-based religion' and Mother Goddess legends in different parts of the world (See Daly 1973, Griffin 1978, Merchant 1983, 1990, Spretnak 1990). In the 1980s, Ynestra King (1983) brought many of the elements of ecofeminism together to argue that men's domination over women was the 'prototype' for men's domination over nature. Some ecofeminists like King, Merchant and Griffin in her later work have veered towards a social construcionist approach. Others such as Plumwood (1986, 1993, 1994) and Mellors (1992, 1997) have striven to set out a nuanced, socialist understanding of the linkages between nature and women. But the broad sweep of popular ecofeminism has been in the celebration of women's bodies and values centred on women's reproductive capacities, birthing, mothering, nurturing, and caring. Globally, ecofeminism has enjoyed a high profile, especially in contesting military and reproductive technologies, although some strands of ecofeminism have been critiqued as essentialist and ahistorical.

In South Asia, the ecofeminist thesis has been advocated by Vandana Shiva (1989: 224) who says: 'Third World women are bringing the concern with living and survival back to centre-stage in human history. In recovering the chances for the survival of all life, they are laying the foundations for the recovery of the feminine principle in nature and society, and through it in the recovery of the earth as sustainer and provider.' This identification of women's biology and capacity for procreation with a 'feminine principle' in nature is elaborated in a collection of essays, *Ecofeminism* (Mies and Shiva 1993). Shiva's particular contribution to the ecofeminist debate is her association of women's roles in subsistence production in forests and agriculture with the 'feminine principle'. *Ecofeminism* holds that the 'capitalist, patriarchal world system' is founded upon and sustained by 'three colonizations': of women, of foreign people and their lands, and of nature. It projects a vision of a 'new sexual and reproductive ecology' rooted in linkages between the ecology of nature and the biology of women's bodies, between the exploitation of nature and the exploitation of women's wombs. Ecofeminism idealizes pre-colonial customary beliefs and traditional practices in South Asia because patriarchy is viewed as the outcome of Western culture and colonial politics. Taken as a whole, the South Asian version of ecofeminism (despite a socialist perspective) lacks the nuanced insights of some ecofeminist philosophers (see Warren ed. 1997) and tends towards an essentialism akin to that of the 'deep ecology' movements of the West.

The question of women's essential relationship with nature has been critiqued by those who advocate a more contextual and gendered approach to the environment, either from a material or/ and social relations perspective (see below and also S4 and S5). Unlike the WED approaches that emerged and operate within the arena of development/ sustainable development, all strands of ecofeminism are ranged in opposition to conventional development approaches. In contrast to WED, ecofeminism rejects positivist approaches to knowledge creation. Yet, paradoxically, both WED and ecofeminisms, which are opposed in the developmental field, share common ideological ground in their understanding of the sexual division of labour as the basis for social organisation. The difference is that for WED the basis of sex role differentiation is located in natural factors while for ecofeminism the basis lies in biological factors.

Gender and development

Women's special relationship with nature has been challenged by many (e.g. Joekes, Leach and Green eds. 1992, Leach 1994, Braidotti et al 1994,) who emphasize context-specificity, intra-household dynamics, access and control of resources, property rights and other aspects of gender-environment-development relations. Critiques of both WED and ecofeminism have pointed out that these approaches do not consider the structural and institutional character of gender-power relations, like class (or caste in India), through which gender inequities are established and reinforced. The attempt to address social relations more explicitly led to the Gender and Development (GAD) approach. The central focus of GAD is empowerment from below rather than simply integration into existing development programmes. GAD (like ecofeminism in this respect) is an engaged approach. It is unlike ecofeminism in challenging the assumed natural and biological basis of gender role differentiation and in seeking to transform gender relations. GAD uses the analytical method of gender analysis and gender analysis frameworks, which have been developed by various agencies in varied circumstances, and are a kind of tool kit that practitioners use in the field.

GAD is supported by several international donor agencies and academic institutions and has grown swiftly on a theoretical level; there is now a vast literature reflecting varied local natural resource contexts across the world. Drawing upon this, Caroline Moser brought 'gender planning' into the vocabulary of the World Bank; her clear articulation of this in *Gender Planning and Development: Theory, Practice and Training* led to a cluster of gender terms being incorporated into project documents and 'gender training' manuals around the world. Moser (1993: 1) asked whether it was possible to 'plan for the needs of low-income households generally' or whether it was 'necessary to plan for the needs of women in their own right?' She said this was a 'very simple question' that:

> ... provides the basis for the development of gender planning, as a new planning discipline with a specific focus on the issue of gender. It also allows us to recognize that because women and men have different positions within the household and different control over resources, they not only play different and changing roles in society, but also often have different needs. It is this role and needs differentiation that provides the underlying conceptual rationale for gender planning and defines its long-term goal as the emancipation of women. The fundamental planning principles, therefore, derive from the need to disaggregate households and families on the basis of gender, when identifying needs.

Although she emphasized that this was not an end in itself but a means by which women could emancipate themselves, many of those who broadly share a GAD approach take somewhat different positions. They include Naila Kabeer's *Reversed Realities* (1994) approach to development, Bina Agarwal's feminist environmentalism (1972) and the feminist political ecology approach of Dianne Rocheleau, Esther Wangari and Barbara Thomas-Slayter (1996). Kabeer's *Reversed Realities*, which focuses on development theory, identifies the household as the primary site for the construction of power relations, but also emphasizes the role of the market and the state. Kabeer's emphasis on social relations and transformatory politics has had wide appeal for feminists. Feminist political ecology brings a gendered perspective to the ideology of political ecology (itself a broadening of theories of political economy) and is concerned with a broad range of issues. Besides context-specificity, intra-household dynamics and the ownership and control of resources, questions relating to the construction of knowledge and the political linkages between local and global issues are also addressed.

Taking the cue from feminist economics, feminist sociology etc., Bina Agarwal (1997) has advanced the concept of 'feminist environmentalism' as an alternative to ecofeminism. She points out (op. cit: 191) that, 'People's relationship with nature is centrally rooted in and shaped by their material reality. Ideological constructions of women and nature impinge on this relationship but cannot be seen as the whole of it. People's responses to environmental degradation thus also need to be understood in the context of their material reality, their everyday interactions with nature, and their dependence on it for survival. To the extent that both women and men of poor peasant and tribal households are dependent on natural resources for livelihoods or for particular needs, both are likely to have a stake in environmental protection and regeneration.' She goes on to suggest that whether or not 'this leads to their initiating or participating in environmental action would, among other things, be contingent on the extent and nature of their dependence and their ability to act in their own interests. Gender specific responses can typically be traced to a given (unequal) gender division of labour, property and power, rather than primarily or solely to the notion of women being closer to nature than men, or to women's biology, as is suggested by the ecofeminist perspective'. The gender division of labour is clearly connected to gendered interests (see also Agarwal 2003).

In the developmental and NRM fields in India, there is considerable resistance to all of this, because it means recognizing the politics of gender-power relations. So, regardless of the language that may be used in policy statements and programme documents, projects continue within a WED mode, valorizing women's nurturing roles and their supposedly intimate essential connection to nature. Some of the methods and tools of gender analysis (used by the GAD/GED approaches), have seeped into NRM practice. But there is a constant slippage into the more instrumental WED approach. This indicates that the attitudinal, conceptual and methodological leaps required for GAD are actually quite elusive.

THREE APPROACHES IN THE INDIAN CONTEXT

In the Indian context, I have sketched a broad typology of approaches to women in the environmental field in general, which also apply to NRM. I have called these approaches (outlined in Table 3.2): conventional, celebratory and gendered (Krishna 1997; 2001, 2004). The three approaches draw upon South Asian gender ideologies and roughly correspond to the three environmental approaches (managerial, popular and progressive) sketched in *Environmental Politics* (see Introduction and Krishna 1996a). WED feeds into both the conventional and celebratory approaches. The nationalistic approach of the Indian freedom movement has had both conventional and celebratory elements. This is apparent in Gandhi's ambiguous valorization of Indian womanhood together with a belief in women's place being in the home in normal times (as opposed to the abnormal conditions of the freedom struggle). Ancient Indian patriarchal and romantic traditions and modern ecofeminism together constitute the celebratory approach. The gendered approach owes much to the understanding emerging from GAD but is not confined to the developmental field.

Conventional approaches

Conventional approaches recognize the gender-bias in economic development and resource management but the task is seen as improving women's capabilities and access. Science and technology are rather naively perceived as neutral. The thrust is to compensate for deficiencies in women's lives through education and wider opportunities. This was expressed even at the dawn of Independence and helped further women's participation in several domains. In the 1970s, with the emergence of contemporary feminism and the women's movement in India, academic and policy interests were re-focused on women's unequal share of developmental benefits. This led to a spurt in activities that ranged from encouraging girls' education to aiding women's economic activities. Home based income generation, for instance, was seen as the means to alleviate women's dependence on male 'heads' of households.

Conventional approaches fluctuate between treating women as invisible (subsumed under umbrella categories like 'people', 'farmers', 'scientists' etc.) to treating women as skilled in tasks that can presumably be performed in the vicinity of the home, food-gathering and processing, collecting fuel, fodder and water. Some conventional approaches (like the celebratory approaches) valorize women's 'natural' strengths of nurturing and caring but (unlike celebratory approaches) tend to see women's nature and sexuality as threatening and needing to be controlled. Men are viewed as the 'natural' heads of households, 'instinctive' hunters and fishers, endowed by male biology with the capacity to range over large areas. Conventional approaches to women are held not only by government developmental agencies but also by many of those who are otherwise opposed to conventional development.

In the conventional approach, women's work in NRM is either invisible or devalued; their capacities and capabilities, such as physical strength or intelligence, are doubted. This leads to a strong male bias in NRM with women being treated as instruments of conservation who provide labour and skills, a feature shared with WED. Even where a certain equality of women and men is projected there tends to be a hidden male standard; this too is shared with WED. The conventional approach, thus, tends to reinforce existing hierarchies.

Celebratory approaches

The celebratory approaches valorize sentiments that identify women with nature. Some early Indian strands of the celebratory approach treat the worlds (and work) of women and men as naturally separate domains. The glorification of women-in-nature can be traced far back into India's varied cultural history. Consider, for example, the strand expressed in Sanskrit poetic drama. Kalidasa's bird-woman Shakuntala is named for the birds (*shakuntas*), who nursed her and with whom she could converse. Kalidasa's Shakuntala and her 'coy maidens' in an unspoilt forest reflect women's assumed closeness to nature. As already mentioned, modern ecofeminist approaches take this further, based on what is seen as an essential linkage between women's procreative capacity and a 'feminine principle' in nature. In South Asia, this has been related to women's subsistence production, and has been set in opposition to Western science and technology, which are seen as masculine projects to subjugate both women and nature (Mies and Shiva 1993, see also S4).

All celebratory approaches (popular ecofeminist or/and some Gandhian approaches) focus on women exclusively, valorizing their biological, emotional and intuitive capacities and their subsistence lifestyles. Some ecofeminist strands may also devalue men's work. As mentioned earlier, women tend to be treated in an essentialist way as natural managers of the environment, and their roles in NRM are seen as naturally determined (WED) or biologically determined (ecofeminism). Like WED, celebratory approaches accept a hierarchy of dual norms, but the system of values is reversed with the feminine being exalted and the existing hierarchies reversed.

The problem with both the conventional and celebratory approaches is that they rest on claims that grow out of the sexual division of labour, which is seen as essential and universal. Context-specific class and caste differences are blurred, neglecting inequities of access to natural resources within communities and households. The understanding is that traditionally demarcated occupational roles are somehow 'natural' and contribute to resource conservation. This may lead to exaggerating women's natural resource knowledge (see Jewitt 2000) and even to overlooking men's natural resource and provisioning responsibilities (see Leach, Joekes and Green 1995). Socio-cultural practices and gender ideologies that restrict women's autonomy, mobility and capacity to participate in resource management are not admitted and, therefore, not addressed.

Gendered approaches

In contrast to the conventional and celebratory approaches, gendered approaches seek to challenge dual norms for women and men (Krishna 2001, 2004). Indeed, gender is seen as central to power relations, and to the dichotomization of physical spaces and mental capacities, not just between men and women, but also between women and women, men and men (Faith 1995:

61). Women's exclusion and alienation from different domains of knowledge is charactezised as the result of a process of historical and cultural construction that derives from men's power over society and also reinforces it. Gendered approaches seek to interrogate cultural stereotypes of masculinity and femininity, and to understand how ideologies influence the acquisition of beliefs and the production of knowledge. As I have commented elsewhere (Krishna 2004a), the knowledge, attitudes and practices of NRM carry a gendered (i.e. male or female) imprint but women's claims to participation and equity in resource management should not be based on the sexual division of labour, roles and responsibilities. Conventional approaches seek to promote women in the natural sciences, integrate gender-responsiveness into policies and programmes and use gender-sensitive tools in projects. In contrast, gendered approaches go further to argue that the practice of natural science cannot be separated from the cognitive content of the discipline and discourse of natural science. (This is taken up in Chapter 4).

Gendered approaches (drawing upon GAD) focus on the gender relations of women and men, and treat women's roles as socially constructed by gender ideologies. Varied contexts and historical changes are encompassed more easily than in the other approaches, so that shifts in work relations and the division of labour are related to both material and ideological conditions. Gendered approaches treat both women and men as having the capacity to manage resources. They go beyond the conventional and the celebratory approaches, which address 'women's needs', to question the social relations that have given women these needs. Gendered approaches would seek to address both 'gender justice' and the question of 'basic needs', seeking to explore the linkages between women's subordination and poverty in situations of environmental stress.

By dealing with the physical-spatial, socio-economic and socio-political aspects of women's subordination, gendered approaches challenge existing hierarchical dichotomies and are thus potentially transformatory. Characteristics which are shared by gendered approaches can be summarized as: a) recognizing particular feminist standpoints b) not seeking a simple regularity of cause and effect; c) accepting multiple paths, explanations and solutions; and d) encompassing different analytic methods. Two other characteristics of gendered approaches that are of significance: e) taking into consideration the entire lifecycle of women and men; and f) aiming to transform gender relations.

Women's subordination, poverty and basic needs [2]

The impact of economic and environmental change on gender roles and relations would depend on the socioeconomic level of households and the communities in which these are nested; on the kind of occupations in which members of the household are engaged and even on the location and topography of settlements. The Indian environmental movement, however, has been particularly resistant to class analysis, while recognizing diversity across geographic locations (Krishna 1996a). One consequence is some ambivalence in conceptualizing poverty. How women's poverty is characterized shapes views of the environmental and gender impact of particular structural changes and the analysis of the various coping strategies that women adopt.

Several studies have shown that poverty is multi-dimensional rather than the monetary equivalent of a minimum consumption level. Amartya Sen (1992: 116) says:

> Poverty analysis that concentrates only on incomes can be quite remote from the main motivation behind our concern with poverty (viz. the limitation of the *lives* that some people are forced to live.) It may also fail to provide empirical guidance regarding the genesis and prevalence of deprivation. Concentrating on the right space is no less important for poverty study than it is for the general investigation of social inequality.

Jackson (1998: 59-60) goes further to argue that 'gender justice' is not a poverty issue' and favours 'rescuing gender from the poverty trap because the subordination of women is not caused by poverty'. Recognizing that many gender concerns are not related to poverty, it is still necessary in the Indian context to pay attention to the gendered aspects of poverty and gender-specific indicators. It is now accepted that economic growth is not always reflected in human development, and that income level is not strongly correlated with gender equality (Haq 1997). But it is more difficult to relate indicators of women's status (Rustagi 1998) with specific conditions of environmental stress.

Some significant dimensions of poverty mentioned in the literature are: demographic factors like life expectancy and infant mortality rates (IMR); purchasing/bargaining power arising from household income or the ownership of assets; the fulfilment of basic needs including food consumption, shelter and clothing. If the primary factor in assigning the position of rural households within the system of production relations is 'whether the household exploits the labour of others, is self-employed or is itself exploited by others' (Patnaik 1987:201), some women's domestic labour might render them poor members of better-off households; so too widows and old people. The use of IMR (the rate of mortality of infants aged below one month) as an indicator of impoverishment has been modified by UNICEF in recent years; the preferred indicator is now the mortality rate of children below five years: U5MR (the Under 5 Mortality Rate). This age group accounts for roughly half of all recorded deaths. Because the U5MR also has linkages to environmental conditions and to women's empowerment, it is probably the single most effective indicator of gender susceptibility to illness and disease. Karlekar (2000) has cited *Towards Equality*, the Report of the Committee on the Status of Women (ICSSR 1974), which had noted that childbearing was a 'health hazard' for Indian women. I would suggest, therefore, that the Maternal Mortality Rate (MMR) could be a key measure of environmental stress and impoverishment, especially in times of economic transformation.

The concept of basic needs is more complicated because the perception of need is not static. At one extreme are some strands of environmentalism that romanticise poverty and subsistence lifestyles. At the other extreme is the typical middle class view which sees any difference from its own way of life as a deprivation which has to be made up—this is sharply evident in urban attitudes to tribal attire, for instance. Environmentalists would also include within basic needs the availability (through gathering) of diverse food and biomass resources, such as seeds, firewood and fodder.

Of particular interest are possible linkages between the quality and availability of common biomass resources and women's health and literacy. For Vandana Shiva (1988), the subsistence lifestyle of food-gathering tribes who live close to nature is a lifestyle of affluence. Without taking the argument so far, Madhav Gadgil and Ramachandra Guha (1992) argue that till the early twentieth century and the disrupting inroads of colonialism, some hunter-gatherer groups were very nearly affluent societies living in harmony with nature. Historically, certain subsistence economies have survived because of the richness and diversity of freely available natural resources. Yet, I find D.D. Kosambi more convincing when he says that subsistence lifestyles have been sustained over time only by incorporating inputs provided by the 'enveloping' society. Moreover, a community which is 'affluent' in terms of a rich natural resource base, may be impoverished in terms of life expectancy at birth and freedom from disease. For poor tribal groups, today, the importance of biologically diverse—and free—resources is that in times of stress these provide a buffer against the intensification of poverty. In many parts of India, this is so also for non-tribal peasant communities for whom the produce of the home garden is a significant source of sustenance. In Kerala, backyard cultivation of a range of produce is a major contribution to household consumption and compensates for low productivity and purchasing power, but whether this contributes to gender equality is not clear.

Judgements about the impact of change on the lives of poor women have to be tempered by an understanding of the many dimensions of poverty (not all of which can be neatly quantified). Various factors need to be considered: food intake, assets including land holding; position in the production system; fulfilment of basic needs, including biomass; women's empowerment, including female literacy; women's health/MMR; and child mortality, especially female child mortality (U5MR). As N.S. Jodha (1988) points out, rural socioeconomic change is often inadequately captured. Because of methodological inadequacies and the perceptions of researchers. His ground-breaking micro-study of two villages in Rajasthan shows that households that had become poorer by conventional measurements of income appeared better off when seen through other qualitative indicators of change. These indicators include several factors which are of considerable environmental and gender significance, such as: less reliance on the support of rich patrons for employment and sustenance; the rejection of low-status, low-paid jobs including gathering of declining common property resources; increased liquidity and the ability to make bulk purchases in cash; improvements in the quality and quantity of food consumption, including maternity diets for women; and an 'impressive' change in the possession of consumer durables, *pukka* houses, separate living spaces for animals and humans, and private bathing places for women. The only negative nutritional change was a decline in milk consumption, a direct result of the growth of milk-marketing—which had, however, raised household incomes. It is not possible to generalize from this study, as Jodha himself points out. Official data on nutrition (GoI 1993: 3) show that while impressive gains have been made since the sixties in eradicating 'extreme hunger and starvation', there are still 'different degrees of chronic and endemic hunger which, in the context of the prevailing patterns of intra-household food distribution, particularly in rural families, translate into a grave danger for the nutritional status of women and children.'

Gender and technology

The gender-technology question is of especial relevance to NRM. Questions relate both to particular technologies and to the crosscutting issues arising from a range of technologies. We need to ask what assumptions are being made in the process of technology development, the design, manufacture, marketing and use of products; whether women are involved in the decision-making process of technological development; and whether and how such development is transforming gender relations and women's work.

The feminist approach to the relationship between gender and technology is not homogenous. The liberal and conventional approach does not critique technology, which is seen as inherently neutral. Therefore, the problem is naively perceived as one of improving women's access to technology (and their capacities to do so) in a society that is gendered by stereotypical sex roles. The ecofeminist and celebratory approach is that technology is inherently masculine and has been used by men to subjugate women and nature. The forces that shape society and technology are not distinguished separately, and particular technologies are not studied. Ecofeminist arguments have been tellingly used against military and reproductive technologies, and have valorised 'feminine' technological knowledge and skills arising from women's biology and presumed closeness to nature.

From a gendered perspective, this is essentialist and ahistorical. The gendered approach rejects both the liberal/conventional and ecofeminist/ celebratory approaches (of technology being inherently neutral or inherently masculine) and views women's exclusion and alienation from technology as the result of a process of historical and cultural construction of technology as masculine, and of masculinity as involving technical capabilities. This inter-weaving of masculinity and technology is seen as both a product of men's power in society and as reinforcing it. (This position has been advanced among others by Cynthia Cockburn 1983, 1992, 1999, J. Wajcman 1999, Rosalind Gill and Keith Grint 1995). Gender divisions of labour shape the process of technology-development and technological products carry a gendered, male or female, imprint.[3] Some would go further to argue that gender itself is shaped by technology—'the construction of men as strong, manually able and technologically endowed and woman as physically and technically incompetent' (Cockburn 1983: 207). The gendering of both traditional and modern technologies has influenced development policy broadly and NRM in particular, as well as the different approaches to women's work and their roles in resource conservation and sustainability.

For those who have not been exposed to either feminist or social-construction perspectives, it may be difficult to grasp the idea that the processes by which science and technology are created (and not just their application) are shaped by class, gender and other divisions of society and that scientific theories and technological artefacts themselves carry this imprint. The next chapter unpacks some aspects of this process in the natural science disciplines.

NOTES

¹ In conversation with the author, Chennai. 2003.

² This is based on part of a section of my chapter in *Shifting Sands: Women's Lives and Globalization* (Krishna 2000).

³ One of the best known examples, although not from the NRM field, is the computer keyboard (see Webster 1996). The initial design of dedicated word processors in the 1970s was developed to mimic and automate the office typewriter—typing in the West having been almost entirely female work. However, as in the earlier case of typewriter development, the needs of the women keyboard operators were not considered. So, the inappropriate QWERTY typewriter keyboard, which overloads the fingers of the left hand, was simply replicated in the word processor. This is only now being re-examined as the spread of the technology has altered the word-processor's specific link with low paid women's secretarial office work, and as both men and women users of personal computers have begun to suffer from repeated stress injuries.

Table 3.1: Gender Implications of Approaches to Rural Development

Overlapping Periods	Approach/ goal	Main rural intervention/ method	Response-model thrust of village community	Main focus of intervening agency	Implications for gender equity
1950s–late 60s	Centralized economic reconstruction	Community Development Block structure–village level workers	*Shramdan*, community self-help and co-operative enterprise	Administer, motivate, guide	Women rendered invisible; work not recognized; welfare approach to domestic roles;
Mid-60s–early 80s	National economic self-sufficiency	Major technological interventions	Individual agency/ spread through demonstration effect	Provide technical know-how, teach new technical skills	Improved quality of life for some; increased labour; marginalization of women
Late-70s–early 90s	Decentralized administration	Local decision-making; mediation through NGOs	New social groupings/ pressure from 'below'	Advocacy, provide information/ managerial skills	Increased awareness and articulation of women's rights
Late 80s–present	Global economic integration	Local management; savings and micro-entrepreneurship	Participatory decision-making; Self-Help Groups	Participatory appraisal/ organisation for credit management	Empowering? Or instrumentalist use of women's knowledge, labour, skills?

Source: Krishna, Sumi 2004a

Table 3.2: Approaches to Women

Aspects	Conventional	Celebratory	Gendered
Focus	On people, women are assumed to be included	Concentrated on women	On women and men
Women's role in NRM	Uncommitted; seek more research	View as naturally-determined (or in some cases biologically-determined)	View as socially constructed
Use of Gender Analysis (GA) (see Chapter 9)	No GA, but the term 'gender' is used	Neither GA, nor the term 'gender' is used	GA is used; gender is seen as one of many social determinants
Place of women's concerns in projects	Tag women on to projects	Valorise women's subsistence skills and lifestyles	Has difficulties in converting GA into practice
Implication for women in relation to NRM	Use women in instrumentalist ways, ask what women can do for NRM; Address 'women's needs'	Essentialize and treat all women alike as skilled nurturers and resource managers Address women's needs	Attempt to address gender relations, and ask what NRM can do for women in the long term
Gender labels/ stereotypes	Reinforce existing hierarchical dichotomies	Reverse existing hierarchical dichotomies	Challenge existing hierarchical dichotomies

Source: Adapted from Krishna, Sumi 1997 and 2004a.

4
The Natural Sciences: Recognizing Gender Bias

'Thus man has ultimately become superior to woman. It is indeed fortunate that the law of equal transmission of characters to both sexes prevails
with mammals. Otherwise it is probable that man would have become as
superior in mental endowment to woman as the peacock is in ornamental
plumage to the peahen.'
—Charles Darwin (*The Descent of Man*, 1871: 874)

This chapter and those that follow explore substantive issues and
themes that lie at the core of natural resource management. Here
I deal with some aspects of the discipline of natural science. I am
especially concerned with how gender-bias in the basic natural
science disciplines moulds the attitudes of scientists and the technologies and practices related to natural resources. The chapter
starts with a brief introduction to the context in which feminist
resistance to masculinist ideology in the natural sciences emerged.
The next section then highlights certain widely prevalent gender-
biased attitudes. Scientists are not trained to recognize that the
sciences, no less than the humanities and the social sciences, are
constituted by the cultures of their time and location. In the third
section I suggest that gender bias is related to the gendered assumptions embedded in 'key-stone stories' of the natural science
disciplines, which are uncritically passed on through natural science education. Of particular interest from the perspective of NRM

in India are the discussions around the gendered conceptualization of gathering-hunting peoples. In the final section, I argue that it is necessary to understand and resist such biases in order to transform resource management practices.

FEMINIST RESISTANCE

During the 19th century, religious and political concepts of a 'great chain of being' and a hierarchy of human types seemed to be reinforced by the modern natural science disciplines. Racism and ethnocentrism sought a biological basis to explain inequalities among peoples. However, by the mid-20th century, following the racial holocaust in Europe and World War II, political pressure brought sociologists, anthropologists, biologists, geneticists and others together under the aegis of UNESCO (1952) to rethink ideas related to race. Drawing upon a growing wealth of scientific evidence on variation in population genetics, two influential statements were issued that held that for all practical purposes race was more a social myth than a biological phenomenon, and that according to the available knowledge, groups of mankind did not differ in mental characteristics, intelligence or temperament. A humanistic ethic of universal brotherhood was being propagated but this was implicitly gender-biased. The science historian Donna Haraway (1992: 201) has drawn attention to 'the inherited cost of unexaminable, unintentional, and therefore particularly powerful, scientific sexism.' Nevertheless, as she points out, re-visioning of the complex relations between biology and culture with regard to race did help to create a climate within anthropology and other related disciplines in which new questions could be asked about the construction of essentializing human categories.[1]

It was only in the late 1960s that Western feminists began re-evaluating the 'scientific' evidence to reveal how gender is written into processes of knowledge creation and shapes our conception of nature and women's nature. Since then, feminist studies of the content, culture and workings of science and technology have shown how women have been rendered invisible and marginalized in the human story. Richly nuanced and varied approaches have contested theories of women's inferiority, the rejection of different ways of knowing, the exclusion of women's perspectives and the reinforcement of gender hierarchies. Critiques of the gendered character of particular disciplines and technologies gained strength and clarity in the US and in parts of Europe. Feminist theory opened up an exciting cross-disciplinary area for collaboration between scientists and social scientists engaged in socio-cultural studies of natural science (Harding 1991, 2000, Shiebinger 1999, Reid and Traweek eds. 2000). Biologist Evelyn Fox Keller (2004) led the feminist resistance to masculinist ideology in the natural sciences; she said that 'being a scientist' she 'chose to extend the kinds of analysis feminists were employing in the humanities and social sciences to the natural sciences.' In particular, she 'sought to understand the genesis of the sexual and emotional division of labor, so conspicuously prevalent in my own generation, that labeled mind, reason, and objectivity as 'male', and heart (and body), feeling, and subjectivity as 'female', and hence, that underlay the historic exclusion of women from the scientific endeavor.' She further said:

> My hope was that to identify such traces of masculinist ideology in the natural sciences would lead to their purging, for surely, here of all places, they ought not to be tolerated. It was a heady time, and like so many of my colleagues in feminist theory, my aim was ambitious to the point of grandiosity: perhaps less ambitious than seeking to change the world, I sought merely to change science.

In India, we have had some attempts to challenge the gender bias in scientific institutions and in particular the 'glass ceiling' for women in science, but none to change the nature of science. Social science research and the women's movement have had close and mutually beneficial links. Activists have drawn upon the lived experience of women to theorize gender, femininities and masculinities. Action researchers have established linkages with other social struggles, notably those for environmental and human rights. Since the 1970s, issues related to the science and management of the environment and natural, living resources have been in the foreground. Factors related to the political economies of forestry and agriculture in different parts of India have been studied. Yet, the historical gendering of natural science has not been effectively interrogated (except to some extent in the area of women's health). and this is apparent in the attitudes and practice of conservationists and other natural scientists.

GENDER BIAS IN ATTITUDES AND PRACTICE

What one sees depends on our belief systems and mental outlook. The act of obtaining natural resource data is gendered. For instance, there is a widespread tendency to view women's agricultural tasks as less arduous than men's, although the evidence from the field often points to women bearing a greater load of physical tasks than do the men (Mencher 1993, Krishna 1998a). On field visits, I have continually come across contradictions between what I am told by researchers about women's roles and what the women are actually doing. In one instance, a team of male scientists told me that women do not row boats to fish but I pointed out a photograph taken earlier by other team members that showed a woman rowing. When queried, one of them initially said, 'No, no it can't be a woman.' Then he scrutinised it and said, it must have been an exception. Subsequently, at the same location, I saw a few young women using oars to row or a long pole to propel their boat along the backwaters. It was not very common but certainly not exceptional. Yet, the young men had simply not noticed this because in the prevailing gender ideology women and girls 'do not row'.

Over the years, I have interacted professionally with biological and life scientists of varied ages and socio-cultural backgrounds, at different universities and institutions, with different sub-specializations but with a shared interest in the conservation and sustainable management of natural resources. Several are gender-sensitive, feminist men but most are not. Some are humanist in their outlook but harbour unexamined assumptions about women. Here is a small verbatim sample of comments made to me in all seriousness by young scientists. The comments were made in both formal and informal settings with the confidence of articulating a proven fact; only occasionally would a younger scientist hedge his statement by saying it was what he had heard or read, not what he himself thought:

Biased comments related to women's weaker physique: It is a scientifically stablished fact that women are weaker than men. Women cannot carry heavy loads. Men require more rest because they do more laborious work in the field.

Biased comments related to anatomical and physiological differences: Women undertake transplanting and weeding because they can bend at their waists, which men cannot do because of men's more muscular physique. Women carry head loads of firewood because their necks are naturally stronger than men's. Women cook because they are biologically more capable than men of bearing the heat of the hearth or stove. The division of roles in the family is based on biological (i.e. physiological) attributes.

Biased comments related to bio-chemistry and genes: Men are heads of households because they have the advantage of male hormones. Idleness is in the male tribals' blood. The only way to change female tribals' bad character is to marry them to change their genes.

All these comments happened to come from men but women scientists (and men and women who are not scientists) could just as well hold the same views. Patriarchal, ethnocentric bias is not the preserve of male scientists. Many scientists pride themselves on their rationality and objectivity and they do acknowledge gender-bias in the natural resource arena, but they see this as an attitudinal problem of the individual or a social problem of application in the field unrelated to the relevant natural science disciplines. They do not question the neutrality of science and technology. It seems to me, however, that natural scientists in India who have trained in ecology, biology and other life science disciplines are especially influenced by elements of sociobiological theory and more recently by genetic determinism. Many of the elements that make up sociobiological and genetically deterministic approaches are embedded in and derived from the narratives of natural science. I now turn to some of these narratives, which I have called the 'keystone stories'.

GENDERED CRITIQUES OF SOME 'KEYSTONE STORIES'[2]

Feminist analyses have uncovered the gendered epistemology of several scientific disciplines—paleo-archaeology and anthropology, anatomy and physiology in medicine; botanical and zoological taxonomy and evolutionary biology in the life sciences. The works of Donna Haraway (1992), Evelyn Fox Keller (1995), Keller and Helen Longino (1996), Emily Martin (1996), Londa Schiebinger (1991), Linda Fedigan (1986), Sally (Linton) Slocum (1971), Susan Sperling (1991/ 1996) and others have successfully unraveled many of the 'master' romances of science. Most notably, in recent years, primatology has been transformed by feminist perspectives. Keller has a fan following in gender studies circles in India, but, with the possible exception of her biography of Barbara McClintock, *A Feeling for the Organism* (1983), students of the natural and life sciences are unfamiliar with this entire body of rich and varied work. The examples in the following sections have been selected because of the clarity with which they reveal how gender structures natural science, whether it be at the level of metaphors, systems of classification or of theory.

Metaphors: 'Sleeping Beauty' and the warrior knight

The anthropologist Emily Martin (1996) has shown how pictures of the egg and the sperm in both popular and scientific accounts of reproductive biology are shaped by cultural stereotypes of female and male. The cultural stereotypes that pass into biology carry a distinct loaded message that female biological processes and women themselves are 'less worthy' than their male counterparts. Analysing the language of numerous scientific reports, Martin (1996: 105-106) says: 'It is remarkable how "femininely" the egg behaves and how "masculinely" the sperm. The egg is seen as large and passive. It does not *move* or *journey*, but passively "is transported, is swept," or even "drifts" along the fallopian tube. In utter contrast, sperm are small, "streamlined" and invariably active. They "deliver" their genes to the egg, "activate" the developmental program of the egg, and have a "velocity" that is often remarked upon. Their tails are "strong" and efficiently powered . . . so that with a "whiplash like motion and strong lurches" they can "burrow through the egg coat" and "penetrate" it.' The egg is most commonly pictured as a passive, fragile 'damsel in distress', a 'sleeping beauty' (Schatten and Schatten 1984), protected by sacred 'vestments' till the heroic warrior sperm attacks and accomplishes the 'mission' of rescuing her.

Martin points out that new researches have now altered the earlier understanding of the biophysics of egg and sperm. It is now known that they are mutually active partners and 'stick together because of adhesive molecules on the surfaces of each'. The egg in effect traps the sperm; the mechanical force of the sperm's tail is actually very weak but it releases digestive enzymes that enable it to move in. Yet, although these new scientific interpretations seem to break through the cultural barriers, the researchers continue to conceptualize the story through the old imagery, with the sperm actively attacking and penetrating the egg. One recent study even talks of the sperm harpooning the egg. In another, the 'imagery of sperm as aggressor is particularly startling' says Martin because the 'main discovery being reported is isolation of a molecule *on the egg coat* that plays an important role in fertilization!' Even when the active role of the egg is recognized, it is pictured as a spider lying in wait, drawing upon images of the *femme fatale*. Martin argues that the stereotypical imagery of egg and sperm are not 'dead' metaphors and that the 'feminist challenge is to wake up the sleeping metaphors of science'.

Classification: The loves and marriages of plants

The image of the passive female and other such metaphors have shaped the organization of particular disciplines. This is vividly reflected in Londa Schiebinger's (1991) historical analysis of the emergence of botanical taxonomy. She shows how the 'universal laws of nature' have been read from the viewpoint of 18th century social relations in Europe. Till the 17th century, the botanical interest in plants had centred on their use as medicines, fibres, condiments, dyes and foods. The emphasis then shifted from local and particular herbal knowledge systems to abstract and universal methods of categorization. This coincided with growing interest in studies of plant sexuality. The many different classificatory systems in use were overtaken by the system put forward by Carl Linnaeus in 1735 based on the difference between the male and female parts of flowers, their sexual morphology. In the Linnaean system, and the later phylogenetic systems developed by Engler and Prantle and by Hooker and Bentham, the 'vegetable world' of plants comprises of classes that depend on the numbers, relative proportions and positions of the male parts (stamens). Classes are subdivided into orders, similarly based on female parts (pistils). Schiebinger points out that the gender hierarchy of 18th century European society was replicated in botanical nomenclature with the male classes taking precedence over female orders. (Today, the classes and orders of plants are not used but the lower rungs of the Linnaean classification into family, species, genus and variety continues; Hooker and Bentham's 19th century *Flora of British India* is still a major taxonomical reference.)

Schiebinger argues that not only was gender used to structure botanical taxonomy but human sexual metaphors were explicitly introduced into botanical literature. Both Linnaeus and Erasmus Darwin viewed plants as highly erotic creatures. Schiebinger argues that Linnaeus saw everything female, even a plant, as 'wife' and interpreted plant reproduction in terms of human marital relations. He did not use asexual terms like 'stamen' (derived from the word for warp thread in fabric) and 'pistil' (pestle) but used the Greek words for husband and wife, *andria* and *gynia*. The classification of plants depended on types of marriage: The class of *monandria* are monogamous; the order of *polygamia* are polygamous, plant 'husbands' live with wives and harlots (concubines) in marriage beds. (Indeed, the scientific term 'gamete' for the mature germ cell that unites with another in sexual reproduction is derived from the Greek word for marriage.)

Unlike the politically conservative Linnaeus, Erasmus Darwin was a democrat and materialist but both scientists followed conventional notions with regard to women. The sexual imagery in Erasmus Darwin's poetic treatise *The Loves of Plants* may seem to be rather at odds with his traditional advocacy of distinct roles for women and men in society. But Schiebinger points out that like Rousseau, Erasmus Darwin 'held that the female character was to possess mild and retiring virtues rather than bold and dazzling displays . . . female learning and refinements were not to lead to professional employ, but were to be directed toward enhancing the home life of prospective husbands.' Schiebinger suggests that this was actually in keeping with broader political trends that emphasized sexual difference and complimentarity between unequals. Middle class prescriptions of sexual complimentarity, thus, actually served to maintain gender hierarchy (Schiebinger op. cit.): 'The theory of sexual complimentarity fits neatly into dominant strands of democratic thought by making inequalities seem natural, while satisfying the needs of European society for a continued sexual division of labour'.

The unequal sexual division of labour is not just a matter of the metaphors and systems of nomenclature and classification in science but this has had an even deeper imprint on theories of human evolution for a century and more from Charles Darwin to Owen Lovejoy, to which I now turn.

Theory: Women tag along in human evolution

It was the 18th century Scottish economist and philosopher Adam Smith (1776) who postulated that all of human history was a progression through four economic stages, each with its characteristic social and political structures: hunting-gathering, pastoral-nomadic, agricultural-feudal, and commerce-manufacturing. In his view, Scotland was on the brink of entering the fourth and final stage. Today, however, it is apparent that the concept of hunting and gathering societies, so deeply ingrained in our thinking since Adam Smith, may not have emerged from field ethnography, empirical studies, or exploration but was an *idea* advanced by the 18th century Scottish thinkers. Barnard (2002) has recently argued that the very conception of hunter-gatherer societies was constructed in the 18th century, an 'invention' of the Scottish Enlightenment.[3] If this is so, one could further argue that the gender-differentiation of economic activities in these societies is also a social invention. All of the Scottish thinkers were men who lived and worked in a gender-differentiated world. The theoretical understanding of these men and others who laid the foundations of some of the academic disciplines that we recognize today was certainly shaped by their European middle class milieu. This has had a pervasive influence on subsequent generations of ethnographers and natural scientists possibly, if not certainly, colouring their reports from the field. It can also be argued that these perceptions later seeped into public policies in the European colonies, as in India, and contributed several erroneous ideas, including that of the pristine subsistence lifestyle of tribal peoples. But let us return to Charles Darwin and the ideas of natural science.

In the latter part of the 19th century, scientific interest in models of human evolution centred around sex roles and inter-relations between men and women in early human society. Darwin explained the role of secondary sexual characteristics on the basis of competition and choice. Linda Fedigan (1986) argues that Darwin's thesis that sexual selection had occurred in humans was based on the belief that human males were 'more courageous, energetic, pugnacious and sexually assertive' than females, besides being bigger. According to Darwin, men had the advantage of size in primitive times because they 'fought to the death for access to women' and in modern times because they had to work harder than women for their subsistence. Darwin saw women as more nurturant, reclusive and altruistic than men because in their case nature does not work to select the assertive male traits and be-cause women's 'maternal instincts' are extended to infants and others in the group.

Darwin also argued that traits are selected for in males but because of what he theorized was 'the equal transmission of char-acters' women are able to tag along in the evolutionary process. In a now infamous passage in *The Descent of Man* (1871: 874) Dar-win concluded: 'Thus man has ultimately become superior to woman' (see epigram above). As many have noted, it is apparent that Darwin simply mapped upper-class Victorian culture onto nature. In the 20th century, his notion of 'equal transmission of characters' was succeeded by a new understanding of human ge-netics. But his model of social relations between the sexes contin-ued its hold on the scientific imagination. The sexist aspects of Darwinian theory have been widely critiqued but, despite a mass of contrary evidence, have proved most difficult to dislodge. More than a century later, Darwin's superior man found expression in stories of Man the Hunter.

Man the Hunter

The late 1960s was a period of upheaval across many parts of the world with a wave of social movements for civil and women's rights, for peace (anti-the US war in Vietnam) and for the environment. The 1950s quest for a universal anti-racist humanity acquired a sharper edge. It was in this milieu that physical anthropologist Sherwood Washburn sought a master pattern, a unifying account of the evolution of 'man'. Functional fossil anatomy and primate behavioural studies were conjoined to produce a theory of adaptation at the origins of human life that did not lend itself to racist exploitation. The neo-Darwinian concept of the evolution of populations was overlaid by the functionalists' concept of social groups with distinct needs and roles. Patterns of behaviour were the key in humanist conceptions of evolution espoused by Gaylord Simpson (1958) and others. In Washburn's view, the critical human adaptation was the hunting way of life (Washburn and Lancaster 1968). Thus, Man the Hunter (Lee and DeVore eds. 1968) was fabricated.

It is ironic that the liberal, democratic humanist quest for a universal man had produced a heroic masculinist narrative. Fedigan (1986) lists the range of aspects that were said to have emerged from men's hunting: 'bipedalism, elaborate tool kits, development of language, appreciation of beauty, male aggressiveness, pleasure in killing, division of labour, nuclear monogamous family, loss of female oestrus, invention of incest taboos, and bonding between males.' The narrative also contained the androcentric picture of women confined to the vicinity of the home, providing sexual and reproductive services in exchange for protection and provisioning.

Woman the Gatherer

Among the first to counter the hunting model was Sally Linton (1971); in an 'oogonial' essay she argued that men's hunting of big animals was a later evolutionary development that came after the establishment of the matrifocal sharing family.[4] In her model, hunting spoils are first shared with mothers and siblings and not with sexual partners. This was elaborated by Adrienne Zihlman and Nancy Tanner (1978) leading to the emergence of an alternative model of Woman the Gatherer. Linton also inspired the shift away from men's hunting tools (projectiles, arrowheads, knives, spears, axes) to women's tools such as digging sticks, baskets, and slings (to carry babies). Most responses to Woman the Gatherer seem to envisage a scenario of either male-hunter/or female-gatherer. Haraway (1992: 340) points out that the narrative logic of

Zihlman's 'woman the gatherer' and Washburn's 'man the hunter' are not symmetrical. 'The stories were not opposites; they involved different doctrines of cause and origin, not simply different central actors or bits of evidence. . . . The presence of the heterosexual nuclear family and the tool-weapon equation in masculinist scientific narratives was about a theory of social reproduction called paternity. . .'

An early response to Woman the Gatherer was co-option. In an invited paper in the influential journal *Science*, Owen Lovejoy (1981) accepted that gathering was the crucial technological invention but argued that it was done by men. His contention was that production and reproduction could not be successfully combined. In his model women continued to be home-based. A third (and less well-known) response came from Lila Leibowitz (1983) who shared Lovejoy's interest in how early humans survived but arrived at an entirely different conclusion. She argued that sex differences did not characterize early human evolution and that all individuals in a group participated in gathering and accumulating surplus food. Commenting on this Fedigan (1986) says, 'Given that primate females are able to combine foraging with infant care, and that women in most societies contribute at least as much as men to subsistence in addition to their reproductive activities, Leibowitz's scenario may be no more or less data-based and plausible than the many models that seek to give preeminence to one or the other sex in the story of human evolution.'

Hunter-gatherers and Gatherer-hunters

One response to Woman the Gatherer is a 'sharing' model (Potts 1984) that superimposes gathering onto hunting to create hyphenated hunting-gathering societies but does not give women (seen as being encumbered with children) full partnership. An Indian version of such a narrative is the hunting-gathering-shifting cultivation model in Madhav Gadgil and Ramachandra Guha's (1992: 16) widely read account of the ecological history of India *The Fissured Land*. Discussing the historical modes of resource use, their model describes 'Gathering' societies thus: 'The sizes of social groups among the hunter-gatherer-shifting cultivators are small. . . . The division of labour within these groups is minimal;

what exists is primarily based on age and sex, and to some extent upon knowledge and leadership abilities. The women will principally be found involved in gathering plant foods and small animals, while the men will be found hunting the larger animals. As regards the gender equation, men play a greater role in organizing information and taking decisions relating to resource use on behalf of the group as a whole.' In this particular model, gathering societies are said to be like all human societies in that they may encounter an abundance of resources, be in equilibrium with resources, or face a shrinking resource base. In the first case of abundance, their demands on the resource base may be small because they have colonized a new habitat 'or on account of a technological innovation such as the bow and arrow' that opens up a wider range of species to hunt. And, of course, men are the chief decision-makers.

An alternative gendered approach, perhaps yet to be fully elaborated, is that of Govind Kelkar and Dev Nathan (1992) who seek to counter the tendency to simply add the gatherer on to the hunter model. They first reverse the usual sequence of the terminology to gatherer-hunter and then draw upon existing data (from Lee and DeVore themselves as others have done earlier) and their own field studies among central Indian tribes to show that gathering tasks are shared by women, men and children. They also suggest that women too may have participated in the hunt, citing Kumkum Roy's study of the Mesolithic stick paintings in the caves of Bhim Betka in central India. More recently, K. S. Singh (in Kelkar and Nathan eds. 2001) attempts to provide other evidence of women's hunting: folklore and the religious mythology of the distant past, the exploits of medieval princesses and queens and the contemporary hunting rituals of certain tribal groups in which women also participate. He suggests that it was only in the colonial period that hunting became associated with male prowess, obscuring women's role as hunters. Singh mentions that it is difficult to discern the gender of figures in pre-historic cave paintings but does not pursue the archaeological enquiry. Yet, even on a casual visit to popular tourist sites in India one can see alternatives to the Man the Hunter stereotype. In the Jain rock-cut shelters dating to the 1st century B.C. at Udaygiri-Khandagiri, on the outskirts of Bhubaneswar in Orissa, a frieze shows two women and a man battling elephants, even as other women (depicted as more timid) try to drag one of the fighting women away. In the ruins of 15th century temples at Hampi, capital of the medieval kingdom of Vijayanagar in northern Karnataka, there are several bas-reliefs of ordinary women with bows and arrows. One panel depicts a woman with a bow, standing on one leg and resting a hand on a young child's head for balance, as she takes out a thorn from the sole of her other foot. This seems to suggest that in that period and place not only did the women hunt, they were not 'encumbered' by their children.

The received truth of science, however, is that for all time women have been home-based and limited by their reproductive roles, and that men have been the main food providers. This is despite continuing evidence from different fields including primatology, archaeology and anthropology that show that women are not dependent on men for provisioning and may even be economically more productive. The passive-female/active-male stereotypes in conjunction with Man the Hunter have had wide influence in different fields of science.[5] Misia Landau (1984) has argued that the different theories of human evolution follow a common narrative structure, which Fedigan (1986) summarizes thus: 'This structure takes the form of a "hero-story" in which the protagonist (= hominid) starts from humble origins on a journey in which he will be both *tested* by environmental stresses (savannah, predators etc) and by his own weakness (bipedalism, lack of biological armaments) and *gifted* by powerful agents (intelligence, technological inventions, social cooperation) until he is able to transform himself into a truly human hominid, the hero's final triumph, which always ends the story.'

Genes and the new hero stories

A counterpart to the romantic evolutionary hero-story is the quest for the 'engineering ideal' in biology that began in the early years of the 20th century with Jaques Loeb (see Pauly 1990). Loeb laid the foundations for a 'technology of living substance', a science that could predict and control life and behaviour, and he achieved iconic status in the field of pure reductive science. This ideal influenced the emergence of behavioural psychology and the later development of molecular biology and biotechnology. It was more than a mechanical view of life for it involved the 'displacement of nature' and the reformulation of biology as an 'engineering science'.[6]

In Richard Dawkins' popular version of the genetic basis of evolution, 'The genes themselves, whether social or anti-social, whether virus genes or 'own' genes, are all just DNA instructions, and they all say, in one way or another, by fair means or foul, briefly or long windedly, "Duplicate me".'(Dawkins 1997: 271.) This particular keystone story of genetic destiny has had enormous influence. Even India's best known environmental activist, Medha Patkar (2004), the woman who has led the Narmada Bachao movement, (whose parents were also activists) told an interviewer: 'Commitment to ideology is something that, you can say, is in my DNA'. In an earlier generation she may have said activism was in her blood. As Dorothy Nelkin (1996: 138) comments: 'The appropriation of DNA to explain individual differences recasts old, pervasive beliefs about the importance of "blood" in powerful scientific terms. Science becomes a way to uphold the status quo as based on natural forces.' The concept of genetic predisposition is indeed a powerful narrative.

The 'de-naturalization' of biology gave women contraception and artificial insemination but also raised questions about the methodologies (approaches, methods and tools) of the new sciences. For instance, feminist critiques have been directed to the anti-feminist bias in the 'new' epidemiologies and the implication for women's health, and have suggested alternative emancipatory frameworks (see Inhorn and Whittle 2001). Despite evidence that 'genetic and social determinants of health rarely operate independently, but undergo myriad complex interactions from fetal life on' (Snow 2002: 167), the genetic paradigm has percolated through both biological and behavioural sciences.

One aspect of this is the genetic interpretation of human evolution that has produced yet another hero story. The period of its emergence is of some significance. In the 1960s when the United States embarked on its war against Vietnam and anti-war demonstrations were being held in many parts of the world, this new story highlighted the innate aggressiveness and territoriality of the human male. Robert Ardrey, Konrad Lorenz and Desmond Morris became best-selling authors. By the 1970s, when modern feminism had already begun to successfully question gendered knowledge in science and social science, this was directly opposed by narratives of male dynamism, intelligence and rationality contributing to male dominance. Lionel Tiger (1970, 1971) set the tone with his notion that males alone have the biological capacity to bond with one another for cooperative productive purposes, as in hunting. E.O. Wilson built upon these popular strands. In *Sociobiology: The New Synthesis* (1975a: 553), Wilson says: 'The building block of nearly all human societies is the nuclear family. . . . During the day the women and children remain in the residential area while the men forage for game or its symbolic equivalent in the form of money. The males cooperate in bands or deal with neighbouring groups.' In his subsequent work, *On Human Nature* (1978), he writes: 'It pays males to be aggressive, hasty, fickle and undiscriminating. In theory it is more profitable for females to be coy, to hold back until they can identify the male with the best genes. Human beings obey this biological principle faithfully'. Regarding gender difference, Wilson (1975b) says that men have the genetic advantage; biology favours patriarchy and the cost of denial would be loss of efficiency: 'Even with identical education and equal access to all professions, men are likely to continue to play a disproportionate role in political life, business and science' Women continue to be seen as helpmates, sexual partners, passive sleeping beauties awaiting rescue, as they were in earlier centuries; the difference is that this is now genetically ordained, and some sociobiologists express regret that biology is so inegalitarian. Thus, the new 'genetic' hero story provides an invidious scientific justification for various power hierarchies including those of ethnicity, class and gender.

The postulates of sociobiology were comprehensively refuted, notably by R.C. Lewontin (1978, 1979), together with Steven Rose, and Leo Kamin in *Not in our Genes* (Rose et. al. 1984); by Philip Kitcher's *Vaulting Ambition: Sociobiology and the Quest for Human Nature* (1985); and by many feminists (e.g. Haraway 1979, 1992; Kaplan and Rogers 1990; Sperling 1991/ 1996). Yet, surprisingly, or perhaps not so surprisingly, undergraduate and graduate scientists and young professionals are scarcely aware of the controversy surrounding these ideas. For instance, although Stephen Jay Gould's essays are popular and widely-read, his philosophic and ideological outlook (which is quite the opposite of the sociobiological point of view) is not grasped. Students are also 'disciplined' to shut out alternative points of view. A bright post-graduate student of Environmental Biology in the University of Delhi was using Dawkins' *The Selfish Gene* (1976) to provide the theoretical frame for his dissertation, which involved research on an empirical problem. I gave him the book *Not in Our Genes* that counters both Wilson's arguments and *The Selfish Gene*. He read it and said: 'Now you have upset everything that I was thinking; it is a chapter-by-chapter refutation, but I am not even going to mention it in my work, because it is much simpler to stick to one point of view.' Most other students would not have bothered to read the book.

It is apparent that the comments of the young scientists mentioned earlier in this chapter are not individual aberrations but part of a wider milieu. Indeed, the 'logical' processes behind the comments are not all that different from the narrative threads that have shaped the received truths of science, from the narratives of evolution to the narratives of human genetics. They start with descriptions of what some women and men are observed to be doing. This is assumed to have cross-cultural, historical and universal applicability. The next assumption is that what is universal reflects the essential natures of women and men. This is then followed by more assumptions: that the division of labour, roles and responsibilities in the family and community are natural; that what is natural is mainly a matter of hormones and genes. Male and female differences are perceived as biologically fixed and determined by evolution and genetics. In sum, three inter-related threads of belief may be discerned: a) genetic predeterminism: that genes produce particular behaviours; b) biological essentialism: that these behaviours are universal for all women, all men, all tribals etc; and c) social Darwinism: that these universals have become fixed through evolution by natural selection. From this follows the argument that the division of labour in society is func-

tional and determined by biology. So men's productive capabilities are perceived as balancing women's reproductive and nurturing capacities. It is then but a short step for conservationists, who
are temperamentally and professionally partial to non-interfer-
ence in nature, to incline towards maintaining the status quo in
social relations as in nature. The power relations in the hierarchy
of dominant and subordinate positions are glossed over. It also
becomes easier to ascribe blame to individuals for their lack of
resources, status and power, and to comfortably and 'scientifically' set aside questions of equity and justice in social relations.
Thus, conservation science and social conservatism are nicely
blended.

RESISTING GENDER BIASED SCIENCE

In a study of the women scientists in the early 20th century in
C.V. Raman's laboratory at the Indian Institute of Science (formerly known as the Tata Institute), in Bangalore, Abha Sur (2001:
120) speaks poignantly of their 'dispersed radiance'. Towards the
end of the essay, she remarks: 'There has been a lingering hope
among feminists that the participation of large numbers of women
in traditionally male-dominated fields of inquiry would change
not only the institutional biases but also more importantly the
very nature of these fields.' Changing the nature of a field, as
feminists have done in primatology, is a stupendous task that depends on a combination of human, social and material factors.
Yet, the fault is also that of the young discipline of gender studies
in India. The major focus of gender studies has been literary, socio-
cultural and political representing the predominant disciplinary
interests of women activists. Women's biology has been specifically addressed by the women's movement in South Asia in the
context of women's health and violence against women. But the
sociology of science and the politics of biology have not been significant areas of interest, except for some celebratory approaches
including that of ecofeminists. Ecofeminist views, however, cloud
the issues. Valorizing women's biological capacity for reproduction and seeing in this a special linkage to nature is as biologically
deterministic as the sociobiological approaches that dichotomize
male and female natures and root this in a predetermined biology.

For those of us who espouse a gendered approach and seek to challenge dichotomies, countering the conventional approaches to women and men, yet maintain a distance from the celebratory approaches, this involves traversing a vastly more heterogeneous and complex path. How do we proceed?

First, we need to agree upon certain basic elements, for instance that: a) Women are not a homogenous category. Women are divided by age, class, caste and ethnicity. There is no universal woman, as there is no universal man. The division of labour, roles and responsibilities related to natural resources are context-specific. b) Natural science is not time-less and value-free. At any given period in its development, it is shaped by social, economic and political forces that are not gender-neutral. c) The institutional funding of scientific endeavours, the setting of research agendas, the act of obtaining information and so on are all implicated in gendered natural science.

Second, we need to change the way in which the natural sciences including biology are taught from junior school to undergraduate college, where the approach is to treat scientific 'developments' simply as a sequence of events unrelated to social forces. As there is little reading beyond the required texts and almost no cross-disciplinary interaction in the universities, the culture of critique is lacking—of asking what is the evidence, whose interest does it serve, identifying and analysing assumptions and different points of view in the context of larger frameworks. The system pushes a student to think in a single track, and the embedded keystone stories in the discipline make it easier to do so. This could be countered by rethinking the boundaries of natural science disciplines and introducing a historical context into every natural science discipline.

And thirdly, we need to search for the unnamed women assistants and students in the history of Indian science. For instance, there is the case of Antonia, the intelligent Konkani servant girl who was assistant to the 16th century Portuguese physician Garcia d'Orta. He came to Goa in 1534, spent the rest of his life in India, and apparently with Antonia's help wrote the pre-Linnaean treatise *Colloquies on the Simples, Drugs and Materia Medica of India* (see Kochhar 1999). Yet, even her name is rarely mentioned by any of the Indian botanists who laud d'Orta's work, and we know nothing of her.

Fourthly, and perhaps most important, we need to develop feminist critiques of natural science in South Asia. The history of gender and science in India is an under-researched area. Most studies (IWSA 1978, Chakravarty, Chawla and Mehta 1984, Krishnaraj 1991, Subrahmanyan 1992, Mukhopadhya and Seymour eds. 1994, Poonacha and Gopal 2004) focus on women's entry into scientific disciplines and their experience of scientific institutions. A very few, such as that of Abha Sur (2001 cited above) have attempted to go beyond this to interrogate 'the modes of intersection of gender, culture and science' in the lives of pioneer Indian women scientists. But to my knowledge there is no sustained feminist critique of the discourse of natural science in the Indian context. Unless we do this, although there may now be a climate within which we can raise the question of gendered natural science, we do not have the body of evidence necessary to shift mindsets, attitudes and practices.

A preliminary step would be to identify and analyse the embedded keystone stories in the scientific literature, popular and academic, unpacking these as the women's movement in India has unpacked the visual images in advertising, television and film, or as dalit women have unpacked brahmanical stories and myths. I will end this chapter with an example of how we could be more alert to the undercurrents in visualization and expression. In 1993, *Seminar* (a prestigious monthly journal with a well-informed general readership) invited seven distinguished Indian scientists 'to interrelate individual biography to the wider issues of knowledge and organization, politics and culture.' It was hoped that each scientist would 'become his own case study', producing through self-reflective stories an oral history of what it meant 'to be a foot soldier or even a sergeant in the grand march of science' (Vishvanathan 1993). Like the metaphors of soldiers and sergeants, all the seven scientists are men. Women do figure in their accounts, in passing, as mothers and wives; one person mentions a daughter. In only one case does a woman mentor, a university teacher, enter the story. The women in the collective story of the making of 'our scientists' are publicly recognized as inspirers and helpmates, and occasionally provide valuable professional support to a male scientist. The opening paragraph of one story is a remarkable metaphorical flourish drawing upon tales from Sanskrit poetics and Indian history. It reads:

> Describing King Raghu's conquest of the four corners of India, Kalidasa likens the Western Ghats to a comely young maiden, her head near Kanyakumari, her feet near Tapi. I fell in love with this damsel at a tender age, may be of three or four, and with time have grown more and more fond of her. I was born on the outskirts of the city of Pune, and from the terrace of our house one saw range after range of hills stretching all the way to the horizon. Prominent among these hills were those of Torna, the first hill fort acquired by Shivaji, and Rajgad that for a time served as his capital. Looming over them all was Sinhagad, conquered with such valour by Tanaji. (Gadgil 1993: 25)

Consider the image from Sanskrit literature of the young attractive and supine woman, a 'maiden', a 'damsel', juxtaposed with the image of the brave conquering Maratha warriors. These metaphors should not be taken to indicate the writer's attitude but they do tell us something about the wider cognitive culture of science in India that legitimizes such ways of seeing and knowing.

For poor dalit and adivasi women, the struggle is against both traditional and modern systems of natural resource management. Attempts to 'integrate' a gendered perspective into natural resource policies have failed to counter the marginalization of women's knowledge and experience. Attempts to 'mainstream' gender concerns into programmes for land and water resource management, agriculture, biodiversity, forestry, fisheries, animal husbandry, watershed or pasture development have had limited success. Among the many reasons for this, in my view, is our failure to problematize gender-biased knowledge systems. We need to unpack the resonances between patriarchal customary attitudes and the sexist assumptions of the biological and natural sciences which together shape gender-biased practices. Recognizing the gendered character of natural science enables us to understand and counter the marginalization of women in environmental conservation and development strategies. Natural resource management cannot be transformed without resisting the gendered discourse of natural science.

NOTES

1 The anthropologist Ashley Montagu who played a central role in the first UNESCO statement was a powerful advocate of the anti-racist positions of the 'modern evolutionary synthesis' popularized by humanist biologists Julian Huxley (1928, 1933) and Theodosius Dobhansky (1937, 1944), both of whom together with J.B.S. Haldane contributed to the second statement. The contributing scientists, however, included some like geneticists C.D. Darlington and Ronald Fisher who did not favour racial egalitarianism believing that races differ in innate mental capacities, and excluded others (despite their professional qualifications) such as the anti-racist physical anthropologist W. M.Cobb presumably because his colour would have made him partisan (Haraway 1992). Montagu's later study, *The Natural Superiority of Women* (1953), counters the Darwinian thesis of woman's natural inferiority and passive role in evolution but also echoes 19th century essentialist concepts of women's less competitive, nurturant nature.

2 In this section, I have drawn mainly on Martin (1996), Shiebinger (1999), Fedigan (1986) and Haraway (1992). Haraway's precision and range is especially helpful in deepening our understanding of the processes of knowledge creation at the interface of nature and culture. Others whom I have referred to but not cited here include Ruth Bleir (1984, 1986) and Fausto-Sterling (1985/ 1992, 2000) on biology, Cynthia Cockburn (1983, 1991, 1992) on technology and Anne Ferguson (1994) on agriculture. Of particular importance in shaping my view of gender as a structuring principle in science is Sandra Harding (1986, 1991).

3 The Scottish thinkers were mainly academics known for their rational and utilitarian approach. They included the economist Adam Smith and the philosopher David Hume.

4 The word 'oogonial' is a playful alternative to the much used 'seminal'. There have been many popular rebuttals of the hunter narrative including Elaine Morgan's speculative reconstruction of the Darwinian model in *The Descent of Woman* (1972)—an account that Stephen Jay Gould (1980: 132) said was 'as farcical as more famous tall tales by and for men—and Evelyn Reed's *Woman's Evolution* (1975). Her collection *Sexism and Science* (1977) includes an angry denunciation of Lionel Tiger's (1969, 1970) popular work.

5 Sperling (1996) cites intriguing examples of the 1960s-1970s Man the Hunter model: Wickler on algae 'showing active males and passive females' and Geist on mountain sheep, besides G.C. Williams' standard reference text on the evolution of human behaviour, *Sex and Evolution* (1975).

6 Pauly comments (1990: 199): 'The core of the Loebian standpoint was the belief that biology could be formulated not as a natural science, but as an

engineering science. More broadly, it meant that nature was fading away. As biologists' power over organisms increased, their experience with them as "natural" objects declined. And as the extent of possible manipulation and construction expanded, the original organization and normal processes of organisms no longer seems scientifically privileged; nature was only one state among an indefinite number of possibilities, and a state that could be scientifically boring. This transformation was not the result of a "mechanistic" view of life—something that could be defined, discussed, and proved correct or not; rather it was a generalization from biologists practice as they saw the extent of artificialisation taking place in laboratories. Nature was disappearing, not as a result of argument, but through trivialisation; not through disproof but displacement. The natural became only one among many results of the activity of biological invention.'

WORKSCAPES

5

Gendered Dimensions of Care among Forest-Dwellers of the Western Ghats[1]

(In collaboration with R. Indira and Jayanand H. Derekar)

> What can be drawn out like strings that tie . . . like water that is guava-sweet?
>
> —Bhagirathi Budho Velip, Uttara Kannada district [2]

In many societies, the gendered dimension of care has meant that women bear the major responsibility for food provisioning, hearth and household maintenance and the well-being of children. Such caring may obscure unequal power relations and is easily exploited. Yet, there is another dimension of care which extends beyond these conventionally-understood boundaries and involves a range of knowledge, skills and work that also enhance women's self-esteem. This chapter attempts to identify and articulate the context within which caring occurs. It explores caring practices among a group of poor hill-forest dwellers in south-western India, concentrating on a small cluster of ten Kunbi villages and one non-Kunbi village in Joida *taluk*, an administrative unit within Uttara Kannada district, bordering the adjacent state of Goa. The first section gives the background of the Kunbi's changing livelihoods; the next considers some aspects of joint living and significant needs. The third section focuses on five women whose lives express different forms of caring work. The last section reflects on the traditional core values of the Kunbi and suggests that caring, like other social practices, occurs within a context of values that have arisen from a specific socio-political history and the economic processes necessitated by living a particular life in a given society, fulfilling particular roles in the family and community.

MIGRATION AND DISPLACEMENT

The Social Context

The Kunbi live in scattered village settlements (see Figure 5.1) set upon the hillsides amidst picturesque semi-evergreen and moist deciduous forests of the Western Ghats, the mountain range that runs all along the West Coast of India. Kunbi settlements extend from coastal Karwar through Yellarpur and Joida in the Ghats and onto Khanapur in the plains of neighbouring Belgaum. Located at the confluence of different cultures, the Kunbi are relatively recent migrants from Goa. Their Kunbi ancestors in Goa are believed to have migrated centuries ago from northern India and the Karnatak plains to the coastal Konkan region of present day Goa. The Kunbi are Konkani speakers (an Indo-European language with affinities to Marathi) living in a Kannada speaking land; a self proclaimed Hindu caste with tribe-like features; non-vegetarians who do not eat domesticated cattle or fowl; members of enormous households of 40-50, even 100 people but having meagre material possessions; a strongly patriarchal community in which some women have quietly fulfilled unconventional roles.

Development has come unevenly to the area (see Table 5.1). Most of the villages in our study are easily approachable from the Hubli-Karwar state highway that cuts through the hills. Three of the interior villages are not connected by a motorable road but telephones have spread rapidly. In 2001 most villages did not have telephones, by 2003 they did. These are usually private connections in a few individual homes. Yet, a village may have telephones but no electricity, or it may have electricity but no primary health care. There is no clear pattern discernible in the spread of communication and welfare services and this puts people, especially women, under enormous coping pressure.

The need for having some ready cash is widely felt. Young women in Anashiwada told us that they quietly keep aside some money (given to them by their husbands) to use for emergencies such as children requiring medical attention in town, because the

Figure 5.1: Deriya village, Sketch by Deepak V. Derekar

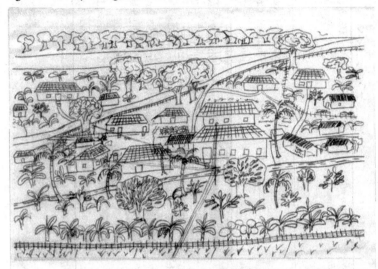

men do not always recognize the seriousness of such needs. Or the women may borrow money from one another. The women maintain kinship ties and neighbourhood networks for communication and support upon which they depend both in their everyday lives and in crisis situations. Kunbi girls and boys are socialized into believing that it is their duty to maintain linkages in their close knit village groups and beyond.

There have been many waves of Kunbi migration into Uttara Kannada district. The area across the Ghats to which the Kunbi migrated offered several occupational advantages for a group of *cumri* (slash-and-burn) cultivators. Sparsely populated Uttara Kannada had rich forests of hard and softwood trees, besides an abundance of varied non-timber forest produce. In recent decades, hundreds of people were compelled to relocate from the nearby Supa area (in the same district) due to a project for the generation of electricity from the Kali river. People say that the dam and reservoir that were constructed submerged over 3200 acres (nearly 1300 hectares) of forest and human settlements. Many relocated to villages in the Joida area where they had relatives; a few took over entire villages that had long been abandoned by previous

Table.5.1: Baseline Data on Villages in Joida Taluk included in the Study

VILLAGE	Distance from Taluk Headquarters	Population of Kunbi Female + Male	Population of Others Female + Male	Number of House-holds	Number of Families	Location of Primary School	Location of Primary Health Centre	Distance from Bus Stop
Sittegali	3 km	25+29	3+3	6	9	Joida	Joida	Nagoda Cross 1 km
Digalamb	4 km	34+41	Nil	5	17	Joida	Joida	Digalamb Cross 0.5 km
Nagarbhavi	1 km	72+73	Nil	13	25	Joida	Joida	Joida
Gavadewada	0.5 km	55+53	(Not Available)	14	21	Joida	Joida	Joida
Chapoli	5 km	52+50	15+19	24	28	Bapeli Cross 2.5 km	Joida	Chapoli Cross 1 km
Bapeli	10 km	Nil	About 150	(Not Available)	(Not Available)	Bapeli	Joida	Bapeli
Mudiye	16 km	21+28	38+43	18	29	Mudiye	Kumbarawada 6 km	Kirwati 5 km
Deriya	14 km	48+51	Nil	9	19	Deriya	Kumbarawada 3 km	Kirwati 2.5 km
Kirwati	11 km	41+43	43+35	20	32	Kirwati	Kumbarawada 1 km	Kirwati
Kateli	12 km	70+61	4+3	17	25	Kateli	Kumbarawada 2 km	Kumbarawada 2 km
Anashiwada	32 km	100+104	11+11	40	49	Anashiwada	Kadra 15 km	Anashiwada

Source: *Collated from personal visits in August 2003; and Jayanand H. Derekar 2001.*

inhabitants during an epidemic, probably malaria; others set up new villages. Some out-migration from the district has also taken place. A large number of Kunbi families are yet to recover from the loss of their agricultural lands. Not all were able to successfully cultivate the new lands allotted to them, and have had to resort to wage labour. Many families are still waiting for the monetary compensation that the government had promised decades ago. The Kunbi who had hitherto led relatively isolated lives have also been exploited in their interactions with other communities in the area. In the past, Kunbi women were very wary of outsiders and shy of meeting and talking with strangers but migration, re-settlement and the demands of a new life have provided the impetus to greater interaction with the surrounding world.

The physical history of Kunbi migration and upheaval is con-cretized in evocative place names. 'Joida' is a corruption of a Konkani word meaning 'shout loudly', and relates to a distant time when the area was densely forested; passers-by were cautioned to shout loudly if they were attacked by a bear. Joida is now a small township and the taluk headquarters. 'Deriya', meaning a 'heap', refers to the gathering of the early settlers at that place, atop a hill. All Kunbi think, speak and converse in Konkani, a warm, earthy spoken language, which did not have a script till some decades ago. It is the language used for song and festivity. The Kunbi also have an old historical association with the Marathi language which is used for drama and for religious purposes. Al-most all older women are illiterate but many men and youth, girls and boys, read and write Marathi which used to be the medium of instruction in local schools. Like Marathi, but at a later stage, Hindi came to the Kunbi through northern employers and land-owners. Kannada has always been used for interaction with non-Kunbis in the area. As the official language of Karnataka it has recently replaced Marathi in schools, so even very young children have to learn a second language. Several Kunbi are linguistically versatile. With another language comes another culture and alter-native ways of viewing the world.

The social structure of the Kunbi consists of sub-groups knit-ted together by intermarriage to form an extended kin group which includes a number of joint and nuclear families in different villages. Each sub-group takes the place name of the presumed first migrant settlement of the sub-group. Marriages are not permitted within a sub-group. The Kunbi are patrilineal and patrilocal. Descent is traced through the male line and married women and their children 'belong' to the patrilineal sub-group. The practice of the boy's family paying bride price is the norm but recently there was a rare instance when this was offset by the girl's family giving the groom a gold necklace as dowry. All women are married between the ages of 17 and 23 and, men from 25 with no upper limit. Marriages are always arranged by the elders. There are very rare instances of young men choosing their own marriage partners. For young women this is unthinkable. There are also only a couple of instances of men marrying non-Kunbi women. Widowed men may remarry but remarriage is not permissble for widowed women.

Until recently Kunbi women had few contacts outside their own villages. Their movements were restricted to foraging in the forests, working in the family fields, occasional visits to their natal villages and those of close relatives, or to worship at the abode of family deities. As even primary schools used to be located far away, few women over forty years of age have been formally schooled. These days, almost all young girls go to school but especially after puberty their mobility is severely curtailed; however, no sharp segregation is practised. Although women bear an equal if not greater burden of agricultural work than the men, several cultural taboos are prevalent. As in many other parts of India, it is believed that women should not handle the plough or bullocks; winnow in certain areas considered to be sacred; touch paddy seeds, or function as priests. Yet, in special circumstances, some women do use the plough.

The Kunbi are a devout people. They have faith in animist (forest) deities and worship Hindu gods and goddesses. Marathi is the language of prayer. The village priesthood is a hereditary male calling. The priest officiates at lifecycle and other ceremonies, and is responsible for the community's spiritual links with the forest. His sanction and blessings are necessary for gathering forest produce. The village head is always male and believed to be imbued with the spiritual powers that enable him to guide decisions and settle disputes. His eldest son inherits these powers. The village elders may, however, transfer the spiritual power to someone else by common consent. Formerly, the head could also be chosen by proving his skill as a hunter of *sambar* deer. Women have no role in these formal observances. (Indira 2002)

Changing livelihoods

Traditionally, the Kunbi cultivated the calcium-rich *ragi* (finger millet) and also some *samai* (little millet) on small hillside plots assigned to families by common agreement. Paddy was also cultivated in the valley areas. In swidden (also called slash-and-burn or shifting) cultivation, people generally work together on one another's plots. Men slash the trees, then women and men burn the vegetation to prepare the land for sowing, which is done by dibbling with a stick. This is low-input organic agriculture; the plough is not used and the crop is rain-fed. After the harvest, the plot is left fallow and the cultivators return to it in a few years allowing the land to recoup its fertility. Over the years, as local use of forest land and resources increasingly came into conflict with commercial and industrial uses, the cycle of rotation on the millet plots decreased and steeper slopes were cultivated. The government considered this to be environmentally unsound, and many decades ago slash-and-burn cultivation was banned by law. In Uttara Kannada, however, the law was not rigorously enforced till the early 1990s.

Hambeer Derekar of Deriya village says slash-and-burn was not just about subsistence, it was a joyous way of life which was transformed by the change from millets to paddy. The paddy crop was insufficient to meet the needs of the large joint families. Paddy involves more labour in ploughing, transplanting and channelling the irrigation from hill streams, and requires chemical fertilizers and pesticides (known locally as 'government *masala*'). In this region, paddy cultivation seems to have added to women's labour.

As indebtedness increased, many Kunbi forfeited their land to moneylenders. Men sought work in manganese mines on the Goa-Karnataka border and brought home cash incomes. This may have contributed to more liquor being consumed and male drunkenness in both Kunbi and non-Kunbi villages, affecting family life. Subsequently, the mines were closed as the devastating environmental impact of open-cast mining had led to widespread protests by environmentalists. This pushed the Kunbi men and women into greater dependence on agricultural wage labour. It has taken many women far afield, and has shifted the responsibility of childcare in the home to the older women who do not go out to work.

Whole families now migrate seasonally to work as agricultural labourers in paddy and sugarcane fields in the fertile coastal plains around Karwar, just south of Goa. Unusually in this area, the agricultural wage rate for migrant women is the same as that for men. Migrant labourers live in the landlord's house. They also eat with the landlord's family, unless (as is quite often the case) the Kunbi labourers consider the landlord to be of a lower caste, in which case they will accept food rations and do their own cooking. The women are acutely conscious of caste hierarchy. In this and other ways, the Kunbi's present economic status does not match their perceived traditional ritual status. Many families have also been compelled to send older children to work in Panaji, the state capital of Goa; the boys toil in bakeries, the girls are domestic helpers with middle-class Konkani families who have had long-standing links with the Joida area.

In the past, the Kunbi's forest dependant lifestyle enabled the community to develop a deep knowledge of the forest terrain, and the use and conservation of its flora and fauna. Their life and livelihood depended on observation. They could read the stars for directions and the forest plants for flowering and fruiting cycles. Gathering was not necessarily a gender specific activity. Both women and men knew where to find what they needed for food and medicine), and what to leave untouched, for example some fruit for seed-setting for the following season. The forest was also closely intertwined with their belief system. Wild animals and reptiles were not feared due to the belief that they harm only those humans who violate certain religious practices. Violations included stealing other people's agricultural produce or destroying their crops, polluting places of worship say by drinking liquor, not taking the sanction of the priest to collect forest produce, and so on. Thus, secular livelihood needs and religious beliefs combined to maintain harmonious and co-operative life in the settlements. Like slash-and-burn cultivation, inland fishing and hunting were group activities and large catches, even if made by a few, were always shared more widely. (Indira 2002)

Changes in the government's forest policies have affected the customary practices of the Kunbi. Contracts for commercial extraction of non-timber forest produce, such as soap nut, black pepper and honey (which was once the sole preserve of the Kunbi) have been given to outside contractors, who are of course men. These contractors are interested in short-term profits and may not be aware of how to maintain the sustainability of forest produce, or may simply not care. As the Kunbi's own gathering practices (for personal consumption or sale in local markets) have been reduced, and boys and girls are being schooled through the formal education system, the repository of local knowledge of the forest has been weakened. All of the older women feel this loss keenly.

JOINT LIVING

Sharing in households

The Kunbi brought with them a Goan tradition of large joint families and built enormous double storey houses of timber and stone, locally available materials in the forests of the Western Ghats. The migrants lived in permanent village settlements and practised slash-and-burn cultivation in a rotating cycle in the surrounding area. While this form of cultivation has now been completely stopped, the joint family structure, although changing, has proved resilient. When a very large family lives together under one roof how does this affect their interactions with one another and with others outside their family? How, for example, do shared living spaces and household chores affect women's routine caring practices?

We visited the house of Vithal Mirasi in Nagarbhavi village (not far from the township of Joida). The house is a short distance from the main road, reached by walking along narrow earth embankments beside just planted paddy fields. The joint family of twelve brothers includes 45 members who live together under

Figure 5.2: Ground floor plan of the Vithal Mirasi house, Nagarbhavi village.

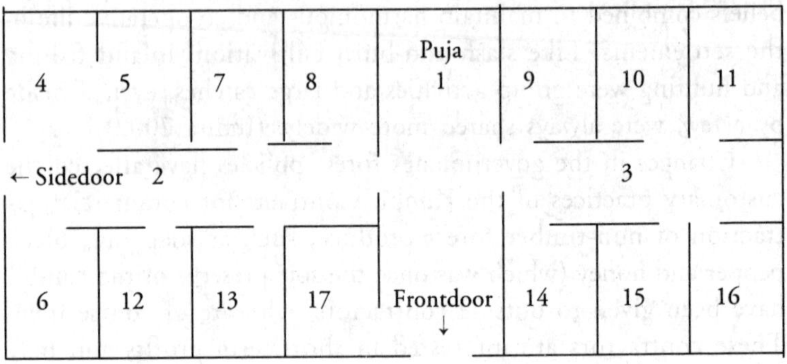

Key:
1. Entrance hall; 2.Corridor; 3.Corridor; 4.Common Kitchen; 5.Special *shradh* kitchen; 6. Kitchen extension (for utensils); 7-16. Family rooms for each brother's family; 17. Work room (for sewing machine).

one roof. Two younger brothers are employed outside the district. The relatively better off condition of the family is reflected in their having bought a small areca (betel nut) plantation a few years ago, and in their newly constructed two-storey-high house, which stands out in an area in which there are very few new constructions of this size. The carved doors are testimony to the family's carpentry skills.

As we removed our footwear at the threshold and entered the Mirasi house (Figure 5.2) our eyes were drawn to the far wall covered with pictures of garlanded Hindu deities. Apart from this puja (prayer) space that loomed over the large rectangular hall there were one or two framed photographs, a wooden cot, a bench, a few chairs. At night all the young unmarried boys in the family slept on mats on the floor of the hall. In the front room on the left of the main door was a foot-pedal operated sewing machine (which was being used by one of the men to tailor uniforms for the family's many school-going children). On either side of the hall were wide corridors that opened into separate family rooms. Each small room was almost bare except for a few rolled up mats and one or two metal trunks for personal possessions. Long bamboo poles suspended on both sides along the length of the corridors served as a common 'hanger' for everyone's clothes. The family kitchen was at the end of the left corridor. On one side of the kitchen was the hearth, very few cooking vessels and some large sacks of grain, and on the other there was a storage area with a few steel plates stacked on shelves. Adjoining the kitchen but not accessible from the corridor was a room with a special hearth that was used only for *shradh* (ancestral remembrance and death ceremonies). The roof of the house was high enough for an upper floor to be added at a later date. The structure of the house reflects and caters to the family's need for cohesion and individual privacy.

What qualities of head, heart and hand does it take to live together and to manage such a large household? We asked this question several times of large families in different villages. In Nagarbhavi, the Mirasi family were somewhat dismissive of the enquiry. They said it was difficult but that is how they had always lived. In Sittegalli village, the women of one family recollected that when they had been ousted from the Supa dam area, their relatives had provided them refuge till they could construct their own house. Welcoming new migrants, making space and time for them, providing food and taking care of other needs was normal, they said; it was nothing to talk about. In Digalamb village, the women were a little more forthcoming. They said that household chores in the family of 17 were shared but no one was specifically assigned a task; when one of them saw that there was a job to be done, she did it, whether it was cleaning vegetables, tending to a crying toddler or providing hospitality to a guest.

If sharing comes so easily, if reciprocity is not a factor, why have the large extended families broken up? All the men said it was because the women could not get along together and quarrelled over the common hearth. All the women said it was because of disagreements and quarrels between brothers. While harmonious community living is clearly dependent on individuals setting aside independent aspirations, the reasons for internal family differences are complex. When men began to take up jobs in mining, some part of the money earned went to support the joint family but a part was kept aside for personal use, mainly to educate their own children. New occupations and individual incomes have affected the composite life of most joint families.

Separation is always painful but divisions have taken place peacefully. For example, in Deriya, four generations of a family of more than 100 people, headed by Ganaba Chudago Derekar (renowned for his hunting prowess in British times), lived together beneath one roof. After his death, the task of managing the family was taken over by his octogenarian wife Ratnabai who had borne 18 children. In 1997-98, after Ratnabai's death, when the joint household split up, there were 108 family members. There was an amicable division of assets, mainly 54 acres (21.6 hectares) of land. Three families continue to live in the old, and now somewhat run-down, two-storey house with three separate hearths in a shared kitchen area. The others live independently in a cluster of small new houses near the big house (See sketch of Deriya by Deepak Vithal Derekar, Figure 5.1). All the families celebrate festivals and other such occasions jointly. The young men continue to derive much satisfaction from the family's Marathi drama troupe and their orchestra. All still take pride in the big house with the tiled roof. Guests are taken on a tour of its many rooms. The younger people especially miss the closeness of joint living even as they take advantage of the wider freedom of life choices that are now before them. Intra-household relations are also changing. We observed one man cutting vegetables, making a pickle, working alongside his wife to prepare the afternoon meal. This may be an exception but would probably have not been possible in the joint family household.

Significant needs

Caring occurs in a context of needs and values, which change as people's occupations and social practices evolve. We attempted to identify the Kunbi's significant needs using the participatory tool of a Focus Group Discussion (FGD). A group of about 35-40 people assembled at Deriya. They included women of different ages from Deriya, Mudiye and Kateli (all interior villages) and young men who had come to interpret the women's Konkani speech into Kannada or Hindi but then became part of the group. We suggested that some practices are so deeply engrained and seem so 'natural' that these are hidden from our consciousness.

Table 5.2: Significant Needs (not ranked) of the Kunbi identified through a FGD.

Need	Expressed by
Krishi and *dev-devta* (agriculture and the blessings of male and female deities for agricultural prosperity)	Older woman
Samay (time—to plan for the future)	Older woman
Water	Older woman
Fire and firewood	Older woman
Cattle and children (both necessary for the future)	Older woman
Deep-diya (lamp and wick for light)	Older woman
School	Younger woman
Money	Younger man
Bhasha (language-articulation)	Younger man
Kala (art-creativity)	Younger man
Health	Younger man
Advice and guidance of elders	Younger man
Ghar-sansar basana (establish one's family)	Younger woman
Co-operation	Younger man

We would, therefore, approach women's caring practices indirectly by first identifying the most significant needs in the lives of the women and their families.

The older women took very little time to express a wide range of needs. Younger women required some urging. Finally, the young men were also brought into the discussion. Table 5.2 gives the list of needs as it was initially compiled without much discussion, only clarifications as to what was meant. Although the list was not ranked, the order does signify a rough prioritization, and many of the needs expressed are also inter-linked.

The large group was then divided, at random, into two mixed groups to discuss some of these needs. The groups were fluid; as the discussions proceeded some women left to attend to their chores, and others joined. Eventually, there were more unmarried girls and boys in the first group and older women in the second. The composition of the two groups and the interests of the respective facilitators seem to have affected the interactions and outcome, which are amalgamated here. On the whole, the younger group was more animated; the older group began quietly but was transformed when the mode of communication changed from speech to song. The general consensus was that there were two things that money could not buy: time and the love of children.

Livelihood, with the blessings of the gods, was the most important felt need; with food, fuel and water being the basic requirements of life. Once these were met, *up-jivan* (finer needs) could be thought about. Both groups talked of the need for time. Older women wished for more time to spend with their children, to plan for the future; indeed, children were perceived as the future. Younger women said time would enable them to pursue their education or help their children to do so. They could learn new income-earning skills or tend home gardens. Health had now become a priority. In the old days people trusted in god and the prayers of the elders; they depended more on traditional practices as they had no money to consult a modern doctor. The young especially missed the co-operative spirit of joint family life. They said work inside and outside the house used to be shared, so one family did not have to be responsible for everything. But the young also recognized that the joint family did not enable individuals to choose a different, independent future. They said it was not just a matter of permission, they themselves could not think any differently.

CARING WOMEN

All Kunbi women (and men too) fulfil multiple routine caring roles within the family and in the community. Apart from this, some Kunbi women (and women of other social groups) are engaged in caring work that has a wider public reach, has gained them the respect of their communities and enhanced their own self-esteem. In some cases, the work fits into the woman's traditional domain but in others it has required venturing out into a new area. The brief sketches here contain accounts of our conversations with women who are engaged in diverse caring practices. They include four Hindu Kunbi and one Christian: a herbal medicine healer, a traditional birth attendant, a singer of folk-songs, a voluntary social worker, and an elected political representative.

Annapurna Krishna Gavda of Sittegali village is a knowledgeable and skilled herbal medicine practitioner, a female *vagdali*. Traditionally, only men dispensed herbal medicines, and this is indicated by the Konkani word *vagdali* which has no feminine equivalent. Annapurna is now over 70 years of age and like the other older women, she wears her sari in the traditional style, a single length of fabric, knotted over the right shoulder in a way that does not require a blouse or petticoat. (Middle-aged and young women wear the modern Indian sari). Married at 18, she has eight children, three of whom are daughters. Her extended family of 15 members includes four sons and their wives and children. The family moved from the Supa dam area to Sittegali about 20 years ago. They do not own any land but have seven heads of cattle and a small house, and work as agricultural labourers on other people's land. Annapurna has never been to school and is not literate but decides all important family matters in consultation with her eldest son.

Annapurna:

'We are living today only because of the forest. It supplies us all the necessities of life, fuel, fodder and medicine. As I grew to adulthood, I witnessed the forest becoming sparser and the rains becoming irregular and this affects animal and human life.

I first learned about herbal medicines to treat fever and wounds in childhood from my mother. I also learnt to recognize medicinal plants according to their shape, leaf, bark or fruits. But I did not practise as a child except in emergencies when I would give medicine for wounds without the supervision of my father or mother. After marriage, when one of my children fell ill I began on my own to use herbal medicines for them. My husband taught me more about herbal treatments for children's illnesses. Then I also began treating others who needed herbal medicines.

Whenever I visited my natal home, my father would come to escort me. We had to walk through the forests for three to four hours. On the way, he would tell me about the medicinal properties of each tree, plant and herb. It was from him that I learnt the most. Different parts of a plant may be used. In some cases, it is the aroma that has healing properties. Or it may be the roots, bark, tender leaves, flowers, fruit. In some cases the medicine is for external use, in others it has to be ingested.

Medicinal plants are not gathered and processed at sunrise because with the sun's ascent to its height at noon it is believed that the patient's illness also increases. So the appropriate time is later in the mornings and afternoons. There are many taboos on women, some trees that they may not touch, even for medicine, during the four days of the month when they menstruate. During the first 12 days after childbirth, women's touch is believed to be polluting. So too that of both men and women for a certain period after a death in the family.

The first time I treated a sick man successfully, I felt very happy. I visited the man several times to understand the stages by which he had improved and become well. I was then confident about managing any illness and was happy about that.

In all the years that I have been a herbal medicine practitioner I have not expected anything from patients except their speedy recovery. No one has ever given me money or clothes in return for treatment and I myself do not think about these things. If someone offers me a coconut, I accept it. But I would never accept money; indeed, this is forbidden. If a healer takes money, then the medicine given by her hand will not bring relief. The spiritual value of the medicine will be lost in the money transaction. As I get the medicine freely from the forest I should not use it to earn money.

I have taught my own children a little but not everything. It used to be said that when a practitioner shows the flowers she uses to someone else, the efficacy of the medicines she dispenses with her hand and her own healing powers are lessened. But now that I have grown old I have shown the flowers to my son, taught him.

The younger generation of school-going children are not teachable. They are not interested in our medicine and prefer going to modern doctors. These children cannot recognize different plant species. If they do not have the confidence to identify a plant, how can I teach them about herbal dosages?'

Sushila (Sunita) Budho Velip of Kirwati village is a 52-year-old *vaijin* (midwife, a traditional Birth Attendant also known as a *dai* in Marathi). Following Maharashtrian-Konkani custom Sushila was given a new first name upon marriage and is now known by both names. Kirwati village lies on the main road through the Joida hills and is linked by bus. It is also an alighting point for many interior villages which can only be reached on foot. Apart from a few years of primary schooling in the Marathi medium, Sushila has had no formal education but is supremely confident and proud of her skills. Her small nuclear family has a little land that they cultivate. Her husband, Budho Velip, told us that Sushila would go immediately to the aid of any woman in labour, even if it meant leaving other work in the household and field, for this was a matter of life and death. Their daughter wanted to join a nursing course after she finished her schooling but did not gain admission and told us that she definitely does not want to be a traditional midwife.

Sushila: 'I have been delivering babies for many years. I learnt the skill in my natal home, from my brother's wife. I collect the necessary herbs myself from the local forest. In earlier years, I only attended to local cases. But in the last few years I have been traveling much further, even as far as Dighe village. Whenever someone comes to take me for a case, I go whether it is night or day, even if it is cold and raining, and regardless of how far I have to walk. Sometimes, the pregnant women come and stay with me for 12 days, and my family and I take care of them.

In the last four or five years, I may have attended more than 400 cases. I've never had a failure. There have been many difficult cases. Sometimes my opinion has been different from the doctors in Dandeli town. But I've always been right. I've saved cases that the doctors could not deal with. Some years ago, I was called for an eight-day government training course. After half a day they told me I could leave because there was nothing more they could teach me. They gave me a set of instruments which I sometimes use. They could have given me some recognition instead. That would have made me proud.

From the poor people who come to me, I do not expect anything. They come because they trust me and they do not have two thousand rupees to pay a doctor. Sometimes they might give me a sari or something like that, or maybe two hundred rupees. Whatever they feel like. If they give, I accept. But whether or not they give anything, I treat them the same. When they stay in our house we also feed them.

I would like to teach younger people, pass on my skill. But who wants to learn? This is unclean, dirty work, dealing with human waste, all blood and body fluids. But, yes, I am satisfied when I see the babies I have delivered as they grow up.'

Bhagirathi Budho Velip of Mudiye village, one of the interior villages, is about 48 years old. She is a cultivator and accomplished folk-singer. Bhagirathi is a woman of unusual energy and independence. A few years ago she lost her son and husband (not to be confused with Sushila's husband who has the same name) in a terrible road accident. Relatives provided comfort and support to Bhagirathi's small nuclear family. Even as she and her young children coped with the tragedy, Bhagirathi broke out of the traditional mould of a widow. She ploughs the family land herself, although handling the ploughshare is customarily taboo for women. She does not, however, broadcast the paddy seed which is the ultimate taboo.

Bhagirathi maintains a cheerful appearance, is outspoken and bold. A couple of years ago, at a meeting with Forest Department officials that was intended to encourage women to participate in village forest management, the women listened for two hours while the men talked (Indira ibid.). It was Bhagirathi who broke the women's silence by saying, '*It is not that we are not interested, and so do not participate. It is because we cannot understand the language* [Kannada] *in which you speak during meetings. What can we contribute when we neither understand nor are understood?*' She asked a senior forest official, '*Why don't you translate the discussions of these meetings into Konkani, so that we can also join?*' One official had immediately retorted, 'You have been living in our state [Karnataka] for several years now, you should have learnt our language.' Bhagirathi answered calmly, '*We know only the language that our mothers spoke* [Konkani] *because we never went to school. Also, we know only the forest. There is nothing like a Konkani forest and a Kannada forest. Our daughters are now going to Kannada schools. But until they are old enough to be in the Village Forest Committees, you must let us know what happens in the committees in a language that we understand.*'

Bhagirathi had told the Forest Department officials to keep the larger interests of the forest and the Kunbi community in mind when issuing permits for the collection of non-timber forest produce (Indira ibid). She had argued that the permits be given

Table 5.3: Some examples of Kunbi Song Genres

Genre	Language	Sung by	Themes
Lullabies	Konkani	Older and younger women	Mainly related to the God Krishna's infancy and childhood
Sibling songs	Konkani	Older and younger women	Brother's concern for married sister who is away; sister's reassurance that she is not alone in her husband's house
Baraat songs	Konkani	Older and younger women	Concern for obstacles the bride must face on her way to the groom's house for the marriage ceremony
Mandap songs	Konkani	Older and younger women	Songs related to the marriage ceremony
Shringar songs	Konkani	Younger women	Description of the Hindu Goddess Parvathy's toilette; actually an idealised guide to a married woman's dress and adornment
Young wife's songs	Konkani	Younger women	Appeal to the husband to bring gifts (sari) for the wife
Grinding songs	Konkani	Older and younger women	Concerns of the daughter-in-law for acceptance by her in-laws
Riddles	Konkani	Older women	Short puzzles for the listener to answer
Agricultural songs	Konkani	Men and women (No longer sung)	Related to 'Slash and burn' cultivation
Nature songs	Kannada	School children from Song book	Peacock dancing in the rain
Patriotic songs	Kannada	School children from Song book	The glory of Karnataka

Source: Informal recordings made at Digalamb, Deriya, Chapoli and Bapeli villages, 2003.

to the Village Forest Committees, '*Give us the permits for collection instead of giving them to contractors who have no real concern for our forests. They are interested only in quick money and are destroying our future, because they do not know how and when to collect. Also, they have built roads in the forest, and these are being used by illicit liquor traders from Goa. When men become alcoholics, it is the women who have to suffer.*'

Bhagirathi is one of the few Kunbi women who still has a complete repertoire of traditional Konkani folk songs and recognizes the role of these songs in holding the community together. The songs express a variety of caring emotions, of mothers for their infants, brothers for their sisters. Some songs provide guidance, others are just fun. The songs celebrate, motivate, console, or draw-in the listener though riddles. Songs related to community agricultural practices are no longer remembered, but there are new songs learnt by schoolchildren. (See below and Table 5.3 below)

Bhagirathi:

'A person who listens carefully can identify the special meaning and values in these songs. These songs have their own importance and are sung for different occasions and purposes. There are everyday songs, like lullabies and grinding songs; songs that express particular relationships as between a brother and sister; and songs for special occasions like marriages, a baby's naming ceremony, and festivals such as Ganesh Puja, Deepavali, and Tulsi "Vivah". But nowadays the younger generation are only interested in film songs, which are meaningless. The style and rhythm of the songs are also changing. The most melodic style is now very rare. I would like to keep the folk songs alive and support those who are interested in learning. I want to pass this tradition to the younger generation and have taught all my daughters. Singing gives them much joy.'

Women's Narrative Folk-Songs

In the Kunbi community, there is an old tradition of women singing community songs. Both women and men like to sing. Although the women's singing style is different from everyday speech, the deep meaning of the Konkani songs can be grasped through their being linked to particular contexts and times. For instance the belief is that a particular song sung during a drought brings the wind god Varun to earth in an invisible form, and the rains follow the next day. The kind of songs sung in the rainy season are different from those sung during festivals. Some songs describe processes step-by-step like the building of a temple from its foundations. Many songs have a rhyming refrain, with a different god being named in each repetition. Others use indirection, a girl may sing of herself using another's name, or of a husband taking a god's name.

Women sing songs from 4 a.m. when they get up to attend to kitchen chores and sweep the courtyard. Children are woken up by sweet tones and hear songs all day till they are put to sleep through lullabies. The women's melodious songs rouse the sun god from sleep, and husbands awaken hearing the names of the gods. Women sing while doing their early morning prayers to the *tulsi* plant-goddess, while drawing *rangoli* (decorative patterns) on the threshold of their houses, getting their children ready, feeding the cattle and preparing to go to the fields to work. The songs help them focus on the purpose of their work and to ease their tiredness throughout the day. They also help women to bond together. Traditionally, twice a month, women and girls from nearby villages gather with their percussion instruments such as the *dholak* (a double-sided drum), *ghumte* (an earthen pot that resounds when struck with the palm and fingers) and *zanji* (cymbals) to sing and dance together.

It is also customary for married women to visit their natal homes to celebrate Deepavali, the festival of lights. This brings great joy. Women sing as they wait expectantly for fathers and brothers to come and escort them home. In the old songs, now not so common, fruits, birds, the sun, moon or wind would become messengers of their longing. One old song goes:

> *Run-jhun* (dancing) bird go to my father's house
> Sit there at the door, *run-jhun* (dancing) bird
> Tell my mother, tell my father
> It's the festival of Deepawali, come take me home.
> (Adapted from a Note by Jayanand Derkar 2003)

Katalin, 38 years, is a Konkani Christian and has for long been engaged in voluntary community service which has brought her in contact with women of many communities including the Kunbi. Her family moved to Bapeli village near Joida town when they lost their lands due to submersion in the Supa hydro-electric project. Bapeli is one of the few villages in the area where there is no Kunbi population; the majority are Marathi or Konkani-speaking Hindu Dessai landlords and traders who moved here from the more densely-forested Castlerock area in the 1960s. There are a few Konkani-speaking Gavli herder families and a couple of Konkani Christian families, including that of Katalin. Formerly the Dessais were particular about maintaining ritual purity and did not invite other families to their festivities because of considerations of pollution. But this has changed with common education for their children.

Katalin:

'Economic conditions have worsened in the last four or five years. Land holdings are small and the population has gone up. Unemployment is severe. This is especially so for women who used to work at the Karnataka Forest Department (KFD) nursery at Bapeli but lost their jobs when it was shifted to Kumbharawada (a distant village). Due to poverty and unemployment, men have taken to drinking liquor and there have even been some thefts in Bapeli. A poor person who does not have work, just thinks about how to get liquor and if there is no money for that, he steals. This social problem is difficult to tackle because almost all the men drink.

Earlier, there were three Self Help Groups (SHGs) but these are not functioning well. After the women lost their source of earning, many of them have defaulted on payments to their group credit scheme. The NGO from Bangalore which initiated these SHGs has no continuous presence in the area and seems to have lost interest. I have tried to get contracts for forest works to help the poor women earn some income. The KFD has been supportive and we did get some contracts for harvesting timber in the year 2003. The SHGs could function more effectively if women had the skills to start and manage small enterprises and for this they need training.

I have also been associated with the government's Ashraya scheme to identify needy persons who have no houses. As a member of the Ashraya committee I have visited several villages in Joida taluk to sanction houses.

I would like to bring changes in Bapeli but people need employment. Some people are supportive of my efforts, but others are not. Factional politics has spoiled life in the village. Some people say that the village will be emptied in a few years as families move away. Yet, I am still hopeful that something can be done to strengthen the existing women's groups and improve village life, and am always willing to work towards that.'

Divyani Dayanad Gavda, just 27 years, is an elected member of the Zila Panchayat, (which takes care of local governance). She is one of the very few women graduates among the Kunbi but can still lead her friends in singing the traditional lullabies and sibling songs. She came to Digalamb village after her marriage; and as a-two-year old daughter named Aishwarya, (after the film star Aishwariya Rai). The joint family owns land and most are full-time cultivators, but her husband also works as a private contractor for the government's Public Works Department. Digalamb village is among the better-off Kunbi villages. Divyani told us that the women generally shared information about wild forest produce, which they gathered for their own use or sale, but if one of them found something in the forest that was likely to be especially profitable, it is possible that they would not tell the others. Divyani is constantly thinking and planning for her people. She was the only one of all the women we met who asked, 'tell me what can you do to help us?' And she was also the only one who said, 'When people like you come and we gather together and talk, it makes us put our minds to things that we would not otherwise think about.'

Divyani:

'My parents did not have any sons; as the eldest of three sisters I had many responsibilities. My father had a good name in society and in the political field. It was always my ambition to enter politics too and accomplish something to make my father proud. But he dissuaded me, saying that I did not understand politics and lacked the skill of making political speeches. After marriage, however, my father-in-law and husband (both of whom were active in local politics) suggested that I stand for the district panchayat elections. I did not have to campaign as the family was already well known. I was happy that I won (a seat reserved for women) and that, despite being a woman, I had brought glory to my father's name. My family gave a feast to the whole village to celebrate, but for me the win was also tinged with sadness because at that time my first child had just died.

During my youth, we sisters were not allowed to take any independent decisions. We had to have our parents' permission if we wished to go anywhere. We had no freedom even to choose the clothes we wore. Nor did we seek any liberties. We girls wanted to study further but there were financial problems. I would have liked to have taken a course to train to be a primary education teacher but was not able to gain admission and took a BA course instead as my father suggested. Today, however, I am free to take my own decisions, although I feel it is natural that I first discuss any decision with my husband and father-in-law.

I have no personal expectations from the Zila Panchayat. Initially, I also faced some problems due to factional differences in the panchayat and could not get their support for certain public work. But this was later resolved. My entire family are supportive of my political role. My mother-in-law and other women of the family look after my child and provide hospitality to any of my friends who visit, even if I am away from home. My family has always told me to help everyone who seeks my co-operation; even if an enemy asks for help, I must help to the extent I can.

The Kunbis in Joida taluk are a most backward community. I want to do something special for Joida in general and the women in particular. The women are shy; they remain separate from the outside world, and are in the dark. I have concentrated on development for the women and have started a 'Svayam-Sahai Sangh' (Self-Help Group) in my village. The majority of women here are uneducated and they have no livelihood avenues apart from agricultural cultivation and labour. Therefore, in free seasons, we have to search for other jobs or learn some other skills. At the very least we can all sit together at one place and plan for the future. In this way we can be energized to strive for organized activities and can work for social change in the village. It is for this reason that after consulting with the women I have started the SHG. The plan is to save, to start small enterprises, to participate in development programmes.

When the three of you came here and Sumi asked the SHG members which was the furthest place they had visited, one woman answered that she had gone to Karwar (the district headquarters). Later, when I had to go Sirsi (in the taluk adjacent to Joida) to attend an official meeting, the same woman wanted to accompany me. Some other women too joined her, just so that they could visit Sirsi. On their way back we stopped at the Krishi Vigyan Kendra (a Government agricultural centre). We learnt that the centre provides training related to agricultural production and the officials told us about various programmes. There was a very good interaction between us. They also said that if a 'batch' of women were ready, they could come to the village and train them. I think we could learn about things like vermiculture. In this way women are thinking in the right direction and I have to do something to help them.'

Annapurna, Sushila, Bhagirathi, Katalin and Divyani's work represent a spectrum of caring practices which have been determined by what is sanctioned by the gendered life-worlds that they individually and collectively inhabit and in which they have also stretched the sanctioned limits. Both Annapurna and Sushila have the gift of healing which they share with great generosity. Annapurna's belief that her gift will lose its efficacy if it is exchanged for money represents a tradition that is now passing, even among the Kunbi. Sushila's daughter rejecting the life of a *vaijin* and seeking to train as a nurse reflects this tellingly. Bhagirathi, the singer of songs, has defied custom in her own life, most notably in handling the plough. There are a couple of other women in similar circumstances in Mudiye village who have quietly begun to use the plough. The stories of the younger women, Katalin and Divyani, show how traditions of care are being shaped afresh to meet new needs in a changing world. Women's self-help groups are fostering different kinds of sharing and social mobility. Taken together, these narratives show that caring practices accumulated over time are dynamic and diverse. The invisibility of caring work in the routine of each day, the disinterest in immediate returns, the emotional investment in a network of social relations and the risk of exploitation are not easily articulated. Yet, by concentrating on practices in particular settings, shifting our vision through different angles, we can indirectly approach that which we cannot readily define.

REFLECTIONS: HONEYED STRINGS

Caring practices occur within contexts of needs, interests and values that have arisen from a specific socio-political history and the economic processes necessitated by living a particular life in a given family, social group and wider society. After many hours of observing, listening, talking, reading and reflecting we drew up a set of what seem to us to be the traditional core values of the Kunbi. Others may interpret the same material in a different way, identify a different set of values. We make no special claims for its validity but found this a useful framework to view the Kunbi's life-world and caring practices.

The *love of children* and *trust in elders* are core values that have shaped inter-generational relations among the Kunbi. For people whose present is physically and materially constrained children represent hopes for the future, even as the young look to their elders for guidance and advice. The time that elders and children can spend together then becomes an urgent need. When parents pass on their knowledge of plants and herbal medicinal skills to their children, or latterly their social and political concerns, the bonds of care are extended to a wider circle of kin and neighbourhood. Children and elders belong to the extended kin group, and when families divide it is they who feel most acutely the loss of kin-elders (who are more than aunts and uncles) and kin-siblings (who are more than cousins).

The Kunbi's *spiritual beliefs* foster *co-existence with nature*. In the past, an abundant resource base ensured the survival of forest-dependent communities. Religious sentiment and economic rationality converged to maintain sustainability; the forest was not valorized, exploited or feared but was used productively within certain regulated limits. Changes in the government's forest and land-use policies and external commercial and industrial pressures have weakened these linkages. When forests have been mined and submerged all around them, time-honoured caring practices such as taking the priest's blessings for collecting forest produce are difficult to sustain. Despite this, knowledge of herbal medicine and other forest lore is widespread among all adults.

For a migrant community struggling to establish itself in a new environment, *co-operative work and responsibilities* and *sharing benefits* were vital aspects of life. The mode of cultivation (slash-and-burn) and the structure of the large joint family made such co-operation and sharing possible. Cultivation practices have changed entirely, and yet common resources continue to be shared; for example, when water is scarce families take turns to channel the hill streams to irrigate their fields. The family structure is changing, but the core values of co-operation and sharing have endured to a great extent. This is perhaps why the Kunbi can so generously extend a welcome, making time and space for home-less kin (and visiting researchers). In all of the Kunbi villages that we visited, doors were always open during the day. Anyone could enter. In any particular Kunbi village there is little economic disparity among the families. An entire village may be better or worse off than other villages but there is relative equality within a village. This is not so in villages that are in the same area but inhabited by a mix of social groups. In such villages, where different economic levels are starkly visible, it takes time and effort for caring practices to overcome the class and caste divisions.

The daily routine of the Kunbi has been so physically demanding that there was little time in their lives to sit down and discuss village matters, although the institutional framework for doing this did exist. Traditionally, women did not have a sanctioned voice in public decision-making. Many decisions however, seem to have been taken by a tangible 'sense of the community' to which both women and men contributed rather than through formal debate. This is possible in small face-to-face social groups where people's characters and outlook are not sharply individualized and the significance of *non-verbal modes of communication* such as song, dance and drama is recognized. Song, as Bhagirathi perceives, is especially important as a mode of communication among women and has contributed to their bonding. The content of the Kunbi songs reflect the strong urge towards the peaceful resolution of conflicts in inter-personal and familial relations that has also marked the division of the large joint families. Today, however, with education being a high priority for girls and boys, the language, mode, content and reach of inter-personal and social communication are changing.

The thread that weaves all of these core values together into the fabric of Kunbi life (and makes caring possible) is empathy rather than reciprocity. The capacity for empathy, an intuitive understanding of the needs of others, derives from their emotional rather than material strength. This strength is not a biological attribute of mothers, nor confined to women, although our study focused on them. It was evident that many Kunbi women and men of all ages (and non-Kunbis too) are capable of drawing upon their rich life experiences to actively empathize with a community that is much wider than the immediate family.

From this small case study of the Kunbi in Joida, we can surmise that the capacity to care reflects processes of socialization and learnings that are passed on—from father to daughter and from mother to son, as Annapurna has done. Caring is more than the giving of material objects in a system of deferred reciprocity. Caring involves giving of oneself, one's knowledge and skills, giving time, giving space, often without weighing this in a balance of exchange. The carer derives satisfaction (and some power) from the self-recognition that she (or he) is performing a vital function and that by fulfilling a social need has gained the esteem of the community.

When we interact briefly, a group of Kunbi and a few researchers, each representing and interpreting the other in myriad ways, it is all too easy to romanticize and essentialize the 'giving natures' of Kunbi men and women, and the moral significance that non-monetary care has in the Kunbi economy. We need to recognize, however, that the life of a social group is made up of a diversity of social practices and care-giving is but one of these. Moreover, these caring practices have evolved in a socio-economic and cultural context that is fast disappearing even in the small pockets in which the effect continues to be felt. In recent decades the abrupt changes that have taken place in Kunbi life are reflective of developments in the larger society of which it is a part. These changes do affect traditional values but also provide opportunities for families and individuals (who have traditionally paid a high price for social harmony) to choose, if they so wish, to develop in new and independently productive directions. Like the syrupy strings of honey in the Kunbi puzzle song in the epigram at the start of this chapter, caring ties are sweet but binding. In their current struggle against poverty and the erosion of the resource base, the Kunbi are especially fortunate to be able to draw upon a strong moral framework and values that blend justice and compassion. Women's caring practices develop within and are legitimised by the worlds in which they live: a framework of norms, a traditional belief system and a socio-economic structure, which have evolved over a long period of time and continue to change.

NOTES

[1] This chapter draws upon an unpublished study 'Honeyed Strings', undertaken in 2003 by myself, R. Indira and Jayanand H. Derekar with Annapurna Krishna Gavda, Sushila Budho Velip, Bhagirathi Budho Velip, Katalin and Divyani Dayanand Gavda, which was supported by Devaki Jain (Bangalore). The study was primarily based upon techniques of participant observation, informal conversations (one-to-one or in small groups and occasionally in larger gatherings), unstructured interviews and Focus Group Discussions, mainly with the women but also with a few men. Community researcher Jayanand Derekar, a Kunbi who grew up in Deriya village and still lives there, is a first generation graduate who worked previously with Mysore university sociology professor R. Indira, on an Indo-Canadian project to improve the Kunbi women's participation in a government forest management programme. The rapport that Indira had developed and Jayanand's familiarity with the Kunbi villages smoothened our passage and eased the difficult logistics of field work. It was polyglot Jayanand, who has schooled in Marathi and knows five languages, upon whom we depended to translate nuances and clarify local idioms; he also revisited some of the women for further conversations which were conducted in Konkani, recorded by him in Hindi and which I subsequently narrativised in English.

[2] This is a free translation of a Kunbi riddle song in Konkani, which was one of many riddles put to me by Bhagirathi of Mudiye village. August 2003.

6

A Gendered Approach to Biodiversity Conservation

> Earlier we used to collect and cook many different greens. These days we go to the forest to collect leafy greens only in an emergency, when it is raining too much and we cannot use the path to the local market to buy provisions. The young people do not like to eat the wild greens. Like city people our boys too prefer market foods.
>
> —Elderly adivasi woman, Wayanad, Kerala.[1]

It was only in the late 1980s that the limitations of dealing separately with the various living components of nature led to the emergence of the over-arching concept of biological diversity or biodiversity, as it is more commonly known. The term biodiversity refers to all living natural resources, fauna, flora and micro-organisms and their inter-relationships in different ecosystems, forests, wetlands, desserts and so on. This integrated rather than sector-by-sector approach gained international prominence with the 1992 UN Convention on Biological Diversity. Since then, the literature on biodiversity and its management has grown swiftly. The need for sensitivity to the social and human dimensions of biodiversity management has also been recognised but biodiversity has rarely been seen from a gendered perspective. The majority of ecologists, conservationists, natural and social scientists continue to be resistant to gender concerns. This chapter takes a gendered view of some aspects of biodiversity conservation. The first section on documenting gender roles in biodiversity management, shows that there is no simple division of labour by sex, and that women's knowledge and role in conservation practises, notably seed preservation, have evolved from interactions in particular social and ecological circumstances. The next section analyses the patriarchal traditions underlying many community practices of preserving sacred groves and species and argues that these practices need to be reassessed. Finally, the chapter argues that a gendered picture of biodiversity conservation is context-specific, dynamic and complex.

SOME GENDER DIMENSIONS OF CONSERVATION

India is among the twelve mega-biodiversity areas of the world with about 6.5 percent of the world's recorded species of wild plants and animals (Nayar 1996, Arora and Pandey 1996, Rani and Swaminathan 1998). Apart from the sheer numbers of wild species (45,000 plants and 81,000 animal species), it is also the diverse range that makes for its unique value. A third of the flowering plants are endemic. India is also a recognised centre of domesticated biodiversity: 166 species of crops and 320 species of wild relatives of crops are known to have originated here. Each crop species encompasses a diversity of varieties. The diversity of livestock, sheep and goat is also high. This richness is paralleled by a socio-cultural diversity of natural resource-based livelihoods and knowledge systems. For example, till fairly recently Indian farming communities were growing more than 50,000 varieties of rice, developed over centuries through different local practices and adjusted to varied soil and climatic conditions. The formal infrastructure for dealing with various biological components of the environment, forests, flora and fauna, was set up under British rule. As with other institutions introduced at that time, these were geared primarily to Britain's imperial interests. The Botanical Survey of India (which is over a century old) and the Zoological Survey, (established in the early 20th century) were expanded after Independence. There are National Bureaus of plant, animal and fish genetic resources and specialised national gene banks for medicinal and aromatic plants. More than two-thirds of the country has been surveyed but little is known of the remoter regions of the

Himalayas in north-eastern India, the Andaman and Nicobar Islands, the wetlands and coastal waters around the peninsula. The various research institutions together with the Indian Council for Agricultural Research and several universities have contributed to the modern knowledge base for the conservation and development of biological resources.

Documenting Gender Roles: no simple division of labour by sex

Women's labour in farming and the collection of fodder and firewood were recognised in the 1970s. At that time, however, there were few who recognised that poor rural women's knowledge and skills also play a central role in the management, conservation, and sustainable use of biological resources, activities critical in maintaining the ecosystems that provide the basis of life. This was not systematically observed and documented till the late 1990s, when studies began trying to draw out the linkages between biodiversity and gender. In one of the earliest of such research[2] (Swaminathan ed. 1998), as the overall adviser and participant I found that it was difficult to isolate women's roles in biodiversity management separately from women's roles in the entirety of their lives, farming, fishing, basketry, household provisioning. This was partly because our research team of women and men were not used to looking at biodiversity as a specific entity but perhaps mainly because women's lives do flow across different domains.

As discussed in Chapter 4, neither gathering nor traditional subsistence production are women's exclusive domain. Women's intimate knowledge of natural resources is not genetically programmed but is the result of social roles, which make women of certain classes, castes and tribes interact more closely with their environment. This 'interactive' knowledge is passed along through generations, only as long as there are no occupational changes. Urban women do not have this kind of knowledge. Nor indeed do young rural women, when modern education gives them the aspiration and the capacity to choose different kinds of work. Our study corroborated this in different locations and for different farming and fishing groups (Krishna, 1998a; see also Tables 6.1-6.4 in this Chapter and 7.5-7.9 in Chapter 7). The study also showed that together with gender, both age and caste were significant factors in the division of labour.

In the Siruvani and Topslip areas of Tamil Nadu, both men and women are involved in gathering tubers and honey from the forest (L. Vedavalli, 1997: personal communication). In the fresh water estuaries among the mangroves of coastal Orissa, both men and women fish but use different means: men cast nets and use boats; while women and children catch fish with their bare hands. In the island ecosystem of Lakshadweep, roles are more sharply gender-demarcated. In this unique tribal Muslim matrilineal community, men and women have different kinds of ecological knowledge: women are more conversant with the resources around their homes and along the reef and shore, while men are more knowledgeable about the land from which they collect coconuts and about the lagoon and sea where they fish. Despite this apparently complementary gendered division of tasks, a favourite pastime of women is to hunt octopus, (V. Hoon, 1999: personal communication). In Wayanad, Kerala, young Kuruchiya girls are adept with bows and arrows, a skill learned over generations— except that now hunting birds for food has given way to shooting targets for sport, and families proudly display the trophies that the girls have won in archery competitions.

Although women do not have access to the kind of technologies that men possess, there are many arenas in which the conventional division of labour does not exist. The women and men in the Kolli Hills in Tamil Nadu undertake most farming activities jointly. This farming community is officially listed as a Scheduled Tribe but practises an entirely peasant way of life; ploughing is traditionally men's work but there is no taboo against women using the plough and occasionally they do use it. In this area, it is the women who are primarily responsible for seed selection and storage, as also for transplanting and weeding although men also participate. Applying green manure, harvesting the crop and post-harvest tasks are shared equally by men and women. Harvesting fruit crops is also done jointly. Among the tribal communities in the hills of Orissa, the selection of the panicles of paddy is done jointly, but women have a greater role in the selection of minor millet and oil seeds. Men plough the land and sow the paddy seed; women weed; harvesting is done jointly; winnowing is the men's task; storage is done jointly and milling by women.

Gender role differentiation is more prominent among upper caste farming groups, as in coastal Orissa, where only men undertake farming activities, be it ploughing and field preparation, raising nurseries, transplanting, harvesting, threshing, or storage. The major activity for women is the post-harvest task of boiling the rice before it is dried in the sun. Wherever brahamanical patriarchy makes inroads, women's roles become more circumscribed. The Kuruchiya of Wayanad are now a 'brahminised' patriarchal tribal community although they continue to follow the matrilineal *taravad* system on matters of lineage and inheritance of property. Men prepare the land and select the paddy seed. Women are not allowed to do so, although older women may sometimes help. Women weed, protect plants from insect damage, harvest and winnow the crop. Other post-harvest activities are carried out jointly by men and women. Men alone are involved in paddy seed storage but women may select and store vegetable seed, and tend the vegetable garden. Since all seed material is considered sacred, menstruating women are not allowed near any kind of seed storage. Despite the oppressive concepts of pollution and purity that women have to uphold, they do have a say in choosing which varieties of paddy are to be cultivated and in which fields.

In India as in the rest of South Asia, gender role differentiation also exists in all natural resource based hand crafts. However, as with farming and biodiversity related tasks, there is no simple division of labour by sex (see also S8). Among the dalit (Scheduled Caste) weavers in Orissa, the men collect the grass for basket weaving, women cure it and weave the baskets. In the Jeypore hills, men and women are equally involved in collection, processing and marketing forest products like grass, bamboo and resin. Among some tribal groups in Arunachal Pradesh, all the tasks related to basket making are considered men's work.

The picture that emerges from field ethnography is varied and complex. This is so even with regard to domestic tasks, conventionally assumed to be entirely within the women's domain. Providing cooking energy and water are major provisioning tasks in poor households. Gender role differentiation exists but there is no simple division. Several studies of degraded habitats in central India and the western Himalaya have shown that women bear the major load of gathering firewood and collecting water. In peninsular Tamil Nadu, women, children and old men gather firewood and graze the cattle. In the estuarine areas of coastal Orissa, children and young men graze the cattle, women collect water and both men and women cut trees and collect firewood. In the hill tracts of Orissa too collecting water is the duty of women and girls; both men and women gather fuel wood but grazing cattle and looking after them is the work of boys and men. In Lower Subansiri district of Arunachal Pradesh, firewood gathering is traditionally a male task, although this is now beginning to change and in Mizoram, collecting water is specifically boys' work that is now sometimes shared by girls in the family.

In various different locations, it is apparent that caste is a significant factor in the gender differentiation of roles but it may sometimes be overridden by external pressures, such as distress migration. As mentioned in Chapter 2, in coastal Orissa upper caste (brahmin and kshatriya) Oriya women are not allowed outside their homestead areas, thus effectively restricting their economic roles to domestic tasks. But Oriya women of other castes, potters and weavers, and migrant Bengali women of all castes have greater freedom of movement. Caste, community, and locally specific social and cultural factors, which change over time, determine the work that men and women do. Collecting fuel wood and water, seed selection, winnowing and so on may be men's tasks in one location and women's tasks in another, or the task may be done jointly. This heterogeneity indicates that there is no simple division of gender roles by sex, as all men or all women are not universally engaged in performing the same tasks. Over time, the tasks assigned to men or women in different contexts reinforce the social construction of gender roles in that socio-cultural group or community. A question that needs to be addressed is the linkage between women's subordination and their concentration in time-consuming and labour-intensive activities. We also need to understand why some gender-specific tasks like cooking for the family have endured for so long, and across so many different social situations. (See also Chapter 7 for a discussion on gender roles in the north-eastern region.)

With regard to the Eastern Ghats region of Tamil Nadu, L. Vedavalli (1997 personal communication) suggests that women do not participate in certain farming tasks that are carried out early in the morning only because of their domestic responsibilities, cleaning and cooking, that also have to be done in the early morning, so this makes it seem that farming activities are sharply gender-segregated, which may not actually be so. This may explain why women do not face any socio-cultural objections when circumstances compel them to plough (as in the case of Bhagirathi in Uttara Kannada district, Karnataka, cited in Chapter 5). Similar complex variations on the ground are evident in traditional conservation practices.

Women's knowledge and conservation practices

Many poor women are adept at using local biological resources for healing and medicine (see also the testimony of Annapurna in Chapter 5). They have a role in preventing genetic erosion, conserving agro-biodiversity through multiple cropping systems, preserving local varieties of critical germplasm, and cross-pollinating crops by hand for fertilisation. Many women also contribute to value-addition through selecting seed, breeding and genetic enhancement. Their ecological knowledge base is a significant data bank of information. Documentation of the resource conservation skills, knowledge and practice of poor tribal and peasant women continues to be fragmentary and episodic.

In areas of traditional farming, among communities and classes that do not practise gender-seclusion, women's participation in conservation-related activities is high. In hill areas where the women are responsible for food production, as in the Apatani plateau of Arunachal Pradesh and Garhwal in Uttarakhand, or share joint responsibility as among the Mizos, Nagas and some of the hill tribes of the Western Ghats, women are primarily responsible for seed preservation. As one woman in the Kolli Hills said, 'It is better to save our seeds, grown in our own field, rather than depending on others'(Vedavalli 1997 personal communication).

Women also exchange seeds between households to increase the intra-varietal diversity of the crop.

In areas where traditional farming is still practised, the knowledge base of both men and women is being eroded. This is especially evident in the plains. In Orissa, it is the elders who predict the monsoon, instruct younger men to prepare the field and younger women to soak the seeds for germination. Irrigation and high yielding varieties have reduced the area under traditional crops, and changed methods of seed selection. Instead of the laborious method of picking out single healthy panicles, a part of the field is simply set aside for seed, or the seed is selected during threshing, obviously affecting the quality. The practice of leaving the straw in the field for composting has been given up. Because the straw is harvested other methods of natural manuring, such as cowdung and ash, are used for improving soil fertility. Formerly, the baskets for seed storage were lined with insect-repellent cowdung, a time consuming process but now seed is stored in discarded cement bags. Food habits are also changing as people prefer eating rice rather than the traditional millets and tubers, which are labour intensive and very time consuming for the women to process. The knowledge of older women who could cook the traditional staples is, therefore, no longer relevant. Decision-making on the farm has also shifted from the elders to young working people. Such changes are primarily age-specific and secondarily gender-specific.

In agriculturally developed areas where the penetration of market forces are much greater, women are less involved with conservation practices, but they continue to have a role in seed preservation. In the relatively prosperous Karamadai block in Coimbatore district (Tamil Nadu), a quantitative survey of women's involvement showed that only 3% of women were occupied in seed-gathering, and 8-10% in selling seed, but that 70-75% of women were involved in seed preservation. All the three activities brought monetary gains for the women. The majority of farm families in Karamadai depend on the government, agricultural universities and private agencies for seed but there is a shortfall in the quantity of seed available from these sources. It is to make up this deficit (30-40%), particularly of cereals and oilseeds, that women are active in seed preservation. In this area, chemical treatment is now the primary method of preserving all kinds of seeds, pulses, cereals, oilseeds and vegetables. Using ash and sun-drying are secondary methods. Less frequently, a coat of red soil may be applied to pulse seeds or neem (*Azerdachia indica*) leaves may be used to protect cereal seed (Devadas 1994).

In an earlier study (Ravishankar 1994, L. Vedavalli 1997 personal communication), researchers working among eight tribal groups, in four districts of Tamil Nadu, identified a diversity of leafy greens, vegetables, fruits, condiments and spices used by the women. The tribal women were aware of seasonal variations in the availability of edible tubers such as the yams of the *Dioscorea* species, and could identify fully-grown tubers by observing the condition of the vine. Women healers could also identify specific medicinal plants and collect them immediately in case of emergencies. In some tribes, the women have also developed ingenious on-farm practices and storage methods to prevent the disintegration of the seeds of millets, maize and sorghum.

More recent studies in Kerala (Ratheesh Narayanan et. al. 2004; see also section on traditional knowledge below) too indicate that tribal women, especially elderly women, have extensive knowledge of wild foods, leafy greens, tubers, mushrooms, molluscs, crabs, and of the medicinal plants, that can be gathered from the forest and fields, near water bodies and along roadsides. Among the younger generation, the knowledge of certain wild foods, such as the leafy greens, is being eroded partly because they no longer relish eating these, as the elderly adivasi woman cited in the epigram at the beginning of the chapter. Many wild plants have multiple uses as food and medicine. In Karnataka, the NGO Aikya, which works in the area of women and health, has been documenting the plants used by village women to treat common ailments (Philomena Vincent 2005 personal communication); among the most efficacious of these is the weed mimosa, or 'touch-me-not' (see *Touch Me Touch Me Not*, 2004).

Traditional knowledge and gathered foods[3]

In the decade since the early 1990s, the livelihood options of the poorest have been steadily shrinking. The process of economic globalisation, international agreements on trade and biodiversity, and national environmental and forest policies have impinged in complex ways on the use and sustainability of the natural resource base. This, together with the displacement and relocation of settlements, and local resource-use conflicts, poses difficult challenges to people's livelihood strategies. The poorest, such as some of the forest-dependant adivasi groups of Waynad district in Kerala, are especially vulnerable. They are on the edge of starvation surviving on free food rations from the government, and in a chronic state of health risk, which undermines their ability to live and work with dignity.

Set on the edge of the Western Ghats and the Deccan Plateau, Wayanad is a region of great ecological and human diversity. It has a varied topography, climate and vegetation, and hence a range of landscapes. Once known as the land of hill forest and paddy fields (*vayal nadu*), Wayanad is now a land of plantations: coffee, rubber and coconut besides cardamom, ginger, pepper and tea. Its formerly lush paddy fields are swiftly being transformed into banana groves, altering the ecology of the region. One sixth of the total population is adivasi; nine groups are currently listed as Scheduled Tribes: these include the Kattunaikkan, originally gatherer-hunters; the Adiya and Paniya, agricultural labourers; the Kuruma and the Kurichya, both settled cultivators. Each of these groups has different resource needs, interacting differently with the natural environment. The district has also been peopled by successive waves of settlers, including Muslims, Christians, Hindus and a small population of Wayanad Chetties, with their own patterns of resource usage.

Because of the prevailing gender ideology of many of these socio-cultural groups, women bear the major responsibility for food provisioning. Adivasi women (poor agricultural labourers and forest-dependent groups in particular) have developed a vast repository of knowledge of lesser-known foods that are foraged from the wild: leafy greens, fruits, seeds, and tubers, mushrooms, honey, crabs, and fish. These 'wild food' sources are found in forests, wetlands, fields and plantations, along wayside paths, and besides streams. Many have multiple uses and some are used as medicines. For the poorest these foods have provided a reliable buffer in lean seasons and enhanced the nutrient quality of their food. In recent times, however, because of the erosion of habitats, invasion by alien species, and the widespread use of agricultural chemicals, the wild foods are no longer as easily available. With changing food habits there is an increasing preference among the younger generation for food bought from the market and the older women's knowledge of these foods is being marginalised.

This complex process of change is at the core of an MSSRF study on wild food management in southern Wayanad, which has documented the ethnobiological (primarily ethnobotanical) knowledge of the Paniya, Kattunaikka and Kuruma. Following a participatory approach, Ratheesh Narayanan and Swapna have attempted to use the adivasi's own frameworks, terms and categorisations. Their study has also tried to blend the disciplinary perspectives, method and tools of social anthropology, gender studies and ethnobiology. This innovative methodology has resulted in a participatory, gendered ethnobotany that provides a richly detailed picture of the dynamics of wild food management on the ground.

The three Adivasi groups studied have different food production systems, and the gender roles also vary. Both the Paniya and the Kattunaikka are foragers and fishers; foraging is mainly women's work among the Paniya but it is more-or-less equally shared by Kattunaikka men and women. Among Kuruma groups, engaged in traditional agriculture, both men and women are involved in wild food collection while homestead farming is mainly women's responsibility. Some Kuruma and non-adivasis are now also marketing wild foods to more distant markets, which could threaten the sustainability of these resources. The Paniya, who are most dependent on foods from the wild and semi-wild areas, know about an amazing number of edible species. Paniya women are skilled in managing disturbed habitats such as the margins of paddy fields, water channels and roadsides.

The broad trend, however, is a marked decline in the adivasi's dependence on wild foods. Women's key role in food production is also undergoing complex changes. While most women continue to be responsible for feeding their families, the resource base available to them is diminishing rapidly. This puts them under great pressure to cope and affects their position in the household and social group.

Poor adivasis have a sophisticated understanding of their situation and of the potential and limitations of wild food resources. They are aware that wild foods by themselves cannot be a substitute for sustainable livelihood strategies. Yet, they are also aware that especially in the difficult food-deficient monsoon season, the wild leafy greens are a key dietary supplement. We now need to build upon their existing management practices to enable more efficient growth of some of these and other food species in homestead gardens.

The adivasi groups are also aware that documenting the disappearing wild food species and declining management practices is necessary to keep alive this knowledge. Yet they are also keenly aware of the risks of such documentation, and the possibility that outsiders could exploit this for commercial gains. It is the moral responsibility of all those who use this study to be alert to possible unethical uses of the knowledge that belongs not to the authors and sponsors of this work, or even to the individual adivasis who are listed as the 'key knowledge holders' but to the adivasi community as a whole. We urgently need to seek ways to enable the adivasi to assert their rights over this knowledge, as also over the resources and the lands that support these resources. The sustainable and equitable management of natural resources cannot be separated from the context of people's resource base, their traditional knowledge systems and the contemporary changes in their life-worlds.

RETHINKING THE SACRED: SPACES AND SPECIES

The customary protection of specific trees such as the neem, various plant species and patches of forest is part of popular environmental folklore and is also sometimes acclaimed by those who celebrate women's roles in conservation. However, such traditional practices have rarely been viewed through a gendered perspective, and in this section I argue that some rethinking is urgently required.

From a nature conservationist's point of view, *in situ* systems in 'hot spot' areas such as north-eastern India are of particular significance because these conserve a range of diversity. Many of these areas fall within the government's protected area network and forest reserves. Their conservation owes less to official efforts than to people's beliefs. For example, in the north-eastern region, some locations such as the Mouling National Park in East Siang are naturally protected by their terrain, and people generally avoid the area, except for some minimal hunting in the periphery. In some remote mountainous and/ or wetland areas, there are taboos on people's entry. Such inaccessible areas are also away from human habitations. For instance, the Pakhuii mountain in Mizoram is effectively protected by its topography, and by the local belief that the mountain is guarded by a spirit, which will harm anyone who enters the area. This has helped to prevent any kind of human intervention near the mountain. Similar protection is afforded to small swamps. People do not venture into areas which are believed to be guarded by spirits, so no enforcement is necessary. These taboos are not gender specific.

In north-eastern India and in many parts of peninsular India, especially in the Western Ghats region, there are also small patches of relatively undisturbed forest, which harbour significant species that are often the last remaining vestiges of local biodiversity. Such forest patches, preserved over a long period, have come to be known as 'sacred groves'. In the north-eastern region, there are well-known groves in Meghalaya and Manipur. Among the tribal Garos of Meghalaya the sacred groves have lost much of their significance, but there are no gendered restrictions on entry (Vasanti Raman 1997 personal communication). There are no groves in Arunachal, except small forest patches controlled by the Buddhist monks at Tawang. In Mizoram there are 'safety forests' which are not really considered *sacred*; their primary purpose was to safeguard village settlements from being engulfed by fires in the *jhum* fields (where the slashed vegetation has to be burned). Sometimes, these also served to protect water sources.

Patriarchal traditions

Elsewhere in India, brahminical patriarchy strictly governs entry into many of the sacred groves. This is so even if the deity is female. In the Kolli hills of Tamil Nadu, women are absolutely prohibited from entering the 'grove of seven deities' at Mettuvillaram. In other groves, Chinnamma kovil and Perumal kovil, women are not allowed to proceed beyond a certain point, or approach the deity. In a grove near Pallathu valaivu village, which belongs to a group of villages, women are allowed entry under certain strictly-enforced conditions: they must wear a white sari *without* a blouse, and are not allowed to wear a bindi on the forehead or flowers in the hair (Vedavalli 1997 personal communication). In effect, what this means is that the women must be in the garb of widows. In coastal Orissa women are not permitted to enter the sacred groves. In Kerala, women are forbidden to go near the sacred grove, known as *kavu*, because of entrenched concepts of purity and pollution that have been strictly enforced. It is only in some of the tribal areas of central and eastern India, as in the Jeypore tract of Orissa, that women have greater freedom to enter sacred groves, with only certain groves being forbidden to them.

Especially where religious practices have evolved around a patch of original vegetation in the vicinity of human habitation and settled agriculture, gender-specific taboos are widespread, women's entry is restricted both for worship and for collection of biomass, and women have no roles in the management. As I have pointed out elsewhere (Krishna 1995 and 1996a) viewed from a gendered perspective, sacred groves do not seem quite such a glowing example of India's age-old conservation ethic that modern conservationists make these out to be. Kosambi (1965: 47) first drew attention to this:

> ... groves sacred to the mother goddess are mentioned in brahmin myth and legend. Such groves still exist in villages away from the road; but women are now generally forbidden entry except in the few cases where the priesthood has remained in primitive hands, not transferred to immigrant settled cultivators. Originally, the ban was on the entry of men. When society changed from matriarchal to patriarchal, the priesthood and ritual were correspondingly transformed.

Natural resource managers and conservation scientists who have celebrated the tradition of sacred groves have largely ignored the iniquitous gender relations upon which 'sacredness' rests (see for example studies by P. S. Ramakrishnan, Madhav Gadgil and his associates). This is so even in a recent lengthy report on the cultural and social dimensions of sacred groves (Malhotra et. al. 2001), which notes briefly that the role of gender in sacred groves can be analysed at four levels: the gender of the deity, the gender of the priest, access to sacred groves and decision-making. The report says that information is scanty or does not exist but fails to go beyond this to analyse the implications of taboos against women's access and exclusion from management. This does not surprise me now, but when I first began looking at the literature on sacred groves in the early 1990s I was puzzled that so many researchers meticulously recorded the taboos related to particular sacred groves but were not sensitised by their own documentation to the iniquitous caste and gender relations that underlay the community conservation practices. Indeed, writing of the sacred groves of Kerala, Gadgil and Chandran (1992, 184) have commented appreciatively:

> The 1921 Census Report stated that Travancore, in southern Kerala, alone had 12,000 *kavus* or groves. *Ayyappan kavus* of Kerala Western Ghats are often patches of dense primeval forests. The sacred hill of Sabarimala where millions flock every year could have been originally a sacred grove. Remanants of sacred groves have become centres of folklore and part of the cultural tradition of Kerala.

The folklore and cultural tradition that they mention is entirely patriarchal and the 'millions who flock to Sabarimala' every winter do not include any women. Some years ago, the District Collector, the administrative head, of the district in which Sabarimala is located, happened to be a woman officer. In keeping with her official responsibilities she wished to visit Sabarimala and obtained a court order to allow her to enter the temple area. Despite this the priests did not permit her to do so. Neither the administration nor the law could overcome the power of the male priests.

Many conservationists are concerned that the biodiversity of sacred groves is being eroded by being converted to common or even private property resources. Indeed, several so-called 'sacred' groves are of recent provenance and owned by individuals rather than by the community. The Centre for Science and Environment's magazine *Down to Earth* (December 2003) carried a special series of articles on sacred groves in different states. The article on

Maharashtra is illustrated by a photograph of a woman praying at a sacred grove near the Kolhapur-Sindhudurg highway. Called the Satichamal grove, it was founded 30 years ago by the woman's grandfather who had been a labourer and when he died, he was buried in the same grove. The story of this grove (as told in the article by Ramya Visvanath) is that during the construction of the road, the labourer became an ardent follower of a saint and his wife who lived in the forest nearby. When the saint died, his wife committed sati. The labourer then set up a sati shrine in her honour, established the grove around it and the village of Satichamal. Some years later, tribal families displaced from the Dajipur wildlife sanctuary were relocated in the same village and they too began to participate in annual rituals held at the shrine. The grove continues to belong to the family who were the first settlers. The article does not mention gender taboos, and perhaps there are none, except in the gendered practice of sati inscribed in the very founding and name of the grove.

The practice of protecting particular plant and tree species also has gender implications. As is well known, snake and tree deities are commonly revered through many parts of India. The Bishnois' traditional practice of protecting the sacred *khejadi* (*Prosopis cineraria*) trees in Rajasthan has become as much of an international environmental icon as the Chipko or Narmada struggles. Yet, few conservationists are aware or concerned that the very same Bishnoi faith that sanctions the conservation of the khejadi also sanctions child marriage, which is especially detrimental to young girls of the community (Krishna 1996a).

In western Uttar Pradesh, tree-protection is gender and location specific: the tending of trees and shrubs in the vicinity of the homestead, or in the *aangan* (courtyard), is done by women along with prescribed religious rituals but village and road-side trees, such as the banyan, neem (*Azadirachta indica*), and mulberry (shisham, *Dalbergia sissoo*), that men look after are not associated with religious practices (Chauhan 1997 personal communication). Indeed, all over India, the nurturance of peepal trees in and around rural and urban homes, and of the *tulsi* plant (the sacred basil *Ocimum sanctum)* in home yards is always the women's responsibility. There are various puranic stories and legends around the tulsi, but all revolve around the unrequited love of a woman (sometimes a princess) for a god (Vishnu or Krishna) and her transformation into the weedy tulsi plant. The tulsi is worshipped by young Hindu girls and women to symbolise the offering of the self in complete surrender. In north India the annual ritual of tulsi *vivah* or marriage of the devotee with the lord marks the beginning of the auspicious season for weddings to be held. Gendered rituals such as tulsi worship are means of socialisation which reinforce the subordination of women to their husbands, or to their prospective husbands. (I recollect being told by my grandmother, when I was about eight or nine years old, that I should perform the tulsi *puja* everyday for the rest of my life to get and keep a good husband.)

It is not clear to what extent the patriarchal taboos and rituals have contributed to conservation, especially the preservation of sacred groves. However, these gendered restrictions should not be relied upon for future biodiversity management. The concept of sacredness, as part of conservation practice (whether of groves, species or seeds), has to be viewed at least with some circumspection if further erosion of women's position is to be prevented.

UNFOLDING COMPLEXITY

In sum, a complex picture emerges when we take a gendered approach to particular ecosystems and modes of farming and/or fishing. The various locations in the study cited in the first section (see also Krishna 1998a) represent distinct bio-geographic, socio-economic and cultural features. Such variations on the ground contribute to overall diversity. Each location is also complex in itself and it is necessary to view this complexity in its entirety.

The many different adivasi groups in the hill forests of the Jeypore tract in the Eastern Ghats of Orissa undertake several activities in joint family groups but some roles are gender-specific. The area is well known for being a unique centre of diversification of rice where both men and women have a wealth of conservation knowledge but this is fast being eroded among the younger generation. Polygyny was widespread in the past and this has implications for women's position. Also in the Eastern Ghats, the undulating landscape of the Kolli Hills of Tamil Nadu are home to a group of adivasi-peasants, among whom gender relations are relatively egalitarian and roles fluid. The area used to be rich in millet diversity with women being mainly responsible for seed selection and preservation. Now, traditional practices of subsistence cultivation and resource use are being replaced by new crops grown primarily for sale, and this is impacting upon social and gender roles. Further south, amidst the mountains of the Western Ghats area, is Wayanad inhabited by several tribal groups whose modes of production range from nomadic food-gathering and hunting to settled cultivation. Gender relations and roles vary across these groups. Among the agricultural groups, brahminical concepts of purity and pollution govern women's lives restricting their entry into sacred groves and their roles in paddy storage. Despite this, the women do participate in taking decisions about certain farming activities and have a critical role in conserving traditional varieties of food crops and medicinal plants.

Moving to the fishing-farming communities of the mangrove-rich river delta of coastal Orissa, yet another picture emerges. Most striking are the socio-cultural differences between the local Oriya groups and the migrants from West Bengal, further north. Migration and caste play a part in determining women's lives both within the family and in the wider community. Across the peninsula, off the coast of Kerala are the Lakshadweep islands, coral reefs and lagoons surrounded by the Arabian Sea. The islanders are a unique Muslim matrilineal community, among whom (as with other fishing communities) gender roles and knowledge bases are sharply defined. Matriliny has given the women a certain status within the family, yet, this is circumscribed by purdah, seclusion and restrictions of physical mobility. The north-eastern region of India is at a bio-geographic and socio-cultural cross-roads. It is a biodiversity 'hotspot' that has been peopled by an immense diversity of tribal groups and varied food production systems. Despite women's greater visibility and social freedoms as compared to patriarchal societies elsewhere in India, the majority of groups in the region are tribal patriarchies, which enjoy special legal sanctions under the Constitution, and where political support for patriarchal customary tribal practices is deeply entrenched (see Krishna 2004b). Despite their greater visibility, social freedoms, and mobility, north-eastern women have low status and are extremely vulnerable. (This is discussed in Chapter 7.)

Although the ecological approach to biological diversity recognises that people are a part of nature, and that elements of the social structure have to be incorporated into the framework of conservation and sustainable management of diversity, its approach with regard to women remains conventional. At an empirical level, women's roles are recognised but this is not incorporated at a conceptual level. This weakens both its social insights and the prospects for biodiversity management. For instance, the recent Biological Diversity Act makes only a superficial attempt to incorporate a gender perspective and treats biological resources as commodities, establishing a patriarchal regulatory mechanism to control access (see also S7).

The sustainability of biological resources is greatly dependent on ensuring livelihood security for men and women. The lack of gender equity undermines both livelihood security and the conservation of diversity. Women's mobility, rights to land, access to credit, markets, information, technology and new skills are important dimensions of biodiversity management. It is the gender-sensitivity and perspective of the researcher, practitioner, or policy-maker, rather than being male or female (see S6) that is critical in determining new initiatives to document people's ecological knowledge base, their conservation skills and management practices, and in framing new institutions and legal provisions.

Many members of a community are living inventories of information on the components of biological diversity, local crop varieties, wild foods and medicinal plants although they may not always be so knowledgeable about the inter-relationships between the different components. But across the country, this rich store of knowledge is being eroded as younger people are becoming alienated from the resource base. At the same time, the workload of older women is increasing; and often biodiversity management programmes contribute to such an increase.

A critical dimension of biodiversity management is that of equity and benefit-sharing within the household and community (see Krishna ed. 2004). This is as important as benefit-sharing at the national and international levels. The majority of biodiversity management programmes, however, are targeted at women's traditional responsibilities for fuel and fodder but ignore women's needs for greater autonomy and decision-making power within the household and community. In India, there is still widespread and entrenched resistance to women's personal autonomy, choice of marriage partners, matters of child-bearing and so on; to their physical visibility and freedom of movement; to their inheritance of property and land in particular; and to their access to modern knowledge and technical skills. Biodiversity projects which fail to recognise these difficult socio-political questions tend to reinforce rather than challenge traditional gender roles. If intra-household equity is not addressed, women's empowerment remains incomplete.

NOTES

[1] Translated from the comment of a Kattunaika adivasi woman in conversation with the author, Aranamala colony, a hamlet adjacent to cardamom plantations within the Aranamala forest, Wayanad district, Kerala.

[2] In early 1997, the M.S. Swaminathan Research Foundation (MSSRF), Chennai, supported by the UN's Food and Agriculture Organisation (FAO), Bangkok, invited me to serve as the overall adviser to a study to map the gender dimensions of biodiversity management in India. As this was to be done in a short span of a few months, I suggested that the foundation's researchers, scientists and social scientists, revisit areas where they had already been working and attempt to refine their focus through a gendered approach. These areas included hill, coastal and island locations in southern and eastern India where the foundation had field interventions: the Eastern Ghats area in Orissa, known as the Jeypore tract (Sharma, Tripathy and Pratima Gurung 1998); the coastal estuarine area of Bhitarkanika also in Orissa (Hemal Kanvinde 1998); Wayanad in the hills of northern Kerala (L. Vedavalli and Anil Kumar 1998); and the Kolli hills in Tamil Nadu (L. Vedavalli 1998). To this list we added the Lakshadweep islands, off the coast of Kerala in the Arabian Sea (Vineeta Hoon 1998) and north-eastern India, because of the extreme significance of the region, a 'biodiversity hotspot' where I covered parts of Arunachal Pradesh (with which I had some earlier familiarity) and Mizoram (Krishna 1998 b and c). Each of the seven case studies, thus selected, represented a distinct ecosystem or area of significant biological diversity that was currently under threat. All of them involved dynamic communities whose livelihoods were in transition, perhaps even in jeopardy. The seven case studies and my overview for the country as a whole (Krishna 1998a) were presented to a peer review meeting at Chennai in June 1997 and the study was published the following year (Swaminathan ed. 1998). Subsequently, FAO commissioned similar studies in other South Asian

countries, Nepal, Bhutan, Sri Lanka and the Maldives and I wrote a synthesis paper for the region, titled 'Involving Women: Ignoring Gender' (Krishna 1999 unpublished), which together with the various country studies were presented at a workshop in Chennai in 1999. This chapter incorporates my experience of this process and the observations of participating researchers, and also draws upon my own independent research both before and after the study.

³ This box is drawn from a Prefatory note 'About the Study' (Krishna 2005a) written in my capacity as Adviser to the study by M. K. Ratheesh Narayanan, M.P. Swapna and N. Anil Kumar (2005) 'Gender Dimensions of Wild Food Management in Wayanad, Kerala'. The study aimed to better understand trends in wild food management by socio-cultural group, gender and age; to correlate people's knowledge with existing scientific information on wild food species; to improve the people's food basket; and in the long term to facilitate context-specific people's plans for using, conserving and developing wild foods sustainably.

Table 6.1: Lakshadweep: Tasks in Lagoon Resources Extraction

Task	Women (18-60 YEARS)	Men (18-60 YEARS)	Children
Extracting coral and shingle		+	
Deep water/open sea fishing (net/trap/line)		+	
Shallow water fishing (cloth/ hand line)	+		
Shark fishing (pole and harpoon)		+	
Octopus hunting	+	+	
Collecting cowry	+	+	
Collecting molluscs	+		+

Source: Hoon (1998: 93)

Table 6.2: Jeypore tract, Orissa: Agricultural Tasks

Tasks	Old Women	Young Women	Girl Child	Old Men	Young Men	Boy Child
Ploughing				+	+	+
Sowing				+	+	
Weeding		+				
Harvesting		+		+	+	
Threshing	+	+		+	+	+
Winnowing					+	
Storage	+	+			+	
Milling, cooking	+	+	+			

Source: Sharma, Tripathy and Gurung. (1998: 120)

Table 6.3: Jeypore Tract, Orissa: Tasks related to Non-wood Forest Products

Tasks	Old Women	Young Women	Girls	Old Men	Young Men	Boys
Leaves	+ P	+ CPM	+ CPM			
Fibres					+ CPM	
Grasses		+ CP	+ C	+ CP	+ CP	+ C
Bamboos	+ P	+ PM	+ P	+CPM		
Resins	+M	+M		+ C	+ CM	
Medicines				+ CP	+ CP	
Edible items	+ M	+ CP	+ CP		+ C	

Key: C—collection; P—processing; M—marketing
Source: Sharma, Tripathy and Gurung. (1998: 120)

Table 6.4: Bhitarkanika, Orissa: Agricultural and other Tasks

TASK	Women	Men	Children
		Agriculture	
All agricultural tasks		+	
Boiling rice before drying	+		
Straw collection, storage			+
		Fishing	
Fishing with cast nets		+	
Fishing by boats		+	
Fishing in nearby waters	+		
Catching prawn	+		+
		Forest-related tasks	
Cutting trees for fuel	+	+	
Collecting dried wood	+		
Collecting honey		+	+
Older boys			
Hunting		+	
		Care of Livestock	
Livestock grazing		+	
Cleaning livestock	+		
Milking/Processing butter	+		
Cleaning shelters			+
		Weaving	
Basket weaving	+	+	
Collecting raw material	+		
Curing (pre-weaving)		+	
Finishing product			+
Marketing		+	

Source: Kanvinde (1998: 144-45)

7

The Gendered Price of Agro-biodiversity in North-eastern India

'A woman's work is never finished, but when the jhum kheti ['slash and burn' fields] rests, we rest. . .'

—Nyayo Bam, West Siang village, Arunachal Pradesh[1]

This chapter continues the discussion in Chapter 6 with a more detailed emphasis on gender ideology within the specific context of rice farming in north-eastern India. This is a region which is characterized by extreme diversity of peoples (see Tables 7.1 and 7.2) and yet shares many common elements. By convention, north-eastern India is taken to encompass seven states, sometimes called the 'seven sisters': Assam (including the autonomous 'tribal' districts of North Cachar and Karbi Anglong), Tripura, Manipur and the 'tribal' states of Arunachal Pradesh, Meghalaya, Nagaland and Mizoram. West Bengal's hill district of Darjeeling and the state of Sikkim are also part of the geographic region of the Eastern Himalaya. The first section of this chapter explores how gender ideology operates in people's life and work, the linkages between gendered knowledge and skills, gender roles and labour, and customary property and power structures in these states. This leads to the understanding that women pay a price for maintaining food sustainability. This is reinforced in the next section by examining gender disparities and dimensions of development in the region. The last section of the chapter looks at the transformation of agriculture and what such development means to women and provides a link between the 'notes from the field' in chapters 5, 6 and 7 to the discussion of development and resource management in chapters 8-9.

GENDER IDEOLOGIES AND RICE FARMING GROUPS

Diversity and shared elements in the region

There is a Naga joke about three men who spoke different languages. They happened to meet at a crossroads and sat down to eat their lunch. Each mentioned what he had brought and each said something different. But when they opened their bags they found that all had rice and chilles (Krishna 1987). As this little joke conveys so succinctly, in Nagaland as indeed in the north-eastern region as a whole, there exists an extraordinary socio-cultural diversity together with a broad band of shared elements. Many of the origin myths of the peoples of the region tell of migration, inter-group warfare and the marking of material and symbolic boundaries between settlements (see Elwin 1958).

North-eastern folktales reflect the difficult, animal-like conditions of life in the forest, before the discovery of farming. A Mishmi tale from Arunachal describes the origin of paddy cultivation (Haldipur 1985: 67). At first there was no rice on earth and people lived on forest roots and leaves. Gallan, the god of the mountains who cared especially for birds, gave the sparrow a grain of rice and taught it how to cultivate. Seeing this the men assembled together and decided to send a messenger to ask Gallan to give them rice too. The sparrow overheard this and knowing it was too small a bird to cultivate rice, offered to teach men provided they let it take rice from their fields. The men agreed. The sparrow took them to the top of a hill and told them to clear the jungle. Gallan sent rain and the seed was sown. Ever since, sparrows feed on young crops in the paddy fields. Sometimes, the natural environment itself is viewed in terms of rice. In an Adi (Ramo-Palibo) story about the coming of snow, a handful of grain overflows the bamboo cooking vessel, fills the house and covers the forests and hills, before it turns into snow (Elwin 1970: 138-139). In Khezankenoma village, in Nagaland's Phek district, a particular slab of stone is believed to have had the power to multiply paddy spread over it for drying. The stone still exists although perhaps not the mysterious power (Anon n.d.)

The cultural and ecological diversity of the region is apparent in the heterogeneity of its rice-farming systems. Paddy occupies a primary position in a composite and varied mix of crops (other cereals, millets, tubers, bananas, squashes, beans, and leafy vegetables), animal food sources including pigs, poultry and fish, and non-food crops such as palms, bamboos, and canes. Land that is not cultivated (e.g. forests, and seasonal or temporary fallows) and water courses, are an integral part of the system. Rice is the major cereal (apart from maize cultivated in Sikkim and parts of Arunachal Pradesh, Meghalaya and Mizoram and some wheat grown in Arunachal's Tawang district). The centrality of rice is reflected in various ceremonies. The Wanchos of Tirap (Arunachal), for instance, believe that rituals to protect paddy in the granary will also protect other grains (Srivastava 1973: 91). The significance of rice is not only because of its place in the diet but also because of the importance of rice stores in ascribing personal (male) status. This must be rice grown in one's own paddy fields and not bought in the market (Marjom Bam personal communication Bam village. 2004). Rice stores are also required for various feasts, and not least, for the nutritious rice-based brew, called *apong* (Adi), *zu* (Wanchos) etc., which is the main liquor, consumed especially in the hill areas.

Mainly indigenous varieties of paddy are cultivated either in *jhum kheti* (swidden or slash-and-burn fields) or *pani kheti* (wet-rice fields). There is some 'dry' (i.e. rain-fed) rice cultivation on terraced hill slopes. 'Wet' rice (irrigated by gravity channels from the perennial hill streams) is grown on the flatter lands in the valleys and near riverbanks. In the hill areas, tilling is entirely done by hand. In Arunachal, only the Sherdukpen and the Khampti use the plough on level lands. In recent years, shallow tube wells have been introduced in the Assam plains, which used to be entirely dependent on monsoon rain. Tractors are also being used in some plains areas. Government policy has consistently discouraged jhum and supported the technological transformation of agricultural production. However, there is a growing public movement for rethinking agricultural policy in the region. The external policy environment and internal processes of social transformation are both underpinned by patriarchal gender ideologies that have significant implications for women.

Gendered knowledge and skills

Several groups in the region associate rice cultivation with female goddesses. The Assamese Hindus believe that the goddess Lakshmi brought rice to earth. The Meiteis of Manipur have a rice goddess, Phoinobi (Panchani 1987:123). The Adi seek the blessings of the female goddess Mopin for a good harvest. The belief is that Mopin gave the first ancestor of the Adi, known as Abo Tani, seeds for cultivation and showed how this was done (Haldipur 1985: 38-39). In the modern Doini-Polo *dere*, community house, at Aalo (or Along) there used to be several pictures depicting deities including Mopin. Prof. M.S. Swaminathan mentions a woman credited with having domesticated rice (Rani and Swaminathan 1998: 17-18) and has a photograph of her picture from the Doini Polo dere in Aalo (Along). When I visited the dere in Aalo in September 2004, however, the alcove where the pictures used to be displayed was entirely bare. The caretaker said that some youth had damaged the pictures in a drunken brawl five or six years ago, and these had then been removed. Later, I learnt from others that there had been tension over the pictures among the Gallo themselves and between them and other religious groups. The Gallo do not have permanent temples or shrines and the elders do not believe in iconography of any kind because of the sun-moon spirit, 'Doini-Polo is in one's heart'. It is not clear whether it was this that led to the destruction of the pictures or whether the incident is at all related to the exhortation on a board in front of the dere: '*Higi ngunnuk yege duge ko moko. Higum kaken be lela ju.* This is our premises. Keep it[s] beauty'.

Whether or not women first domesticated rice, its cultivation has traditionally been in their domain of knowledge. The wide variety of rice in north-eastern India reflects the women's range of knowledge of seeds and of plant breeding. Kohonoma village, which is quite close to Nagaland's capital, Kohima, is being promoted as a tourist attraction for the 20 varieties of paddy being grown in its terraced fields (Anon. n.d.). Studies have shown that the morphological variability of rice in the region is related to a very high genetic diversity, and that the 'gene diversity index' for the region is close to that for all Asian rices (Glaszmann, Benyayer and Arnaud <www.gramene.org>). What this means is that in the proportionately small geographical area of north-eastern India there is as much diversity of rice as in all of Asia. The germplasm collection from the region, despite running into thousands, is still 'felt to be far from exhaustive' (P.K. Pathak 2001: 54). Although Assam and the surrounding hill regions are recognized as a centre of origin of rice, the genetic base of rice may have diminished since the introduction of modern high-yielding varieties in the 1960s (Richaria and Govindaswami 1990). Of the Garo of Meghalaya at the turn of the century, Bina Agarwal (1994: 104, citing Burling 1963) notes that 'some women knew of over 300 indigenous varieties of rice'.

Women carry the knowledge of different varieties with them, even when they are displaced from their original villages elsewhere in the region and have migrated to new settlements or have lost their farms. Several villages in the flood-ravaged Dhemaji district on the north bank of the Brahmaputra in upper Assam have been settled during the last few decades. In Harinathpur Hajong village where most fields have been entirely buried under sand, rendering cultivation impossible, many men have left to seek work in the tea and oil-producing areas south of the Brahmaputra; a few have migrated even further to western India. The women (some who still have cultivable land and others who do not) responded swiftly to a question about the paddy varieties grown. They first mentioned the main classes of rice as they perceived these: *dumahi* ('two months' short-duration monsoon harvest), *ahu* (monsoon harvest), *hali* (or *sali*, winter harvest), *boro* (summer harvest), and *bao* (deep-water 'floating' rice sown in summer and harvested in winter). Then, within minutes they listed some 20 local and improved varieties of rice (Table 7.3). Certain varieties were not favoured because these required more work or were prone to pest-infection. Of the winter rices, they said that while some cultivated the scented fine-grained *joha* only for special occasions or for sale, all preferred the glutinous, sticky *bora* for their own consumption because it gave a feeling of fullness. (Malati Hajong Sr., Malati Hajong Jr.,

Amala Hajong personal communication, Harinathpur Hajong village 2004).

Arunachal Pradesh is yet to be fully explored but 105 land races of paddy have been identified. Together with the local cultivars, this represents an extraordinarily rich heritage of germplasm (B.D. Sharma 2002: 4). This diversity has evolved under different farming practices, at high, middle and low altitudes, in varied upland and wetland conditions. The food-gathering Idu of the Mathun and Dri valleys in eastern Arunachal collect leafy greens, edible mushrooms, berries, fruits and nuts from the forests, and supplement this with jhum cultivation, growing two early-maturing varieties of paddy, *apu* and *entro* (*ng*) and six late-maturing varieties *keochi, ketara, kejari, kebora, kememora* and *kembomar* (Bhattacharjee 1983: 59). Many local varieties are deliberately selected for specific locations, soil conditions, growing durations and for special characteristics. The glutinous rices grown by the Khamptis at low altitudes in Lohit and Tirap are well known for their softness. The Apatani valley, at a height of over 1500 metres in Lower Subansiri district, is world-famous for its unique irrigated wet-rice and fish cultivation. One woman farmer, Nani Duni (personal commmunicationi Sululiya village 1997) told me that she planted five local varieties for different reasons: *pyapi* 'with a black husk', *allang amo* 'which retains its red colour even after it is cooked', *aino ari* 'which can be harvested quickly', *amo hasso* and *rarre amo* which are both suited for different kinds of soil (see also Table 7.4.). Of these, she preferred the quick growing aino ari. Both in the hills and the plains, the women say that different growing seasons allow for a staggered harvest, which is done by hand either by the women and men together, or by women alone. Only the panicle, the grain-bearing inflorescence, is cut. As has been pointed out (B.D. Sharma 2002: 6), 'The logic for panicle selection among local cultivars which together show a long range of discontinuous variation for maturity has been that the farm women can do the manual harvesting operations more comfortably and effectively over the entire crop maturity span in the valley. The widely adapted, high yielding IRRI rice cultures such as IR-8 and IR-26 have been little accepted . . . due to their short stature and, thereby unsuitability for panicle harvesting using the existing manual practices.'

Whether in the wet-rice fields of the Apatani, the jhum fields of other groups, whether in terraced fields or plains cultivation, the combination of particular crops varies from one family to the next in keeping with the ecological conditions of the family's land and its other livelihood activities (like weaving, basketry, service occupations). This mosaic adds up to an overall diversity that reflects a collective wisdom that has evolved over several decades.

Throughout the region it is generally the women who select the seed for sowing although their methods may vary in detail from place-to-place. Years of observation and practice have given them an intuitive understanding of paddy seeds and the ability to select viable pure strains. Some women said they take care to select only those sheaves that do not have different strains 'mixed'. They 'feel the weight' of the seed by holding the sheaf up from the cut end. Some examine the seeds minutely for size, shape and colour. Formerly, the Adi in Arunachal's West Siang district used a basket of closely woven bamboo, called a *hushak*, especially meant for paddy seed storage but this is now being replaced by tins. Many groups do not take any special measures to store paddy seed separately from the rest of the harvested grain, but Mizo women in Aizawl district use wood ash to preserve paddy seeds in bamboo baskets and tin drums, while small quantities of other seeds like maize are kept in dry gourds. (Krishna 1998 c: 203). Despite this reality, popular sayings undermine women's knowledge as in the Mizo saying that 'a woman's knowledge does not go beyond the village water source'.

Gender roles and labour

In much of the north-eastern region, gender roles are more sharply defined in the domestic sphere than in farming (see Table 7.5 Tripura; Table 7.6 Mizoram; Table 7.7 Arunachal; Table 7.8 Nagaland; and Table 7.9 Manipur). Generally, it is the mother's responsibility to socialize her daughter at a young age into her role at home and in the fields. In upper Assam, very young Hajong girls carry siblings slung on their backs. In Kabu village in West

Siang (Arunachal), young girls are urged to cross the swaying bamboo bridge across the Yamgo (also called the Siyem) that connects the homestead area to the fields across the river. In Tirap, Wancho girls aged three or four, carry seeds, farming implements, and even firewood (Srivastava 1993: 89). The traditional practice among the Gallo is that women and girls collect and carry firewood. Among the Apatani and Nishi men used to be responsible for collecting firewood from the forest and chopping it but this is now changing. Young Apatani girls also help with many other domestic and farming jobs; the girls now collect water, which was the boys' task, and also carry heavy loads of husked rice. In the same area, such changes are also visible among the Nishi. I have seen Nishi women chopping wood, although women are not supposed to use the axe (Krishna 1998 b). The Tanghul Naga of Manipur consider collecting firewood a female task. As one man, Phantipang, told a researcher: 'Men do not carry firewood. Why should I carry firewood, it is my wife's job. My job is to cut down tree for firewood.' (U.A. Shimray 2004). However, farming activities may have been less sharply gendered in the past as young men and women worked together in groups, 'ho-ho'-ing and using spades to till the terraced, wet-rice paddy fields (R.R.. Shimray 1985). Among the Mizo all tasks in the jhum cycle, apart from felling trees, are either done jointly or by women alone. Women participate in clearing the slashed and burned debris and they prepare the land for sowing. Broadcasting or dibbling is usually done by women. Weeding is always the woman's task. Harvesting and seed selection may be done jointly (Krishna 1998 c). Among the Apatani, it is said that land preparation is men's work and that only men may handle the spade, but women do use spades in the fields (Krishna 1998 b).

In the Brahmaputra valley, farming tasks are highly gender-specific. A study by Anuva Saikia (2000) of three villages near Jorhat in central Assam shows considerable 'gender-specificity'. Women are engaged in sowing, transplanting, irrigation, hand weeding, harvesting, and post-harvest activities (see Table 7.10). While they perform 80 per cent of transplanting and harvesting they do not participate at all in the spraying of insecticides and other pesticides, using tractors and power tillers, or purchasing inputs. For the rest of the tasks women provide between 10 and 30 per cent of the total labour. She notes that this specificity cuts across all farm sizes and has not changed in some 15 years since 1980-81. This may also be true of some plains groups such as the Mishing but one observes a different pattern in the hill areas. Among some groups there is less visible gender-specificity in farming tasks assigned to either women or men. A particular domestic or farming task (like collecting firewood and water, or sowing and winnowing) may be undertaken by women in certain locations or by men in others. The variability of gender-specific work indicates that socio-cultural factors rather than just physical and physiological attributes determine the assignment of tasks to women or men (see also Krishna 1998a, 1999, 2004a). However, as young men and women are getting educated and moving away from farm work, the burden of farming is shifting to older people and women in particular. Broadly, in the north-eastern region as a whole, women bear a greater quantum of work than do men and are now undertaking tasks that were traditionally in the men's domain.

Yet, as elsewhere in the country, there is a widespread perception that the gendering of tasks is 'natural' (biologically-determined) and that men 'naturally' do the heavier, riskier tasks while women (presumably weaker in body and mind) do the light, easy work. Researchers often reinforce these local stereotypes by carrying their own perceptions into the field. An account from western Arunachal in the early 1960s (Raghuvir Sinha 1962) describes the jhuming practices of the Akas of Kameng: 'The first phase of agriculture begins with the clearing of forest land, which may start in the month of January and continue to the end of March. Both men and women go together to the forest; soon after reaching the spot, the division of work among them begins. Men occupy themselves with the more arduous tasks involving physical labour, such as felling big trees, and removing the logs, while women are given lighter tasks like clearing the smaller growth. The cultivation of land, the second phase in jhuming, starts with the sowing of seed. Sowing of seed, which usually takes place in the month of April and May, is a simple job and so is primarily entrusted to women.' The account goes on to say that women are 'exempted' from burning the forest but do 'the sowing and harvesting almost by themselves' and that men 'do the harder work of basketry' while women 'engage themselves in weaving bags'. It is exceptional to come across an account that does not simply reproduce the stereotype about 'hard, masculine work'. For instance, an account of the jhuming practice of the Sherdukpen of Kameng (R.R.P. Sharma 1961) notes that women pound and sift grain, cook, fetch fuel and weave, extracting fibre from a poisonous plant which is a somewhat risky task. He says 'Men reserve for themselves a majority of less onerous and fatiguing jobs, leaving for the women the bulk of the tedious tasks.' The women 'enjoy no slack season, the whole of the year is spent in hard toil.'

For some women not much has changed since these accounts from the early 1960s. More than four decades later, in another part of Arunachal, a group of Adi women at Kabu village in West Siang expressed the very same sentiments to me. Returning around 4 p.m. from their jhum fields, they said they had been up and working since dawn (which comes early in this region). Old women too go to the jhum fields. The women would spend the evening washing utensils, cooking the meal, feeding the children. As we talked, we looked down on a football field in the village, where local boys were preparing for a game.

In another village near Basar, the sub-divisional headquarters of the district, I met middle-aged Nyayo in her house as dusk was setting in. She had returned from the fields and was grinding bamboo shoots. Interrupting her work to talk with us about women's work in paddy cultivation, she said her family has both jhum kheti (swidden) and pani kheti (wet-rice) fields. Work on the jhum is seasonal. 'When the jhum rests we also rest,' she said. This is not so with the wet-rice, which gives better yields but has increased women's labour. She summed it up simply: 'A woman's work is never finished.' (Nyayo, Karpin and Tumnyar personal communication Bam village: 2004). Wet-rice requires transplantation and more weedings than jhum rice. Women say that men do not have the patience for such work. There is also a perception among women and men that alien weed species have been introduced into the area with the fodder being brought for the establishments of the Indian army. The only circumstances in which weed formation is limited are where wet-rice fields stand in continuously-flowing water from perennial hill streams (Marben Lollen personal communication, Sipu colony, Aalo: 2004).

The contribution of women's labour may be recognized but it is not perceived as a 'cost'. In a comparative study of the labour input of two groups in Arunachal, Gangwar and Ramakrishnan (1992: 126) note that the traditional systems 'respond both to human needs and ecological imperatives'. The Sulung at Tabumah village are mainly gatherers and hunters while the Nishi at Yazali, are engaged in jhum cultivation and animal husbandry. The Sulung get more foods from the forest than the Nishi do, and grow a lesser variety of crops, but in both cases the system ensures a balanced diet. Among the Nishi, animal husbandry supplements farming and cycles the agricultural wastes, increasing the food available for humans with minimal effect on the environment. The study concludes: 'If labour costs are computed, then the financial investment in slash and burn agriculture is high. However, their labour output is geared to the maximum utilizing family labour. As such, it does not have actual financial costs.' The study does not disaggregate the labour input by gender, but ethnographic accounts (e.g. Kiran Mishra 1991) and my own observations in the Yazali area show that among the Nishi 'family labour' on the jhum fields is almost entirely female labour.

It is also significant that whenever additional labour inputs are required in the farming system, this seems to come from women rather than men. Data from a Khasi village in Meghalaya (Ramakrishnan 1993) show that of the two traditional cash crops, ginger and pineapple, the labour input required for ginger was high. Tea and coffee were introduced as experimental crops and of these, tea required considerable labour. From a gender perspective, what is significant is that the male and female labour input is almost the same for the low-labour cash crops i.e., the traditional mixed pineapple cropping and the experimental coffee. But in the case of high-labour crops (whether the traditional ginger or experimental coffee), women's labour is much more than that of men.

Even among groups who share jhuming activities, women almost exclusively do the post-harvest and processing tasks. Time-use studies of post-harvest drying of paddy and seed, husking and pounding show the predominance of women's labour among the Tanghul Naga of Manipur; (U.A. Shimray 2004; Table 7.11). De-husking and pounding grain by hand in a mortar and pestle are laborious and time-consuming tasks that are gradually being replaced by machines. In Arunachal Pradesh there are several thousand bamboo and stone *ghattas* that use the energy of flowing streams to grind grain into flour. In peri-urban and relatively better-off areas in the hill states and in the plains of Assam, women no longer do dehusking. In an Ahom village in upper Assam, families still have the traditional grinding stone, the *dheki*, but no longer use it. Some families have their own mechanical grinders but most take their grain to local grinding shops to be de-husked and ground for a small service charge. This has greatly eased women's labour. Pounding small quantities to make the flattened rice required for special preparations is still done by hand.

Because of the composite nature of agriculture, women also undertake multifarious activities, animal husbandry being one of the most time and labour intensive. Everywhere, it is also women who look after poultry and ducks. Women and children also fish with their bare hands in the water channels beside the fields, or collectively in deep-water paddy fields. Indeed, in some areas, women are spending as much time on animals, birds and fish as in crop cultivation, but this is rarely recognized as work. Saikia (2000: 50) notes of Assam that the 'share of women in livestock and poultry related activities are greater among small and marginal farms than among larger farms. Further, despite the considerable hours spent in caring for animals, since such work is frequently dubbed as household chores, no attention is paid to increasing efficiency or encouraging better management practices in these activities.' In Mizoram women speak of the hard daily work involved in rearing pigs, which is exclusively women's work although the buying and selling of pigs is mainly done by men (Elizabeth Saipari pers. com. Aizawl. 1997). Among many other groups, women have been able to retain control over the cash earnings from livestock and poultry and this serves as an incentive to labour.

Traditionally, women have managed the petty trade and men the larger markets. In Basar town, in the mid-hills of West Siang, the small, traditional daily market is entirely occupied by elderly women who sell miniscule quantities of produce (fish, leafy vegetables, tubers, bananas, etc.) and retain the cash earnings for their own needs. Women run all the small local market stalls in Mizoram. In most parts of upper Assam (where paddy now covers every patch of vacant land, even along roadsides and in narrow water channels running through abandoned tea estates) the little rice that is traded in local markets is entirely in the hands of men. On the Sunday when I visited the large and crowded weekly market in Borbaruah village in Dibrugarh district (Assam), there were enormous quantities of meat (sold by men), fish and vegetables (mainly by women), some salt and spices (by women), baskets and clothes (by men and women). There were only three stalls where men (one of these a long-settled Marwari) were selling rice but few buyers, even for the aromatic *joha*. An NGO, the Rural Volunteers Centre at Akajan village in Dhemaji district has encouraged women to take control of local weekly markets and lease out stalls. But apart from such initiatives, major local markets are controlled by men who may or may not be locals. The only exception to this pattern is the women's rice market in Imphal, Manipur.

Customary norms and power structures

Women's lives are circumscribed by '*niyams*' (laws/rules/norms/ customary practices) that govern social relations in a community. Srivastava (1973: 87 and 183) writing about the Wancho says the Hindi (also Assamese) word niyam is used indiscriminately to signify many things: 'Whatever a Wancho would be doing he says he is doing his niyam. Whatever he cannot explain, he puts it aside by saying it is Wancho niyam.' This was also what one observed in the Adi villages of West Siang where niyam operates at many levels of everyday life. Niyam prescribes the gendered spaces within a house and modes of behaviour: men and women must enter through different staircases; women do not appear on the men's veranda or speak in public, especially if outsiders (males) are present; within the house, the places around the hearth are marked out by niyam, and so on. Yet, while these niyams are clearly stated, underlying the traditional codes, they are not always observed in practice. This seems to reflect a tension between the prescribed ideal way of life and changes now taking place as younger women overcome their traditional socialization and become more casual about the niyams.

A well-known Assamese folk song addressed to the young girl Rohimola captures the subtlety of socialization processes with its message that girls who are free to move around and enjoy themselves in their youth have to restrict their movements and walk carefully after marriage (Tilottama Misra personal communication Dibrugarh, 2004): 'Rohimola, jiyori kalore ujutit siga nokh,/ Bowari, kalothe gaje' (Rohimola, the toe-nail which was broken when you tripped in your girlhood days, will grow again when you are a daughter-in-law.) Other sayings that girls and boys hear from an early age are far more explicit. Among the matrilineal Garo it is said: 'Just as crab meat is no meat, so women have no value.' And the patrilineal Mizo hold that 'Women and old bamboo fences need to be changed' (i.e. when they are worn out).

Compared to many other parts of India, women in the north-eastern region have a more visible role in the economic life of their communities because of their responsibility for the production and processing of food for their families. In Nagaland, the landscape itself and natural resources are gendered in common speech: fields for women, forests for men; domestic animals for women, wild animals for men. Re-examining historical texts, Manorama Sharma (2004: 72) says the Ahom women 'held their own position in society through their participation in productive labour although there is no doubt that they were made the disadvantaged section in the society because of the existing patriarchal norms and values.' This is true even today in Ahom villages in upper Assam. For the Ahom as for other women their role in food production gives them a sense of self-worth and identity. Physical mobility, the freedom to work and to take certain kinds of decisions do contribute to improved gender equity. This has been remarked upon by British anthropologists and by Indian administrators and researchers. However, the ground reality in the north-eastern region is more complicated and far less advantageous to women than it might seem on the surface. This is so regardless of the belief system or religion a community follows, animist, Doini-polo, Buddhist, Christian, Muslim, or Hindu, and holds even for the relatively more gender-egalitarian groups such as the Khasi, Garo and Jaintia in Meghalaya. Critiquing the 'ethnographer's romanticized model' Tiplut Nongbri (1998: 223) says that the tribal women's 'greater economic independence and freedom of movement' compared to 'their counterparts in non-tribal societies cannot be disputed,' but it is 'naïve to equate this with superior social status.' She argues that a 'closer look would show that gender inequality is not alien to tribal societies but it is obscured by their poor economic conditions which forces men and women to co-operate and share in joint economic activities'.

The rich spectrum of cultures in the region encompasses considerable variation with regard to kinship, class and gender relations among the different socio-cultural groups. Inter- and intra-group relations are affected both by traditional hierarchies (ruler-commoner, patron-client) and the social stratifications that have emerged in modern times (Chowdhury 1976, Krishna 1998 b and c, Sinha 1998). Cultivable land is the most productive asset and the basis for livelihood and food security. Some women admit privately that they take decisions about the resources that they manage, which crops to plant and where. ('What do the men know?'). But there is some hesitation in saying this in the presence of men. Women's lack of property rights may not have been as significant in earlier periods when community ownership over natural resources prevailed over large parts of the region. But as markets in land and forest resources have developed, this customary lack reinforces women's subordinate position, exasperated all the more by exclusion from public-decision-making. These are not minor social restrictions but are fundamental to the power structures upon which the rice farming system rests.

These power structures are only masked by the lack of gender-seclusion. Adolescent boys and girls converse with easy familiarity and mix freely in all parts of the region, except among some Muslim and upper caste Hindu groups in the Assam plains. The relatively greater freedom in the choice of marriage partners, the right to divorce, and a widow's right to remarry give the impression of equality among the sexes. Women's low status, however, is maintained by traditional practices governing descent, property and inheritance, and by systematic exclusion from participation in religious ceremonies and community decisions (Table7.12). This has the sanction of customary law, which is safeguarded in certain cases by the Constitutional arrangements between the Government of India and some of the states (see Krishna 2004b for a detailed analysis of this).

Throughout the region, women have no substantial property rights. The Khasi, Garo and Jaintia in Meghalaya are matrilineal, that is inheritance and descent are traced through the female line. However, authority is vested in the mother's brother. The Tiwa (formerly called Lulungs) in Assam used to be a matrilineal group, but are now in the process of transformation to patriliny. The Dimasa-Kachari in Assam have a unique form of dual female and male descent, daughters tracing lineage through the mother and sons through the father. All of the other communities in the region are patrilineal and patrilocal. Most communities are monogamous, but polygyny is also practised, especially among the wealthy. A very few groups are polyandrous. Family structures vary from extended families to nuclear, or may be unique as in the case of the Nishi 'long house'. A man's many wives and their children live together in a literally long house, each wife having her own hearth and access to independent jhum fields where she works to grow food for her own children. All the wives are subordinate to their common husband who pays bride price for each wife and claims full control over her and the produce of her labour. Bride price is embedded in wifehood; in fact, the Taraon-Mishmi word for marriage, *miyabraiya*, means 'buying a woman' (Baruah, 1976: 111). However, bride price does not protect women from exploitation within the family. Apatani women, known to be most hardworking, have a high bride price that is compensated by their labouring in their husbands' fields; so married women are afraid to be seen to be at leisure. Mizo women are liberated to work but their earnings belong to men; a widow's place in society is precarious because she is herself considered the property of her son (Lanipuii personal communication Aizawl 1997). Naga women are generally not allowed to inherit property (Kelhou 1998). However, D'souza (2001: 89) says that among the Japfuphiki (the southern Angami Naga), while 'landed property' is inherited through the male line, 'movable property may be inherited by females', so a woman can buy land on her own and receive land bought (i.e. not inherited) by her parents. It is not clear whether this actually happens in practice.

The Meitei of the Manipur valley are among the few communities in the region who do not socialize women into subordinate status. The women's sphere of work has been enlarged since the early 19th century, when the wars with Burma (now Mynamar) led to a severe decline in the male population. Vaishnavite Hinduism (which had begun to spread in the area before the Burmese wars) was intensely promoted by the ruling elite. But it did not succeed in overthrowing the traditional gender egalitarian practices. Hindu customs such as child marriage and the prohibition of divorce and widow-remarriage were rejected. So too Pangan (Muslim Meitei) women rejected purdah. As I have written elsewhere (Krishna 2004: 385), 'Caste Hinduism was not able to curtail the customary male-female cooperation in the religious sphere or change women's socio-economic role, which centres on the market for rice. Meitei women's control of the rice trade gives them a powerful public voice. So although the Meitei are a patriarchal society and men have the position of authority as fathers and husbands, the women's socio-economic power and collective strength counteracts male domination.' Writing two decades ago about 'the traditional political power of the market network', Chaki-Sircar (1984: 223) commented that 'the women can paralyse the political and administrative system when the need arises.' This power has been demonstrated on more than one occasion, and most recently in the summer of 2004 as the market women led sustained protests against the presence and actions of the Assam Rifles, a para-military force stationed in the state. Yet, as elsewhere in the region, women's participation in public movements has not ensured a place for them in public decision-making bodies, traditional or modern. As Agarwal (1994: 150-51) notes even in matrilineal communities (such as the Garo and Khasi), 'property rights did not alter the overall gender division of labour'. She points out that 'rights in land did not guarantee women the same sexual freedom as men.' Moreover, it was men, husbands, brothers or maternal uncles who had 'formal managerial authority over land', and most importantly, men monopolised the 'customary institutions' with jural power. Even the Khasi women heiresses did not have the 'considerable local influence' that the chiefs commanded.

So, even as the rich diversity of rice in the north-eastern region has been nurtured by women's knowledge and skills, we need to recognize that this is the result of a gendered division of labour, of roles learnt and practised over generations. These roles are reflective of the patriarchal ideology that determines gender relations and the value that is ascribed to different spheres of work.

GENDER DISPARITIES AND DIMENSIONS OF DEVELOPMENT

Gender indicators across the region

Anecdotal, descriptive and ethnographic accounts have begun to undermine the widespread assumption about the gender-egalitarianism of north-eastern India. There is a slowly-growing number of gender-specific studies of different groups, their belief systems, socio-cultural life, land ownership, resource use and so on, but these are still too few and too scattered. We can fill out the picture a little by examining data from sources that cover a larger scale, although these too have many inadequacies. In colonial times and till fairly recently, many of the north-eastern states were a part of Assam. Assam has had historical linkages with the eastern Indian region and is, therefore, often grouped with Bihar, Jharkhand, Orissa and West Bengal. Using the Census and other large-scale survey data, Preet Rustagi (2002) has examined the status of women in these eastern states of India. The analysis is based on 14 district-level 'gender development' indicators, including demographic and work participation data, literacy, mortality and fertility rates. This shows that Assam's eastern plains area (i.e. the upper Brahmaputra valley) is 'among the best' in eastern India with higher work participation, better literacy and health conditions, and that the North Cachar Hills district tops all of the eastern region (ibid. 46).

In a later and more comprehensive all-India study, Rustagi (2003) looks at a wider range of gender disparities using state-wise and gender-disaggregated data. These indicators cover six sectors: women's decision-making and security, besides the more conventional indicators covered by others (i.e. demographic factors, women's health, education and economic participation). Based on Rustagi's compilation and analysis, supplemented by that of Kishor and Gupta (2004), I have selected 11 significant gender indicators (choosing between one and three from each of the six sectors identified by Rustagi) and extracted the data for eight north-eastern states (See Table 7.13). Substantial positive and negative divergences (based on absolute numbers or trends) from the average for all-India are noted for each indicator. Without going into the controversy over methodologies for measuring poverty, for purposes of comparison, the Planning Commission Estimates of 2001 are used. This shows that Mizoram alone fares better than the all-India average (column A). The child sex ratio (column B) is a critical indicator of levels of female discrimination because it is less affected by migration than the overall sex ratio (column C). Although all the states in the region are in a better position than the all-India average, between 1991 and 2001, the child sex ratio improved only in Sikkim, Tripura and Mizoram.

There is some doubt over the accuracy of the National Family Health Survey (NFHS-2 conducted in 1998-99) in certain north-eastern states, and it has been suggested that in Arunachal Pradesh and Manipur the survey does not effectively capture the rural situation. In the absence of other data we have to use this bearing in mind its limitations. The survey shows that one out of two women in India suffer from severe, moderate or mild anaemia, reflecting an aspect of women's under-nourishment. According to the survey, Assam, Meghalaya and Sikkim have high levels of severe and moderate anaemia (column D); Arunachal, Assam and Tripura have high levels of mild anaemia (column E).

Instead of looking at school enrolment or literacy rates, I have taken the gender gap in literacy rates (column F) as more indicative of women's status vis-à-vis the men of their own communities. Mizo and Ao Naga women are well known for their high literacy, on par with Kerala, and indeed all of the states in the region have higher rates than the all-India average. Manipur also shows a decline in the female-male gender gap over the decade 1991-2001. Despite improvement in female literacy, Arunachal continues to hover near the low national average.

Women's economic participation is known to be related to improved social status but women's productive work continues to be under-estimated despite efforts to improve enumeration. For farming communities the proportion of workers in relation to the total population, i.e. the Rural Female Workforce Participation (RFWP) rate, is of great significance (columns G and H). According to the National Sample Survey, between 1993-94 and 1999-2000, the all-India average RFWP rate declined, but it increased in five states in the country: Nagaland, Mizoram and Sikkim in north-eastern India, and Punjab and Gujarat. The RFWP rate in Meghalaya and Arunachal, although still above the national average, showed a decline. In the major paddy-growing states, Manipur, Tripura and Assam, the RFWP rate was already below the all-India average and declined further.

Measures of women's autonomy and their power to take decisions about their own lives are relatively recent. Traditionally, women have been free to take decisions about the domestic sphere. This is borne out by NFHS data, which show that an average 85 per cent of women in India take decisions about what to cook. In Arunachal this is as high as 94 per cent. About one in two adult married women in India are involved (with husbands/ families) in decisions about their own health; women in Meghalaya, Mizoram, Arunachal and Nagaland are especially well placed in this regard (column I). Women's mobility, or its lack, is generally seen as a key indicator of their position in society. One in three women in India needs permission to go to the market. Among those who do not need such permission (column J), Mizoram ranks high, on par with Goa but still far behind Tamil Nadu. Both Assam and Nagaland lag behind the national average. Taking independent decisions on one's own earnings is yet another indicator of women's autonomous position (column K). Here, Sikkim and Manipur rank much higher than the national average but Mizoram and Nagaland fare badly. (I am reminded of a Mizo saying that women are free to work but not to earn.)

Women's safety and security, both within the home and in public spaces, are rarely measured in large surveys but this is perhaps one of the most significant indicators of gender disparity. The National Crimes Record Bureau of the Ministry of Home Affairs provides annual data based on police records of registered crimes against women. These include cognisable offences under the Indian Penal Code and certain other laws, such as those relating to dowry, sati, child marriage etc. While this is clearly inadequate, it does provide a revealing picture of the nature of crimes against women and an indication of the rising trend. In 1999, the all-India figures showed that cruelty at home accounted for 36 per cent of all crimes; followed by molestation, rape, kidnapping and abduction of girls, sexual harassment and dowry death. The 1999 figures for different states are extremely variable, ranging from 246 cases per million in Rajasthan to zero cases in Lakshadweep. In north-eastern India, Mizoram has the highest record of crimes against women with 176 cases, comprising of rape and molestation (column L). Arunachal Pradesh with 148 cases also has a high, and rising, level of crime, comprising mainly of molestation, rape, kidnapping and abduction, and cruelty at home. Nagaland, Meghalaya and Manipur show low levels of crime against women.

As with Rustagi's all-India analysis, the data for north-eastern India shows that all states have both positive and negative indicators of gender disparity. Sometimes, this seems to be counter-intuitive, as in Mizoram's high level of crimes against women, but is comparable to the trends in certain other high female literacy states, such as Kerala and the Union Territory of Chandigarh, although the linkage between high-literacy and crimes against women is unproven. The data reinforce the qualitative findings in certain respects. They show that broadly women in the north-eastern region, like women in other hill areas and rice-growing states, have higher work participation rates, mobility and power to take certain kinds of decisions. This is offset by the fall in the rural female work participation rates in rice-growing Assam, Tripura and Manipur. As in other parts of the country, greater levels of poverty, particularly in Sikkim, Assam and Tripura, may be contributing to women's lower levels of literacy and health. This is again offset by the gender gap in the female-male literacy rate in the north-eastern states, which is high in Manipur despite its relatively lower level of poverty.

Based upon both the positive and negative indicators of gender disparity, I have suggested a composite gender rank (column M). The composite ranking shows that in the north-eastern region, gender-disparity is least in Mizoram and less in Meghalaya and that it is greatest in Assam. Despite greater autonomy for women in certain respects, Arunachal Pradesh also ranks low. While Meghalaya's position may reflect the relative gender balance in the past among matrilineal groups in the state, that of Mizoram is clearly related to all-round development, which is perhaps helping to counter gender-bias in customary practices. The low position of Arunachal undermines any attempt to generalize about gender equity in 'tribal' communities. The similar position of Assam and Arunachal at the lower end of the scale reflects similarities in the child sex ratio, levels of anaemia among women, gender gap in literacy and surprisingly comparable rates of crime against women. Overall, Arunachal ranks somewhat higher than Assam on account of women's greater work participation and mobility.

In the more specific context of gender and rice-farming, it may be useful to relate the gender rank of the north-eastern states postulated in this paper with the position of these states in the *Atlas of the Sustainability of Food Security in India* (M.S.S.R.F. 2004). The *Atlas* uses 17 selected indicators (driven by the secondary data available across states) such as the weighted net sown area, the per capita forest cover, the future availability of surface and ground water, the percentage of degraded area, the percentage of non-agricultural workers, infant mortality, and the percentage of households with access to safe drinking water. Based on the indicators, index values have been calculated and the states classified in five groups, ranging from the extremely unsustainable to the sustainable. According to this mapping, Nagaland is the most unsustainable, and the only such state in the country (mainly because of land degradation) while Arunachal is sustainable because it has more forests and fewer people.

Given the ground situation of the food production system in north-eastern India, as indeed in the rest of the country, any assessment of food sustainability would be incomplete if gender indicators are not taken into account. In Table7.14, I have juxtaposed the composite gender rank (taken from column M of Table 7.13) and the sustainability of food security index (taken from the *Atlas*). This comparison reveals that Arunachal with high gender disparity is sustainable in terms of food security while Mizoram with the least gender disparity is moderately sustainable in terms of food. Nagaland, which is the most unsustainable state for food security in the entire country, has a moderately high level of gender disparity. There are, of course, limitations to this exercise because the gender indicators do not capture critical areas of women's lack of autonomy and subordination within the family and community. However, if such information were available, it is likely to reinforce one inference that can be drawn even on the basis of the available qualitative and quantitative data. This is that Arunachal is paying an extremely high gendered price for the sustainability of its food security, with Assam and Tripura not far behind. Indeed, in all of the states of the north-eastern region, agricultural production has an in-built gendered price.

WHAT DEVELOPMENT MEANS FOR WOMEN

The transformation of traditional farming systems in north-eastern India is taking place within a developmental framework that seeks to reproduce the successes of the 'Green Revolution' of the 1960s in the context of today's globalizing world. The Union Ministry for the Development of the North-Eastern Region (DONER) and state governments envision a 'resurgent' north-eastern India fuelled by tourism, power generation and agro-processing (see official websites of these states and Kyndiah 2004).

This is to be the antidote to insurgency; militancy will be tackled and the region will be rendered conducive for external investment. Massive infrastructure development, roads, bridges and urban projects are planned. The region is to be the biggest exporter of power to the rest of India and neighbouring countries. Arunachal Pradesh also has a New Agricultural Policy centred around high-yielding varieties, as does Assam. Rice production in Assam has risen since 2000, following the introduction of shallow tube wells. Horticulture is being vigorously promoted in the entire region and market linkages with Southeast Asia are envisaged.

Mizoram, Meghalaya and Sikkim have stated their intention to go 'organic' to meet the requirements of niche markets abroad.

The first and most serious challenge facing the region is the network of dams that have been commissioned, proposed or are under construction. These are mainly on the glacier-fed rivers, the Kameng, Subansiri and the Dihang-Dibang of Arunachal, and also on the Barak in Tripura and the Teesta in Sikkim (*The Ecologist* 2003). The region does need electricity but these reservoirs will submerge extensive areas of dense forest and also cultivated lands (orchards and jhum fields). The Subansiri, which originates in Tibet, is the largest river in Arunachal and a major tributary of the Brahmaputra. The Lower Subansiri dam and hydroelectric project will submerge only two villages upstream but it will affect extensive wetland areas downstream, inhabited by Mishings who depend on deep-water rice and fishing (Vagholikar and Ahmad 2003). Recently, there has also been public concern over the proposed Middle Siang dam (one of the smaller projects) but this was met with the rejoinder from officials that jhumia families are not entitled to compensation because jhuming is banned in Arunachal. Administrators are not sensitive to the ecological linkages between the forests, water courses and cultivated areas, and consider jhum lands unproductive and of little economic value. With or without monetary compensation, given the gendered division of roles, women who lose access to land will still have to feed their families. They might have no options other than hiring themselves out as agricultural labour or doing coolie work on the roads and constructions around the dam sites. Their knowledge of farming and their skills would be lost, along with the nutritious mix of cereals, millets and leafy vegetables grown on the jhum plots.

The second challenge stems from various short-term engineering solutions to the problems of transportation in the riverine plains. For example, eastern Arunachal and the areas of upper Assam on the north bank of the Brahmaputra do need a bridge across the river to Dibrugarh town, on the south bank. Crossing the river by small local ferryboats is time-consuming and can be risky both when the river is in spate and when it recedes, leaving sandbanks that the ferry has to negotiate. The nearest road bridge is at Tezpur in lower Assam. Not surprisingly, therefore, the proposed Dibrugarh Bridge is among the region's most prestigious and widely welcomed projects. To provide a small proportion of the total stone required for this, most of the major rivers and hill streams in the surrounding hill states have already been stripped of loose boulders (Ravindranath personal communication Akajan, 2004). The north-eastern hills are fragile and sedimentary in nature; the high rainfall leads to torrential and unpredictable flows in silt-laden rivers, which are known to change their course. (On the north bank of the Brahmaputra in Dhemaji district there is the strange sight of a bridge standing in the midst of rice fields; the tributary that it was supposed to straddle flows far in the distance.) People in the foothills say that when they see heavy rain clouds up in the hills they know that they have five hours before the flood reaches their villages. The river flow is likely to be much faster without any rocks to reduce the force of the water. How will this affect the wet-rice fields in the low-lying areas along the riversides? How will women in the foothills cope with more flash floods from the hills? Even now male out-migration from flood prone areas is high. The women who are left behind may gain space to take decisions independently of the men, but because they would also have to perform the farming tasks that were previously in the men's domain, the labour load will certainly increase.

The third challenge relates to changes in farming which are the result of the growing density of population around the cultivated areas of the region (Burman 2002), and of government policies that curtail the area available for jhuming in order to promote settled wet-rice cultivation. The outcome of this process for the matrilineal Garo in Meghalaya is well documented. Agarwal (1994: 132) says 'Variations in the extent of shift out of jhum into diversified production led to two forms of economic differentiation in the Garo Hills: inter-village, and inter-household within villages. Inter-village variations stem essentially from differential availability of irrigable flat land for settled rice cultivation.' Villages that shifted entirely to wet-rice, with some jhum, are self-sufficient in food production. But those that depended entirely on jhum are impoverished. When such differences occurred within a village, inter-household inequality increased. She notes (ibid. 158) that wet-rice cultivation has reduced the need for labour cooperation between villages, which was essential for clearing jhum forests, and that women have become 'helpers' to men. 'This includes harvesting, an operation in which, under jhum, men were women's helpers.' Wet-rice cultivation has affected the traditional land ownership pattern of the Garo. Privatization has resulted in *pattas* for land ownership being granted in men's names and this in turn has eroded the customary matrilineal inheritance and marriage patterns. As Agarwal points out, the pressure of increasing population might have led eventually to the decline of jhum, but the erosion of women's rights in land is directly attributable to the male bias of state agencies.

Positive indicators of women's status, such as higher rates of literacy, work participation and greater autonomy in the north-eastern states, do not seem to be sufficient safeguards against the erosion of women's traditional knowledge and skills, increase in their labour, and regressive changes in gender relations. The significant correlation between high levels of gender disparity and even moderate levels of food sustainability in some states is a clear pointer to the gendered price of rice. One can speculate on the reasons for this correlation but it seems to be linked to a greater emphasis on increasing agricultural productivity at any cost. Gender disparities in customary practices are reinforced by conventional approaches to development and together these serve to advance patriarchy. The clearest reflection of this is in greater control over women's sexuality, increasing violence against women and the declining trend in the sex ratio in some states. The adverse gender outcome of conventional development in north-eastern India is, thus, similar to trends in the rest of the country. These are major social changes forming the substratum, the power structure, upon which the rice-farming system rests.

In some areas, government interventions in agricultural development may have enabled people to make more productive use of their lands, perhaps even reducing intra-village inequalities. However, there is little genuine appreciation of the complex diversity of the region's landscapes, people and farming systems. These are served up as tourist attractions, in which the women figure prominently, but not at all assimilated into policies.

Moreover, far from recognizing the 'gendered price' of rice, the cost of food security which is borne by poor women in the region, agricultural extension continues to be geared to men as in the Green Revolution years, four decades ago. Commenting on women in Indian agriculture, M. S. Swaminathan (1975) said, that women had played a pivotal role, attending to various field operations like transplanting of rice, weeding crops, and scaring birds, and 'have also been practically in complete charge of many harvest and post-harvest operations like reaping, winnowing, threshing and storage'. So too, women have done 'much of the work in plantation crops like plucking tea', and in 'tending farm animals and saving farm-yard refuse for use either as fuel or manure'. While women in the plains 'provided much of the unpaid family labour in agriculture', he further said:

> When we go to hill areas, like most parts of Himalayas, we find that women occupy even a more important place in agriculture since they attend to most of the operations connected with crop production. In spite of such an important role played by them in our agricultural economy, the attention paid to training farm women in modern skills has been very poor. It will not be incorrect to say that quite often they have been bypassed by many of our extension programmes. In my view, this is one of the reasons why we find it difficult to get full benefit of modern technology like rice.

Despite this awareness and two decades since, a watered-down version of the early 1950s middle-class American Home Economics model and the 'welfare' approach of Indian development planning (see Krishna 1995a, S3) continues to provide skilled farming women with lessons in home-based activities like juice-making and embroidery, even as DONER prides itself on its new generation projects for women: fashion 'technology' and toy-making.

Traditionally, rice was the people's primary need as depicted in the Buddhist Sherdukpen variation of the common Arunachali tale of a young woman who marries a snake (Elwin 1970: 307-313). In the Sherdukpen story a widow is abandoned by her daughter (who marries the king of water snakes and goes to live in his palace below the lake). But the girl presents her mother with five bundles containing different apparently useless things, sand, pine cones, stone etc. When the mother grows old and tired and can no longer grow food for herself, she happens to open the bag of sand, which overflows with rice. Later, tiring of a diet of rice, she wishes for some dry meat and finds this in another bag. Then she wants some variety, a little fish, which is in the third bag. With the onset of winter, she needs clothes and finds hides in the fourth bag. She had thrown the fifth bag away and does not know that the stone it contained would have turned to gold. The Sherdukpen ranking of needs is simple and clear: rice, meat, fish, cloth, and money. Today, however, government policy and people's own aspirations have overturned these priorities. Despite successful attempts by sections of the Nagas and the Mizos (AMFU 1995, Thansanga 1997) to combine the diversity of jhum with permanent farming, the focus in the region is not on preserving the rice diversity but simply on improving productivity and cash incomes. There is little realization that food and livelihood security cannot be 'engendered' without addressing the structural aspects of development. In an era of globalization, the 'Green Revolution' approach cannot just be grafted onto existing farming systems without sensitivity to the known problems of intensive agriculture (see Krishna 1996a, 2000). This could have disastrous ecological, social and gender consequences for the region.

So, what does it all mean for women? In brief, it means: ecological changes and habitat loss, changes in the cropping pattern, increasing male control over agriculture with women as helpers and youth perhaps withdrawing from farming, and changes in labour relations. It also means that women's knowledge and skills are likely to be eroded, perhaps quite swiftly. Their workload and incomes may or may not improve but their autonomy and self-image will decline. The trend points to the reinforcement of customary laws and more crimes against women. All of this shows the advance of new forms of male domination in the region, which resonate with elements of brahminical patriarchy. A somewhat unusual Manipuri saying seems to recognize the value of girls: 'Who will cry for me when I die if I don't have daughters?' Perhaps, we should now ask, who will cry for the knowledgeable, skilful and labouring mothers and daughters, the farmers and food producers of north-eastern India? Women in the region are just beginning to recognize this and collectively struggle against it. But there is a 'long and winding road' ahead.

NOTES

[1] Translated from Hindi. Interview with the author, West Siang district, Arunachal Pradesh. September 2004.

Table 7.1: Naga communities recognized as 'Scheduled Tribes' (ST), 1991

Nagaland	Manipur (Tamenglong, Senapati, Chandel and Ukhrul districts)	Arunachal Pradesh (Tirap and Changlang districts)	Assam (North Cachar and Karbi Hills districts)
1. Angami*	1. Anal	1. Tangsa	1. Zeliangrong
2. Ao.	2. Chiru	2. Wancho	
3. Chakhesang	3. Chothe	3. Nocte	
4. Chang	4. Kabui (including Puimei)		
5. Chirr	5. Kacha Naga (Zeme and Liangme)		
6. Khienmungan	6. Koireng		
7. Konyak	7. Lamgang		
8. Lotha	8. Mao (including Poumei)		
9. Makhori	9. Maram		
10. Phom	10. Maring		
11. Rengma	11. Monsang		
12. Sangtam	12. Moyon		
13. Sema*	13. Tanghul		
14. Tikhir			
15. Yimchunger			
16. Zeliang			
17. Pochury			

* Also recognised as ST in Manipur
Source: Population Census of India (1991) and U.A. Shimray (2004: 1699)

Table 7.2: District-wise distribution of main 'tribes' in Arunachal Pradesh

District	Headquarter	Tribe*
TAWANG	Tawang	Monpa
WEST KAMENG	Bomdila	Monpa, Sherdukpen, Lishpa, Chugpa, Aka (Hruso), Miji, Bugun (Khawa)
EAST KAMENG	Seppa	Nishi, Bangni, Sulung
PAPUMPARE	Itanagar	Nishi/Nishing
LOWER SUBANSIRI	Hapoli	Apatani, Nishi, Hill Miri
UPPER SUBANSIRI	Daparijo	Tagin, Gallo (Gallong), Nga-Fagin, Hill Miri
WEST SIANG	Along (Aalo)	Adi-Gallo (Gallong), Adi-Bokar, Adi-Minyong, Adi-Bori, Memba
EAST SIANG	Pasighat	Adi-Minyong, Adi-Padam, Mishing (Miri)
UPPER SIANG	Yingkiong	Adi-Ramon, Adi-Bokar, Adi-Palibo, Adi-Minyong, Ashing, Tangam, Khamba
DIBANG VALLEY	Anini	Idu-Mashmi
LOHIT	Tezu	Idu-Mishmi, Idu-Kaman, Idu-Taraon, Idu-Muu Adi-Padam, Khampti
CHANGLANG	Changlang	Tangsa-Naga Lisu/Yabin
TIRAP	Khonsa	Nocte-Naga, Wancho-Naga

* Former names in parenthesis
Source: Krishna (1998 b: 153) derived from various sources

194 GENDERSCAPES

Table 7.3: Women's perceptions of different kinds of rice, Dhemaji district, Assam

Classes and varieties of rice as categorised by women

Classes:

dumahi ('two months' duration, monsoon harvest), ahu (monsoon harvest), hali (or sali, winter harvest), boro (summer harvest), bao (deep-water/ floating rice, monsoon to winter harvest)

Varieties for various seasons (undifferentiated in the listing):

bach, bar jahinga, bachimali, bara, mala, halpuna, jaha (joha), memlahi, lauduvi, padumani, aiare, pacha, katinali, surai kini, baima bichi, sunamukhi, bihari (aijang), hungmoni and bora

Source: Malthi Hajong Sr., Malthi Hajong Jr., Amala Hajong personal communication recorded by Gyananda Gogoi, Harinath Hajong village. 2004.

Table 7. 4: Local rice germplasm in the Apatani Plateau, Lower Subansiri district, Arunachal

Prevalent rice germplasm in the Apatani plateau

(representing a unique set of intermediate types between the indica and japonica, evolved with a high degree of location specific adaptability)

emo, emo elang, emo empu, emo enkhe, empo are, empo hat, ji pyat, nipya pyani, mipya pyare, mipya pyat, mishing (jhum), owe impo, pyapin, pyapin pyankha, pyapin pyat, pyapin pyani, pyapin pyare, pyat kogya, pyani, pyat pyapu and rade amo

Source: Extracted from B. D. Sharma (2002) based on Kochar and Chandel (1996), Hore (1999)

Table 7.5: Gender roles: Herma village, West Tripura

Women	Men	Women and/ or men
husking rice	jhum cutting	sowing seeds
pressing oil seeds	setting fire to jhum	weeding
collecting firewood	fire protection	watching over jhum
gathering banana leaves	basket-weaving	harvesting crops
fetching water	house-building	threshing paddy
feeding pigs	hunting	shelling sesame
feeding poultry		ginning cotton
carding cotton		cutting and separating
spinning yarn		jute from stalk
weaving cloth		transporting jhum to market
cooking food		selling jhum products
brewing rice beer		purchasing goods from market
cleaning house		fishing

Source: Collated from J.B.Ganguly (1993 a).

Table 7.6: Gender roles (selected activities): Aizawl district, central Mizoram

Women	Men	Women and/or men
jhum weeding	cutting large trees	clearing forest
small storage	protecting jhum (youth)	
vegetable marketing	large storage	sowing
animal husbandry	marketing	harvesting
home-gardening	collecting fuel (youth)	celebration
cooking		collecting water (youth)
child care		

Source: Sumi Krishna (1998 c).

Table 7.7: Gender roles: Nishi, Arunachal Pradesh

Women	Men
clearing undergrowth	slashing and burning the
sowing	forest cover
weeding	removing unburnt logs
harvesting	building and fencing fields
storing grain in baskets or granaries	keeping watch over crops
preparing old plots for next season	searching for new plots
spinning	hunting
weaving	fishing
making earthen pots	tending mithuns

Source: Collated from Kiran Mishra (1991).

Table 7.8: Gender roles: Japhuphiki (southern Angami), Nagaland

Women	Men	Women and men
work in the fields	demarcate plots	harvest
carry agricultural implements and food to the fields	cut trees for jhum; burn branches	
clear paths	till soil	
sow	cut trees for firewood	
weed	or other uses	
collect firewood in the forest		
carry firewood from the forest to the village		

Source: Collated from various sources: mainly Alphonsus D'souza 2001, Nikita Mehrotra 1992.

Table 7.9: Gender roles: Tanghul Naga, Manipur

Women	*Men*
tending saplings	clearing forest for cultivation
transplanting	ploughing
weeding	building dykes
harvesting	preparing land
husking and pounding	hunting and trapping
storage of food crops	construction and repair of fence,
lighting the hearth	shed and house
cooking	collection of materials for
taking care of children,	house-building materials and
taking care of sick, elderly	agricultural implements
tending kitchen garden	construction and quarrying
cleaning and washing	collection of honey
knitting and weaving	
cane and bamboo work	

Source: Adapted from U.A. Shimray (2004: 1706)

Table 7. 10: Gender-specific roles in cultivation, Jorhat district, Assam

| | Average person days (8 hours) per worker | | | | | | | | | |
| | Marginal | | Small | | Medium | | Large | | All Sizes | |
	Male	Female	Male	Female	Male	Female	Male	Female	Male	Female
Land preparation, ploughing etc.	25.6		31.0		38.5		42.6		34.4	
Irrigation	9.4	2.4	11.3	2.9	14.5	3.4	16.8	3.6	13.0	3.1
Fertiliser application	8.6	1.6	10.6	2.3	12.9	3.5	15.9	4.8	12.0	3.1
Sowing	8.8	2.5	12.8	3.4	15.9	3.5	17.2	4.2	13.7	3.4
Transplanting	4.7	24.5	5.8	29.6	6.4	32.8	8.9	35.5	6.4	30.6
Use of insecticides, pesticides	4.2		5.3		7.4		8.5		6.3	
Hand weeding	8.3	2.8	10.7	3.4	14.3	3.6	16.3	4.2	12.4	3.5
Use of weeder/ herbicide	4.2		5.3		6.8		8.5		6.2	
Harvesting	6.0	26.5	7.0	30.4	8.1	32.0	10.2	36.4	7.8	31.3
Post-harvest operations	38.7	9.0	40.5	8.7	51.0	8.5	53.5	11.7	45.9	9.5
All operations	118.2	69.3	140.0	80.6	175.6	87.3	198.5	100.4	158.1	84.4
Total working days	187.5		220.6		262.9		298.9		242.5	

Source: Anuva Saikia (2000: 47)

Table 7.11: Weekly average time spent* in selected post-harvest activities, Tanghul Naga, Manipur

Feeding domestic animals		Home garden		Drying paddy and seed		De-husking and pounding	
Female	Male	Female	Male	Female	Male	Female	Male
2.00	1.42	2.25	1.12	6.00	5.00	8.19	0.30
	2.10		2.00		6.15		4.60

* Weekly average time disposition = Total hours spent by Total number of persons.
Source: Extrapolated from U.A. Shimray (2004: 1708-09)

Table 7.12: Aspects of Patriarchy among selected groups

	Descent and family structure	Property inheritance	Women's participation in religious and public decision-making
Mizoram			
Mizo	Patrilineal, patrilocal; extended family	Youngest son inherits; women have no property rights	None
Meghalaya			
Garo	Matrilineal, matrilocal, may be virilocal	Men cannot inherit but land may be gifted to sons; Youngest daughter inherits	None
Khasi	Matrilineal, matrilocal	Youngest daughter inherits	None. Women's participation in public affairs is ridiculed by the saying 'a hen has crowed'
Arunachal			
Monpa	Buddhist, patrilineal, patrilocal; extended and nuclear family	All sons inherit; daughters inherit mother's ornaments; in the absence of sons, daughters can claim property which reverts to the male line in the next generation	None
Sherdukpen	Buddhist, patrilineal, patrilocal	Women have no rights of inheritance but can independently rear livestock and poultry, and keep money earned from the activity.	None
Sulung	Patrilineal, patrilocal	Women have no rights but under certain circumstances widow may have a share in husband's property	No role but sometimes allowed to attend village meetings as onlookers.

Contd.

Table 7.12 *Contd.*

	Descent and family structure	Property inheritance	Women's participation in religious and public decision-making
Nishi (also Bangni Hill Miri)	Patrilineal, patrilocal; polygynous; 'long house' (many wives in one house) family; bride price	Eldest son inherits; women have no rights except to ornaments and utensils (brought as dowry)	None
Apatani	Patrilineal, patrilocal; monogamous, polygyny permitted to wealthy; bride price	Eldest son inherits; mother may be consulted on property matters; women inherit clothes and ornaments	None
Adi-Gallo	Patrilineal, patrilocal; formerly, elder brother's wife could be 'shared' by younger brothers; polygyny also permitted to wealthy; bride price	Sons inherit; rarely daughters may receive land in dowry; unmarried daughter can retain their own earnings; women inherit beads and ornaments	Participate in religious ceremonies; no role in public decision-making; (Adi women recently appointed to the traditional council, kebang, make tea for members but are not allowed to speak.)
Idu-Mishmi	Patrilineal, patrilocal; polygyny permitted to wealthy; extended and nuclear family; bride price	Sons inherit; daughters inherit ornaments	Participate in religious activities; no role in public decision-making
Khampti	Hindu, patrilineal, patrilocal; monogamous but polygyny also permitted to wealthy, nuclear and extended family		None
Tangsa	Patrilineal, patrilocal; Monogamous	Women have no rights to property but have free access	None
Nocte	Patrilineal, patrilocal; monogamous but polygyny permitted to wealthy; extended and nuclear family		None
Wancho	Patrilineal, patrilocal; monogamy and polygyny practiced	Women have no rights	None

Source: Collated from various authors and interactions with some tribal groups.

Table 7.13: Selected Gender Disparity Indicators: North-eastern States

States (Listed in order of poverty levels)	Demographic, survival factors			Health: Anaemia		Education	Rural Female Work Participation		Private Decision-making %			Crimes against Women	
	(A) Below Poverty Level % 2001	(B) Child sex ratio 2001	(C) Sex ratio above 6 years 2001	(D) Severe & moderate anaemia % 1998-99	(E) Mild anaemia % 1998-99	(F) Gender gap in literacy rate 2001	(G) RWFP rate 1993-94	(H) RWFP rate 1999-2000	(I) Involved in decisions on own health 1998-99	(J) Freedom to go to the market 1998-99	(K) Freedom to decide about own earnings 1998-99	(L) Recorded cases per million population 1999	(M) Composite Gender Rank (B to L) 1999
Mizoram	19.5	971	932	12.8	35.2	4.6	31.7	44.0	73.2	64.2	26.4	176	1
Manipur	28.5	961	981	7.1	21.7	18.2	30.8	25.3	43.3	28.6	52	29	3
Nagaland	32.7	975	899	9.7	27.8	9.9	21.6	44.1	69.4	17.3	17.8	11	5
Arunachal	33.5	961	888	11.9	50.6	19.8	40.9	31.0	70.0	46.8	46.4	148	7
Meghalaya	33.9	975	974	29.9	33.4	5.7	49.3	41.8	78.9	46.5	40.7	25	2
Tripura	34.4	975	947	16.3	43.0	16.1	12.8	7.3	51.2	27.4	37.7	98	6
Assam	36.1	964	926	26.5	43.2	15.9	15.9	15.1	65.1	13.2	40	138	8
Sikkim	36.5	986	858	23.8	37.3	15.3	19.8	24.1	60.2	38.2	69.8	56	4
All-India	26.1	927	934	16.7	35.0	24.5	32.8	29.9	51.6	31.6	41.1	127	

Notes: Derived from Rustagi (2003), Kishor and Gupta (2004). Sources: as below.

Figures in **bold** font indicate negative divergence, underscore positive divergence from national average, except where indicated. Column A. % of population Below Poverty Level, Planning Commission, Central Statistical Organisation, 2001. Column B. Child sex ratio (number of females per 1000 males in population below six years), calculated from Census of India, 2001. Bold font most unfavourable ratio among north-eastern states, underscore improved ratios over the previous decade. Column C. Sex ratio in population above six years (number of females per 1000 males). Census

Table 7.13 *(Contd.)*

of India 2001. Column D. and E. % of women with Severe and Moderate Anaemia (taken together); and Mild Anaemia, National Family Health Survey-2, 1998-1999. Column F. Gender Gap in Literacy, difference in % of literacy of females and males, Census of India, 2000. Bold font: most unfavourable position among north-eastern states, underscore: among the five lowest gender gaps in literacy (all-India). Column G. and H. Rural Female Workforce Participation Rate (proportion of total workers among population above six years), calculated from National Sample Surveys 50th and 55th Rounds, 1999-2001. Column H. bold font indicates decline, underscore increase in RFWP rate over the previous decade. Column I., J. and K. % of ever-married women (aged 15-49) involved (with husbands/family) in decisions about their own health; who do not require permission to go to the market; who are free to take independent decisions on their own earnings, National Family Health Survey-2, 1998-1999. Column L. Crimes against Women, number of cases per million population, National Crime Research Bureau, 1999. Column M: Estimated on basis of B to L.

Table 7.14: Comparison of Gender Disparity and Food Sustainability

States by Gender Rank	Gender Disparity Level	Food Sustainability
1. Mizoram	Least disparity	Moderately sustainable
2. Meghalaya	Some disparity	Unsustainable
3. Manipur	Moderately high disparity	Unsustainable
4. Sikkim	Moderately high disparity	Unsustainable
5. Nagaland	Moderately high disparity	Extremely unsustainable
6. Tripura	High disparity	Moderately unsustainable
7. Arunachal	High disparity	Sustainable
8. Assam	Extremely high disparity	Moderately unsustainable

Note: Gender Disparity Level: Estimated on basis of Composite Gender Rank (Column M of Table 7.13)

Food Sustainability: Derived from 'Sustainability of Food Security Index Values' (MSSRF, 2004)

Extremely unsustainable: Below 0.300

Unsustainable: 0.301–0.350

Moderately unsustainable: 0.351–0.400

Moderately sustainable: 0.401–0.460

Sustainable: Above 0.460

ACTIONSCAPES

8

'Mainstreaming' Women in Resource Management

What do you mean by mainstreaming? To make some room for us in all that is going on? But that is not what we want. We want no part in planting thousands of eucalyptus trees that rob our soil of water and other plants, leaving our children and cattle hungry. We want to *change* these processes. If we have our way, we will call the scientists to work with us, adding their knowledge to ours, and look for solutions that would be good for everybody.

—Malati Mandi, Santal peasant woman, Manila, 1990.[1]

During the late 1980s 'gender mainstreaming' came into international prominence as a strategy which refers to integrating women into all areas of policy and programmes, and at every level from the identification of needs, to project planning, implementation, monitoring and evaluation. This was seen as an advance over the earlier strategy of separate programmes for women. Advocates of mainstreaming also explicitly articulated the goal of gender equality. In India, separate programmes for women were the norm for many years but 'mainstreaming' is now also being advocated, although on the ground the distinction between these strategies is not always as clear as it is in policy and programme documents. In this chapter, I first highlight some aspects of the policy environment, and then touch upon recent approaches to 'mainstreaming' in participatory forest management and watershed development to understand why these are not working in favour of women. The third section discusses the emergence of the Sustainable Livelihoods Approach to poverty alleviation and the concept of biovillages. The fourth section then reviews a range of different innovative interventions that have tried to change the process of resource management and expand women's livelihood options. This helps to further our understanding of the different ways in which resource management may be engendered, and the potential and limitations of such approaches.

GLOBAL TRENDS AND THE POLICY ENVIRONMENT

In recent years, the women's movement and academic research in South Asia have effectively asserted women's centrality in conserving biological diversity and managing local ecosystems and resources. Women constitute the major part of the labour force in subsistence crop production, agri-silviculture, and sea-food harvesting. In some parts of the country, women are the most stable labour because the men migrate to distant locations for wage-employment. Researchers and activists have shown that the degradation of fragile ecosystems and the displacement of communities affects poor women in particular, together with young children and the elderly.

Such advocacy and experiences from the field have helped gain national and international recognition for the significance of gender in resource management. International conservation circles have slowly come round to recognizing women's concerns. For instance, the 'Preamble' of the *International Convention on Biological Diversity* (1992) acknowledges 'the vital role that women play in the conservation and sustainable use of biological diversity', and affirms 'the need for the full participation of women at all levels of policy-making and implementation of biodiversity conservation'. Apart from this, there are no specific references to women. The *Agenda 21* reinforces the concerns of the Third World Conference for Women (Nairobi 1985) enunciated in the *Forward Looking Strategies for the Advancement of Women*: the need for strategies and government actions which would strengthen women's involvement in managing ecosystems and controlling environmental degradation. These concerns were expressed yet again in the *Plat-*

form for Action, adopted with the *Beijing Declaration* at the Fourth World Conference on Women (Beijing, China 1995).

As a signatory and a major contributor to all these international agreements, India has a special responsibility towards developing gender-disaggregated data bases on conservation practices, integrating gender analyses and perspectives into policies and programmes for sustainable development, and ensuring the equal participation of women and men at all levels of environmental decision-making. Some see the current national policy focus on 'mainstreaming' women in NRM, agriculture, forestry, watersheds and so on as an externally-imposed foreign, donor-driven agenda. In my view, this is somewhat simplistic because it seems to disregard the range of initiatives and experience within the country that have also helped to shape policy. Indeed, externally funded programmes are not necessarily characterized by gender sensitivity.

In the post-Independence period, India's policy towards women was conventional and welfarist (see Chapter 3), clubbing women with children and the disabled. Since the Sixth Plan (1978-79 to 1982-83), there has been a more specific focus on women although this has lacked consistency and has wavered between the earlier welfarist and the more recent instrumentalist approaches. This is also so with regard to women and natural resources. Whether it is watersheds, wastelands, animal husbandry (poultry, fishing), forestry or any other aspect of resource management, policy documents increasingly reflect an awareness that women contribute a major part of the labour and that they have special responsibilities. Specific polices, such as those for agriculture or for water, and the recent Tenth Plan document, as also state-level initiatives, show that policy-makers are conscious of the lack of gender-equity. For instance, the Tenth Plan even makes a commitment to gender-sensitive rehabilitation for displaced peoples and to the special educational needs of girls of the Scheduled Castes and Tribes. But apart from an acknowledgement of equity concerns, what all of this really amounts to is giving women 'a greater role', involving them in a more 'appropriate' manner in participatory programmes, providing employment, and sometimes providing assets (including access to land). However, it is not women's empowerment that is the real focus of policy but rather the strengthening of women as the most effective instruments to improve family welfare, environmental conservation, wasteland regeneration and so on. Such an approach has been called the 'efficiency' argument but I prefer to use the term 'instrumentalist' because it more clearly shows where the focus lies.

Consider the following: Taking its cue from successful NGO interventions, the Tenth Plan document (e.g. paras 5.1.54, 5.2., 5.3) advocates 'giving wastelands on lease to women' with credit subsidies and technical support. It acknowledges that a sizeable number of the one million tea plantation labourers in the country are women and advocates 'micro-financing through self-help'. It recognizes that women constitute 70 per cent of the labour force in animal husbandry and suggests 'backyard poultry farming'. It wants to 'involve more women in the fisheries sector' and wants to 'train fisherwomen to improve their participation'. The New Agriculture Policy, 2000, which is part of the Tenth Plan, is explicit about the instrumental rationale of giving women land rights (see also Rao 2005):

> Strengthening the conditions of female farmers and female labourers would also help improve the food security at the household level. This is because generally women spend most of their income on household expenditure unlike men and this would help improve the nutrition of the children.

Likewise, the Plan chapter on Environment and Forests states that rural people, particularly women and tribal communities, have an intimate knowledge of species, their growth characteristics, utility, individual value etc. It says this knowledge is 'utilized' for the community under JFM. In the past, similar arguments have also been explicitly put forward regarding professional women forest officers; the forest service could use them as instruments to carry the message of forest protection to village women, and through them to village communities. The assumption was that women officers would have skills of communication and interaction, and succeed where their male colleagues had failed. (See S6)

The National Water Policy, 2002, sees the need for legal and institutional changes to ensure appropriate participation of women:

Management of the water resources for diverse uses should incorporate a participatory approach; by involving not only the various governmental agencies but also the users and other stakeholders, in an effective and decisive manner, in various aspects of planning, design, development and management of the water resources schemes. Necessary legal and institutional changes should be made at various levels for the purpose, duly ensuring appropriate roles for women. Water Users' Associations and the local bodies such as municipalities and *gram panchayats* should particularly be involved in the operation, maintenance and management of water infrastructures/facilities at appropriate levels progressively, with a view to eventually transfer the management of such facilities to the user groups/local bodies. (para 12. April 2002)

At the state level too, similar sentiments are expressed. The intention is clear: increase women's management of resources to improve conservation and family welfare. For instance, a policy note of the Tamil Nadu State Environment and Forest Department (2005-06) states:

In order to ensure household food security, millions of rural women are burdened with the duties of collection of firewood, fodder and water. Dwindling forest resources further make their work very difficult. Hence, emphasis will be given to ensure that the poorest women with greatest dependence on bio-resources secure access to decision-making and control over their livelihood resources. To ensure this, many women Self Help Groups are being formed under Joint Forest Management.

There are three main prongs in this policy thrust: a) implementing services to meet 'women's responsibilities' of providing the family's water, fodder, and fuel needs; b) generating employment and assets for women, together with skills-training, credit and marketing to increase family incomes; and c) utilizing women's knowledge and labour for enhancing community resources. The provision of services is intended to open up a space for women's knowledge to be utilized, and the provision of assets to helping strengthen women's capacity to meet the needs of the community. The equity concerns that are sprinkled through policy statements and programme documents effectively mask the reinforcement of women's traditional roles and the release of men from responsibilities for household food-provisioning and community resource conservation.

The Planning Commission's mid-term appraisal of the Tenth Plan is also revealing: it lists 59 priority actions that it says could yield results immediately. These include enacting legislations to confer ownership rights to tribals living in the forests in keeping with the National Forest Policy of 1988 (Overview, action point 23); and providing social security for unorganized sector workers (action 48). One of the priority actions that has been elaborated is the promotion of participatory NRM (action 13):

> Participatory management practices seek to empower the rural communities who would decide and prioritise their requirements and accordingly prepare and implement micro plans appropriate to local conditions and needs. The building of community based organizations, flexibility in technical and financial norms, facilitation through a multi-disciplinary professional groups, independent reliable and on-going monitoring and evaluation are the basic premises and procedures of these participatory processes. There is need to revisit the guidelines and the content of all programmes in natural resource management in the light of this valuable experience and also strengthen the coverage and funding of these programmes. More specifically, vacant and under utilized land areas can be used for creation of forest resources. Currently, there are 2,34,676 village Panchayat institutions in 31 States and Union Territories in the country in addition to the traditional councils in Meghalaya, Mizoram and Nagaland. If every Panchayat is entrusted to identify a reasonable area of land for afforestation through community participation, a substantial area can be covered under green canopy in total. The right of use of such resources should be left to the communities and opportunities for value addition and marketing provided.

Gender concerns are not separately addressed in any of these priority actions. However, women do find mention under a separate section on 'Women and Child Development' (actions 21 and 22). Two priority areas listed in that section: the need to restructure ICDS to integrate crèche services and pre-school education; and the need to move beyond gender-budgeting (i.e. ensuring separate allocations for women in all programmes) to improve mechanisms to measure the outcome for women of various development programmes. While these are laudable goals, elsewhere, the mid-term appraisal also points out that information on the 'Women's Component Plan' (which is supposed to have been mainstreamed, i.e. included as a part of every 'women-related' ministry or department), has not been provided even by those ministries/departments which had done so earlier.

Given this policy scenario, it is not at all surprising (as the Santal peasant woman Malati Mandi so eloquently points out in the epigram above) that women's empowerment has been far from being the focus of modern scientific resource management. Poor adivasi and dalit women whose livelihoods depend on work within natural environments have acquired a vast amount of experiential knowledge and skills in resource management. Yet, their productive participation in the household and larger economy, and their contribution to the conservation and sustainability of resources, is either ignored by policy makers or appropriated in instrumentalist ways.

MODERN MANAGERIAL APPROACHES

In the main, modern approaches to resource management are geared to the conservation and sustainable use of resources for what policy makers see as wider national or global goals. During the 1960s and '70s new social movements (for peace, environment, women) brought a global perspective to people's concerns. The UN Conference on the Human Environment, at Stockholm in 1972, was among the first markers of this change. The spiralling international price of crude oil had affected the productivity of industries worldwide and at about the same time environmentalists became increasingly concerned that more alarming than the depletion of fossil fuels was the dwindling supply of fuel wood for the world's poor. The decline of common property resources became a focus of research, policy and action and provided an impetus to many donor-aided development programmes for poor countries. However, resource management programmes, such as for wasteland development, did little to ease the condition of the poorest (see below).

Common property resources

The decline in community management systems and common property resources (CPRs) has been comprehensively documented by N. S. Jodha. Between 1982 and 1985 Jodha (1990) surveyed 82 villages from 21 districts in seven large states, Rajasthan, Gujarat, Madhya Pradesh, Maharashtra, Karnataka, Andhra Pradesh and Tamil Nadu. This study shows the significance of such resources especially in arid and semi-arid areas. The common resource area has shrunk, its productivity declined and its management worsened leading to a crisis situation. Because CPRs do not provide high returns, Jodha argues that the poor depend on these resources more than do the rich. Indeed, such resources help to reduce income inequalities. Access to common resources also complements privately owned resources because common grazing lands, for instance, sustain farm animals and provide a buffer during droughts. Jodha points out that development planning and welfare programmes have neglected to consider common resources and that land distribution policies have led to large scale privatization of common lands. Together with population pressure, this has resulted in severe loss of biological diversity in CPR areas, more time and effort having to be spent on gathering the produce of these areas and structural changes such as a shift from cattle husbanding to rearing goats and sheep. His conclusion is that the poor have experienced a collective loss that has not been compensated by their individual gains. This has significant implications for natural resource policy and management.

JFM and non-timber forest produce

Till the mid-1970s, India's development programmes were, in the main, internally funded. This began to change after the Stockholm Conference. The prevailing understanding at that time, which is now discredited, was that deforestation was caused by poor people's need for firewood (see Eckholm 1976). This formed the core of the 1980s policy (mainly driven by the World Bank) to use village lands to grow trees for people's needs, i.e. fuel wood, fodder and small timber, so as to safeguard government forest lands for industrial plantation. Unlike earlier farm forestry and afforestation schemes, social forestry had been envisaged on a much larger-scale. The forestry sector was among the first to attract donor funding: besides World Bank support, there was also bilateral support from USAID, the British Government's ODA, Denmark's DANIDA, Swedish SIDA, Canadian CIDA and IDRC, and even from international voluntary organizations such as the Aga Khan Foundation and Oxfam.

By the mid-1980s, however, it was becoming clear that social forestry was not producing the desired results (see Krishna 1996a: 75-85). This led to a sharp policy reversal with the focus seemingly shifting to a more participatory process by which environmental regeneration, ecological stability and people's fuel and fodder needs could be ensured. Participatory forest management became the guiding principle. Regarding the global rhetoric of development, N. C. Saxena (1997: 155-57) has commented that 'in most Third World countries forestry and women had both remained neglected stepchildren of development'. In India, recently, 'the pendulum has taken a full swing, as both forestry and women have become buzz words.' He remarks that along with other buzz words such as 'computers, liberalization and structural reforms', such rhetorical references are expected 'to launch India into the 21st century'. As he points out, translating 'lip sympathy for women' into action requires radical changes in attitudes to the use and management of forest lands.

Yet, thus far, supplies to markets and industry have occupied centre-stage, and not the needs of women, of forest dwellers and the poor. This is very apparent in the Joint Forest Management (JFM) programme, the tussles over non-timber forest produce (NTFP), and the opening up of forest areas for mining and quarrying.

People's participation was institutionalized under the JFM programmes in the 1990s; these were even more massively funded than social forestry in the previous decade. Aid came from the World Bank, the EU, ODA and the Japanese OECF (see Saxena 1997). Sharing of authority and responsibility between the Forest Department and the people was structured into JFM agreements. Under these agreements, which vary from state-to-state, the village is expected to protect forests in return for a share of the usufruct. This refers to poles and small timber that would be produced when felling takes place after the restored tree plantations have matured. Villagers are also guaranteed use of NTFP for their own use. NTFP, formerly called 'minor' forest produce because they did not have commercial value, include fallen branches, twigs and dry leaves, fodder grasses, and various food sources, tubers, mushrooms, leafy greens, fruits and flowers. The 'major' non-timber produce, bamboos, fibrous grasses and some nuts like cashew, with significant commercial value, were excluded from these agreements. Collection rights for the more valuable NTFP continue to be leased to private contractors, or in some cases to tribal cooperative societies.

A *van samiti*, or other local forest management committee, formed in each village was the village-level institution set up to oversee the JFM agreement. Membership in these samitis was supposed to follow the national guidelines but the majority of states implementing JFM did not make clear provisions for women's representation, and households have invariably been represented by men. The implications of this have now been well-documented for both India and Nepal (Sarin et.al. 1998, Locke 1999, Correa 1999, Singh 2004, Lama and Buchy 2004). Sarin et. al. (op. cit.) have suggested that the incentive of a future share in the sale of timber shifted the stakes in the forest trees from poor women to better off men. Both the forest bureaucracy and the male dominated local committees have said that only 'dead, dry and fallen twigs and branches' should be collected. In degraded forests, this is so scarce that women 'head-loaders' (i.e. the women who gather firewood from the forest and carry it away on their heads) have little choice but to violate this rule leading to sharp clashes. The collection of firewood and other produce is assumed to be only for household needs but due to the lack of alternative livelihood options, for decades, poor women have been selling small loads of firewood and other produce in local markets (Fernandes and Menon 1987). The JFM agreements 'criminalize' all of these activities.

Furthermore, under the provisions of PESA, the Panchayats (Extension to the Scheduled Areas) Act, 1996, state governments were supposed to transfer ownership rights over NTFP to village panchayats and gram sabhas. Accordingly, in March 2000, Orissa changed its NTFP policy and the local institutions were given limited control over 60 specified items. The Forest Department retained control of the rest, which included the more profitable and marketable produce. In Orissa, the most valuable NTFPs are the seeds of the sal tree (*Shorea robusta*) and the leaves of the plant *Dispyros melanxylon* (known as *kendu* in Oriya and *tendu* in Hindi). Kendu leaves are used for wrapping tobacco in bidis; the leaves are primarily gathered by women. A study by Vasundhara (1998) in five villages in Bolangir and Nuapara districts showed that 88 per cent of the gatherers were women; in one village this was 100 per cent. As Neera Singh (2004: 312) and others have pointed out, Orissa has one of the most regressive NTFP policies in the country, 'guided by the principle that all forests and forest produce are state property'. She says further,

> Till very recently, most of the 29 marketable NTFP items were leased to a joint sector company. According to JFM, 100 per cent of the intermediate produce and 50 per cent of any major harvest is supposed to go to the Vana Suraksha Samiti VSS (Forest Protection Committee). Yet the VSS members and NTFP gatherers get only wages for collecting the produce. Thus, even in jointly managed forest lands, the people, who are supposedly co-managers, are treated as mere hired labourers whose earnings are based on the minimum wage rate and not related to the value of the produce.

Observations in the field show that JFM may be increasing women's labour while continuing to keep them out of the decision-making process. Women may be spending more time in fuel wood collection because the forests in the vicinity of the villages are now protected. This is also borne out by studies in Bankura, West Bengal and in the Panchmahals, Gujarat (see below). So too in the Hazaribagh and East Singhbum districts of Bihar where autonomous van samitis have been functioning. As Saxena (1995) has noted, 'merely shifting the protection role from the Forest Departments to the community does not provide any immediate relief to women. Further, the gender-differentiated impact is not restricted to firewood—it applies equally to other forest produce. For example, protecting sal trees with the existing technology of multiple shoot cutting results in the leaves getting out of reach. This affects the making of sal leaf plates, which is a common source of income, primarily for poor women in many parts of West Bengal, Orissa and Bihar'.

It is now increasingly becoming clear that JFM has been unable to address gender-related issues within the household and the village. A review of the Western Ghats Forestry and Environment Project in Uttara Kannada district in northern Karnataka, during the 1990s found that the philosophy of joint forest planning and management was widely accepted by all levels of the state forest department, and that there was significant change in the earlier 'adversarial relationship' with the village level committees (Saxena and Sarin 1999). Nevertheless, there remained institutional and policy constraints which limited the effectiveness of the project in empowering the people and in ensuring the sustainability of such forest conservation efforts. One of the problems is that when the village is treated 'as the unit of intervention,' the participation of women and disadvantaged groups is 'likely to remain superficial' (Correa 1999). Elaborating on this, Catherine Locke (1999) argues that currently there is no adequate conceptual or operational basis for gender policy and planning in JFM. She suggests that institutionalizing women's bargaining strength within JFM would require that forest professionals collaborate with social scientists and community development practitioners to understand gendered roles and relationships. This is not happening. So, despite the appropriation of progressive and gendered terminology, women's participation in JFM has remained fragmentary and limited.

Watersheds and water-use

Paralleling the externally-funded forestry programmes, since the mid-1980s, the Government thrust has been on watershed development. The integrated 'watershed plus' approach is geared towards multiple goals: improving the productivity of the land, increasing the availability of food and easing the burden of poverty. Technically, the watershed approach is expected to increase the water-holding capacity of the soil by planting trees along the ridges, creating soil-bunds to prevent run-off, and building check dams to store rain water. During the 1990s, these programmes extended throughout the country and were massively funded by some of the same external sources (mentioned above) and others like the German KFW and GTZ, the Swiss SDC, national agencies like NABARD and state governments.

Partly influenced by donor requirements and in response to local activist pressures, the watershed projects have also focused on capacity-building so that villagers could implement and manage the watersheds themselves. Many projects specifically aimed at involving women, and supported 'self-help' savings-and-credit groups and small enterprises.

Yet, village-level studies of micro-watershed projects funded by various different agencies in several states have shown clearly that the environmental benefits of watershed manangement have been appropriated by land-owning groups. Chhaya Datar and Aseem Prakash (2004: 158-59) have argued that 'the economics of the market requires policies that are based on environmental regeneration.' So, the emphasis of watershed programmes is on environmental sustainability and financial sustainability, which really translates to the financial benefit of land-owners. Such an approach is geared to securing food security at the national rather than the household level. They point out that this leads to an inherent conflict between social and private benefits in watershed development: 'The economics of the market results in investment in soil and water conservation measures, both on private land as well as common land, primarily benefiting the landed class while giving less importance to marginal and small farmers and almost ignoring poor women and the landless.' Datar and Prakash (ibid.) point out that the medium and big farmers 'now exploit groundwater with increased intensity'. This has led to a shift to commercial 'cash crop cultivation at the expense of food crops' and has increased the vulnerability of those who lack assets, amidst the growth in productivity. Contrary to the main trend, there are a few instances as in Ahmednagar district, Maharashtra, where the landless have benefited through the increase in agricultural wage rates, the regeneration of common grazing land and local forests (especially beneficial to women); some landless people have also stopped migrating because they are able to lease lands to cultivate. However, whether the gains to disadvantaged groups could be sustained is somewhat uncertain because inter-village inequality has increased and traditional institutional codes of conduct show signs of change. Despite success in reaching the landless in some pockets, and the reduction of inter-regional inequality, Datar and Prakash (ibid.) argue that the broad picture is that the watershed schemes deepen inequalities within a village, as the benefits and facilities 'provided at public cost' have become 'a privilege for a few', resulting 'in licence to overuse and waste'. They point out that this has 'also prompted a rent-seeking behaviour, whereby a new class of water lords, taking advantage of heavily subsidized energy, sell water to the poor and needy at exorbitant rates.'

Indeed, this is true for South Asia as a whole and has a gendered impact. Unless a policy on entitlements is clearly enunciated and implemented, programmes such as watershed development that aim to improve the natural resource base do not necessarily benefit those who are dependant on it (see Seely, Batra and Sarin 2000). In an analytical study of water user organizations in Sri Lanka, Pakistan, Nepal and India, Meinzen-Dick and Zwarteveen (1998: 179-180) have shown that women's participation is 'much lower' than men's. This is so despite women being involved in irrigated agriculture and even in agricultural decision-making. They point out that in 'most cases, low female participation is also in conflict with official policy statements, which almost always claim that the involvement of all farmers or water users is the ultimate objective.' They show that the extent of participation, of men and women, depends on the rules which determine eligibility, and 'the balance of costs and benefits to be derived from involvement'. In India, there are a few instances of women's involvement in participatory irrigation management (Dalwai 1997; Ahmed and Hari Krishna 1998, 2000). But the broader picture is one of exclusion. Thousands of water-user associations have been formed in Andhra Pradesh, under new policy initiatives for decentralization and local control of resources. These are membership organizations, and only land owners are eligible; as women do not own land in their own names, they are not part of the water user groups (see Jairath 2000). As I have written elsewhere (Krishna 2004a), 'when land-ownership becomes the basis for new and emerging rights in resources this reinforces class, caste and gender-based divisions of society.'

The environmental conservation achieved in watershed development is of limited value without social sustainability. The contradictions between these 'two sides of the coin' have been part of the environment-development debate since the early 1970s, and different approaches have been advocated to overcome the contradictions. One of the more recent of these is the concept of Sustainable Livelihoods.

SUSTAINABLE LIVELIHOOD APPROACHES

The concept of 'Sustainable Development' was outlined in *Our Common Future*, the influential report of the World Commission on Environment and Development commonly known as the Brundtland Commission (WCED 1987). The report defined sustainable development succinctly as that which 'meets the needs of the present without compromising the ability of future generations to meet their own needs.' This was elaborated upon by many others and it soon became a buzz phrase, widely used throughout the 1990s. It gave room for almost any kind of interpretation; so, every study, report, speech, or conversation ended with a rhetorical reference to sustainable development. The grand vision that it reflected was an attempt to encompass a future in which historical conflicts, both between humankind and nature and between different sections of people, would be peaceably reconciled. It recognized three inter-linked elements, the need to conserve ecological systems and resources, maintain the sustainability of economic growth, and ensure the equitable sharing of benefits. The concept gave an impetus to shifting the indicators of development from narrow economic concerns of Gross Domestic Product (GDP) to matters related to human development and poverty, but glossed over many social, political and ethical issues. In particular, ideological conflicts, including those related to gender, were not addressed. This was in keeping with the Women-Environment-Development approach (see Chapter 3).

The underlying assumption that the sustainability of economic development would be assured was, however, open to question. Among those who critiqued the concept of sustainable development was Sukhamoy Chakravarty (1992) who identified three obstacles: achieving equity at the national and international levels; establishing the necessary institutions; and political conscientisation. He saw an important role both for the market and for the central planner at intermediate levels of decision-making, but was not optimistic about co-operative endeavours, 'what induces people to co-operate and what induces people to look for co-operative solutions'. He pointed out that 'unless we bring in a certain ideology and value orientation which is broadly acceptable to the masses, any intermediate level of decision-making will succeed only in a few cases. It cannot be replicated on a wide enough scale'. As I have written elsewhere (Krishna 1996a: 252-253), 'Sustainable development requires changes in socio-political attitudes and structures, and in the specific instruments of development, which at present are not taking place. So both nationally and internationally, behind all the . . . rhetoric of equity, it seems to be business as usual. Indeed sustainable development itself has become big business.'

Concerns for the sustainability of people's work and livelihoods came as an advance over sustainable development, and this was at least partially a response to the lessons of failed or ineffective interventions on the ground. Many NGOs and development practitioners view 'livelihood' as a straightforward term as defined in dictionaries: the means of living and sustenance. For people's struggles, such as the Chipko movement the 'means of living' encompasses the sustainability of the resource base. The Chipko leader Chandi Prashad Bhatt has repeatedly said: 'Saving the trees is only the first step, saving ourselves is the goal'. Such perceptions from 'below', rooted in the everyday reality of poor people's lives, contributed to the emergence of the concept of sustainable livelihoods in the 1990s. Robert Chambers (1995) defined livelihood as the 'means of gaining a living, including tangible assets (resources and stores), intangible assets (claims and access), and livelihood capabilities' that included coping abilities, opportunities and sundry freedoms. Such an interpretation covered a cluster of factors that went beyond employment and income-generation in specific sectors that had marked earlier approaches to 'poverty-alleviation'.

The broader focus on livelihood rather than incomes gained some prominence in Agenda 21, the non-binding 'Plan of Action' adopted at the 1992 UN Conference on Environment and Development at Rio de Janeiro, Brazil. 'Enabling the poor to achieve sustainable livelihoods' is up-front in the chapter on Combating Poverty. It states: 'While managing resources sustainably, an environmental policy that focuses mainly on the conservation and protection of resources must take due account of those who depend on the resources for their livelihoods. Otherwise it could have an adverse impact both on poverty and on chances for long-term success in resource and environmental conservation'. Further: 'The long-term objective of enabling all people to achieve sustainable livelihoods should provide an integrating factor that allows policies to address issues of development, sustainable resource management and poverty eradication simultaneously'. The first programme objective is to 'provide all persons urgently with the opportunity to earn a sustainable livelihood'.

Also in relation to poverty, the 1995 Fourth World Conference on Women at Beijing, China, in its Platform for Action urged governments to provide adequate safety nets and strengthen state and community-based support systems so that women living in poverty could 'withstand adverse economic environments and preserve their livelihoods, assets and revenues in times of crisis'. It urged multilateral financial and development institutions to create 'an enabling environment that allows women to build and maintain sustainable livelihoods'.

These concerns provided the impetus for the United Nations Development Programme (UNDP) to adopt a 'Sustainable Livelihoods Approach' (SLA) as one of its main planks. UNDP defines this as 'the capability of people to make a living and improve their quality of life without jeopardizing the livelihood options of others, either now or in the future'. The approach promises a poverty reduction strategy through linking employment with the social dimensions of sustainability and equity. Since 1998-99, several international agencies including the Food and Agriculture Organization (FAO), the International Fund for Agricultural Development (IFAD), the International Union for the Conservation of Nature and Natural Resources (IUCN), the British government's Department for International Development (DFID), and a host of international NGOs, have adopted variations of the approach.

Government departments and NGOs in India have also adopted SLA with enthusiasm. The broad sweep of the sustainable livelihoods approach retains resonances to WCED's sustainable development approach and is open to wide interpretation. It is sometimes seen as an objective, sometimes as a framework for analysis, and at other times as a method of implementation, or as all three.

International agencies, government departments and NGOs have used SLA variously to deal with access to resources but have generally not been able to cope with issues of resource control and conflict. This limits their effectiveness in reaching those most affected by economic and environmental distress. On the other side of the spectrum, are agencies and organizations that tend to valorize subsistence lifestyles, especially those of adivasis and forest-dwelling peoples. This too limits their effectiveness in dealing with the many dimensions of poverty, nutritional and health impairment and the lack of livelihood capabilities (see Chapter 3, Box 3.1). In whatever way it is used, the approach perhaps needs to more clearly define the power relations (including gender-power relations) that form the substratum on which livelihood systems rest. For it is these power relations that determine the emergence of particular occupations and livelihoods in particular places and times, and the value that society places on these occupations and livelihoods.

The biovillage model

One of the most widely-publicized of sustainable livelihood interventions is the biovillage model of the MS Swaminathan Research Foundation (MSSRF), Chennai. The conceptual framework of biovillages is attractive because of the elasticity with which it can be stretched to encompass several different objectives. The biovillage has been presented as a model of human development, based on the conservation, equitable utilization and sustainability of natural resources. It envisages groups of poor people improving their economic condition through enhanced skills and knowledge, by applying sophisticated science, biotechnologies, information and communication technologies to local needs in a participatory manner, without harming the ecological and natural resource base. It shifts the emphasis from WCED's sustainable development approach to a more people-centred livelihood approach. From the initiation of biovillages in 1991 in three coastal villages of Pondicherry, within four years, MSSRF extended the model to 19 villages, and subsequently to a couple of villages in coastal Orissa and also to villages in the dry and semi-arid areas around Kannivadi, in Dindigul district of Tamil Nadu. The model has drawn support from governments and has been taken up by a clutch of international agencies; a biovillage 'network' is also being promoted in other parts of India, and in East and South East Asia.

As enunciated by agricultural scientist MS Swaminathan (2001a and 2001b) the biovillage is a model of rural and agricultural development, a 'blueprint' for the future, which is based on the foundation of sustainable human development. The model is expected to concurrently address natural resources conservation and enhancement, poverty eradication and women's empowerment. Its principal components are eco-farming and non-farm employment through remunerative marketing. Ecofarming substitutes chemical and capital inputs by knowledge and biological inputs, such as vermiculture, bio-fertilizers and bio-pesticides, which in turn create new eco-jobs and multiple livelihood opportunities in the villages. So, both on-farm and non-farm employment are addressed.

> New opportunities for earning a living are devised through analysing a family's resources. As a result, landless labouring families take to household mushroom cultivation, ornamental fish-rearing, coir rope-making, rearing small ruminant animals under stall-fed conditions and other enterprises which are within their means. Those with a small plot of land can take to hybrid seed production, floriculture, dairying, poultry and other high value enterprises. Groups of assetless women engage in aquaculture in community ponds. All these exercises are based on micro-level planning, and enterprises supported by micro-credit. (ibid. 2001a)

A perusal of the Annual Reports of MSSRF and occasional publications, over a decade, reveals that the model did not emerge full-fledged although it is now generally projected as such, but that it had the elasticity to evolve in keeping with ground-level experiences and shifts in development policy at the national level. In its earliest stages, the purpose of the biovillage was simply defined as job-led economic growth rooted in the principles of ecology, equity, energy efficiency and employment generation (MSSRF 1991-92). It was seen as a means to take the benefits of new technologies to economically and knowledge-disadvantaged people. Translating the concept into activities meant participatory field testing of different technological options to promote the 'sustainable productivity' of crops and farm animals. The technologies included the adoption of hybrid rice, bio-fertilizers, later bio-pesticides and aquaculture in common ponds. Having established the feasibility of the technologies, specific 'target groups' were also identified including, women, landless labour and marginal farmers (Vijaylakshmi and Hopper 2000), and local institutional mechanisms, biovillage societies (later called councils) and biocentres, were set up in each of the villages selected for the purpose. By the mid 1990s, the concept of biovillages was braided together with the concepts of ecotechnology and sustainable livelihoods (MSSRF 1995-96). Subsequently, yet another braid was added, micro-planning, micro-credit and micro-enterprises. Biovillages, thus, became a 'model' for sustainable development that integrates resource use 'to control degradation of the resource base and alleviate rural poverty through knowledge and skill empowerment' (MSSRF 1996-97). Research and development were focused on seed production, crop management and farm machinery. As these were sectors involving a high level of women's labour, all of these technological interventions had a gendered component. Viewed from the perspective of ecotechnology, biovillages were said to be a model of 'ecotechnologies in action' (MSSRF 1997-98). Although this does not amount to a 'biovillage paradigm' as it is now termed (MSSRF website, 2005), the biovillage-ecotechnology model has been able to identify relevant technologies and facilitate 'ecoenterprises' for asset creation especially for small groups of poor women.

Ecoenterprises require technical, organizational and marketing skills and go beyond earlier interventions, such as the government's Integrated Rural Development Programme because of the clearer emphasis on local participation, the development of local skills, and establishing local institutional mechanisms. For example, a women's SHG in a small hamlet in Tamil Nadu has taken up the production of a the biopesticide, *Tricogramma*, which is a parasitic moth used to control the bollworm (*Heliothis armigera*) that affects cotton and vegetable crops. Technologically, this is a sophisticated intervention but the women have acquired a range of necessary skills to manage this enterprise. The rise in the women's confidence, their incomes and the beneficial impact on the environment are significant gains. Among other such small successes is that of a group of about 12 dalit women who have set up and manage a handmade paper enterprise, using local crop residues, mainly the waste stem of the banana plant and vegetable peelings. The women, who were formerly agricultural labourers, had to overcome resistance from the community, from the men in their families and also their own notions of what a dalit woman was capable of doing (P. Thamizoli 2004 personal communication). The evolution of grassroots women's groups and federations of groups, and the emergence of local leadership are high points of the biovillage. As the emergent women leaders point out, because the approach is one of learning by doing, their illiteracy is not an obstacle in the process of acquiring new skills.

ENHANCING WOMEN'S LIVELIHOOD AND
RESOURCE OPTIONS

Since the 1980s, two major trends in resource management that have had far reaching gendered implications are political decentralization and the promotion of groups of resource users. Local self-government was a dream in the early years after Independence. The model of Community Development Blocks was established but the aim to bring them into close working cooperation with village panchayats proved very difficult to achieve. In the 1980s, new systems of local self-government were started in some states, notably West Bengal, Karnataka, Andhra and Maharashtra. These initiatives covered local bodies from the village to the district, through three tiers of panchayats, mandals and zila parishads. The reservation of seats for disadvantaged groups, dalits, tribals and women provided an impetus to women's political participation, and the experience clearly demonstrated the political effectiveness of administrative decentralization (Mathew 1992, 1997). In these states, women members were able to wield some limited influence over decision-making in the local bodies. Recognizing that women's political participation was key to altering gender relations, the *National Perspective Plan for Women 1988-2000* recommended 30 per cent reservation for women in the local bodies. Attempts to amend the law, however, did not succeed for several years till 1992 when Parliament passed the 73rd and 74th Amendments under Part IX of the Constitution. The 73rd Amendment invests local bodies with control over local resources and the authority to shape the pattern of local land use and development. The law is revolutionary in reserving a third of the elected seats of members and chairpersons for women.

The Amendments did not apply to the tribal areas covered by Schedule V of the Constitution, the autonomous councils of Schedule VI, and to certain tribal states in the north-eastern region (except Sikkim and Arunachal Pradesh). This led to protests and in 1994 after considerable public debate a committee was set up to examine the extension of the 73rd Amendment to the Scheduled Areas. The committee's report resulted in the Provisions of the Panchayats (Extension to the Scheduled Areas) Act, 1996, commonly known as PESA. Under the 73rd Amendment, a third of the seats in the local bodies are statutorily reserved for women, and PESA extends this reservation to tribal women in the Schedule V areas. While PESA takes forward the political process of decentralization initiated in the 73rd Amendment much of the biodiversity-rich north-eastern region continues to be excluded from its provisions.

Shifting the control of local resources, land use, mining leases, water harvesting etc. to elected village and district-level bodies, the panchayat, taluk and zila parishads, should improve resource management and give women more say over these matters. This is happening in a small way in some pockets. For example, an elected woman from northern Karnataka told me that since water-harvesting was now within the purview of the panchayat she had been able to take a Junior Engineer to task about an incomplete water-harvesting structure (Krishna 2004c). Apart from several such anecdotes from different parts of India, there are also well-documented cases particularly from the southern states of women panchayat presidents and members successfully taking on the local administration.

In December 2002, according to press reports, the Association of Women Panchayat Presidents in Tamil Nadu meeting in Madurai said that quarries, tanks (water reservoirs) and trees, which were under government agencies, were actually being controlled by traditional caste panchayat mafias, and that local tank beds were being converted into plots by land sharks. The women leaders demanded that trees, fishing and mining rights should be transferred to the elected panchayats. They pointed out that if the management of local natural resources, especially the water bodies, was handed over to the elected panchayats, this would ensure that the resources were not misused and would provide a permanent income to fund-starved local bodies. The Tamil Nadu women Panchayat Presidents' call to government to hand over local natural resources to the elected panchayats is significant on many counts. This seems to be among the very few concerted efforts by any group of Panchayat Presidents to collectively demand their right over local natural resources, although this is in keeping with the provisions of the 73rd Amendment. (Tamil Nadu has had a relatively efficient block administration but no elected panchayats for years till the Constitutional Amendment made it mandatory.) The collective stand of the local women politicians was two-pronged: against the local officials and the traditional male-dominated panchayat 'mafia'. The pervasive distrust between elected panchayats and block-level officials in Tamil Nadu, as elsewhere, is well-known. Local officials claim that the newly elected panchayats are corrupt, do not understand developmental needs, and work against the best interests of the people, a sentiment which is reciprocated by the panchayats. Local officials may be criticized for not understanding that the panchayats are democratic local government institutions. But this criticism also applies to some NGOs, government line departments and donors, all of whom are encouraging the formation of local NRM user groups, independent of the elected panchayats.

Side-stepping the sharp tussle for space between the politically elected panchayat and the local administration at the block or taluk level, various departments of the state government are directly forming user groups for particular resources, such as forest produce or water. Dalits and women are frequently excluded from such groups. For example, women and the landless have virtually no role in thousands of village-level water-user groups that have been formed in Andhra Pradesh. Despite the National Water Policy (see above) that speaks of making necessary legal and institutional changes at various levels for ensuring an appropriate role for women, the criterion for membership in these bodies is land ownership and women do not have land in their own names. So, although there has been some progress, poor tribal and rural women have not gained a greater or more sustained voice in resource management through the local bodies.

However, several agencies and NGOs have also attempted to develop strategies that integrate various empowering processes into sustainable livelihood projects, and this has also been recognized by state governments. Among the earliest of such NGO interventions are those by the Self-Employed Women's Association (SEWA) with Ahir water users in Banaskantha, Gujarat and the Centre for Women's Development Studies work with Santal women in the wastelands of Bankura, West Bengal. Interestingly, in both cases the state governments had invited the NGOs to work with the women and help change very difficult local conditions.

Water and embroidery in Banaskantha

In the arid and saline areas of Banaskantha district in Kutch, Gujarat, livestock herding is a major occupation; agricultural productivity is low and seasonal migration of families for work is the norm. Fetching water for domestic use is the responsibility of women and girls. This chore can take four to six hours a day, involving several trips carrying head loads of water from the source. Besides domestic and health needs (such as during childbirth), the women also carry water required for a variety of livelihood occupations in which they are engaged, horticulture, animal husbandry, food-processing and handicrafts. In 1986, the Gujarat government's Water Board asked SEWA to help strengthen the local pani panchayats (village water committees). About a hundred villages in two taluks of Banaskantha were getting piped water from borewells located 100 km. away. Pani panchayats had been set up to manage water use but these were inactive, the infrastructure had deteriorated and the system was floundering. SEWA, a pioneer among women's organizations, had considerable experience in organizing poor urban women who were excluded from male-dominated trade unions. Building on this, SEWA began its innovative work with rural women in Banaskantha by linking their livelihood needs, household provision responsibilities, and natural resource conservation. (Crowell 2003; SEWA 2005)

Surveying the pattern of water use in the area, SEWA found that most of the pani panchayats were inactive; when they did function the women on the committees were excluded from participation. Often, neither the local government officials nor the village people were even aware of the existence or the responsibilities of the committees. SEWA's interventions revealed that people desperately needed non-water based livelihood options and that they wanted to restore their traditional water conservation methods. SEWA got many of the local water management groups working and helped the women to revive and maintain traditional water conservation structures, such as check-dams and ponds. It then mobilized the women into groups under the government programme, Development of Women and Children in Rural Areas (DWCRA). These women's groups took up a range of livelihood activities including water harvesting, resin collection from forest trees and embroidery (a traditional skill).

During the Eighth Plan (1992-97) the Union Government had recognized the need for local management of water systems, and later in 1999, guidelines for the participation of women were issued. But on the ground, water management was perceived as being in the male domain. With continuous facilitation by SEWA, despite male resistance and their own misgivings, the women began to take over water management, either through all-women *samitis* (committees) or in mixed committees with the men. The women learnt management skills to maintain the democratic functioning of the samitis and many women also acquired the technical skills of maintaining the water infrastructure. As water availability became less time-consuming, women of the Ahir community who have an ancient tradition of embroidery began to revive the craft. A marketing cooperative was formed to exhibit and sell the women's needlework which fetched high prices in urban markets. The water-user groups thus developed into artisan groups; for many families in the area, women's embroidery has now become the major livelihood occupation.

The entire process has been extensively documented and there is also a documentary film on it made by Sewavideo, another group of SEWA women. Building local institutions, gaining new managerial and technical skills, and enhanced incomes have all contributed to the women's greater self esteem.

Tussar silk cultivation in Bankura

Another well-documented NGO intervention that has primarily focused on women's empowerment is the Centre for Women's Development Studies (CWDS) project in Bankura district of West Bengal (Banerjee 2004). The Santal tribes of Bankura had lost control of their land; most remaining lands were degraded and the formerly dense forests were severely depleted. Impoverishment forced the women to migrate to distant places in search of work. Operation Barga, the West Bengal government's programme to determine the rights of sharecroppers and distribute land to the landless, had not been particularly beneficial to women, because homesteads were not being given to them. In 1980, the state government invited CWDS to work with the women. The project began by forming village level women's samitis for the cooperative greening of wastelands. Tree species were selected to support the rearing of tussar cocoons to improve women's livelihoods. Men's resistance had also to be overcome because of customary taboos in the community against women handling tussar cocoons. The samitis then obtained land which was donated by individual owners. Within three years, with help from the State Tribal Welfare Department and other agencies, and from CWDS (whose staff were funded by ILO), the first plots of land had been afforested for tussar cultivation. In later years, the project spread to other villages and the membership of the samitis increased significantly. Men's resistance to land being owned and controlled by women was overcome by making this a pre-condition for participation in the project. The women gained representation on official local development cooperatives, and those concerned with trade in forest produce. The income from the annual yield of tussar cocoons helped to finance a range of individual and group enterprises. Participating in a business and planning ahead has given the women a sense of security. In their own perception, the enterprises were much more than businesses; they were an expression of the women's new found self-esteem. This is clearly reflected in Malti Mandi's remarks in the epigram at the start of this chapter. While migration has not completely stopped, the women's material resources and personal strength enables them to choose when to migrate.

Interestingly, from the very beginning, CWDS emphasized professional management skills and the women were specially trained for this. Indeed, much less attention was paid to the technology of afforestation and tussar rearing. It is also significant that the coordinator, the management specialist and the majority of the field staff in the Bankura project are all men. That the men were able to establish rapport with the women is an indication that gender-sensitivity is not a woman's preserve. When a gendered perspective is integrated into a project from the very beginning, as the Bankura project has done, women need not just be involved in raising nurseries and planting trees, and a range of issues related to women's autonomy and self-image and their immediate resource needs can be effectively addressed. Over the years, the role of the facilitating NGO has also changed as the women's samitis have gained strength and a measure of independence. Organizational skills, representation on official local bodies, increased decision-making power, and greater self-esteem are important long-term gains and could be the basis for gender-equity and benefit-sharing in community resource management. However, despite all these gains, the Bankura women continue to struggle because their livelihoods are threatened by the import of Chinese silk yarn under the new trade regime.

Wastelands for biomass

Working among the Bhils in the Panchamahals district is SARTHI an NGO whose primary focus has been on women's empower-

ment. A means to this end was the process of organizing to enhance local natural resources. SARTHI's interventions have, therefore, been geared more to the organizational aspects than to the
technical aspects of the resource base itself. In this area, women's
work includes the gathering of biomass, an increasingly difficult
task because of extensive deforestation. Madhu Sarin (1993) notes
that several women of the area have remarked: 'Men just expect to
be served cooked food. They aren't bothered about where the firewood comes from. That is our problem!'. The women's status was
low; they own little land or property, and generally it was the
men who took decisions about how the land was used. SARTHI
helped to set up several women's wasteland development groups
to grow biomass and included a range of group activities geared to
enhance women's self-esteem. In 1989, a SARTHI team also
began to record the local knowledge of medicinal herbs used for
women's health problems, and medicinal plant cultivation was
integrated into the wasteland programme.

Long before SHGs had become the buzz word in development circles, these women formed 20 'savings groups' in different
villages to get emergency funds and to be free from money
lenders. The interaction with women of other villages was empowering. In this region, women have few opportunities to meet
and cooperate with other women outside their family and community networks. Even within the community, the only time
women get together is for events such as marriage, death or religious ceremonies where they are expected to perform their traditional roles. Through the SARTHI programme, women were able
to share experiences with women of diverse castes and communities. Besides acquiring new knowledge, they were able to shed
some of their traditional *sharam*, shyness and inhibitions.

Most difficult, however, was the task of obtaining tenurial
rights to the common lands. As a first step each group had to
obtain a 'no objection certificate' (NOC); they also needed
panchayat resolutions supporting their right to work on the land
and use its usufruct. But the legal validity of this arrangement is
uncertain. There is also the fear that the panchayat may reverse its
decision. This is why, as Sarin has pointed out, women need a
greater political voice in the local bodies.

Changing gender relations through lift-irrigation

In the same arid and drought prone Panchmahals district of Gujarat, there is some evidence (Ahmed and Krishna 1998) to show that small lift-irrigation cooperatives have benefited women, contrary to the general trend of women losing control over farming with the introduction of large scale irrigation. The Bhil cultivators of the Panchmahals are a patrilineal tribal group. The division of labour is traditionally gendered: men plough and market but all other farming and domestic tasks are done jointly or by women. Male migration is high and women have traditionally taken on the role and responsibilities of the household head, including farm management. Improving water supplies both for domestic uses and irrigation is a critical need. Ahmed and Krishna (ibid: 2) point out that the wider irrigation sector has all along been gender-resistant and suggest three reasons for this: First, the nature of the irrigation system itself, in which equity is viewed 'spatially' as equal sharing by all irrigation users along the line. This overlooks the wealth status of water user communities as also gender-differentiated needs for water. Second, the separation of irrigation and agriculture development, which results in underestimating women's role and contribution to irrigation, which has been far less documented in comparison to their role in agriculture. Third, the division between water for domestic uses including cooking (seen as non-economic usage) and water for productive use, i.e. water for industry and irrigation for agriculture.

It is against this background, that the Gujarat-based NGO, NM Sadguru Water and Development Foundation, used lift irrigation schemes as an 'entry point' and directly addressed gender needs from the start. Lift Irrigation Cooperatives (LICs), which included women, were set up in the villages to manage the schemes locally and oversee equitable distribution of water. Traditionally, both men and women have been involved in irrigating the fields, or this has been done by women alone in the absence of the men (due to migration). However, under the law governing cooperatives in Gujarat, only land holders, that is male heads of households, were recognized as members. Following advocacy from Sadguru and other NGOs, the law was amended in 1996 to enable women to be part of the LICs and serve on the executive committees. The impact of three lift-irrigation schemes on gender roles in agriculture shows that improved irrigation has brought about agrarian transformation and that women's participation in decision-making has been enhanced to a limited extent Both incomes and food, fodder and fuel supplies in the area have improved, with immediate benefits to women. Many of the women interviewed by the researchers felt that the lift irrigation scheme had changed their lives dramatically. The women had stopped migrating, although in families with surplus labour and in critical times, men continued to migrate for work. The researchers conclude (Ahmed and Krishna ibid. 32) that while the 'women's participation in irrigation management varies depending on the extent to which they are involved in agriculture', the women in the executive committees 'have shown that gender differences play a part in mediating people's access and control of water resources.' They say further that the women's 'keen participation in irrigation management and other community issues has given them a new confidence and enhanced their self-identity. However, the extent to which economic empowerment can be translated into social and political empowerment (greater control of resources and decision-making) remains to be seen.'

Animal healing skills: from fathers to daughters

The work of Anthra (an NGO set up by women veterinarians in Andhra Pradesh and Maharashtra) and its associates is a unique example of facilitation related to animal husbandry (see Ramdas, Ghotge et. al. 2004). Generally, all the tasks connected to animal husbandry are women's responsibility but animal health care is firmly in the hands of male healers. Anthra began with the premise that for half a century 'mainstream' development had ignored the existing knowledge base of communities and was designing programme interventions that were unrelated to the existing local conditions and expertise. It felt that a vast resource of mainly oral knowledge on livelihoods, cultural practices and local natural resources was being lost. Anthra saw women, dalits and adivasis as marginalized groups within this larger framework. Working with local people's NGOs in six different agro-ecological regions in Andhra Pradesh and Maharashtra, Anthra's participatory research project looked at gender issues related to livestock development, and interlinked livelihood systems, agriculture and forestry. A key focus of the work was on local animal healing practices.

On the one hand, macro development policies (such as changes from traditional multi-crop agriculture to mono-crop cultivation) were displacing and marginalizing women. On the other, traditional gender-power relations had also excluded women from local knowledge systems. Women performed all the daily care and management of livestock, but the knowledge and skills of animal healing (with the exception of poultry) was entirely in the men's domain. Although there were a very few women healers, knowledge of herbal medicine and veterinary practices was customarily passed by male healers to their sons. Women recognized that this was a constraint in their work in livestock production, and together with Anthra they began to challenge this. The traditional male animal healers were aware of the need to document and validate their practices and feared that this knowledge would soon be lost because their sons were not interested in carrying on the tradition. Taking advantage of this apprehension, Anthra began negotiating for space for women healers, and elicited the support of the men healers. Women were trained in the specific knowledge and skills related to veterinary practices and their own health care. This was placed all along in a large context of issues of gender and the sustainability of resources and livelihoods. Unlike their male counterparts the women animal health healers were always reachable and they soon gained the confidence of the community.

Organizing around seeds and grain banks in Medak

The Deccan Development Society's work related to enhancing food security for dalits in the dry and semi-arid areas of Medak district in Andhra Pradesh is well-known (DDS 2005; Rao). The traditional crops in the area are sorghum and millets, 'coarse' grains suitable to unirrigated rain-fed land. These crops used to be supplemented by a diverse variety of vegetables (greens and tubers) and medicinal plants. Food production was in the women's domain and women also selected and conserved seed. The official Public Distribution System (PDS) provided milled rice (procured from the paddy-rich coastal areas of the state) at subsidized prices through identified 'ration shops'. This replaced the nutritious sorghum and millets and altered diets in the area. DDS had been working with dalit women's sanghams (groups) around Zaheerabad in Medak for several years. In 1995 it took the lead in implementing an unusual government-funded programme based on the principle of local procurement and distribution of locally-grown coarse grains through a public system of ration shops, an Alternative Public Distirbution System (APDS).

DDS devised a well-planned four-stage programme. It first addressed the household needs of the dalits by encouraging them to collectively improve their small patches of land, which they had got through the state government's land reform programme. Appropriate bunding, trenching and the addition of top soil resulted in higher crop yields. Next, DDS helped the sanghams identify lands that had been left fallow by marginal farmers and, in keeping with the stipulations of the project, these barren lands were leased and cultivated. The cultivators repaid the small government loan in kind with grain, mainly sorghum, over three years. This grain and a small additional amount contributed by the participating cultivators went into a village 'grain bank'. This store of grain was then used for the neediest families, identified by the sanghams themselves, who could buy the grain at subsidized rates. This decentralized alternative public distribution system enhanced the livelihood and food security of marginalized people. Dalit women reclaimed their decision-making role in food production and regained their self esteem as community seed keepers. At the same time marginalized lands were improved and the local diversity of food crops maintained. Some children attended special innovative DDS 'green schools' where among other things they also learnt craft skills from local craftspersons. Simultaneously, DDS has been active in getting women to speak out and fight the local patriarchal system, and has also established a 'safe home' where women, who faced domestic violence or other problems, can find refuge.

The remarkable success of the DDS-led APDS in Medak for promoting local self-sufficiency for poor farmers was achieved despite many odds. Very early in the project, government funding was stalled and then withheld on technicalities. Political leaders rubbished the project, DDS and the dalit women. Writing about this experience, Rukmini Rao of DDS points to the 'clear alliance between political and bureaucratic elites in the district.' DDS steadfastly refused to pay bribes to hasten the flow of project funds. It had no links with any political party. Moreover, the dalit women's struggle for higher wages and their reduced dependence on local landlords aggravated the wealthy. Affronted by the self-reliance of dalit women the caste backlash was swift. The women had 'fought to escape the corrupt labour relations of bondage, thereby denying the local elites cheap child labour'. Rao (ibid) points out that although some senior administrators were sympathetic to the dalit women's cause, they did not want to risk censure from the political leadership. As she says, 'it is difficult to avoid the conclusion that this conflict is about power, control and superiority.' The silence of the administrator is 'a political mechanism which preserves the status quo'. This means preserving the poverty, social discrimination and subordination of dalits, which seems to be essential to maintaining the elites' own sense of personal security.

Beyond 'gender-balance'

Government programmes continue to be conventionally premised on a sexual division of labour and responsibilities. Household needs for water, fuel wood, fodder, seeds etc. are characterized as 'women's needs' serving to reinforce women's familial nurturing role. At the same time, men's natural resource and provisioning responsibilities are overlooked. This was most tellingly apparent at a seminar in New Delhi (at which I happened to be present) where the Secretary of the Ministry of Environment blandly stated that if there was a problem about drinking water the women should take out a demonstration and demand water from the civic authorities! It simply did not occur to him that water for the household might also be seen as men's responsibility. Such attitudes result in an instrumental approach of using women's labour and skills to improve the efficiency of programmes rather than empowering women to gain control of resources and take management decisions. Rarely do large-scale projects interrogate the unequal power relations which make women more often than men fill the role of responsible nurturers and resource managers, and which give them 'women's needs'. The great reluctance to address the socio-cultural practices and gender ideologies that restrict women's autonomy, mobility and capacity to participate in decisions reflects the patriarchal framework and substratum of institutionalized resource management.

Unlike the large scale NRM programmes that have attempted to enhance the natural resource base by using the skills and labour of rural or tribal women, instrumentally, and have assumed that women will inevitably benefit from an improved resource base, the NGO interventions discussed above did not make this assumption but attempted to reconcile different objectives. The more innovative NGO strategies attempt to extend women's mobility and their ability to reclaim public spaces. This requires improving women's access to and control of productive assets. These may be in the form of joint ownership of land with husbands, or independent titles to land, and collective ownership of common resources including non-timber forest produce, ponds for fishing and aquaculture, newly created water supplies and so on. The ownership of assets gives women some negotiating authority. In order to build upon this, however, women also need opportunities to develop skills and access to credit and technology. While this enhances women's self esteem and helps to counter subordination, it is women's collective strength ('sisterhood') in grassroots organizations that could give them the confidence to cope with discrimination and violence, whether in the community or the family. In order to participate effectively in public action, women also need lowered workloads and more leisure.

Social acceptance for such empowerment and changes in gender relations do not come painlessly. Many interventions, however, tend to sidestep conflicts that arise in the process of asset creation for the poor (dalits, tribals) at the community level, and shut their eyes to intra-household gender-power conflicts. Women's public gains can be undermined by male 'backlash', entrenched elite and caste opposition, male alcoholism and domestic violence against women, as well as men's resistance to sharing domestic and caring responsibilities. Addressing such issues, of course, requires different kinds of interventions over a longer term than is possible within the ambit of a development and natural resource programme. Failing to address issues of conflict at the community and household level could undermine the social sustainability of gender 'mainstreaming'. Gender equity in resource management requires more than gender 'balance' in programmes.

NOTES

[1] Spoken in 1990 at a Seminar in Manila on 'Gender Issues in Agriculture' (convened by the Asian Development Bank) translated and recorded by Vina Mazumdar (1998: 258) who was present as the interpreter.

9

Reflections on Research and Research Methods

The master's tools will never dismantle the master's house.

—Audre Lorde (1984: 110)

The previous chapter looked at different approaches to achieving gender equity in development and resource management, at the level of policy, programmes and project interventions. In this chapter, the focus shifts to the challenge of 'mainstreaming' gender in the research process itself. I turn first to a few selected studies that 'open up the community'. Such studies are useful in uncovering a historical legacy of conflicts over resource usage among sections of the community since pre-colonial times but they tell us little about the gendered patterns of such usage. I then look at other studies that 'open up the household' to reveal the intricacies of women's lives and livelihoods in diverse present-day communities. Insights from these learnings provide the background to the second section where I discuss a range of participatory and gendered approaches to research, including Gender Analysis. The chapter also reflects upon the difficulties faced by researchers in giving up control of the 'master's tools' (see epigram above) and striving towards more inclusive research processes.

LEARNINGS FROM RESEARCH

Opening up community resource usage

The depletion and degradation of India's natural resource base is linked to the industrialization of the British economy and the expansion of the British empire in the nineteenth century. The natural resources of the colonies fed a narrow range of British manufactures and the new colonial markets provided an outlet for manufactured goods from Britain. Iniquitous trade relations helped to finance imports of food into Britain and raw materials for its urban growth. The objectives of NRM in British India were, therefore, geared to this process; for instance, forestry was primarily intended to augment forest resources and provide the timber to supply British industry and the needs of British forces during the World Wars. This has been documented since the late 19th century by Dietrich Brandis, later by E.P. Stebbing, and subsequently by H.G. Champion (Champion and Seth 1968; see Guha 1989). British interests influenced the land use pattern and the spread of irrigation as in the canal colonies in the Punjab. Strategic and imperial interests also governed the growth of the metropolitan port cities, Calcutta (Kolkata), Bombay (Mumbai) and Madras (Chennai) on the coast. After Independence, the pressures of modern development continued to alter India's natural resource base, as raw materials were used to feed India's own industrial expansion and growing urban needs. In recent decades, commercialization, economic liberalization and globalization have intensified this process with far-reaching consequences.

While recognizing that colonialism altered community resource use patterns and that contemporary market forces have a powerful corrupting influence, we need to be wary of popular environmentalism and celebratory approaches, including strands of ecofeminism, that sentimentalize the traditional community-environment interactions of the past. Village communities in many parts of pre-colonial India did have well-established practices of resource management but such community-regulated access to forests, pasture lands, or water sources was not always egalitarian, especially in settled agrarian communities. Recent historical studies from different regions of India reflect the complex and changing patterns of natural resource usage in particular local situations. Power and dominance in pre-colonial India were related to the control of resources, land, labour and capital.

Opening up the community enables us to understand how traditional non-market systems of managing common resources were linked to the relations of power within a community. For instance, David Mosse's (1995) work on the extensive spread of tank irrigation in Tamil Nadu reveals the existence of power structures that were contested and negotiated. Entitlements to water were based on caste and kin networks, and related to the control of land and other resources. Unequal access to water, the amount available, the times when it was available, all of this was institutionalized. Later, under the British, the colonial systems of revenue collection and consolidation of private property broke the old political linkages, undermining traditional water management. In the post Independence period, the government took over minor irrigation. Reciprocal caste-based relations were weakened by new market relations but the privileged continued to exercise control over water. Water usage was facilitated by community management, or by panchayat management, both of which tended to protect the interests of dominant caste groups. Mosse's historical perspective shows that the local resource management system is embedded in and influenced by changing sets of social relations and the wider process of political transformation.

Similarly, in a micro-study of ecological and land use changes in Gorakhpur, in present day eastern Uttar Pradesh, Meena Bhargava (1999) uses historical sources to detail processes that took place two centuries ago. The *sarkar* (principality) of Gorakhpur, which was part of the Awadh *suba* (state) was ceded to the East India Company in 1801. Gorakhpur's economy was vibrant in the late eighteenth and early nineteenth centuries. New crops were introduced to enhance productivity and the acreage under cash crops increased rapidly in response to market stimuli. The cropping pattern was determined by the suitability of the soil, and conflicting demands were overcome by more land being brought under cultivation in the terai, in the Himalayan foothills. There was no decline in the acreage under food grains and the different crops grown for consumption as food and for sale as commodities complemented one another. Changes in the 'forest-line' were already taking place when the East India Company came on the scene, and it furthered these changes within a new structure and policy framework for the twin objectives of providing an adequate and profitable source of timber and expanding cultivation. Much later in the 1850s, the Company was 'overcome with the fear of a deforested Gorakhpur'. From then on the Company's approach changed, conservation was perceived as 'an indication of agrarian prosperity', which 'could not be abandoned for material interests'. So, 'rigid plans' were made to save and preserve timber, conserve forests and create a balanced ecosystem. Despite the Company's understanding that forest conservation and agrarian prosperity were connected, somewhat contrarily the Company was also re-formulating and re-structuring landed property rights to facilitate the clearing of land and the expansion of cultivation. Landholders and cultivators responded by converting forests and wastelands into areas of settled cultivation, extending the frontier northwards into the terai and ensuring the rapid growth of the economy.

Initially, there had been no subversion of indigenous knowledge, customs or Mughal institutions, which were appropriated and woven into the new revenue system. Yet, in order to underline its power and authority, Bhargava says the Company 'soon shifted to simplification, modification and reinterpretation of the local custom and law.' This caused conflicts and resistance, and contributed to the 1857 revolt against Company power. But even as the 'large imperial Mughal cities were in disarray, there was a smooth flow of capital in Gorakhpur. Inland and foreign trade were a stimulant to growing commercialization and markets. Expanding market forces engulfed Gorakhpur and redirected the productive capacities of the rural and urban class to suit market requirements' (p.259). In the case of Gorakhpur, urban development did not undermine homogeneity and independence in the social structure but reflected the people's flexibility and capacity to respond to market stimuli.

The study documents the 'strong affinity' of the peasants with the land and forests but this is not romanticized: 'It was their home, a shelter and if ever their actions caused any adversities, they were so mild as to have little impact on the environment.' However, this does not mean that there was ecological equilibrium in pre-cession Gorakhpur. Bhargava points out that 'the landholders and cultivators were not "natural conservators" of their environment.' They knew 'the value of the forests—as a source of moisture, fodder, firewood and timber' and 'exploited it either themselves or through merchants and traders to earn profits' (p. 71). She goes on to say that 'The institution of forestry in Gorakhpur provides an interesting case study of the evolution and changing attitudes towards forests and land use. For the local inhabitants and the villages, this vast expanse of vegetation represented perpetuity, a way of life, an unawareness that this mass could even be exploited or extracted for more than what was required for local use or local consumption. There were, nevertheless, no signs of rigidity or 'status quoism' in their upbringing and approach' (p. 87). She notes further that 'As commercialism and material concerns penetrated into the villages, changes in attitudes became visible. The zamindars of the villages, who had once adamantly stood by their trees, protecting them from human compulsions, bent before the forces of commercialism, cutting down trees and even growing trees for timber trade.'

A similarly complex and nuanced picture of change is reflected in the study by M. V. Nadkarni (with Pasha and Prabhakar, 1989) of the political economy of forest use in the areca nut (betel nut) growing areas of Uttara Kannada district of Karnataka in the early years of the 20th century. The study explicitly shows the class bias that has always existed within the local economy. Class differentiation determined the control over land and forest benefits; the commercialization of the local and larger economies encouraged privatization rather than the evolution of local community management. The study points out that rich farmers, the land-controlling class, were the main beneficiaries of free rider resources like green manure and small wood from the forest. The richest gained the most both in absolute terms and in terms of their share of the total benefits accruing from forest use. But it was the poor peasants who were the greatest beneficiaries in terms of their own income. The study also points out that there were no local conventions for the equitable use of forest resources (p161): 'In the long drawn struggle against the Forest Dept, the locals rarely raised any environmental issue or gave any evidence of such awareness. If the local use of forests in the pre-commercial past was sustainable, it seems to have been due more to the limited commercial pressures from the larger economy than to the environmentally sound local practices. This is contrary to the popular impression that, traditionally and everywhere, forests are a community reserve equally shared by all. Deflating many populist assumptions, Nadkarni argues that we cannot now go back to a supposedly idyllic stage of exclusive local use of forests, just as the state cannot expect to protect forests purely by oppressive regulation of local use. (Krishna 1996a)

As these studies show, community-environment interactions are specific to particular ecosystems and resources, at particular points of time. While there have been many examples of non-market community resource management systems these should not be idealized and taken as the norm. Contemporary mismanagement of natural resources does not mean that past systems were always ecologically sound, socially harmonious and gender-equitable, although such a vision of the past is most seductive for certain sections of Western and Indian environmentalists (see Krishna 1996a and Rangan 2000). Moreover, even insightful studies (such as those cited above) tell us little about the gendered dimensions of resource usage in the past.

Opening up households in the community

Since the mid-1980s, as we have seen in earlier chapters, there has been a slowly growing interest in the significance of gender in understanding livelihood systems, patterns of resource use and conflict, and the strategies adopted by women to cope with external pressures. Most researchers (like practitioners) have found it difficult to open up the household and have tended to confine themselves to studies of women's waged work and employment in the 'public' sphere. However, some researchers with feminist perspectives have focused on women's work and labour both in the non-monetized and the market economy to comprehend intra-household dynamics within the wider community.

Anita Agnihotri, an administrator in Orissa, points out that for very poor adivasis it is 'hard to judge the problems' of men and women separately because 'both are so steeped in economic disadvantage.' Yet, for poor women the 'problems of living' are indeed different from those of the men, which is why Agragami, a local activist NGO in the tribal belt of western Orissa, has had to address women's concerns:

> The problems of living are much worse for women, because of several interconnected factors. One: because of the high infant-and-child death rate, mothers can't commit to birth control, and giving birth to so many children ruins their physical health. Two: almost sixty per cent of the responsibility for producing and collecting food lies with the woman. Yet, she's excluded from, or ineffective in, the political decision-making processes even at the local level. Three: absolutely no hard information about the available development schemes reaches these women. Planning and implementation is a male-driven machine. (Agnihotri 2001: 7)

Agnihotri goes on to say that at 'the same time a variety of legal and social restrictions constantly circumscribe' women's lives and that they have no 'direct way to overcome the adversity of their environment' except collective organization. Vidya Das of Agragami (2000) has remarked that economic initiatives such as women's collective marketing of non-timber forest produce and their striving for a fair price in the local markets do have the men's support, but that it is difficult to address intra-household issues.

Yet, all the three factors that Agnihotri mentions as contributing to the marginalization of women, i.e. poor health, exclusion from decision-making and lack of information, are linked both to public policy and to intra-household gender-power relations. This is so even in contexts where the women are not involved in the local market economy as in parts of Himachal Pradesh. Writing about two villages in the 1990s, Brenda Crawley (2001) has suggested that because the Himachali men are 'pulled into capitalism' and more active in the local markets, 'when the economy changes, they are affected more directly than women'. The women are not directly affected by the market forces because they do not work outside the home but they are affected indirectly.

The commercialization of forestry, especially timber extraction, has led to a deteriorating environment and the burden of coping has fallen disproportionately on the women. Crawley suggests that while men 'despair as they lose income as well as self-esteem' and, therefore, 'turn to alcohol', the women who 'also despair' are able to face hardships better than the men 'because they have always had to rely on their own skills in collecting fuel and fodder and making do with what little resources they have'. Crawley's gendered insights are derived by looking at the community from the vantage point of the household. Because women's work in household provisioning already constitutes the 'mainstream' of local livelihood systems, this is often the more critical to family survival in times of stress compared to the men's entry into the conventionally understood main stream of the economy.

A few researchers have also shown that women and men experience and respond to environmental stress differently. Studying seasonality and drought in a village in Ahmedabad district of Gujarat, Martha Chen (1991) highlights women's close linkage with non-market livelihood resources and the different responses of various members of the household to the loss of resources. Unravelling the linkages between environmental and economic stress experienced by poor rural communities, Chen underlines two factors: the significance of women's work and gender as a means to understand household behaviour; and the critical importance of non-market resources, relationships and institutions. The study shows that since the feudal period, the privatization of common property resources (CPRs) has changed both the cropping pattern and the occupational pattern, but all the landless are not poor. Unskilled self-employment consists mainly of collecting, processing and selling natural resources for a small profit, which contributes significantly to livelihoods. Entry into the migrant labour market and flexibility of occupations are strategies for survival. For the poor (landless labour/tenants and small land-holding households), CPRs provide a seasonal buffer against shortages. But this buffer capacity is limited by several factors, such as privatization, over use and degradation, and conflicts between different sections of the village community. For instance, the shepherds have a greater commercial interest in CPRs. Village institutions and kinship ties have a role in providing access to free goods and traditional social security. But market forces are far more significant in the tenancy, labour and credit markets, and traditional transactions themselves are sensitive to the stimulus of the market. As the study points out, the problem with the market is that it does not guarantee subsistence in lean seasons.

Although severe drought does not mean starvation, Chen's study shows that the ability to build up surplus is greatly reduced, local employment opportunities (like share cropping) become more risky, the scope for reciprocity is limited, common pastures and water resources are over-used leading to conflicts over rights of access, and traditional security systems are strained beyond capacity. The findings suggest that in normal years labourers are the most vulnerable, but that in drought years while labourers get government employment, the vulnerability of peasant and shepherd households increases. For rural households, whether peasant, pastoral, artisinal or labourer, adjusting to seasonality and drought is integral to their overall livelihood systems. The government responds effectively in a severe drought with short-term measures like providing employment on relief works, but it does not respond to seasonal difficulties. Chen (ibid p.224) points out that 'By focusing on the short term, public drought management does not address the need to develop dry land farming technologies (crop, soil, water management), to regenerate and conserve the biomass, to provide employment on a regular basis, and to provide seasonal loans and inputs in normal years.' Therefore, she argues that what is required is 'drought-proofing', rather than drought management.

It is, of course, not possible to generalize from one village about rural phenomena but the insight into what makes different households in the study village adopt different coping strategies has wider implications. Regarding the significance of gender, Chen (p. 109) makes four points. First, women work in all sectors of the local economy and they do so for longer hours than the men. Second, some livelihood activities are women's special responsibility, 'notably, the domestic and reproductive activities associated with household maintenance and the gathering, collecting and storage of free goods (especially, fuel, fodder and water).' Third, she points out that women's roles and responsibilities, as compared to men's, 'cut across self-provisioning, income conserving and market activities to a greater extent.' Fourth, women play 'a significant role in networking caste and kinship relationships to help manage seasonal shortfalls' and they participate fully both in the local labour market and in the migrant labour market.

The labour of women and girls is critical not only to the economies of their own households but also to the wider economy of the productive systems in which they are engaged, whether this is undervalued and underpaid work, such as family coir-yarn production by very poor women and girls in Kerala (see Nieuwenhuys 1999) or paid employment in the formal economy, such as the tea plantations studied by Piya Chatterjee in *A Time for Tea* (2003). Carefully unstitching the politics of women's labour in a north Bengal tea plantation in the 1990s, Chatterjee points out that the euphemistically named 'tea gardens' in the lap of the Himalaya were actually acquired for plantation through the Wasteland Rules of 1838 that designated blocks of forests as waste and opened them up to tea companies. These virtual fiefdoms recruited plantation labour from the adivasi belt of Chotanagpur (Jharkhand) and elsewhere because local communities in Assam and Bengal resisted the call to work for wages. By the turn of the century, migrant women were doing the most labour intensive job of plucking tea and the gendered stereotype of women's 'nimble fingers' and delicate touch had emerged. The suggestion of women's delicacy also imbued the romantic depictions of women tea pluckers on the tea packets. In post-colonial (and now neo-colonial) times the feminization of labour in the production process continues, even as the image of upper class feminine gentility in the consumption of tea is reinforced. When Piya Chatterjee (ibid. 4) discusses these depictions with the women tea pluckers, they are amused and derisive; their hands are hardened, cut and stained black with tea juice: '*Hath dekho . . . Yeh kam . . . yeh natak nahi he, didi.*' (Look at our hands . . . this work . . . this is no play-acting, didi.)

Chatterjee points out that the company's profits, and the planter's power and efficiency in managing the estate, rest on the disciplining and surveillance of labour. Much of this is achieved through ideologies of sexuality, grafted feudal norms of gender roles and behaviour, bodily controls and individual coercion. The political economy of the field is a sexual economy. At every level of power, men wield the planter's *hukum*, a regime which gives working men the 'right' to rule over women in labour. Yet, in village households there is also a 'displacement' of power with customary masculine authority and honour being eroded because women are the primary wage-earners and male unemployment is high, resulting in alcoholism and violence. The women know that their wage-earning is one of the reasons they are beaten. 'Violence is the modality of both power and its lack.' (ibid.: 284)

By opening up households within the tea plantation community, Chatterjee's research reveals the many layers of exploitation, the complexity and context-specificity of gendered livelihood practices. Such nuanced analysis shows that gender is not simply a problem of paying attention to 'women's needs', and that 'integrating' women into systems of productive labour may benefit the political economy but may not necessarily change women's position unless gender-power relations, constructions of masculinity and femininity, and the 'sexual economy' of the household and field are also addressed. ·

Each of the researchers cited above 'speaks' from a different place, that of an administrator, a development practitioner, an activist researcher-photographer, a social anthropologist. Located as 'participant observers' and viewing the community from the vantage point of the household, and of marginalized women, they bring an engaged perspective and a gendered approach to their research. Contrary to Audre Lorde's (1984: 110) well-known feminist precept (see epigram), they each extend the 'master's tools' of their own disciplines, bending these both to express the voices of disadvantaged women and to yield fresh insights. Research that opens up the community and the household, from the inside out as it were, helps us to a conceptual understanding of several threads that make up the pattern of women's lives: a) Although women may have more in common with the men of their class than with other women, the 'problems of living' are indeed different for women and men; b) Women's household provisioning responsibilities gives them a resilience based on skills and coping strategies that men may not have; c) Even as households in a community are not homogenous and vary in their responses to environmental stress, the significance of gender in understanding household behaviour cuts across households; and d) The wider economy depends on the continuation of underpaid, undervalued gender-disaggregated work. Community resource usage cannot be researched without opening up the community. The complexity and context-specificity of women's livelihood activities, in which inside-outside spaces are not clearly defined, cannot be discerned without also opening up households within the community. This process of unstitching requires many different kinds of tools. My own view is that the 'master's tools' can be used to dismantle patriarchal epistemologies, but that we do need more inclusive research processes and other kinds of tools to build other kinds of houses.

PARTICIPATORY AND GENDERED RESEARCH METHODS

The feminist focus on the family as the 'central site' of women's oppression has had wide influence on women's movements and on gender studies but it has not had much effect on disciplines like forestry, ecology and social anthropology, which are basic to NRM. This is partly a problem of internalized biases and partly a problem of how to make the linkage. As Henrietta Moore (1988: 126-7) has commented, 'The sexual division of labour in the home is related in complex and multifarious ways to the sexual division of labour in the workplace and in society at large. Women's subordinate position is the product of both their economic dependence on men within the 'family'/household and of their confinement to a domestic sphere by ideologies of mothering, caring and nurturing.' Moore says the feminist anthropological position on these issues is 'not clear-cut', partly because 'the available data are of such extraordinary richness and complexity that they defy even the most serious attempt at synthesis, let alone generalization.' However, she also points out that 'it is clear that any straightforward explanation of women's subordination which does not take into account the enormous variation in women's circumstances and in gender and "familial" ideologies would be not only reductionist but extremely ethnocentric.'

The struggle to overcome ethnocentricity and express 'grassroots' experiences and people's voices is a matter of concern for people themselves, and for activists, development practitioners, natural resource managers and academic social scientists, all of whom may have something to contribute to the evolution of relevant research processes. Over the last many decades, different methodological approaches have emerged, shaping both development research, communication and interventions. By methodology I mean the guiding philosophy or approach, the methods and the tools. The approach chosen influences (either implicitly or explicitly) the choice of research topics, the methods and also determines the tools used. Different tools lend themselves to different methods. Here, I briefly discuss a variety of methods and tools used by practitioners and action-researchers and a few of my own attempts to find a creative and rigorous synthesis of methods. But the first step is overcoming bias in the researchers' own minds.

Overcoming research bias

Researchers and practitioners who have been trained in conventional approaches to resource management, have to go through a difficult process of 'unlearning' to overcome biases in outlook that have become ingrained in resource management. Many researchers find it difficult to envisage the power equations of class, caste and gender that determine who does what in both traditional and modern societies. For instance, descriptions of women's roles and responsibilities in farming, biodiversity and forest conservation often reveal a researcher's own nostalgia for the subsistence lifestyles of the past. Poor tribal and local communities in the pre-colonial period are naively romanticized as having 'simple lifestyles' and 'few wants', without recognizing the vulnerability of such lives. The widespread assumption that 'traditional' subsistence lifestyles were always a matter of choice, governed by a concept of ecological sustainability needs to be re-examined and critiqued (as has been done by Kelkar and Nathan 1992; Krishna 1996: 89-92; Jeffrey 1998 and others). Moreover, as Amartya Sen (1990) has emphasized, when women whose lives are severely deprived express contentment with their situation, this reflects the limitations of their experience and is not an adequate measure of their quality of life. Nor are historical (or contemporary) instances of elite women enjoying political power a reflection of the status of the average women of their period.

Many researchers and practitioners struggle to shed their own previous assumptions and training in the natural science disciplines to undertake a gendered analysis of the inner dynamics of the household and community. They may accurately note that women do not own property but yet conclude that women and men are treated equally. Despite considerable evidence to the contrary, the conviction persists that male and female roles are invariably complementary and equitable. They note the restrictions on women's movements but this is seen as being in the women's own interest, for their 'protection'. As already mentioned, the 'traditional wisdom' of conservation practices is lauded even as the gendered and caste character of those very same practices is uncritically recorded (for instance, taboos regarding women touching the seeds of certain food plants or entering sacred groves). It is not recognized that denying women resource ownership and curtailing their mobility, ostensibly for 'protection', is a deeply embedded patriarchal strategy of using different norms for men and women to reinforce inequitable relations of power. Indeed, the acceptance of dual norms for men and women is so firmly embedded in theory and practice (see Chapter 3) that researchers and practitioners find it difficult to distinguish between what women do in the household and community (their gender roles) and what is natural for them to do because of their biological/ sexual attributes (see also Krishna 2004a). In order to re-vision resource management, therefore, we need to recognize and counter our own biases; doing gender in the field cannot be separated from internalizing a gendered perspective into one's life. This is the first step towards building new frameworks and developing the new tools required to re-construct the 'master's house'.

A variety of methods

The conventional anthropological method of participant observation is attributed to B. K. Malinowski in the early years of the 20th century but may have had an even earlier lineage. The attempt by colonial anthropologists to grasp a 'native' perspective from a 'native' point of view through long months of observation and continuous interaction in the field have not had much impact on modern development practice in India. Perhaps the only exception is the work of Verrier Elwin that influenced independent India's tribal development policy in what was then the North East Frontier Agency (NEFA), now Arunachal Pradesh. At the other end of the scale, in more recent times, are anthropological inputs that have facilitated the administrative recognition and certification, at the district-level, of particular socio-cultural groups so that they are included in State lists of Scheduled Tribes (Thamizoli and Sudarsen 1998), thus gaining the special benefits of such inclusion.

The conventional development studies method is an economic or demographic study based on established survey techniques and heavily dependant on the collation of quantitative data. Women's concerns are often submerged in such information because of the manner in which categories such as work or households are defined. Despite this limitation, some of the large surveys do provide useful gender-disaggregated data. For example, the comparative analysis of different indicators of women's position in the north-eastern states in Chapter 7 is based on a range of secondary national and state-level data. One of the most striking examples of the value of large scale quantitative data is that provided by the Census of India on the declining trend in the female child sex ratio. This spurred sustained feminist action against female infanticide and foeticide, leading to the national law against sex-selection and foeticide. When smaller units of large-scale data are examined, as in the work of Satish Agnihotri (2000) at the district level in Orissa, this provides a revealing picture of the specific locations and the directions of spread (from urban to rural) of the decline in the female sex ratio at birth. Small studies that examine specific demographic groups can also be very revealing. For instance, a recent study in Delhi (Sehgal 2005) of the sex ratio of third-borns in families with two surviving girl children shows how alarmingly low this is, 219 girls for every 1000 boys born, indicating the extent of sex-selective foeticide, which is against the law.

In comparison to quantitative surveys that may take months

or years and require teams of several investigators (who may or may not be involved in the process of analysis), there are the much quicker methods of development communication. These draw upon speedy information gathering techniques and a modified form of participant observation to put a qualitative 'human face' upon the economic substratum. Among the earliest examples was economist Kusum Nair's interview-based *Blossoms in the Dust* (1961/1971) that reflected farmers' perceptions of agriculture in different parts of India. Among contemporary practitioners is journalist P. Sainath of *The Hindu* whose researched reports from the field (such as the 1996 collection, *Everybody Loves a Good Drought*) combine observations, interviews and policy analysis to create richly detailed pictures of ordinary people's lives.

My own entry into the field of rural development was also through this route. In 1969, B.G. Verghese, editor of *The Hindustan Times*, New Delhi, started the column 'Our Village Chhatera' to open a window on rural transformation for urban readers. This pioneering experiment in development communication provided an intensive and continuous focus initially on one village and later on three villages in Haryana state. Those of us who were associated with the column had to devise ways of maintaining this focus over several years, serving as catalysts in village development and guarding against becoming a crutch for the villagers themselves. This was an extraordinarily difficult task, despite the editor's own interest and support, because at that time there were no precedents nor training, and many logistical, attitudinal and institutional obstacles had to be overcome. Yet, within a short span of time the column acquired considerable influence and led to many ad hoc developmental interventions in the area. However, the productive work of women in agriculture was entirely ignored (see S1). One of my sharpest recollections of those days is the struggle with male colleagues on the Chhatera team who, despite the evidence before their eyes, unrelentingly opposed the very idea of village women being consulted about agriculture. They were not interested in writing about women in agriculture and I (a woman) was not supposed to write about agriculture! Although the column adopted the photograph of a young shepherd girl as its logo, it was also very difficult to address the problems of lower caste, landless groups, perhaps because we did not have the skills to work our way around the land-owning elite with whom we were most in contact. It was only by extending the coverage to a group of weavers in an adjacent village that the livelihood concerns of a marginalized community were brought within the ambit of the column.

A most influential method that emerged in the late 1970s was Rapid Rural Appraisal (RRA). Based on field experiences in India and other countries, RRA evolved into a systematic method of intensive information gathering to uncover the knowledge and perspectives of local people to plan for immediate development projects. Using background information, short field visits, followed by discussion and analysis within the group, the aim of RRA was speedy investigation and identification of specific rural problems, in particular locations, to provide a basis for interventions. Observation, informal conversation, short questionnaires, semi-structured interviews and in-depth interviews with key persons in the community were part of the RRA tool kit. Small, multidisciplinary teams drew upon this range of tools to understand not only the elements in a chain of problems but the inter-linkages between them. Although envisaged as a flexible and creative approach, RRA did not succeed in overcoming the divide between the researcher and the researched. This was especially so with regard to rapid assessments and evaluation of project interventions.

Many variations of the RRA approach evolved independently as researchers tried to find methods to suit their own purposes.[1] The case study method lends itself to many different uses. It is especially effective, although more time-consuming and expensive, when the researchers in different locations are able to meet and share their understanding. There are various ways in which a research team can work on a set of case studies. The conventional path is to have a clearly laid out pattern of steps that all the researchers follow in their different locations. This makes for easier comparisons and perhaps greater coherence but tends to curb individual initiative, reducing the possibility of original insights, and perhaps does not reflect the complexity on the ground. A less conventional path is to establish some broad common parameters for the team within which individual researchers use methods suited to their own professional training and their varied individual skills and temperaments. This is more difficult to coordinate but may provide a richer output because researchers do not come in one mould and different methods do work for different people.

Since the 1980s, the methods of participant observation and case studies to understand and express invisibility and powerlessness have been given greater depth by feminist narrative and interpretive approaches. Such approaches emphasize the 'embedded' and 'situated' character of all knowledge and are more reflexive (see Chapter 2). Although we all realize that the knowledge gained by participant observation in the field is a totality that includes the researcher's own messy experiences, this usually remains unarticulated. Indeed, in the collision of the personal and the professional, there is tension between the inside/outside roles of the researcher at the grassroots. This is difficult to express without self-indulgence. In an attempt to do this through a narrative (see S10), my first draft was a 'portrait' that I subsequently cast in a theoretical 'frame' for a social science audience; the inside/outside of the title reflects my own dilemmas not only during the experience but also in writing about it.

Conscientization to participation

For many in my generation Paulo Freire's *Pedagogy of the Oppressed* (1970) provided the inspiration and rationale for participatory methodologies, shifting the focus away from teaching, research and writing to action. The power of Freire's philosophy of education as conscientization continues to be influential. For example, in India it has helped to shape the process-oriented education-as-empowerment programme called 'Mahila Samakhya' (MS). In states such as Karnataka, it was the success of the MS programme upon which women's self-help groups have built. Ideally, participatory research of any kind should involve a power-shift with the 'other' voices becoming 'the voices'. In such a process, people at the grassroots are not the objects of research but the agents who define their own priorities and agenda. The researcher is a facilitator and the primary purpose is developmental action, not contribution to a body of knowledge. Among the many Freire-type approaches is Participatory Action Research (PAR) advocated by Fals-Borda and Rahman (1991). The Centre for Development

Studies (CWDS) project in Bankura (see Chapter 8) has successfully used PAR methods to organize women through wasteland development. Banerjee (2004) points out that the very purpose of women's empowerment in Bankura is participation.

PAR has now been overtaken by Participatory Rural Appraisal (PRA) that evolved in the 1980s from the influential critiques by Robert Chambers and others (Chambers, Pacey and Thrupp eds. 1989) who argued for putting the 'farmer first' (Chambers 1995). This was in reaction to the almost complete absence of farmers' voices in programmes designed for their benefit. PRA overcame some of the limitations of RRA and developed techniques to bring farmers voices into the processes of development. PRA tools include diagramming and ranking exercises that represent ideas and quantities symbolically through locally available materials such as twigs and pebbles, with finger drawings on the ground, or coloured markers on chart papers and whiteboards. There is a vast and easily available literature, including PRA guides and toolkits. PRA exercises are easy to learn and fun to do. They build rapport among participants and between them and project staff. As a research method, however, PRA is not just about bonding and enjoyment but also about testing ideas in the field and understanding conceptual issues. A PRA facilitator needs considerable skills for this and also to ensure that the voices of women and other silenced groups are not excluded.

PRA is now the most widely used method by government, development agencies and NGOs in India. But one of the consequences of this rapid spread all over the country is that PRA has been reduced to a mechanical tool. There are many examples of the superficial use of PRAs. For instance, the 2005 calendar of a Bangalore-based NGO features photographs of its work in promoting ecological agriculture. The picture for the first quarter of the year shows more than 20 men and five women seated together on the ground, undertaking a PRA exercise. The women can be seen at the far end, *behind* a stand that supports a whiteboard. The caption says the organization 'favours participatory methodologies which are enriching and empowering'. When I commented to one of the staff that the picture spoke more loudly than the caption, he took it as a compliment, till I explained that in my view the picture clearly underlined the exclusion of women and their powerlessness. This was all the more ironic because it was supposed to be depicting an empowering exercise. A few years ago, I also came across a case of 200 PRAs being mechanically undertaken in one north-eastern state by an international natural resource organization simply to fulfil project requirements stipulated by an unrealistic project schedule. Even when PRAs are carried out with sincerity, they may provide only partial views. For example, two similar PRAs on 'social mapping' of the same village were conducted through focus groups, organized by the same institution but at different points of time for different projects. There was vast variation in the results of the two exercises because the composition of the participant group had changed for the second project giving rise to two different pictures of the village (Saujenendra Swain 2002 personal communication). On reflection, it was obvious to the team that the project and its staff needed the PRA more than did the community. In such cases, sensitive project staff do feel some unease that such exercises may be used to legitimize a project's 'participatory' character.

Indeed, the assumption that participatory methodologies and tools would somehow automatically take care of the interests of different 'stake-holders' in the community is very simplistic. Neither communities nor women are a homogenous group. In India, the initial political challenge that participatory approaches may have posed to dominant power structures has been diluted as PRA is being treated as a technical/management solution unrelated to the politics of power on the ground, including gender-power relations. As the language and tools of PRA are widely accepted (co-opted?) by 'mainstream' development approaches, PRA comes to be used only as an instrument to build rapport and gather information to fulfil the goals of the intervening agency. This undermines the progressive and idealistic philosophy of participation, in which as Thamizoli (2004) points out, participation is envisioned as 'the goal, an end in itself', and thus empowering. When participatory tools are used without skill and sensitivity, or only to fulfil project requirements and as a means to achieving project goals, such 'participation' may itself be disempowering for women.

Gender analysis

One way of making participatory methods more inclusive for women is to combine these with Gender Analysis. As we saw in Chapter 2, feminist perspectives have given rise to many different approaches to women. The WID/WED approach was oriented towards 'integrating' women in developmental and environmental programmes while the GAD approach went further to address the larger framework of social relations including gender relations. The GAD approach led to the evolution of Gender Analysis (GA). The systematic analyses of the impact of developmental interventions on women and men was seen as essential to identify needs and implement programmes in a gender-equitable manner. Different agencies developed their own methods, often inspired by variations of a gendered approach, suited to their own specific situations. Together with sets of tools, activities and checklists, these make up 'frameworks' for analysis. Some of these frameworks are discussed briefly in the following paragraphs. (I have drawn mainly upon March, Smith and Mukhopadhyay, 1999, who provide a more detailed analysis).

Perhaps the best known of GA methods is that developed in the early 1980s by Caroline Moser and the Development Planning Unit of the University of London. The Moser framework is intended as a 'gender planning' method (see Moser 1993). Its theoretical underpinning comes from an understanding that: a) women perform reproductive, productive and community work, a triple burden; b) that they have both practical and strategic needs (an adapatation of the differentiation drawn by Molyneaux (1985) of practical and strategic 'gender interests'); and c) that different planning interventions have different impacts (characterized as welfare, equity, anti-poverty, efficiency and empowerment approaches). The framework goes beyond the conventional approach to planning, recognizing the strategic need to challenge traditional gender role differentiation and to transform gender relations in order to overcome women's subordination. It also has a variety of tools that are easy to use in different situations. The Moser framework was adopted by the World Bank and gender planning became part of the Bank's development discourse. Despite its attractiveness, critics point out that the framework does not take into account the inter-relatedness of the work that women and men do, and that it ignores other forms of inequality. In the Indian context both these limitations are crucial. The distinction between practical and strategic 'gender needs' is also not so useful. For instance, in some contexts, learning to ride a bicycle may be classified as a practical need for getting around but for young rural girls in India, enhanced mobility serves a strategic interest for autonomy and self-esteem, for themselves and in some cases for their communities. (In a recent episode in rural Orissa, a young dalit girl asserted her right to ride a bicycle to college, challenging the gender and caste oppression of the brahman village elders who opposed this. Her courageous stand compelled the district authorities to protect her rights by providing a policewoman as an escort.)

Almost as influential as the World Bank-Moser framework, is the Harvard Analytical Framework, which was specifically devised to meet the needs of USAID projects around the world and was intended to support the economic reasons for integrating women into development. Its tools include recording gender role differentiation in productive and reproductive activities and profiling the gendered access to, and control of, resources. In my experience, natural scientists are especially comfortable using the USAID-Harvard framework because it generates considerable data and they can identify with its objective of increasing the efficiency of projects. Among several variations of the Harvard framework is the People-Oriented Planning Framework, developed by the UN High Commission on Refugees with support from CIDA, which aims to target resources more efficiently and reduce gender disparities (Anderson 1992). Both frameworks rely on Moser's differentiation of practical and strategic gender needs and are useful to understand the gender division of labour. However, they are not participatory and remain bounded by a WID efficiency approach. Therefore, they are unable to draw out power relations in a community and the dynamics involved in contesting and negotiating resource-use.

Others who have attempted to develop frameworks or/and toolkits that address some of these limitations include the UN Commission for Human Rights (UNCHR); UNIFEM; Sara

Hlupekile Longwe; Christine Okali; and Naila Kabeer. UNCHR's Gender Analysis matrix is based on the understanding that 'Development is a process by which vulnerabilities are reduced and capabilities are increased' (Anderson and Woodrow 1989). While this helps to encompass greater complexity (particularly in emergency situations), it does not explicitly address women's empowerment and is not participatory. Working with NGOs in the Middle East, Rani Parker (1993) developed a matrix for UNIFEM that scores women, men, household and the community against labour, time, resources and culture. Despite the fluidity of the categories 'community' and 'culture', it is very simple to use especially in mixed groups of women and men and generates a lot of information quickly. But it requires a skilled facilitator to overcome the limitations of a 'snapshot' view and draw out underlying conflicts. Yet, another GA matrix, developed by Sara Longwe, is based specifically upon field experiences in West Africa (see March 1999 et. al.). Longwe goes beyond practical versus strategic needs to suggest five hierarchical stages along which the advance of women's equality and empowerment may be traced: welfare, access, conscientization, participation and control. These stages are seen as a continuum towards the clearly defined goal of empowerment. Also working out of Africa, Okali (personal communication, Chennai: 2001) and her colleagues have attempted to go beyond the Harvard and Moser frameworks to conceptualize processes of 'gendered bargaining' around project interventions. Okali suggests that for improved project planning, monitoring and evaluation, it is not the shift in gender relations that needs to be addressed but the process by which gender relations are re-negotiated. Both Longwe and Okali have a more nuanced awareness of gender-power relations in the household and community, although Longwe is the more radical.

In South Asia, for those who follow a gendered, rather than conventional or celebratory approach (see Chapter 3), the most useful framework is that derived from Naila Kabeer's social relations approach to gender and poverty that is enriched by her experience in Bangladesh. Kabeer identifies four key institutions, the state, market, community and family/kinship, each of which has five distinct dimensions: rules, resources, people, activities and power.

Policies may be 'gender-blind' or 'gender-aware', neutral, specific or re-distributive. For our purposes, this framework has significant advantages because it links institutions and levels of analysis. Although some critics say that the community is not an 'institution', my own view is that it is sometimes necessary to see the community as an institution because this reflects the tangible reality of South Asia where communities govern religious practice and gendered behaviour. While the approach provides a good basis for training development practitioners, the framework is difficult to apply in a participatory way.

Qualitative assessment

A significant aspect of participatory and gendered research and action is project assessment. Many of the PRA exercises can be reduced to mini-surveys and numerical scores of how many women, men, households, responded to particular aspects. I suspect that the apparent rigour of quantification is one of the reasons that conservation scientists find PRA appealing. In contrast, all the GA frameworks and tools are premised, implicitly or explicitly, on achieving qualitative insights, because of the feminist perspective from which these frameworks have evolved. Yet, this has had little impact on governments and international donor agencies who invariably assess programmes through quantitative indicators.

The chosen quantitative indicators may be financial targets: expenditure of the project budget, the quantum of savings made by a women's group etc., or they may be physical targets: the extent of land reforested, the number of women's groups formed etc; or both. Every practitioner is aware that monitoring programmes and projects in this quantitative way is unsatisfactory and that it does not indicate levels of participation. Yet quantitative indicators have become the basis to judge the success or failure of projects and project staff. The government's reliance on budgetary expenditure as an indicator of 'success' has a long history. The annual performance of ministries and departments is mechanically evaluated by the percentage of the allocated budget utilized for a given activity. The assumption is that if the budget has not been spent/disbursed by the concerned department, planned works have either not been initiated or have not been implemented effectively.

At the level of the government there may be some validity in that assumption. The problem is when quantitative financial and physical indicators are unthinkingly applied by donor agencies and NGOs themselves on the assumption that this is more rigorous. Unless, qualitative indicators are incorporated, it is not possible to fairly assess a participatory programme.

There is also a deeper question which relates to whether people's participation is to be limited to involvement in a particular programme or whether it would also extend to monitoring and evaluation. Where participation is used only as a tool, a means to improved performance of a watershed or any other programme, evaluation would invariably be based on quantitative indicators. But if participation is understood as an approach, and empowering in itself, then evaluation of success or failure would also have to be participatory and disaggregated by gender, caste and age. To my knowledge, there are very few examples of such participatory assessment. Therefore, at the project level, we need to strive to evolve methods to facilitate participatory social and gender impact assessments, by enabling people to develop their own tools and criteria for assessment. If this were to be done, the question would not be how to evaluate participatory programmes but how to develop participatory evaluation of programmes.

An experiment in participatory gendered assessment

One of the problems both with PRA and gender analysis, in my view, is that the tools are devised by 'us' for 'them'. This goes against the philosophy and spirit of participation. In 2000, in my capacity as gender consultant to an innovative mangrove conservation and management project of the MS Swaminathan Research Foundation, I attempted to take this thought a step further in a tangible way to enable the 'other' voices to assess the project impact according to their own criteria, as in a normal participatory project, but without using conventional PRA tools. Instead my idea was that the people would be facilitated to use their own cultural tools, which is fairly normal practice in Non-Formal Education but is far less common in NRM projects. I was fortunate that the project staff, the institution and the donor agency were all supportive of the experiment. A workshop was first held with the staff (from locations in three different states) to build their capacity to undertake the experiment and to 'unsettle' the prevailing assumption that gender concerns had already been well integrated into the project through PRA and gender analysis. It was recognized that there was a methodological challenge in evolving context-specific tools for participatory social and gender impact assessment, but the joint decision of all concerned was that we should go ahead.

At the first location, a tribal village, team members facilitated a meeting of men and women in the village school room. The first task was to identify significant project interventions/activities. The group swiftly identified four interventions and the women added a fifth: formation of SHGs. We suggested that these be represented by symbols, as in a normal PRA. At this point, imperceptibly, one of the village women took over the facilitation. The symbols were swiftly drawn and evocative. Those drawn by the women seemed to reflect a greater interest in process rather than product, although one should not read too much into this. The discussion then shifted to the existing cultural tools and how these could be used to show the impact of the project on women and men. There was animated discussion without any facilitation, and near unanimity among the villagers that the interventions/ activities could not be matched to cultural tools one-to-one, that all was a whole and could not be 'separated-separated'. Instead, they envisaged a kind of 'cinema' in which everything would be depicted. The next day the people, on their own, spent a few hours planning how they would do this and were ready with their 'cinema' that evening.

The tribal villagers' cinematic presentation was a unique and moving experience. It consisted of more than 50 scenes, presented by men and women over six hours, spread over two consecutive nights. There was no written script but the scenes followed in chronological sequence without any hesitation. It included music, mime, narration, song, dance, and finally a tableaux, which was presented with sophisticated dramatic skill. The dialogues and actions depicted incidents that had occurred two or three years earlier with utmost accuracy, or with occasional exaggeration to make a point. The entire village was involved and the audience participated with witty asides. Most interesting was that their perspective extended over a much longer time span than the project, going back to the origins of the hamlet and the difficulties of settlement at that site. It was only after a whole hour devoted to this 'pre-history' that the project actually entered the scene. This pre-history was very important to the village and it also helped the team see the project in the larger perspective of the totality of village life. In the dramatic presentation, the women and men took on the roles of the project staff, effectively capturing the voice, behaviour and actions of each team member. For the men and women in the team, this view of themselves inspired reflection. The finale was a tableau that summarized the project impacts, highlighting material improvements from the people's own point of view: for instance, they attached great significance to the change from using clay pots to metal utensils. The gender impact was not addressed directly at all but could be gleaned throughout the drama: the gender equity that existed in the past with women participating equally in decisions; later changes with women remaining in the background, particularly in dealings with government officials (all men); and the more recent self-confidence of women and men after project interventions.

Some months later, we repeated the same experiment in another state. In this case, the project staff facilitated focus group discussions with the women alone. The idea of a 'drama' to depict the project's impact emerged from the women and they drew up a plan for this. They intended to rehearse but could not do so because of certain logistical problems. The women's unrehearsed 'drama' was actually a role simulation, which began with an imaginary scene that provided the context to talk about the project interventions. The team 'representative' was brought into the scene quite early. This extemporary exposition went on for two hours. Compared to the mixed, male and female, tribal group in the first village, the women's drama in the second village was much more focused on the project. The team members were also not personalized or explicitly identified. The women seemed to be less concerned with the dramatic elements than with discussing the issues and showing how their concerns and those of the project had been reconciled.

The women in the audience also spontaneously became role players. As audience participation increased, even the physical distance between the 'stage' and the audience space vanished. Above all, the entire process was controlled by the village women.

At both locations, the dramas seemed to accurately reflect the institutional understanding and at the same time expressed the grassroots view, the perceptions and doubts of the 'other' voices. The growth in the women's confidence was marked in both locations. However, my view that the process of participatory impact assessment was a success and reflected the innovative methodological possibilities in the project was not shared by some of the staff. Letting go control of the process of assessment was difficult for many of them because they had been trained differently and felt responsible for any mishaps. It was also unsettling for some in the institution that established participatory methods like PRA were being 'overturned' by an outsider and the approach was seen as 'interference'. Indeed, this led to much intellectual and emotional discomfort all around. For the village women too taking hold of the process was not easy because the conventional government-NGO system has made them accustomed to the idea that someone else knows better. This is one of the challenges of re-visioning grassroots development and reshaping patterns of governance with a gendered approach.

Transforming the research process

The gap between participatory methodologies and gender analysis is not easily bridged. However, when interventions address the methodology of research alongside research and development goals, the process of research itself may be empowering. For instance, in Anthra's work in sustainable agriculture (see also Chapter 8) men and women from the community were trained as 'barefoot researchers' in a range of skills to document different aspects of their livelihood and knowledge systems. (The concept of the 'barefoot' doctor, engineer, or other professional has had a fairly long history in India going back to the early 1970s when it was adopted by NGO initiatives such as that of the Social Work and Research Centre, in Tilonia, Rajasthan.) Writing about their work in livestock development and agricultural conservation with poor communities, Sagari Ramdas, Nitya Ghotge and their colleagues (Ramdas et. al. 2004) say:

> 'the skills included participatory research methodologies, communication and, most important, having a development perspective. Gender awareness and equipping the team with the tools of gender analysis formed an integral and ongoing component of the work. Participatory research methodologies including PRA, case studies, informal group meetings, focused group meetings, as also more conventional research tools such as household surveys, were used according to the need.'

> They say further that, even as information was being documented and analysed, 'the issues were immediately discussed and shared with the wider community of men and women. This was done through institutions such as women *sanghams* and *gottis* (groups). Information was also shared with a wider audience through innovative media such as theatre, village *jatras* (folk theatre) and mobile exhibitions where many critical issues were visually depicted through posters, banners, and slide shows. The issues were discussed and debated in intensive workshop-like situations with farmers of both sexes. In some areas and on some issues this resulted in concrete community action; in others it brought the issues to the forefront and for the first time people were engaged in a process of discussion and debate on gender questions in the context of livelihoods, knowledge systems and natural resource uses and their management.'

By combining a clear 'development persepective' with a variety of tools, Anthra was able to build the capacities of 'barefoot' researchers and engage the wider community in a process of charting its own developmental route.

Reshaping resource management practices, reconstructing systems of governance, creating new political spaces, finding new ways of listening requires that we build bridges between the priorities of grassroots voices, programme requirements and the conventions of academic scholarship. The new frameworks and tools that we need to re-construct the 'master's house' are not out there just waiting to be found but have to be fashioned in complex detail, piece-by-piece.

NOTES

[1] An early 'door-opener' as Devaki Jain called it were the five case studies that constituted *Women's Quest for Power* (Jain with Singh and Chand 1980). This sought to identify how women in different parts of India had successfully leveraged themselves into greater participation in national development. When studies are rooted in the 'grassroots' experiences of women they do produce fresh insights.

For instance, in the early 1980s, I used a combination of participant observation, development communication and RRA tools for a short study comparing water supply, sanitation and health in two Indian villages (Chauhan and Gopalakrishnan 1983). Somewhat surprisingly this showed that the smaller, poorer village with fewer facilities was the more healthy. A similar approach, along with a team of development writers in different countries (Chauhan with Bihua et. al. 1983), assessed community participation projects in water, sanitation and health that had been hailed as success stories. Taken as a whole the case studies showed that 'success' was much more nuanced and often followed years of struggle and failures that were not recorded.

GENDERSCAPES

10

Revisioning Natural Resource Management

> Then we were veiled. Now that our ghunghats (veils) are off, and we have
> seen courts, katcheri (collectorate), attended meetings in Delhi, Calcutta,
> Orissa, Gujarat, Madhubani how can we go back to the hearth? . . . Just to
> meet the collector to persuade him to give us the ponds, we made so many
> trips. Every such trip costs at least Rs.100 and the collector says 'go'. If
> they take away our livelihoods, they will be guilty of *tiriya vadh* (murder
> of women—femicide).
>
> —Bhulia Devi, Mallahin women's inland fisheries
> cooperative, Madhubani, Bihar [1]

Why does gender-bias persist in NRM, despite policies and
programme interventions that appear to be geared towards women's
concerns? This seems like a simple question but as we pursue it
from different angles and at different levels, it becomes increasingly
multi-faceted and more layered. I do not think there can be an
over-arching gendered design for NRM. However, by challenging
traditional and modern gender ideologies in specific contexts and
imaginatively and sensitively comprehending these contexts in their
entirety, we may be able to construct a different vision of NRM
than the patriarchal and instrumentalist interventions that have
characterized NRM policy and practice. In this final chapter,
therefore, I begin by recapitulating the main threads that have
run through the book thus far, revisiting what I have called

'wordscapes', 'workscapes' and 'actionscapes'. I then foreground issues related to institutionalized gender ideologies, processes of hegemony, resistance and the appropriation of women's dissent, and the limitations and potential of women's collectivity. Finally, I sketch the concept of genderscapes, as a more nuanced way to move beyond gender analyses and encompass greater complexity.

GOING OVER THE GROUND AGAIN

Wordscapes, workscapes and actionscapes

Feminist scholarship has established the significance of locating the researcher on the same 'critical plane' (Harding, 1987) as the researched. The researcher is not a disembodied, authoritative voice (what grammarians call 'passive impersonal') but has a historical particularity, with interests and views that have evolved in specific contexts over a period of time. Therefore, in Chapter 1, looking back through a gendered lens, I traced some of the trails through which I have passed. It is only through the passage of time that such trails come to be defined and recognized as paths.

In the three chapters in Part I, Wordscapes, I tried to unpack the words that shape our everyday lives, our life-worlds, to show how gender ideologies are embedded both in social institutions and in human minds and are expressed through the physical-spatial, socioeconomic and socio-political planes. Conceptual categories such as gender are difficult to grasp in the mind's eye. I suggested that this is a little like trying to view the patterns embedded in stereoscopic pictures (that are deliberately designed to obscure); some people can see the patterns immediately, while others need to look at it this way and that before the pattern comes into focus. Yet, gender is also something more than a fixed pattern, a variable or category with clearly defined limits. Indeed, it is increasingly being realized that gender is a fluid power-relation that is acted out, 'performed'. The roles, responsibilities, knowledge, activities and behaviour of women, men, girls and boys in normal, daily life are determined by how society visualizes a spectrum of gender positions from femininity to masculinity, and femininity vis-à-vis masculinity. Gender inequity is reflected in common sayings, songs, rituals and other cultural practices. These *word*-views and ideas are internalized within each one of us at a very early age through processes of socialization and reinforced by socioeconomic and socio-political institutions and practices throughout our lives. Women's subordinate position in patriarchal societies is characterized by the control and management of their sexuality and their labour. The family and kin groups—both the natal family into which we are born and the extended family established through marriage relations—are involved in shaping gendered ideals and practices. Gender relations are also governed by the gender ideology of one's community, caste or ethnic group. Patriarchies shape traditional stereotypes of womanhood and manhood, just as they shape modern developmental approaches.

In Chapter 3, I contrasted the gendered approach to women and the environment with the conventional and celebratory approaches. I suggested that the conventional approaches, which ignore women or see them as 'beneficiaries' of welfare programmes, and the celebratory approaches, such as the ecofeminist valorization of women's 'intrinsic' qualities, shared certain ideological roots in their conceptualization of the sexual division of labour as naturally rooted in male and female biologies. Going beyond the conventional and the celebratory, a gendered approach looks at the historical and social construction of gender relations in societies. This is especially relevant in the creation of modern knowledge. Discussing women's exclusion and alienation from technology, I noted that this is the result of a process of historical and cultural construction of technology (including agricultural technology) as masculine, and of masculinity as involving technical capabilities. Viewed from a gendered perspective, this inter-weaving is a product of men's power in society and at the same time, reinforces it. As we then saw in Chapter 4, the processes by which some of the theories of the natural sciences have been created clearly reflect the gender ideologies of their times. Carried forward through word and metaphor, these ideologies have influenced the wider cognitive culture of science, legitimizing ways of knowing, of seeing and writing, that appear to be gender-neutral but are in fact deeply gender-biased. I argued that the sexist assumptions of the biological and natural sciences resonate with patriarchal customary attitudes and that together these shape gender-biased practices. And further that recognizing and resisting the gendered character of natural science in India is essential to understand and counter the marginalization of women in environmental conservation and development strategies.

In Part II, Workcapes, the concepts and ideas discussed in Wordscapes were placed in the contexts of women's *work* in diverse, complex and dynamic field situations. Chapter 5 depicted the caring practices of a group of women in the Western Ghats, practices that have evolved in particular socio-economic and cultural contexts through joint living and perceived familial needs, which are themselves the result of multifarious historical processes of migration, displacement and relocation. The chapter showed that the abrupt changes that have taken place in Kunbi life in recent decades are reflective of developments in the 'enveloping society' of which the community is a part, and that while these changes do affect traditional values, they also provide opportunities for families and for women (who have traditionally paid a high price for social harmony) to develop in new directions. We saw that women's caring practices take new forms, as in modern systems of health care and local governance.

In Chapter 6, I examined the variability in women's roles as conservers of biological diversity, reinforcing the gendered conclusion that women's work and responsibilities are socially rather than biologically-determined. Many different examples illustrated women's repertory of information of the components of biological diversity, local crop varieties, wild foods, medicinal plants etc., but it is apparent that this rich store of knowledge is being eroded as younger persons are getting educated and alienated from the resource base. I also argued that with regard to women the ecological approach as it has thus far been developed is distinctly conventional. So, although women's roles are recognized at an empirical level, this is not incorporated at a conceptual level. A striking instance of this is the manner in which environmentalists acclaim traditional conservation practices, such as the sacred groves, without enquiring into the gendered roots of these traditions. Some of the same themes were taken up in Chapter 7 in the specific context of tribal patriarchies in the rice farming societies of north-eastern India. The chapter pointed to the 'price' that women pay for food sustainability, the increasing burden of labour on older women in particular, and the challenge of imminent macro changes in farming and labour relations that threaten to erode the ecological and socio-cultural diversity of the region. I argued that the trends point to the reinforcement of customary laws, increase in crimes against women and the advance of new forms of male domination in the region, all of which reflect the influence of elements of brahmanical patriarchy superimposed on the traditional tribal patriarchies. Both Chapters 6 and 7 pointed to the need to bring gendered insights into resource management policy and practices.

Wordscapes and Workscapes led to Part III, Actionscapes. In Chapter 8, I considered some of the governmental and non-governmental *actions* to 'mainstream' women's work in resource management. The chapter highlighted some of the assumptions made by the makers of policies and the framers of programmes: that there is an inevitable convergence of interests between women's needs and resource sustainability; that community control will inevitably benefit women; that poor women have inexhaustible resources of time and labour; and that cultural constraints to women's participation are best left untouched. I suggested that all of these assumptions are in keeping with an approach that uses women's participation in resource management as a means to conservation and sustainability without being concerned whether such participation also transforms women's position. As I have also written elsewhere managerial 'mainstreaming' strategies ask what women can do for conservation rather than what conservation can do for women. Innovative NGO attempts to change the process go beyond seeking women's labour inputs and gender-balance in programmes. Some interventions have also succeeded in 'unpacking' the community and sometimes even the household to create new spaces for women. Yet, the problem remains of how to extend the empowering effects of these interventions across a wider expanse and ensure that such empowerment is sustained.

Focusing on the methodology of research, in Chapter 9, I first looked at learnings from selected research studies that have 'opened up' the community. I suggested that such studies are useful in uncovering conflicts over resource usage among sections of the community since pre-colonial times but that they tell us little about the gendered patterns of usage. I then went on to look at feminist researches that have opened up the household to show that the efficiency and productivity of the political economy rests upon the sexual division of labour, and that the gender ideologies that determine women's roles and behaviour also give men the power to control women's labour and sexuality. Poor women's lives and natural resource-based livelihoods are not clearly demarcated into worlds of work and home. In the next section of the chapter, my concern was with the extent to which various participatory and gendered approaches to research and interventions, provide gendered insights. I suggested that uncovering bias in the outlook of researchers and practitioners is the first step towards countering gender-power relations. The next step is the need to look beyond both conventional research tools, such as quantitative surveys, and newer tools, such as PRA and gender analysis (although all of these have their uses), to search for more inclusive non-conventional tools fashioned by the people themselves in their own cultural contexts. Describing efforts to bridge the distance between the researcher and the researched, led to reflecting upon the difficulties faced by researchers in giving up control of the research process and the 'master's tools'.

It is evident that simply adding a women's component into existing NRM programmes has limited value and that we need to change the ways in which we talk, observe, live, think, plan and act. Women's rights in natural resource management need to be seen as empowering human rights that are not premised on the sexual division of labour. Interventions that do not address the difficult socio-political question of intra-household equity tend to reinforce rather than challenge traditional gender roles. Thus, women's empowerment remains incomplete.

ADDRESSING GENDER IDEOLOGIES

In order to envisage how communities can manage their natural resources in a gender-equitable way, it becomes necessary to understand the role of natural resources in local gender-power relations. For this we need to understand how gender ideologies develop and are expressed in society. And we need to find ways of encompassing both the ideological and material features that make up the specificity and entirety of women's life-worlds.

control of their sexuality in the family and wider community. As we have seen in earlier chapters, this complex ambiguity derives from the ideologies that characterize many different belief systems and religious practices, whether it be brahmanical or tribal patriarchies.

Patriarchy does not come full blown but is a process by which men's control over different spheres is established and is continually reinforced. This process has been intertwined with the formation of the state, which is founded as it were on the village community, caste hierarchy and the patriarchal family. The experience of colonialism did not fundamentally alter gendered hierarchies in state structures, although colonialism introduced elements that seemed to be in favour of women. This process is continuing today. In India, as in the rest of South Asia, the conventional models and administrative structures of development and resource management are being adjusted to include women but this is being done without addressing patriarchal structures and gender-power relations. This is so across a range of informal and formal, traditional and modern NRM systems. Patriarchy has left its footprints on the policy environment and the practices that characterize both large government programmes, like watershed development and JFM, as also smaller resource management projects. The thrust towards decentralization of resource management and control is undermined by new forms of exclusion that are tied to the old forms of marginalization. As mentioned earlier, thousands of membership-based water-user groups were formed in the late 1990s in Andhra Pradesh (Jairath 2000), but membership was based on land-ownership effectively excluding women and the landless, both traditionally marginalized groups.

While certain traditional livelihood systems may even now be characterized by a more equal division of labour and decision-making roles, these systems are changing due to developments in technology and markets. As women's knowledge and skills are increasingly being marginalized, their decision-making power is curtailed and they are restricted to providing labour. So, on the one hand, the gender ideologies embedded in customary practices have become enshrined in traditional and modern institutions and in modern law in a cyclical process that reinforces and often solidifies customs that may have been more elastic and malleable in the past and, on the other hand, new resource rights have strengthened traditional gender, class and caste divisions of society (as in the case of Andhra's new water-user associations). Both these processes undermine women's position in the household and community.

Dissent, resistance, negotiation and appropriation

The robustness of gender-power relations derives from the combined material and ideological subordination of women, and women's apparent complicity. Yet, gender-power relations are constantly being destabilized by subtle processes of negotiation and contestation that reflect women's daily resistance. Traditional taboos and restrictions have been countered by women, either symbolically through ritual painting and song (see S8), or materially. In some cases, such as that of the few hill and forest-dwelling peasant-tribal women who use the plough, this is the result of women's own initiative. In other cases, it requires interventions by the state or by NGOs. For example, in Bankura, West Bengal, the Centre for Women's Development Studies found that tribal women were prevented from participating in tussar silk cocoon culture in the forest because it was feared that the women's touch would kill the silk worm larvae. The project staff had to convince the community that women also processed and cooked food without a supposed deathly touch. Similarly, as mentioned in Chapter 8, the work of Anthra in Andhra and Maharashtra helped male healers break with customary practice and pass their veterinary knowledge to their daughters.

Bina Agarwal (1994) has drawn attention to the range of hidden and overt protest by individuals and groups; forms of resistance involve the actual diversion of food, income and other resources as well as attempts to undermine male power through song and dance. Kamala Ganesh (1999: 236-237) suggests that women's agency should not be seen only in terms of dissent and resistance but in terms of negotiating positions that draw upon 'alternative conceptions of gender in the larger culture' and that make use of 'structural lags and ambivalences within patriliny.' She points out that the 'capacity to adjust, given so much importance in the socialization of girls and women, does not consist of acceptance alone but includes the acquisition of negotiatory skills.' Yet, negotiation may not be in women's favour because of the patriarchal power relations within the household.

Patriarchal institutions too retaliate to resistance in varied ways, ranging from outright force and violence to subtler responses that seek to co-opt and appropriate dissent. A few years ago, I was facilitating a discussion among a group of village women and men in southern India. They wanted to identify income-generating activities that they could take up to supplement their natural resource-based subsistence occupations (in which both women and men played a role). One man suggested introducing knitting machines for women; he had seen women using these machines to make woollen garments in the hills of north India where he had worked some years earlier. Others dismissed the idea arguing that there was no local supply of wool and no local market for woollen items in the hot and humid plains of the south. Other suggestions were made, all for activities that the women could undertake. When I asked whether the women had the time for such work, the men said, of course, the women had plenty of time. So, I asked the group about their daily activities to find out how much spare time men and women actually had to take up a new activity. In a little while it became clear that the men had many more hours to spare than did the women who had additional household chores and other time-consuming tasks that the men did not share. That being so, I suggested that perhaps the community could think in terms of activities that the men could undertake. All the women in the group started to clap, spontaneously, but almost at once the clapping stopped and there was a hush. The woman sitting nearest to me, said quietly: 'Why are you speaking like this? Do you want us to get beaten?' The men did not have to say anything. The women, who were acutely aware of the unequal burden of labour, themselves dismissed the possibility that the men could contribute more to household incomes or household work. This was obviously a 'contested domain' that they feared to enter.

Woven into the fabric of gender relations are a spectrum of strategies from visible force to subtle forms of appropriation that undermine women's dissent and resistance. Violence is the most visible strategy to maintain women's subordination and, as in the above incident, even the unspoken threat of violence often suffices to silence women. I believe that the tactics adopted to negate and deflect women's resistance in the household and community have resonances with the tactics used by the state to appropriate dissent in the wider society. Elsewhere, I have delineated three such 'tactics of illusion': false projection, safety valves and smokescreens (Krishna 1996b, see Table 10.1). False projection, entailing deliberate inversion and misrepresentation, is the first stage in a strategy of appropriation. This is a simple tactic of deliberately and falsely representing subordinated groups and individuals as being aggressive and dominant. Among many common instances are men's jokes that project women as sexually predatory and domineering although the reality is usually the reverse. False projection is easily seen through as being false. Safety valves are a more ambiguous tactic; they serve to 'let off steam' by using the appropriate jargon, words unlinked to actions. The rhetoric of empowerment in natural resource policy statements and programme documents, such as those cited in Chapter 8, are safety valves that create a democratic and progressive façade while doing little to change basic conditions. Discussing the 'inappropriate and partial borrowing of feminist vocabularies in government planning discourses', Saraswati Raju (2005) has pointed to the limited outcome of such 'empowerment' for project women. The third tactic, the smokescreen, creates the illusion of change without affecting the underlying contradictions but is more subversive than safety valves because it uses programmes and terminology to negate the very purpose that these are supposed to advance. The majority of conventional women's 'welfare' programmes are designed to reinforce gender-biased stereotypes and may even be viewed as a deliberate strategy to perpetuate women's subordination. For instance, projects that increase women's work in conservation activities may add to their labour but leave them with little time or energy to participate in decision-making, thus effectively undermining women's influence over community management of common resources.

False projection, safety valves and smokescreens are ways by which dominant groups maintain inequitable gender-power relations, and negate, deflect and absorb elements of women's empowerment. Among some of the tribal and other groups in north-eastern India, patriarchal domination has been countered by other socio-cultural factors such as matriliny among the Khasi and Garo, the high literacy of the Mizo and Ao Naga women, the socio-economic power of the Metei women and so on. But this has had little impact on gender-power relations, on women's autonomy and political subordination (see Krishna 2004b). Micro-studies from southern India, such as that of Geethakutty (personal communication 2005) on Kerala, and M Indira (2005) on Karnataka suggest that in particular circumstances land-ownership does not necessarily enhance women's self-esteem and decision-making power. Even the empowerment of women in public leadership positions, say as elected women representatives in panchayats and local bodies, may be undermined within the closed precincts of their own homes (Mendhapurkar 2004).

The experience of several NGOs concerned with rural development and resource management is that when the family's livelihood interests are at stake men's support is generally forthcoming. In such cases, women are able to undertake activities traditionally seen as male work. However, most government agencies and NGOs hesitate to venture beyond what Gram Vikas (an NGO working in rural Orissa) termed 'uncontested domains', apprehending that this might jeopardize all the rest of their developmental or resource management interventions. It is rare for this to be explicitly stated but Subash Mendhapurkar (2004) has described the professional and personal dilemmas of those who seek to address gender politics within the socio-cultural domain beyond the sanctioned developmental arena. NGOs may facilitate women's inclusion and participation in village development and NRM committees, but organizations that work in a project-mode lack the mandate and persistence (apart from the inclination and skills) required to address contested domains such as male alcoholism and domestic violence. Nor are they likely to concern themselves with the customary laws that govern marriage, inheritance and public ritual status, all of which reflect the relative position of men and women in a community and impinge upon resource management.

Consider, for instance, the case of Mizo women who bear a major responsibility for resource management in the exceptionally harsh terrains of this small state in north-eastern India. In Chapter 7, we noted the contradictions between the Mizo women's economic freedoms and growing social constraints reflected in increasing violence and crimes against women. In Mizoram, as elsewhere in the country, customary practices are widely perceived as being 'traditional' and given. However, such practices have a socio-political history and their enshrinement as 'law' in modern times reflects the understanding and interests of dominant groups, usually men. The Mizo Customary Laws were originally drafted in 1927 when the region (then known as the Lushai Hills district) was under the British superintendent N.E. Perry. Some changes were subsequently made in 1982 when Mizoram was governed by the People's Conference headed by Brigadier T. Sailo. The Indian Constitution explicitly protects the customary practices of certain north-eastern states, including Mizoram. This covers customary marriage and property laws. Mizo society is patrilineal and women do not have inheritance rights. Women have no standing under customary law; wives can be discarded for a whim by husbands who pay a nominal fine; and the position of widows (who are considered the 'property' of their sons) is especially precarious. Yet, the paradox of Mizoram is that on most conventional demographic and economic indicators, such as literacy and work participation, Mizo women rank among the highest in all of India. A sustained struggle to change customary practices is only just gathering momentum. MHIP (the acronym by which the all-Mizo women's organization Mizo Hmeichhe Insuihkhawm Pawl is popularly known) has been among the most organized and outspoken of women's groups in north-eastern India. In 1997, Lanipuii (then President of MHIP) told me, the Mizo women were free to work but not to earn, and that their position in the home was like that of 'good servants' who may be consulted but may not take decisions (Krishna 1998c). The women's groups in Mizoram want representation in the state legislature and they want to be part of the decision-making process in the enactment of new laws that concern them. In 2005, the present MHIP president, B. Sangkhumi was reported as having stated that the condition of Mizo women was 'miserable' under customary marriage, divorce and inheritance laws. She said that these laws are 'male-dominated' and need to be changed but she also pointed out that some aspects of the customary law are favourable to women (Anand 2005). So, led by MHIP, the Mizo women are now campaigning to replace the customary marriage law by a Mizo Christian Marriage Act that would combine customary and modern laws, and give women the right to inherit parental properties. Commenting on the oppressiveness of Mizo customary codes, Sangkhumi makes a fine distinction between institutionalized practices and the actions of individual men: 'I do not say that Mizo men are oppressing their women, but our customary codes do'. The point is that when patriarchal structures are taken for granted, individual men do not have to exercise their agency to gain from the hierarchy of power.

The dynamics of gender-power in households and communities are important influences on women's autonomy, their control of resources and their ability to take decisions. Yet, these are issues that environmentalists and natural resource managers prefer to ignore. As I have written elsewhere (see Krishna 2004a), 'Experience from a range of project and activist interventions in the field shows that women's rights to share community spaces may be more easily asserted than rights to familial spaces. Women's claims to economic/ livelihood rights, forest produce or wasteland for example, do enlist male support. It is within the family that power equations of age or gender are more difficult to challenge, and where both hegemony and resistance take covert forms. Improved livelihoods and enhanced political space do not automatically translate into greater negotiating power within the closed-doors of the family.' Therefore, it would seem that conscientization, articulation and a 'shared platform', what Vina Mazumdar calls the 'magic of sisterhood' (Krishna 2004c), may be far more vital in attaining a gender just resource management system than any other single 'empowering' element such as literacy, economic power, inheritance of land and property, government programmes for women, formal inclusion in village-level resource management committees or representation in panchayat raj institutions.

Women's collectivity and gender relations

Sisterhood or women's collectivity may be built both through political activity and through seemingly apolitical groupings. During the Independence movement, women's collectivity acquired greater legitimacy and a political purpose. Indeed, there is a fairly long history of Indian women coming together in groups for social purposes such as dealing with male drunkenness, as the Meira Paibeis (bands of women 'night- patrollers') have done in Manipur. In the mid-1970s, the initiative and participation of women's groups in the Chipko movement to safeguard the hill forests of Uttarakhand acquired iconic status. Less well-known are the struggles of mahila mandals (women's groups) in Madhya Pradesh, Orissa and Bihar for land, forest and fish resources (see Marathe 2004; Singh 2004; Tewari-Jassal 2004). Smita Tewari-Jassal's study of the Mallahin fisherwomen's cooperatives, facilitated by the NGO Adithi, in Madhubani Bihar traces the tortuous process of empowerment of the low caste Mallahin pond fisherwomen. The evolution of the women's 'collective consciousness' is reflected in their ability to negotiate and maintain their rights, overcome the 'initial hostility' of the men of their own families and village, 'brave the taunts and jeers of neighbours' and build diverse bridges with the district forest authorities, Muslim fishermen and upper caste Brahman men. Tewari-Jassal (ibid. 42) says, for these women the shift from agricultural labour 'to collective ownership of a productive resource also opened up other opportunities within the agrarian economy.' Yet, these considerable societal gains fashioned over 10 years were threatened in a moment by the District Collector withdrawing their hard-won fishing licence because of an apparently inflexible government policy that restricts the number of years for which such a licence can be held. With the expiry of the pond leases, and no other alternatives, the women were faced with the prospect of having to go back to labouring on upper caste farmers' fields. As one of the pond fisherwomen Bhulia Devi says (see epigram above), the loss of their livelihood is akin to the loss of life. Indeed 'the episodic nature of this experiment with women's empowerment' shows that for poor women such empowerment may be 'ephemeral' against the combined power of the state, an unsympathetic bureaucracy and upper caste/class adversaries.

On a much larger scale is the Indian government's Mahila Samakhya programme, which began in 1988-89 as a process-oriented programme for education as empowerment through mahila sanghas (small groups of about 20 women) in 10 districts in Karnataka, Gujarat and Uttar Pradesh. A decade later the programme was extended to 50 districts in Assam, Madhya Pradesh, Andhra Pradesh and Kerala, and the original three states. At an MS *sammelan* (conference) in 2002, sangha women from north Karnataka told me that their group gave them a *bedike*, platform, and *dhairiya*, literally courage which they themselves translated for me into Hindi as *atma-viswas* or self-confidence. The collective solidarity of the sanghas was a significant factor in supporting the women elected to panchayats through special quotas. One of my favourite stories relates to a tribal banjara woman, an elected representative, in a panchayat in one of northern Karnataka's drought-prone areas. She asked me whether I was aware that water-harvesting was now within the purview of the panchayat. She spoke in Hindi but used the English term 'water-harvesting'. She said that she had taken the JE (Junior Engineer) to task because a particular water-harvesting structure had not been properly completed. He said: 'Who are you to ask me that?' She reported this to the women's sangha. In response, the sangha women and some men accosted the JE and asked him: 'Who are you not to keep her *maryada* (dignity). She has the right to question you'. The common platform, especially a publicly recognized group, has given women legitimacy, self-confidence and courage, the strength of 'sisterhood'. But the point is whether this can be sustained and lead to the control and management of productive resources, or whether this too will be just another episode in the story of the 'empowerment' of poor women.

The question becomes especially pertinent with the recent 'discovery' by donor agencies and governments of SHGs (self help groups) and micro-credit as levers of development. The promotion of SHGs is related both to the earlier small scale successes of women's groups, such as the sanghas, and the new market orientation of public policy. Within a very short span of time, some Indian states like Karnataka have gone from having a few thousand groups (formed slowly over a decade) to a hundred thousand groups. While the experience of SHGs is very mixed and far better in the south of India than in the north, even in the southern states, the majority of SHGs are simply rotating credit groups that help women to meet immediate consumption requirements and avoid dependence on moneylenders—these are, of course, vital needs that also have to be addressed. It is only a minority of groups, usually with effective facilitation by NGOs, that are able to take the next step from savings and credit towards micro-entrepreneurship and collective action for resource management.

Development practitioners and women activists are sharply divided on the government's SHG programme. Some critics believe SHGs undermine rather than advance women's agency, that they are a kind of smokescreen. In this view, SHGs are being used by government as a deliberate strategy to depoliticise the collective activity of poor women and hasten corporate entry into the rural market. It is true that the products of corporate houses may be in direct competition with the products made for sale by women's groups themselves. For instance, the government's Khadi and Village Industries Commission (KVIC) and NGOs have widely disseminated the technology for making soap on a small scale. This is an easily learnt income-generating activity for individuals and groups in rural areas. The soaps are marketed locally under brand names registered by the KVIC or the NGOs. This market for soaps is now being taken over by the aggressive attempt of big business houses to sell their own branded soaps through women's SHGs. Yet, there are also a few instances of women's groups withstanding the pressure of corporate marketing agents. In one such instance, the head of an SHG in a village in the interior of Wayanad district, Kerala, told the Hindustan Lever agent that they would be happy to stock the soap he was pushing, if in turn he agreed to buy the notebooks that the women made, which they found difficult to transport. She told me that the agent left quickly and did not return! It is, of course, an extremely difficult task for resource-poor women to use their group strength to resist gender hierarchies and power structures, to 'construct alternative truths and develop a vision' (Thamizoli 2004) in order to manage local natural resources collectively and equitably. Yet, it needs to be emphasized that in their own perception, a formally-established group provides them with a common platform, which fosters their self-image and confidence to take on 'male' tasks/activities, increases their negotiating power and strengthens their participation in local familial and social issues.

In my view, women's collectives, whether SHGs or other groups, are indeed quite adept at negotiating their path at different levels. So they may use the groups in the limited ways that are formally expected of them for micro-credit savings and loans, even as they subvert the agendas of outside agencies, drawing upon the groups as formal, legitimized public spaces to establish an informal 'constituency' that provides a support system and enables a more spirited encounter with the world. In a small, interior village in coastal Orissa, the women office-bearers of an SHG organized around resource management, told me how important it was to them to get dressed in a 'going-out' sari, independently handle the SHG finances, and go out of the village without male escorts to visit the nearest bank where the group's savings account was maintained. They said these may seem like small things but had enhanced their self-esteem and made the men (and women) in the village look upon them differently. The sense of dignity and worth that the women had not experienced earlier enabled them to voice their preferences on common matters in the village, such as where to locate a solar street light, which they had not been able to do in the past.

Women's groups enhance women's agency both within the household and in the community. When women have assets (even minimal savings), earn incomes, have more mobility and deal with institutions, government departments and banks, these changes in their physical-spatial and socio-economic activities do have socio-political implications. These significant gains cannot be measured by conventional quantitative indicators. But government and NGOs continue to assess the performance of SHGs by the target number of groups, number of members and amount of savings and disbursements. I would argue that the tangible qualitative benefits of publicly sanctioned collectivity are of equal if not greater significance than credit for poor women. This is also in keeping with studies from elsewhere in South Asia. In their paper on micro-credit and gender relations in rural Bangladesh, Govind Kelkar, Dev Nathan and Raunaq Jahan (2003: 40), conclude that the women 'have made a substantial change in overcoming some aspects of the hegemonic concepts of masculine domination'. While there is 'still a long way to go in extending the critique' in particular to the intersection of domestic and other household labour, they point out that it is significant that structures that were taken for granted as 'natural' or religiously sanctioned were being juxtaposed against 'competing possibilities and practices', opening the way for discussion. Furthermore, this shift to 'competing discourses' is not being conducted only in terms of tradition ('adherence to purdah') but 'in terms of new ideas and concepts'.

Countering the politics of gender-power relations and gender inequitable ideologies in the practice of NRM requires collectively challenging the institutional basis of subordination, exclusion and discrimination. In order to do so, it is necessary to recognize the historical invisibility of women's work in diverse subsistence activities like dairying and livestock rearing, fishing, hunting, cultivating fruit and vegetable gardens, food preservation, family health care and tasks related to the conservation of environmental and living natural resources (protecting water sources, collecting and processing medicinal plants, selecting and storing seeds) and so on. We then need to understand how women have been confined to certain kinds of subsistence labour and nurturing activities, and why these are undervalued. We also need to understand the gender-power relations that have shaped communities, their traditions and the hierarchical division of labour. The interactions of women and men with the natural resource base are broadly context-specific, but there are also some persistent continuities across time and space. If our understanding is to be rooted in specific contexts, it is necessary to trace continuities and discontinuities, opening up the structure of community institutions from the perspective of those women (and men) who are oppressed by gender ideologies. Recognizing the centrality of gender in power relations, 'between men, between women and between women and men' (Faith 1995: 65), is crucial to understanding that women's experience of oppressive power is related to their sexual and economic subordination. So too, recognizing that in varying contexts women have demonstrated the capacity to question and challenge gender ideologies is essential to understanding that sexual and economic subordination can be transformed.

GENDERING THE LANDSCAPE

The struggle to challenge traditional and modern gender ideologies is a continuing process. At the same time we also have to constantly explore new ways to understand the linkages between people's knowledge systems, their livelihoods and the natural resource base, as also the linkages between happenings at the local level and larger institutional structures. It is difficult to keep gender-power issues in focus in these wider debates and to comprehend the specificity and complexity that make up women's life-worlds. In this final section, I suggest a possible way of doing this. Appropriating the term 'genderscape' (occasionally used in art, film studies and landscape architecture), I sketch a way of moving beyond gender analysis frameworks to encompass a more nuanced and layered complexity. I use the word 'genderscape', together with 'wordscapes', 'workscapes' and 'actionscapes', to understand and represent the ideological and material features that make up the entirety of women's life-worlds. My use of the postfix 'scapes' (which is derived from the word landscape and literally just refers to a view or a representation of a view, such as a moonscape or a seascape) reflects the many-layered spread and dynamic complexity of concepts and terms of discourse (that is, *words*), ethnographic accounts of women's day-to-day life (their *work*), and research, policy and programme interventions (*actions*) that elucidate or have an impact upon women's natural resource-based livelihoods.

Let us begin by considering the more familiar concept of landscape. A landscape is commonly defined as an expanse or scene that includes material features of land, water courses, vegetation and fauna, and the built environment, all of which may be 'taken-in', absorbed in one view. The term 'landscape' became a scientific term over two centuries ago after it was used by Alexander von Humboldt, scientist-explorer and geographer, to represent the total character of a region integrating the natural and the human into a complex system. The discipline of landscape ecology evolved in more recent years to represent the ways in which ecosystems interact. Landscape ecologists are not concerned with particular ecosystems but with spatial patterns and ecological processes, how spatial heterogeneity influences and is influenced by ecological processes. Since the 1990s, conservation biology has also shifted focus from particular ecosystems or sites to wider expanses. (A protected biodiversity 'hotspot', say, would then be seen not in isolation but as part of a larger landscape that includes unprotected areas.) An understanding of how landscapes are constructed over a period of time, and the diverse components, processes and relationships that characterize different landscapes, is vital to traditional and modern systems of managing natural resources.

The concept of landscape is also intertwined with historically specific socio-political ideas of land, nature, art and poetry, with national cultures and heritage. David Lowenthal (1991, 7-10) has pointed out that, in fact, the now familiar visual picture of the English landscape is quite recent. The distinctively crafted 'patchwork of meadow and pasture, hedgerows and copses, immaculate villages nestling among small tilled fields', suggests 'national virtues', a stable, ordered and controlled world. This is linked with the English national ethos 'imprinting its heritage role: insularity, artifice and stability.' National identity, thus, has a 'scenic essence'. This is not wild nature in the raw but a landscape that reflects the seemliness and propriety of ancient harmonies and an ordered society. 'Heritage is above all chauvinistic' (Lowentahl ibid.). In the US too, landscapes have been the means to assert nationalistic identity. According to Alfred Runte (1979), in the latter half of the 19th century, spectacular and monumental natural sights were celebrated to bolster American heritage against the grandeur of Europe's castles and cathedrals. The demarcation of wilderness areas, such as the Yosemite Valley in 1864 and Yellow Stone National Park in 1872, was part of the American national aspiration for monumentality and visual spectacle, rather than just the expression of an early conservation ethic. So also in India. As I have written elsewhere (Krishna 1996a: 262), a 'picturesque landscape of self-contained village communities is a central and powerful image in Indian environmentalism and some strands of global environmentalism as well. This is an imagined landscape shaped by many different influences —by foreign anthropologists and Indian nationalists. It is above all a visual image of village communities, living close to the land, in harmony with one another and with nature.' A landscape is both a physical-social place within which one is located and a space which one experiences mentally. A landscape is endowed with both material and ideological values that are also gendered.

One of the best known instances of the blending of the material and ideological is the unique categorization of landscapes in ancient Tamil poetry. Between the 1st and the 3rd centuries, Tamil poetry was framed by five context-specific poetic themes (see Ramaswamy 1997: 228-35, Dubiansky 1998). Five such zones or *tinais* were recognized in the poetry of the period (also called Sangam poetry), each with a dominant landscape: the *kurinji* (mountain forest), *mullai* (undulating pastureland and forest), *neydal* (littoral coast), *marudam* (river valleys and wet-land), and *palai* (parched and arid hot desert). Each landscape zone had its own characteristic inhabitants or *kudi* engaged in particular occupations, with their own modes of food production and ritual traditions. The social meanings invested in the mountain forest or other landscape were built up by the poetical convention, which in turn was reinforced by its natural and climatic associations. In each theme a particular poetic situation corresponded to a natural landscape and a season or time of day. The kurinji was visualized as a zone of hunter-gatherers, the mullai of shifting cultivation and animal husbandry. The marudam was the zone of plains agriculture, and the neydal of fishing, salt manufacture and trade. Both the marudam and the neydal, as also the dry palai were associated with crafts.

The elements in a landscape, the flora and fauna, were gendered as male or female and these symbolic correspondences were expressed in the landscape (see Dubiansky 1998). In the kurunchi-tinai, the poetical situation is of erotic romance; the meeting of young lovers in the mountains is expressed in terms of mythology and landscape elements, with plants taking on anthropomorphic identities. The golden red flowers of the *venkai* (the big tree *Pterocarpus bilobus*) were associated with the male god of war and worn by warriors into battle. The edible tubers of the forest vine *valli* (*Convolvus batatas*) symbolized fertility; its clinging tendrils, which encircle the venkai tree, reinforced the association with the female. Similarly, in the mullai-tinai where hill forests form 'the background for the situation of a devoted wife, waiting patiently for her husband, we see that its dominant idea—female chastity— is also expressed symbolically by numerous details of the landscape.' (ibid.: 22). The most important of these is the jasmine (*Jasminium trichotomum*) the symbol of female chastity. At one level, the five conventional landscapes of Sangam poetry reflect a sensitivity to local natural environments and a deep conservation ethic. Yet, at another level the very same landscape metaphors and iconography reflect stereotyped attitudes to men and women. Modern conservationists who seek to revive the conservation ethos reflected in the poetry may or may not consciously be aware of the dichotomy of the warrior male and the clinging, patient, devoted female, but the resonances with some of the metaphoric ingredients of modern natural science discussed in Chapter 4 are unmistakable.

From the imagery of ancient Tamil poetry, let us turn to the materiality of everyday practice. Anoja Wickramasinghe (2004) has studied the evolution of the ecological and cultural landscape, in the recent past, in the dry zone of central Sri Lanka. She points out that the spatial zonations, which 'maintain the security of the habitat, livelihoods and the environment', are constructed by 'human values and attitudes'. The landscape zones are intimately connected with the gendered division of knowledge and work in a patriarchal society. Gender-differentiation has resulted in greater diversity and distinctive ecological-cultural spaces that men and women occupy. The lateral interaction of the landscape elements, home gardens, *chena* (swidden) fields, forests and water courses are sustained and balanced by the gender-differentiation of work. Yet, the gender-differentiated spatial zonation, which seems to be required to maintain ecological sustainability, also reflects the patriarchal relations of society that have shaped both the landscape and the stereotyped gender roles that continue to hinder 'women's potential contribution to modern ecosystem management and the entry of extension services to enhance traditional practices' (ibid.183).

A landscape is both a rich source of symbolic value (as in the aesthetic zonations of Tamil poetry) and an intricately-evolved gender-differentiated pattern of work zones (as in the dry region of Sri Lanka). The seeming ecological complimentarity and balance of a landscape is, in fact, a contested terrain that 'needs to be understood as enmeshed within the processes which shape how the world is organized, experienced and understood' (Seymour 2000: 214). Landscapes are also vulnerable. Judy Whitehead (2003) has suggested that 'concepts of abstract space are often forcibly imposed on local places, resulting in a radical reconfiguration of class and gender relations'. This negates the customary ways in which people relate to landscapes and waterscapes and cannot contain processes such as nomadism. She points out that in the Narmada valley, the concept of abstract space has enabled 'developers to maintain a highly objectified and external relation to the landscape, which becomes emptied of people, history, entitlements, myth and magic', and is 'replaced by a quantifiable area consisting of commodifiable resources, in this case, water and electricity'. Therefore, 'most development maps of the areas surrounding the Sardar Sarovar Dam in the valley do not contain the names of villages that hold historical importance for the tadvi, vassawa, bhils and bhilalas, even ones they consider centres of their cultural history.' Following Lefebvre (1999:87), Whitehead sees this as 'immense waves' of spatial change, colliding rather than intersecting. She argues that both neo-liberal capitalism and scientific-managerial attempts to reorder landscapes reflect an environmental approach that is narrowly utilitarian, that 'measures and surveys the landscape in terms of its commercially viable features'.[1]

When we think of people's life-worlds as complex, experiential centres in which people, dwell and work, the 'taskscape' as conceptualized by Tim Ingold (1993: 152) provides an especially insightful approach. For Ingold, a landscape is a bounded space 'constituted' by the activities of people. It is 'an enduring record of—and testimony to—the lives and works of past generations who have dwelt within it, and in so doing, have left there something of themselves'. The criss-crossing paths in a landscape are not just routes to and from particular locations but the social imprint of generations, 'the taskscape made visible' (ibid. 1993a: 167). The taskscape constructs the physical environment and gives the landscape its character. It is incorporated into bodily experiences and known through the senses. Tasks and landscape are transformed through time. The temporality of the landscape involves patterns from the past and projections into the future. Ingold illustrates the taskscape through a painting, called 'The Harvesters', done by the 16th century Flemish artist Pieter Paul Bruegel (also spelt Breughel). A humanist and naturalist, Bruegel keenly observed and depicted the social relationship between peasants and nature through the seasons. (He was known as the peasant's painter because he is believed to have been born in a peasant family and also because peasant life is a major theme of his paintings.) Analysing 'The Harvesters', Ingold says: 'The landscape . . . is not a totality that you or anyone else can look *at*, it is rather the world *in* which we stand in taking up a point of view on our surroundings . . . not so much the objects as "the *homeland* of our thoughts".' (ibid. 1993: 171). Ingold's concept of a landscape is a world, a homeland, a standpoint, which seems to me not unlike the Angami Naga *ura*, 'my place, my village, my nation' (Krishna 1991: 207).

'The Harvesters' is not so much a snapshot as a narrative; it tells a story through time, from the perspective of the peasant. The painting illuminates Ingold's powerful and dynamic concept of taskcapes. However, the pathways and social imprints of a landscape do not automatically render visible a gender-differentiated taskscape such as the gendered landscape zones of Sri Lanka described in Anoja Wickramasinghe's (ibid.) study. From a gendered perspective, therefore, we need to build a concept that deepens and enlarges the taskscape. This would mean not just bringing in another dimension, another view or a different lens. It would mean altering the frame of vision to encompass both the rootedness and particularity of a taskscape and the gender-differentiation and 'layeredness' of a genderscape. The concept of a genderscape, as I have described it earlier (Krishna 2004a) deepens the taskscape-landscape by drawing out the material and ideological dimensions of gender-power relations—conflict, contestation, resistance, negotiation and transformation from the standpoint of the 'outsider-within'. Genderscapes are relevant to NRM: economically, because gender relations are meshed in physical and natural environments; socio-culturally, because gender relations are diffused through belief systems and ideological constructions which shape both individual and communal life-worlds; and socio-politically, because gender relations flow through a range of different traditional and modern institutions.

The evocative metaphor of the 'outsider-within' upsets the more familiar metaphor of the existentialist outsider, the detached observer of life, who may or may not struggle to overcome her/his disinterest. As used by feminists, the outsider-within denotes engagement and interest rather than disinterest. It is the experience of a participant and an observer, being part of a social group or community and yet distinguished from it because of a particular set of attributes. Speaking as a Black woman academician in the US, Patricia Hill Collins (1986, 1990) said 'the outsider-within position of Black women academicians encourages us to draw on the traditions of both our discipline of training and our experiences as Black women but to participate fully in neither.' The concept of the outsider-within can be elaborated by Sandra Harding's (1991, 2001) concept of standpoint epistemology, the creation of knowledge from marginal positions. As a feminist and a scientist, Harding questioned positivism, the supposedly objective scientific 'voice from nowhere' and she argued that every researcher occupies and speaks from a specific lived location. Yet, even as specific locations are recognized, this does not mean a multiplicity of subjective views because knowledge-making is a collective process. So, if we start from the perspectives of women's lives, not women in the abstract but particular groups of women in specific social locations, marginalization itself becomes a strength (generating what Harding calls 'strong objectivity'; see also Hirsch and Olson 1995). Marginalization provides a new angle of vision from which gender relations in the community may be observed and examined. I have argued that the apparent equilibrium of gender relations, their stability and robustness over time are maintained by other systems of social relations, such as class, religion and caste and socio-cultural attitudes and practices, which are so deeply internalized within the self that they seem natural. The flux in gender-power currents only becomes apparent when viewed from a different standpoint, from intermediate, outside-in perspectives. However, despite the turbulence in the undertow, hegemonic gender relations are continuously being reinforced or recreated with the aid of mechanisms that contain, accommodate, or overcome transformative forces, for instance by isolating subversive forces at the local level, or within the family.

A genderscape would, therefore, start with the family and the household and trace the complex and multifarious linkages between the sexual division of labour in the home and the division of labour in the wider community. It would seek to uncover patterns of women's subordination, whether through economic vulnerability or through coercive/forceful confinement in domestic arenas by 'ideologies of mothering, caring and nurturing' (Moore 1988). While gender analysis frameworks differentiate gender roles, responsibilities and patterns of resource usage, I see genderscapes as ranging further and dwelling deeper to render visible the subterranean currents that are not discernable in a 'normal view'. They would do this by combining formal and non-formal research tools, especially oral history and literature, narrative techniques, song and drama, hand crafts and so on, uncovering the nuances in everyday gendered practice to reveal the linkages between 'the homeland of our thoughts' and patterns of resource management.

When I visualize a genderscape, the picture that comes to mind is abundantly detailed, many-layered, diverse and complex, like a rainforest or a tropical sea. We need richly-textured genderscapes of gender-egalitarian systems, how these are being changed, maintained or eroded; genderscapes that blend different ways of knowledge creation, exploring traditional knowledge systems and customary practices, how these circumscribe women, how these are changing to enable women to claim their stakes; that uncover the inclusion and exclusion of women in traditional community resource management practices and trace the linkages between changing patterns of resource use and control, ecological sustainability and women's well-being. We need genderscapes that look at women's health, mobility and decision-making power within the family, in the public sphere, and in the fluid interstitial spaces between them. More specifically in the context of the management of natural resources, genderscapes would:

a) construct a gendered and trans-dsiciplinary picture of resource management over time, drawing upon the collective memories of poor women in a particular landscape;
b) establish linkages between the local heritage of resource values and gender-power relations;
c) build a gendered taskscape of the natural-resource based livelihoods of marginalized women;
d) reveal the gendering of landscapes, through gender-differentiated knowledge and work, and the implications of this for maintaining ecological sustainability and challenging patriarchy;
e) examine the conflict between different conceptualizations of resources in a landscape, from a gendered perspective; and
f) seek to understand how the material and ideological subordination of women are mediated through natural resource use and management.

Genderscapes may be varied in scope and application but would look at the process of interventions and women's agency in the context of structures of domination. Localized genderscapes (as in Chapters 5 and 7) would help us to get away from simplistic 'master-stories' and 'grand narratives' of women's subordination, to understand the diverse processes by which power is gendered, and to explore sites of resistance. Broader genderscapes (such as Chapters 4 and 6) would help to provide a strategic ground for transformative collective actions. Making the linkages between these levels (as in Chapter 8) is an extraordinarily difficult theoretical and practical task that can be accomplished by the collective efforts of researchers, practitioners and activists seeking new paths.

Walking new paths

I believe that we can make these paths by walking them with minute observation, by-passing preconceived stereotypes of the mind, perceiving details on the ground as they are, highlighting unseen edges and boundaries and building micro-level pictures with 'head, heart and hand'. We need to construct more inclusive and encompassing approaches that are 'gendered' rather than 'conventional' or 'celebratory'. As repeatedly stated in this book, women are not a homogenous group. Their life-worlds are shaped by class/caste and other factors. Re-visioning NRM does not require bringing women into the picture or taking men out of it, but altering the frame of our vision to encompass the varied and layered experience of women and their gendered relations in specific locations and in different physical-spatial, socioeconomic, socio-political planes. The division of gender roles, family responsibilities, household labour etc. are not natural or permanent but have been shaped through historical circumstances and reflect a hierarchy of power. These traditional roles will have to be challenged if approaches to the management of resources, whether these be watersheds, forests, wetlands, ponds, soil, seeds, medicinal plants, livestock, fish etc., do not just perpetuate gender-discrimination.

The policy of treating each natural resource sector as a bounded entity is a view from afar and above based on disciplinary and technical knowledge that is deeply sexist. It entirely shuts out the complexity of women's lives in which the use, conservation and management of different resources are almost always inter-linked. Instead, policies need to be geared to the genderscape, centred on the local spaces that women inhabit, the places where they dwell and whose surroundings provide the resource base necessary for their survival and development. The question of resource rights is especially difficult to address because women are at once independent constituents of the household-community and integral members of family-kin networks. However, if new resource rights are to be egalitarian, these will have to be de-linked from old conventions that determine unequal access and control of resources. This could mean that poor women's resource entitlements need to be separately addressed. How this is done may vary for different natural resources but, basically, it is all the same issue of recognizing that the so-called 'women's rights' to natural resources are human rights to survival and development choices.

Even as they step out of their traditional veiled lives, the mallahin women of rural Bihar recognize that without the rights to the fish in the ponds, or viable alternatives, their empowered survival is at stake. Re-visioning resource management is not simply a matter of resources but a matter of people and resources, and so has moral, political and human consequences. Gender bias in NRM cannot be overcome, nor can communities manage their natural resources in a gender-equitable way, unless the role of natural resources in gender-power relations is understood and collectively addressed.

The diverse circumstances in which women's leadership has emerged from women's collectivity are reflective of the kind of capabilities that women have to change existing resource management practices. If empowerment is not to be ephemeral, however, women's economic and livelihood needs cannot be separated from their socio-political interests. Transformations that threaten to subvert the existing order cannot come without struggle. Yet, unless such a long-term goal is kept in sight it would be all too easy to lose our way in policy measures and interventions that seem to be in women's favour but are no more than safety valves or smokescreens, changing little, if not actually aggravating women's subordination.

NOTES

[1] The vulnerability of customary ways of relating to landscapes is especially pronounced in the context of globalization. In an innovative adaptation of the suffix-scape, Arjun Appadurai (1996) has expressed the cultural aspects of globalization that involve dynamic movement. He identifies five global flows across boundaries that were earlier impenetrable: ethnoscapes, the mass movements of peoples; technoscapes, the speedy trans-boundary transfer of technologies; financescapes, the speculative flow of global capital; mediascapes, the dissemination of information, images and narratives; and ideoscapes, the transmission of political cultures of nation states, ideologies and counter-ideologies. Appadurai points out that the globalization of culture is not the same as its homogenization but that globalization involves using various homogenizing 'instruments' that are absorbed into local political and cultural economies, a process in which the State plays an increasing role. He sets the contest between 'sameness and difference' at the core of global cultural processes.

Table 10.1

	Suppression	Appropriation			Structural Change
			Illusion		
Characterized by	Violence	False Projection	Safety valves	Smokescreen	Politicization
Tactics Instruments	Force	Defensive Law and order machinery	Conciliatory Administrative machinery, Activist leaders	Subversive Planning and Administrative machinery, People's groups	Conscientization

Source: Adapted from Sumi Krishna 1996 c.

APPENDIX I
SIGNPOSTS: ESSAYS

S1
Women on the Farm: Holding up the Ladder

Chhatera's peacocks perched calmly on the neem tree over-spreading the *chaupal* (the village meeting place) quite unmoved by the hubbub below. More than 50 farmers were clustered around seven dairy experts from the National Dairy Research Institute, Karnal, to discuss the pros and cons of modern crossbreeding techniques. There was nothing surprising in this, the peacocks would have told you—this juxtaposition of old farmers in bespattered dhotis, puffing away at their hookahs, young ones in terylene shirts and trousers, city-bred specialists armed with pamphlets and charts—and children laughing, scrambling all over the place, hanging monkey-like over the roof of the chaupal for a better view. This was a familiar scene. Now what would have startled the peacocks out of their perches would have been a couple of women in swirling Haryana skirts and jingling bangles come up and settle themselves among their menfolk to ask: 'Aren't cows our business too? Who do you think is going to wash them and milk them and bring in the fodder?' But that, alas, has never happened, not in all the six and a half years that *The Hindustan Times* has been watching the comings and goings of 'Our Village Chhatera'.

As the men talked of Holstein Friesians, frozen semen and green fodder, I slipped off to corner a woman striding by, a great green sheaf balanced firmly on her head. 'Why aren't any of you women here?' I asked abruptly, and was shamed into silence by her serene reply. 'But there are no women among them either', she said, meaning the Karnal experts. No, indeed there were not. 'And although my family has land', she continued patiently without lifting her veil, 'I don't have a field of my own, you know. Besides, now I have housework to do and no time to sit down and talk.' As she walked away it struck me that there in a nutshell I had some answers to the question I had been struggling with: what was the role of women in village agriculture? This was a vexing question because though many of the women were old friends and I had been in and out of the village for nearly three years, I did not really know.

A role rarely reported

Attempting to find out I first thumbed through our clippings file armed with a sheet of paper marked 'Agriculture' with columns for 'women' and 'men'. There were three jottings for 'women' when the 'men' column was halfway down the page; there were five jottings for 'women' when the column for 'men' had gone on to page 2. At this stage I gave up what had become a futile exercise. One hundred and fifty reports dating back to February 1969. Agriculture predominated: sowing, harvesting, new seeds, fertilizers and pesticides, new varieties, new crops and farming techniques, irrigation problems, marketing problems . . . the list went on and on. But where were the women? My instinct told me they were there, so did my observation. You could see the women bringing in fodder for the cattle, cutting grass or tough stalks of *jowar* (sorghum), carrying these loads over slippery field bunds. Yet this was a role that rarely got reported, a role that all the men and women in our team had perhaps deemed not worth reporting. This was a sobering thought that if the story of agricultural progress in Chhatera were written the record would show that the women did not have any major role. Was this the true picture? The nagging question remained: where were the women during all those years when the agricultural pattern in the village was undergoing a sea change?

Let us forget the women for a moment and consider the agricultural scene. In 1969 there was no tractor in Chhatera; today there are at least eight with a variety of fittings for different agricultural operations. As the farmers switched to the high-yielding varieties, traditional irrigation methods were abandoned in favour of the modern energized tubewell. Wheat continues to be the major crop, but the once popular *desi* (indigenous) varieties have been replaced by the new high yielders. When a new variety is released, say by the Haryana Agricultural University, it now gets to Chhatera almost immediately. Yet six years ago, the village had not even heard of the hybrid varieties of coarse grain and paddy, which the National Seeds Corporation had been selling since the early 1960s. It was only the persistent efforts of scientists and extension workers of the Indian Agricultural Research Institute (IARI), New Delhi (commonly known as the Pusa Institute), which succeeded in setting off a minor agricultural revolution. Insecticides were unknown and Pusa's agronomists had to hold demonstration after demonstration both for *kharif* (summer) and *rabi* (winter) crops before the farmers were convinced. The bigger farmers were the first to be won over and with their co-operation the IARI conducted a water and soil survey. Each individual farmer was then advised what crops, varieties and rotations were best suited to his land, and given specifications for the amount of water and fertilizer he should use.

There were a few sceptics but also many progressive farmers who even began to visit IARI regularly to buy seeds, seek expert advice and keep in touch with the latest developments. Such a farmer who took the trouble to make the 40 km. trip to Pusa would be among the most enlightened and energetic in the village. And there were many like him. What about the women? Suppose, I thought hypothetically, we took the most progressive, enlightened, energetic woman in Chhatera, would she be able to match that? The women's response was obvious. The young ones and the old one, the conservative ones and the enlightened ones, every one of them said no, they would not.

The ladder held by women

And yet such agricultural novelties as a modern storage bin designed by Pusa and a soybean crop claimed to be better than

Pusa's own, were achieved by men who climbed up the ladders of progress, which their women were holding steady below. There were elderly brahmin women like Lakshmi and Phulo who worked on other people's land without any prejudice, gathering fodder from field bunds and canal banks. There was ancient Khazani, the harijan [dalit/ Scheduled Caste] woman who even at 85 would go out at dawn to graze cattle or cut grass for landowners in the village, only to earn a paltry Rs.1.50 a day. There were couples like Jog Lal and Bharto who would spend a month harvesting, brushing chaff with their brooms and winnowing. Together they earned about seven quintals of wheat in a season, at the rate of four sheaves for every 100 they reaped. There were others like Parvathy who spent half a day cutting a sugarcane field and got Rs.3.50. These women who were at the very bottom of the agricultural pyramid were too far away from the fruits of modern agricultural techniques to care particularly about them one way or the other. As they said over and over again, 'we do not have fields of our own.' Village agriculture might collapse without their labour, but it was a fact that their work could be done more efficiently and quickly by machines. And so the role of such women in agricultural decision-making was not even peripheral, and it had always been like that.

If the very poor and the harijans had for long been left out of the agricultural scene, this was not so for many others such as the tough jat women who worked with their husbands on their family fields. The women were in fact more adept than the men at many field operations—sowing, weeding, harvesting, threshing and winnowing. In the old days, a joint family council of men and women had decided what crops would go where and when, but farming was no longer an extension of domestic activity. The women, perhaps educated only up to the primary level, hampered by purdah restrictions and household work, just cannot cope any more with the complexities of modern agriculture. Today's farmer offering his field for an IARI demonstration might consult a brother or a son, standing beside him at the chaupal but not the women-folk who would be out working in that very field or cooking in the house.

The nagging question and answer

And there I had got a possible answer to the nagging questions: why did it appear that the women were nowhere on the scene during the years that the agriculture of their village was being transformed? Where were they? They were being left behind, just simply and quietly being left behind. For the story of agricultural progress was the story of long conversations with male experts from the city, of reading pamphlets which discussed the comparative merits of different fertilizers, of travelling to marketing centres and research institutes to keep abreast with the latest in the agricultural world. In these activities there was no room for a woman.

Would there be any incentive for women to break out of this and start taking agricultural decisions on their own, I wondered. Were there any women planning their own farms, working their own fields, organizing it all by themselves? There were three women the villagers said, Bhim Kaur, Maya and Chalthi, all widows. Maya's had been the greatest struggle of all, they said. The young brahmin widow had brought up her small children and pulled her family out of desperate poverty by dint of courage, patience and hard work. I remembered that Maya had once donned her very best skirt to show visitors how voluminous a Haryana garment could be. But in her laughing face there had been no trace of the struggle she had been through. Maya, true to her reputation, was away at her field and on two subsequent visits I could not get to meet her.

Bhim Kaur, now a grandmother was at home spinning her *charkha*. This outspoken and determined woman was ahead of her time as the first woman farm manager and the pioneer of birth control. She also has the distinction of having brought up the most enlightened young man in the village. Widowed when her son was under 12, she was too proud to take help even from her brother-in-law, the richest farmer in the village. Managing her 12-hectare (30 acre) farm single-handed, she had kept to her resolution to educate her son through school and college till he qualified as an Ayurvedic doctor. But to return to Bhim Kaur's early struggle: The village helped by providing her farm labourers whenever she needed them. Too intelligent and too practised a farmer herself she did not need and would have felt insulted to follow anyone else's judgment. But despite this progressiveness, Bhim Kaur never once left the village to market her own produce at the *mandi*. A neighbour would take it along with his, and her young son would go with him to keep an eye on it. Even today she maintains that a 'nice woman' would not go to the mandi. This is all the more surprising because she has travelled to many parts of northern India as a part of a group of women panchayat members. That the trip was government sponsored and there were other women with her seemed to make it all right.

Thirty three year old Chalti did not have Bhim Kaur's self-confidence. Widowed when she was scarcely 16 and with a one-year-old son, she had no alternative but to go home to her parents. A youthful, attractive widow could not stay alone in the village; it would neither be considered proper nor safe. But now [1975] her son is 17, studying at Sonepat, and Chalti is back in Chhatera trying to pick up the old threads again. This is her first crop and she has many problems. Irrigation is dependent on energized tube wells but the electricity is only turned on at night; 'what can a woman do?' she asks. Hired labourers do not work at night and a woman cannot go out to her fields in the dark. Her neighbours help, but how often can she ask them, Chalti said. Because she was a woman on her own, her crop would suffer some loss, she felt but could not estimate how much. And like Bhim Kaur so many years ago, she too would send her produce along with a friend to the mandi, with her son going along to keep a watchful eye. Her son, like many other educated boys and girls in the village could handle some farm jobs but did not have the thorough grasp of farming that she and others of her generation had. What would the future hold? Chalti, perhaps superstitiously, refused to speculate. 'Let's see how this harvest goes,' she said.

What would the future hold? Would the woman once so closely associated with the process of agriculture, taking decisions and making assessments and forecasts, be left further and further behind as the green revolution turned greener and greener? Would each new breakthrough in technology only increase the existing gap between the men and women, making it a great gaping chasm?

Perhaps not, but only if . . . if she had a little more education, if specialists from the city included women who (instead of addressing meetings at the chaupal) went from home to home talking to village women as they cooked, cleaned and washed, if women had land of their own or held it in trust for their minor children as the widows did, if some far-seeing organization arranged joint excursions to take groups of women to marketing centres and research institutes . . . then and only then would women regain their old position and stop playing a merely supportive, behind-the-scenes role in the process of agricultural change.

Adivasi women: Short-changed in local markets

Forest-dwelling adivasi communities in central India have struggled with the lack of economic opportunities, the erosion of their lifestyles and resource bases. Gathering and marketing forest produce is a major occupation for many women in Bastar (Chhatisgarh) and Jharkhand. The weekly *haat* (local market) is the hub of the local economy, where a variety of forest products are bought and sold, and sometimes exchanged. There may be seasonal variation in the items, and lean seasons, but generally some forest produce is available all year round: firewood, *tendu* leaves, tussar cocoons, sal leaves and seeds, *mahua* flowers and seeds, gums, resins, medicinal herbs, and so on.

The haat is also the centre of adivasi social life, a place where people from several villages collect to renew old ties or make new ones (through arranging marriages). It is also the place for relaxation and entertainment. The air may be heavy with the smell of *sulfi*, the toddy-like liquor fermented from the sulfi palm in Bastar, or with *handia*, a rice beer popular in adivasi Bihar. In a medley of images and sounds, fighting cocks shriek as bedecked adivasis, squabble, laugh and jostle each other; heaps of white salt glisten against a stack of brightly coloured petticoats and ribbons fluttering in a nearby stall. There are mud pots, iron implements made from melted down rock, green vegetables, onion and garlic, and food stalls selling biscuits and savouries. For many years now, the adivasi's traditional boiled or mildly-fermented food has been varied by fried and spicy savouries bought in the markets.

In the past, the haats were dominated by women from various adivasi groups, each of which had different levels of ,interaction with the market. The women's independent income provided the 'oil and salt' money for subsistence-level households and gave them a degree of autonomy, which is increasingly being undermined. The women sell their produce, often in minuscle quantities, for low prices. Some products are bought up by non-adivasi *mahajans* (traders-cum-moneylenders), who have a monopoly over particular markets and can, therefore, strike usurious deals. Indebtedness is. widespread, even though going to the moneylender is a last resort. A common adivasi saying reflects the mahajan's power to accumulate wealth: 'You enter our country thin as a needle; you leave it thick as a ploughshare'.

The adivasi women's responsibility for marketing and their experience in this has made them more adept than the men at bargaining and accounting. The women are skilled and patient in striking the best deals. But coping with the mahajan's agents is a difficult task. A Munda song makes the point that the mahajans, like kites or geese, should not be allowed to enter the village precincts but should be made to wait in the tree groves beyond.

Different government agencies have recognized the importance of the market in the local economy, but tribal welfare societies and cooperatives have not been able to intervene effectively. Well-intentioned schemes are easily subverted. This is illustrated by a case in Singbhum district (Jharkhand). In 1979 the Central Silk Board had established a tussar cocoon 'bank' at Chaibasa, the district headquarters, to ensure that the adivasi women got a fair price for their cocoons. At that time the prevailing market rate for a *páan* (a counting unit of 80 cocoons) was between Rs 5 and. Rs 6. The cocoon bank offered to pay Rs 10 directly to adivasi sellers, but before it could begin to do so, the mahajans' agents had fanned out all over the district, buying large quantities of cocoons at the lower rate. When the bank opened, the mahajans simply employed adivasis as a cover to sell the cocoon stocks that they had already acquired. The adivasis got paltry wages for the labour of carrying the sacks; the mahajans made a cool Rs 5 on every paan off-loaded onto the government's cocoon bank.

Having been out-manoeuvred by the mahajans, the following year (1980), the Silk Board decided that its officials would buy the winter cocoon harvest, directly from the haats in Chaibasa and other towns. I was travelling through Singbhum at that time, and followed the markets from the southern border of the district to Chaibasa. At each haat on the road to Chaibasa, the Board officials would arrive, lay out their cloths and open their account books to buy the cocoons, but they did not get any. In the meanwhile, the mahajans' agents did brisk business; they spread themselves out on the periphery of the market, covering every path leading to it. They reached more adivasis more quickly. The officials could only offer the declared rate of Rs 10 for 80 cocoons. The mahajans hiked the rate to Rs 10.50 in the market furthest away from Chaibasa. Lured by the higher rate, the women were cheated as the agents juggled the figures while counting the cocoons and the money. However, the mere presence of Silk Board officials did ensure a kind of support price. At the end of the day, the smaller agents and traders would sell their cocoons to the big mahajans, who paid them a small profit of Re 1 per paan.

In the meanwhile, the government announced its intention to hike the rate per paan to Rs 15. This was known to the officials and the big traders but very few of the adivasi women were aware of it, and others did not want to risk waiting. So, at the large haat at Hatgamaria, south of Chaibasa, the women sold their cocoons at Rs 11. per paan to small agents who in turn sold to the mahajans at Rs 11.50. The Chaibasa-based officer who should have authorised the higher rate had been sent temporarily to Assam to set up an oak tussar centre, and his return had been delayed because road and rail communications in Assam had been disrupted due to an on-going agitation there. No one knew when he would be back. As a result, in the peak buying season, the Board was not getting cocoons. The concerned officer arrived at Chaibasa on the eve of the weekly haat. In a few hours, he had organized a jeep with a loudspeaker to announce the new rate throughout the town. The next morning, the mahajans as usual offered a marginally higher price, but at the Board's shed the cocoons were now piling up at a much quicker pace. This might have been because the adivasis (both men and women) around the urban area of Chaibasa were more aware, or because the traders had already bought up sufficient quantities at the lower rates and were surreptitiously disposing off their stock to the Board, as they had often done before. It was hard to tell.

Even if the mahajans had not taken advantage of the spurt in cocoon prices at Chaibasa, they could still have gained a good profit as their major bulk buyer was the Government's own Khadi Board which supplied yarn to weavers of Bhagalpur in north Bihar. The Khadi Board's buying rates would be determined by the Silk Board's rate for the cocoons. The innovative attempt by the Silk Board to buy tussar cocoons directly from the adivasis was only partially successful. The profits of the traders may have been far greater than the benefits to the adivasi sellers. Government intervention did succeed in raising the buying rates, although considering the women's labour involved in collecting tussar cocoons, the rate worked out to much less than the official minimum daily wage. The government too had a problem because the weavers who used the yarn were also extremely poor people, and a higher cocoon price would have affected them.

If the women do not have the capital, the reeling equipment or the skills required for turning cocoons to yarn, they can have no part in the production of tussar yarn, a more valuable product. But the technological upgradation of activities in which women are primarily involved has rarely engaged the attention of policy makers and programmers. The division of labour in adivasi societies makes the women responsible for the household's 'oil and salt' money, but they are easily exploited not only because they are women but because their economy is vulnerable against unregulated markets.

S3
Women and Environmental Activism: A Patchwork Quilt

When one thinks of 'women and environmental activism', the image that comes to mind is of a patchwork quilt in shades of green. How does one make sense of the variegated hues, the assorted textures and patterns, the partial and conflicting visions? Perhaps, we should hold the quilt up to the light, to try and discern its history, the fraying and tangled skeins that lie beneath. Perhaps, we should then look at the individual human beings, the women who fashion the patches. And then maybe we would be in a position to ask that most difficult question of all: not what women have done for environmentalism, but what environmentalism has done for women.

During the previous century, the extension of the British colonial administration, its systems of law and order and land revenue into the hills and forests eroded peoples' rights to land and forest resources, and led to diverse movements of resistance. We do not know the part women played in the protests that erupted in the tribal heartland of Chotanagpur and the Santal Parganas in central India, or in the mountain tracts of Kumaon in the northwest. But in Manipur in the northeast, it was the Meitei tradeswomen who controlled the commodity market and led the *nupilan* (women's wars) against the British administration's policy of exporting rice from the valley. The need to restore the livelihood rights of poor people, to conserve the soil, protect water courses, and maintain vegetative cover were deeply felt issues, which were intertwined in the struggle for Independence. Even more prominent were the commitments to women's education and efforts to free women from oppressive social customs. However, after Independence, through the 1950s and 60s these issues were overshadowed by the more urgent concerns of new nationhood. Women and the environment were both on the neglected fringes of development planning, and the linkages between the two were not made.

Activism from Chipko to Narmada

It is against this 'pre-history' that we should view the current phase, beginning in the mid-1970s, of both the environmental and the women's movements in India. This was a period when diverse new social movements were seeking to alter the fabric of conventional politics. As these movements matured, they found that they shared many concerns.

Towards Equality (ICSSR 1974), the pioneering report of the Committee on the Status of Women had not considered the warp and the weft by which poor peasant women were bound to natural resources, their problems of access to fuel, fodder and water, and matters of resource management. But less than a decade later, this had changed. Today, both women and the environment have become buzz words fastened together in all kinds of ways.

How this happened is a story of many women and men. The story begins in the 1970s, in Garhwal and Kumaon in the western Himalaya. This is a region of breath-taking beauty and much poverty. The land and the forests alone cannot support the population, and most adult men seek employment in the plains. The women bear the burden of agriculture on the steep slopes, and the day-to-day responsibility of caring for the household. The forest provides the villagers with timber for house beams and agricultural implements, twigs and branches for fuel, leaves for fodder and a variety of herbs for medicine. But commercial extraction was fast depleting the Himalayan forests, threatening watersheds and forcing women to trek longer distances to gather fuel and fodder.

In 1973, in the border district of Chamoli, the Forest Department denied a local cooperative 10 ash trees that were needed to make lightweight yokes for the small hill bullocks. The very same trees were allotted to a private sports goods manufacturer from Allahabad to make cricket bats. The village men and women first considered burning the trees down, but decided otherwise when someone suggested that a mother saves her child from the wrath of the tiger by hugging the child to her breast. They would hug the trees rather than let them be cut down. The threat sufficed, the contractor withdrew and the people's movement got its method and its name *angwaltha*—the Garhwali word for embrace, later modified into the more direct Hindi exhortation *chipko* (to cling or hug).

In another episode at Reni village in the spring of 1974, a young girl spotted a group of contract labourers preparing to go into the forest, and raised an alarm. All the village men were away, summoned to the district headquarters. So, the women led by middle-aged Gaura Devi swiftly got together, singing songs and barring the only path into the forest. The action at Reni transformed Chipko from an obscure movement of poor peasants to a celebrated environmental icon.

However, women's protests against mining in the neighbouring Pithoragarh and Almora districts evoked much less media and public attention, although the objectives of the anti-mining group were similar to those of the movement against commercial forestry. Perhaps this was because the method that the women adopted—slitting sacks of soapstone and spilling the contents—lacked the emotional nuances of hugging a tree. And there was no catch-all slogan like chipko.

Chipko raised the issue of people's rights to resources, and the ecological value of forests. Reni dramatically provided the link between women and the environment. Chipko emphasized women's nurturing role, and in later years, local *mahila mandals* (women's groups) in some villages took the lead in growing trees and fodder grasses to meet household needs. In those villages where women participated more actively in afforestation programmes, they gained some control over the use and management of local resources, and the drudgery of bearing loads from the forest has eased. But the movement has not questioned lower wages for women, the denial of land rights to them, or the patriarchal authority structure. So, the women's position within the household and community has remained virtually unchanged.

This has generally been the pattern of environmental activism, whether of forest-dwellers or fisherfolk, of rural peasants or the urban poor. This is so even in the Narmada Bachao Andolan (NBA), led by Medha Patkar, arguably the most famous environmentalist in the country. Although large numbers of women have been an integral part of the movement, taking part in meetings and *dharnas* (demonstrations), this has done little for their own subordinate and often oppressed position within their families.

At present, land is the critical environmental resource. The Gujarat government's rehabilitation package provides for alternative sites for each male householder, and to his adult sons, but not to wives and daughters. But the NBA (in common with other environmental movements like Chipko) has been little concerned with the question of land rights for women. Why is this so? Is it because while the struggle for environmental rights may threaten many interests, the struggle for women's rights is even more destabilising?

Indeed, during the last two decades there have been many instances of women's environmental activities being thwarted even when they have legal rights to the land. This is either because of traditional local customs, or the inertia of government functioning. The case of the nameless Bhil hamlet attached to the village of Brahmano-ke-verda in Udaipur district, Rajasthan, is well known. The women had applied under a government scheme for the allotment of government-owned wasteland, but they found that there was confusion over whether the law allowed transfer of land to women. Eventually, the women did get the land but only after a year of struggle and the persistent intervention of a local non-government organization (NGO) Seva Mandir.

Women in the environmental debate

Leaving these troublesome questions aside for the moment, let us examine more closely some of the colours and patterns in the quilted patchwork of environmentalism, and the positions that women, along with men, have taken. The heart of the debate concerns the impact of the development process: is development the cause of environmental problems or is it the cure?

On the global stage, the late Prime Minister Indira Gandhi captured world attention at the first United Nations conference on the human environment at Stockholm in 1972, with her comment that "poverty is the greatest polluter". She upheld the position that development was the instrument to improve the quality of life, and sought a managerial solution through the institutionalization of environmental concerns in law and the administration. The National Committee on Environmental Planning and Coordination was set up. This was later to become the Department of Environment and in the 1980s, the full-fledged Ministry of Environment and Forests.

However, a much wider spectrum of popular environmental advocacy draws its inspiration from back-to-nature philosophy and Gandhian ethics. Here the patchwork becomes very intricate, as women of all kinds of persuasions have adopted a variety of populist stances. Radha Bhatt, of the Kausani Ashram in Kumaon, who led the women's protests against mining, appeals to age old Hindu religious sentiments, urges the preservation of traditional lifestyles, and a rejection of what is seen as a western model of industrial development. Radha Bhatt and her associates draw their inspiration from an earlier generation of women disciples of Gandhi, notably Sarla behn. Rejecting her Swiss-German heritage to follow Gandhi, Sarla behn had adopted an Indian name and way of life. She spent her later years in the Pithoragarh region advocating environmental conservation and women's welfare. In the late 1970s, I had some correspondence with her and recollect her pragmatic concern for easing the drudgery of hill women.

Celebrated NBA leader Medha Patkar who moved from an academic interest in social work towards popular advocacy, describes herself as a mixture of green and red values—Gandhian environmentalism and socialistic egalitarianism. More than any other environmentalist in the country, male or female, her integrity and dedication have helped to arouse public opinion and force a rethinking on conventional development. Yet, somewhat conservatively, Medha Patkar tends to treat rural society as a homogenous whole, undifferentiated by class, caste, tribe and gender. It is difficult to tell whether this is part of her philosophy or a tactical approach in the strategy of protest that the NBA has adopted.

The surprisingly diverse back-to-nature school includes Maneka Gandhi, who gained prominence as the estranged daughter-in-law of Indira Gandhi, and went on to become the Union Minister of State for Environment and Forests. With a more narrowly focused concern for vegetarianism and the welfare of animals—from silkworms to stray dogs and performing bears—Maneka Gandhi sees ecology as an approach, not a science. She is more concerned with intuitive perceptions of the whole of nature, than with understanding the complex linkages between poor people and their resource base.

Yet another thread of distinctly sharper hue is Vandana Shiva's brand of back-to-nature ecofeminism, which equates women's procreative power with a so-called feminine principle in nature, and this 'feminine principle' with women's role in subsistence production and forestry. The ecofeminist vision is to forge 'a new sexual and reproductive ecology', rooted in imagined linkages between the exploitation of nature and the exploitation of women's wombs. Ecofeminism tends to the view that female biology endows women with a monopoly over holistic and ecological knowledge that men lack. Yet, in emphasizing women's biological, procreative and maternal roles, ecofeminism curiously mirrors the very motifs of conventional development which it seeks to repudiate.

Between them, the managerial and populist strands have tacked together much of the patchwork quilt. Progressive approaches are only sporadically visible among the patches. However, in the few instances where progressive approaches have been adopted, the focus has been more on women's strategic interests and less on the environment as an end in itself.

Activism takes many forms. Among the best examples of progressive village-level initiatives is the work of NGOs like SARTHI in the Panchmahal district, Gujarat, and the Centre for Women's Development Studies (CWDS) in Bankura district, West Bengal. In both cases, the greening of wastelands and the generation of income were means to the greater goal of empowering women. (See Chapter 8)

Untangling the patchwork

Nani Duni lives on a small plateau, cradled in the high mountains of Arunachal Pradesh. On her face, she sports the traditional tattoo marks and the large flat nose-buttons of an Apatani woman. She no longer weaves her own sarong-like *gale*, and instead wears one of the dark-striped Himachali shawls that flood the market. A thin blue wind-cheater protects her against the winds which tear through the plateau, but her feet are clad only in a pair of ordinary rubber slippers. Nani Duni is not what you would call an activist in the conventional sense of the word. She has carried no banners, made no statements. Yet she has resolutely held on to a way of life and skills that have come down to her through generations (and which she cannot pass to her daughter who is away at college and building a new life). She selects the seed and cultivates five different varieties of paddy—the red for wholesomeness, the black-husked for special occasions, a fast-growing variety to fill the granary, and two others to make the best of different kinds of soil. Women like her are not closer to the earth, simply because of their sex, but because the arduous role of producing food for the family has been foisted on them by their society. These women are the last bulwarks against the erosion of agricultural diversity. The irony is that conserving this diversity also means conserving their own marginalization in society.

Environmental activism has to untangle such knotted skeins in the quilted patchwork. Emphasizing women's ecological knowledge and their role in conservation may help to ease women's labour and even further their contribution to resource management. But unless women's familial and social status is strengthened, the effectiveness of environmentalism can only be of limited value to women themselves. If women acquired greater control over the natural resource base, the processes of production, and of their own labour, they would be better equipped to cope with the problems of transition under India's new economic policies. Such empowerment has been most elusive. Yet, this is what women and men must strive for, if a design is to emerge from our patchy fragments, our bits and pieces of colour.

S4

Ecofeminism: A Review

The ecofeminist world view, which has been hailed as a radically different version of women and of nature, has been propagated in India by environmental activist Vandana Shiva. Ecofeminism links women's procreative power with a so-called 'feminine principle' in nature, and attempts to project this into the public domain. It equates the ecology of nature with the biology of women's bodies, and men's exploitation of nature with men's exploitation of women's wombs. Women's 'sexual spirituality' is seen as a fountainhead from which emerges the ecofeminist vision of a 'new sexual and reproductive ecology'.

In Vandana Shiva and Maria Mies' book of the same name (*Ecofeminism*) the authors speak of 'their shared belief in the grand unifying formula of ecofeminism upon which everything in the universe—biology, economics and politics—is based.

The theme of *Ecofeminism* is that 'the capitalistic, patriarchal world system' is founded upon and sustains itself through 'three colonizations'—of women, of foreign peoples and their lands and of nature. Ecofeminists view modern science and economic growth as 'reductionist' responses of a violent male ethos which ignores 'the interconnections that nurture and sustain life'. Instead, ecofeminism envisions a world of subsistence lifestyles, in harmony with nature and pervaded by the 'feminine principle' of loving and caring.

There is much that is valid in the ecofeminists' analysis of the adverse impact of colonialism on the natural resource base, and in their critique of the hegemony of international trade, consumerist production and technological fixes. Ecofeminists are also right in emphasizing the patriarchal character of many aspects of modern development—although it needs to be pointed out that not all development is patriarchal and anti-women.

However, the powerful advocacy of ecofeminism rests on a dubious base. Ecofeminism does not specifically seek to exclude men, but it assumes that female biology endows women with a monopoly over holistic and ecological knowledge that men lack— 'to create a child is quite different from constructing a car or other machine' argues Maria Mies. This biologically deterministic view has been critiqued by progressive feminists. For if insight into nature is women's biological heritage and intrinsically humane qualities like caring for nature and people are rooted in women's reproductive capacities, then it would follow that men are biologically incapable of such knowledge and nurturance. Therefore, the implication is that men's violence and aggression are also biologically determined and unchangeable. This is pernicious politics.

The book is a mixture of persuasive arguments and selective interpretation of facts to fit the ideology. This results in many half-truths and distortions. Modern economic theory is criticized for being based on the 'principle of self-interest'. Charles Darwin is summarily dismissed for the same reason. Yet, Darwin's contribution to shaping the modern world view was surely in showing that the human position in life is *not* a privileged one apart from the rest of nature?

Ecofeminism denounces the 'fathers of natural science' and Francis Bacon in particular for attempting to control 'the power of creation which hitherto lay with women and with nature', and transforming this into 'the art of production'. It is true that Bacon advocated the extension of man's power over nature, as ecofeminists contend, and in today's world his 17th century language would be considered sexist. But Bacon was also deeply concerned about the ethics of science—an aspect of his work which ecofeminists completely ignore. Bacon was motivated by a 'love of God's creation' and believed that nature could not be commanded except through obedience. He recalled the warning of the Faust legend, arguing that the quest for knowledge and practical skills should not merely be for mental pleasure, disputation, superiority over others, profit, fame or power, 'but for the benefit and use of life'. Ecofeminists completely miss the variety, depth and complexity in Bacon's attitude to nature, and this is characteristic of the single-track along which ecofeminism proceeds.

To criticize all of science as reductionist is also particularly biased. Reductive analysis, which represents a whole in terms of the functional relations of its constituent parts, has proved to be particularly effective as a tool in some branches of science and social science. It does not mean that the whole is a mere sum of its parts. Intuitive experience may be a valid method of perceiving and understanding complex wholes. But this does not negate the understanding gained through the intellectual analysis of compli-cated structures—indeed this helps to concretise the synthesis and wholeness for which ecofeminists yearn. There are, of course, limits to the usefulness of reducibility, just as there are flaws in a nebulous holistic approach.

Vandana Shiva's particular contribution to ecofeminism is that she relates the 'feminine principle' in nature to women's key role (as compared to men) in forest-based food-gathering and subsis-tence agriculture. But there is considerable historical evidence to show that there is no simple division of labour by sex. In India, neither gathering nor the traditional knowledge of subsistence production had been women's exclusive domain. Women relate to nature not because of their biological distinctiveness as women, but because of their gendered role in the household and commu-nity. Women's experience is also more closely linked to men of their own socio-economic class, than to women of other classes.

The authors assume that prior to colonialism and modern development communities existed in idyllic harmony with their local environments. They argue that traditional and subsistence economies which satisfy basic survival needs through 'self-provi-sioning' are not poor. Since subsistence is not deprivation, for ecofeminists emancipation from poverty becomes unnecessary. This reflects a strange blindness to the human dimensions of poverty.

Basic needs are a matter of perception; over time these change, extending beyond the physical and biological needs of survival. Health, education and an enlarged range of occupational choices are also vital needs of today. For those who have themselves moved beyond subsistence, it is all too easy to advocate subsistence lifestyles for others.

For ecofeminists the soil is the 'sacred mother', the womb of life in nature and society, which is desecrated by colonialism and conventional development. This shifts sovereignty from the soil and soil-linked communities to the nation state, ecofeminists say; so the country as Motherland is replaced by a masculine nation-state. From this follows Vandana Shiva's thesis that the socio-political violence in the Punjab was the result of profane agricultural development that violated the sacredness of the soil. In her simplistic view, social disintegration, separatism and ethnic violence are ecological matters of high-yielding seeds and the intensive use of fertilisers and irrigation. Such ecological fundamentalism overlooks the complex linkages between the emergence of agrarian capitalism and the political process. Although the processes activated by agricultural dynamism may have contributed to political developments, there was clearly no facile one-to-one linkage between the 'violence' of Green Revolution technology and the 'violence' in Punjab.

The celebration of female 'sexual spirituality' as the pervasive unifying principle in nature to counter all of modern science, technology, industry and economy is singularly biased. Despite its radical stance as a rediscovered philosophy of nature and women, ecofeminism shares many of the ideological roots of political conservatism—the belief that biology determines social divisions and that monopolies of knowledge derive from male and female reproductive capacities. The appeal of the 'new cosmology' of ecofeminism seems to derive from the cult-like power of inventing a seductive mythology, rather than from insights into historical and socio-political processes.

It's Time to Clear the Cobwebs: The Gender Impact of Environmentalism

All poor 'Third World' women do not constitute a homogenous group who experience the same kind of changes. All rural and tribal women are not poor. In order to understand how different groups of women are affected by environmental transformation, it is necessary to clear away some of the cobwebs in our perception.

Women are producers, consumers, conservers and distributors of environmental resources. Concentrating exclusively on women's position as consumers and distributors, some environmentalists cast women as *victims* of ecological degradation, bearing an increasing burden of work due to the depletion of water, firewood and fodder resources. Others focus attention on women as producers and conservers, locating women in an apparently more positive role as *managers* of natural diversity. Both approaches mask distinct socio-political attitudes. (Krishna 1994, 1996a)

Viewing women as environmental victims is a comfortable position for middle class, city-based, male environmentalists. (It is also a comfortable position for middle class urban female environmentalists.) Championing the cause of poor rural women does not affect the patriarchal pattern of their lives, because the women in their own households do not have to perform tasks such as fetching water or gathering fodder and fuel wood. So too, seeing 'Third World' women as victims of developmental and environmental stress, makes it easier for Western environmentalists to advocate gender equality, without examining their own biases too deeply.

Many development interventions are based on the understanding that women are environmental victims. So, environmental programmes with a 'women's component' may ameliorate a specific condition—schemes to ease women's burdens by increasing biomass or water resources, for example, but these are not designed to change women's gendered roles. Women are now participating in both government and non-government programmes in large numbers. But such programmes have had little impact on women's status within the household and community. The approach that sees women more positively as environmental managers (rather than as victims) is apparently more positive—but only apparently. This is notably so in the advocacy of ecofeminism. . . . [See S4]

In emphasizing women's biological, procreative and maternal roles, ecofeminism curiously echoes some strands of the conventional development theories which it seeks to repudiate. For instance, Shiva (1988) attempts to relate the so-called 'feminine principle' in nature with women's role in subsistence production in agriculture and forestry, and argues that women-gatherers—as compared to men-hunters—play a key role in the forest economy.

In fact, historical and anthropological evidence shows that there is no simple division of labour by sex. In certain parts of India, poor women do bear an increasing burden of work due to the depletion of environmental resources, and the degradation of village commons. Walter Fernandes and his associates have documented the tribal woman's extensive role in gathering forest produce in Central India; much of this labour goes into gathering firewood (Fernandes and Geeta Menon 1987). In the caste society of Garhwal and Kumaon in the Uttar Pradesh [now Uttarakhand] Himalaya, where patriarchal systems are even more firmly established, women bear the major burden of collecting fuel, fodder and water.

However, neither gathering nor the traditional knowledge of subsistence production is women's exclusive domain. Govind Kelkar and Dev Nathan (1991) argue persuasively (in their study of the Jharkhand region in Central India) that the division of labour between men and women is a matter of culturally-determined gender roles rather than biologically-determined sex roles. They cite studies of the Mesolithic period in Central India which show that apart from gathering, women also participated in the hunt. They point out that in many foraging societies, where gathering provides the major part of the diet, it is not all done by women. Their estimate is that men's labour accounts for 30 per cent of firewood collection and 40 per cent of the total. Moreover, much of the work is actually done jointly. A. K. N. Reddy's well-known study of the very different conditions in Karnataka has also shown that men do participate in gathering firewood; the ratio of domestic labour in the study villages was: men-24: women-56: children-20.

The weakening of tribal society and the transition to the caste order is characterized by changes in the status of women, such as in their control of resources, their right to property, and freedom of movement. Little is known about the very earliest stages by which women on the Indian subcontinent lost control over land, but in certain parts of India the decline in woman's status appears to have been a prelude to the formation of class society. It also seems that women lose even access to natural resources with the rise of patriarchy, caste domination and the erosion of their ritual and social status.

The women's movement and the growing area of gender studies have concentrated attention on the household. The significance of gender and women's work in understanding household behaviour under conditions of environmental and economic stress, such as droughts, has been rightly stressed (Chen 1992). From a gender perspective 'opening up' the household for economic analysis yields many insights (Ranadive-Deshmukh 1994). Environmentalists, on the other hand, are more concerned with communities than with households, because for the purposes of conservation, the community as a whole is more important than the interacting households within it (Krishna 1994).

Perhaps because of the emphasis on entire communities—which is valid upto a point—environmentalists have generally avoided analyses which sharply define the conflict of class interests among different sections of rural or tribal society. For instance, the Narmada Bachao Andolan (NBA) has tended to coalesce the conflicting interests of the two groups which will be affected by submergence—the well-to-do non-tribal *patidar* landowners in the Narmada valley and the much poorer tribals. In the case of the NBA, this is perhaps due to strategic reasons. Yet, popular advocacy that treats tribals, forest-dwellers, villagers as a composite category, threatened by a menacing urban industrial society, does not help our understanding of how different groups of poor women are affected by changes in the natural resource environment.

Environmentalism and feminism have overlapping concerns, but every social and environmental issue is not a matter of gender. For instance, the controversy of fuel and fodder trees versus timber and pulpwood trees has been projected as a gender issue of 'women's trees' versus 'men's trees'. The controversy takes off from one singular episode at Dongri-Paintoli village in Chamoli district [Uttarakhand state] where such a conflict between women and men was first reported by a woman researcher Gopa Joshi (Chauhan 1980). I am now somewhat skeptical of this kind of simplistic distinction, which equates women with nurturance and men with commerce. Would the host trees for tussar silk worms, which have been cultivated by the women of Bankura district, be categorised as women's trees, despite their commercial use—or as men's trees because of that? The socio-political question regarding tree species is not one of gender. The conflict here is rather between the interests of different agricultural economies. (For instance, if fuel and fodder trees are grown in areas of subsistence agriculture, and timber and pulpwood trees in areas of productive agriculture, would this increase existing imbalances?)

Modernization affects the interaction of both men and women with the natural resource base. In some parts of the Himalaya, improved roads, better transport and greater accessibility to markets have reduced the people's dependence on the local forests for food and medicinal plants. This weakens the linkages between communities and their local environments. J. Bandhyopadhyay (1993) has noted that upper caste women of all ages, and younger women of all castes, are now much less knowledgeable about the biological diversity of their local forests. A corollary of this trend would be an erosion of women's role in conserving community resources. This is the outcome of economic forces, for there is, after all, nothing intrinsic about women's interaction with nature.

In some parts of Central India, and in Garhwal and Kumaon, economic and environmental stress has intensified male migration from the hills, increasing the workload of women who are left behind. In these areas, environmental stress, male migration and high female work-participation rates coincide. It has been suggested (CSE 1985) that because of their greater workload, women then neglect traditional soil conservation practices, and that the end result would be further environmental degradation—a cyclical process, which has been noted in Kenya. However, it is not clear that this cycle can be assumed for India, where both social and environmental conditions are markedly different. In fact, it is possible to argue that the monetary remittances of male migrants have helped to ease the pressure on local resources in Garhwal and Kumaon.

Development actually poses wrenching choices. An environmentally damaging development may not necessarily be detrimental for women. Consider the case of roads. Environmentalists have argued against feeder roads, which provide easy access to isolated parts of the country, as doing more harm than good. In Uttarakhand, a network of border roads built for strategic reasons (after the 1962 war with China) brought in timber contractors and busloads of pilgrims, increasing the pressure on fuel wood and other resources. Environmentalists have also criticized the process of road-building by using explosives on the fragile Himalayan slopes. Yet, for the people who live in remote areas, roads are a lifeline to the outer world, better health care, education and employment. In some parts of Garhwal and Kumaon, villagers want motorable roads and are agitated that the Forest Conservation Act is being used to prevent the cutting of trees for road-building (Krishna 1996a). Even in the early 1980s, tribals in Orcha block in the isolated Abhujmar area (in Bastar district) [now in Chhatisgarh state] told me that they were anxious that their forest tracks should be made into proper roads, so that they could more easily go out to get work (Chauhan 1981).

Are village roads important for women? Among the larger states those with more than half their villages linked by all-weather roads also tend to rank relatively high in terms of rural female literacy. Village roads may or may not be a factor in the level of female literacy, but an analysis by UNICEF India (1990) does show that rural infant mortality tends to be higher in places which lack motorable roads or bus stands. This might be because village health services are unreliable, and people need all-weather roads and bus routes for access to better medical care in an emergency (Krishna 1994).

Changes in a community's mode of interaction with the environment can be particularly stressful for women with their multifarious responsibilities, but traditional systems of resource use may also entail a burden of drudgery for women. For instance, data from a Khasi village in Meghalaya (Ramakrishnan 1993) shows that ginger and pineapple are traditional cash crops; pineapple is cropped in mixed systems along with rhizomes and tubers. Coffee and tea have been introduced more recently as an experiment. The labour energy input required for tea (experimental) and ginger (traditional) were high throughout the year, while it was low for the mixed pineapple cropping (traditional) and coffee (experimental). What is significant from a gender perspective is that the male and female labour input is almost the same for the low-labour cash crops. But in the case of both the traditional and experimental cash crops, which require high labour inputs, women's labour is much more than that of men. This would suggest that changes in land use and cropping patterns need to be assessed both from a gendered and an environmental perspective (Krishna 1994).

So too with technological changes. For example, picturesque as it may appear to the onlooker, pounding and grinding grain to flour, and whole spices to powder is one of the most exhausting and time-consuming of women's traditional domestic chores. The introduction of commercially-run electric grinding machines in the villages of agriculturally dynamic regions, such as Haryana, has released women from this task (Chauhan 1979), and in some cases has shifted the chore to men.

Nostalgia for the natural environments and traditional lifestyles of the past is understandable. But the uncritical tendency among administrators, activists, academics and media persons to idealise days gone by has the very real danger of imprisoning women in traditional roles. It is ironic that many middle class urban women, who have themselves broken out of traditional moulds in their personal and professional lives, should be averse to less privileged women doing the same.

Towards women's autonomy

All environmentalists agree that women's participation is necessary to tackle the environmental crisis—'ask the women first', give them a greater say in the planning of projects (what species of trees to plant in an afforestation project, for example), let them decide how the community will share the available resources, and so on. Yet, significantly, almost all these modes of participation are limited to consultation, planning and management, avoiding the political questions of women's autonomy within the household and community.

Among the most important factors for women's autonomy are the right to land, control of local markets, and access through education and training to occupations that enhance their self esteem. Environmentalists strongly advocate community control of local resources, but have neglected women's right to land—which for the present is the critical resource—and have been indifferent about girls and women's access to education and modern skills.

In an informal survey of a Haryana village (see S1 above), at the start of the International Women's Decade in 1975, I had found that only three women—all widows—owned land either in their own name or in trust for male sons (Sridharan 1975; see S3). Although the women farmed the land themselves, they depended on male relatives to market the produce. The marginalization of women followed from their lack of control over land, the critical resource, and their lack of mobility. They were not encouraged by custom, or empowered by education and training to participate in the new learning; middle class male scientists and extension workers (with strong gender biases) transferred the new knowledge and skills exclusively to male farmers. As Kelkar (1981) points out, 'Women with no control over expenditure or marketing lose authority at home. This has been the natural consequence of their displacement from the spheres of work and market.'

Considering the ecological implication of excluding women from both community and government-owned forest management, Kelkar and Nathan (1991) have argued that the demand of land for women should be taken up within the Jharkhand movement, that women's participation should be used to prevent the destruction of forests and to strengthen institutions like the panchayat. They suggest that strengthening surviving tribal collectivism, while providing individual access of women and men to land and other productive resources, could be the beginning of a development that is not patriarchal.

The question of land rights also reflects the government's patriarchal attitude to development programmes. Many instances of this could be described. The experience of a small tribal hamlet of Brahmano ke verda in Udaipur district (Rajasthan) is fairly typical. In 1984, the Bhil tribal women applied under a government scheme for the allotment of government-owned wasteland, only to find that there was confusion over whether the law allowed transfer of land to women. They did get the land a year later, after the persistent intervention of Seva Mandir, a non-government organization working in the area (Krishna 1986).

The problem of women's control over land has rarely figured even among the many agitations and protests that have marked the environmental movement in India. The Gujarat government's rehabilitation package for those who will be displaced by the Sardar Sarovar dam on the Narmada provides for alternative land sites to each male householder, and to his adult sons. What of the rights of wives and daughters to land? The Narmada Bachao Andolan—led by Medha Patkar, arguably the most famous woman environmentalist in the country—has not been able to integrate women's rights into the campaign, although these are no doubt recognized. Feminists too have concentrated on the human rights violations of women rather than on land and economic rights. For instance, women's right to land does not figure at all in Ratna Kapur's (1993) impassioned argument that the Narmada Bachao Andolan should not treat women's rights as extraneous to its goals. Nevertheless, her analysis of the movement's attitude to women is pertinent. Although the women have taken part in meetings and demonstrations in large numbers, they 'are forced to return to their chulas

(hearths) and beatings after the dharnas (demonstrations) are over';
she goes on to say:

> If the Andolan continues to mobilize women in large numbers without
> addressing their specific needs their movement will be limited, in so far as
> it will continue to operate within a patriarchal framework. Although
> women's participation in the movement can be empowering, their em-
> powerment is incomplete because the movement as a whole is not in-
> formed by a feminist perspective and an understanding of the specific
> issues that women experience in the public and the private spheres.

In concentrating on women's ecological role in gathering and
producing food, environmentalists have also by-passed women's
economic role in local markets (Krishna 1996a). It is apparent
that for some tribal women, their control over the income from
gathering forest produce has enabled them to retain a certain degree of social autonomy. For tribal women, therefore, the market
is an important social and economic space, a place for interaction
and mutual bonding, and the means by which their status in
tribal society is protected. This is quite unlike traditional Hindu
society, in which the market is virtually 'out of bounds' for upper
caste village women.

In tribal areas throughout India the market is not perceived as
exclusively for males. (This is, of course, also increasingly true of
urban India.) The significance of women's interaction with the
market is particularly striking in Manipur, in North-Eastern India. The Meiteis of the Manipur valley are a patrilineal society
noted for the women's independence and collective solidarity. The
Meitei women have retained their identity and status despite the
pressures of 'Hinduization' and the upheavals of colonial rule.
What is the source of the Meitei women's enduring power, which
has few parallels in the Indian Subcontinent? The work of
Manjushri Chaki-Sircar (1984, 185) suggests that the women's
strength is derived from their primary socio-economic role, based
on control of the commodity market, and from the alternative
role of high ritual status for priestesses. In the colonial period, the
tradeswomen who controlled the commodity market led the protests against the British administration's policy of exporting rice
from Manipur. The historical antecedent of these nupilan (women's

wars) of the early 20th century have spurred other protests after Independence—notably against the government policy on increasing the rent on market plots, against public drunkenness and most recently against drug addiction. The women's power to influence the political and administrative system is not easily eroded.

The strength of the women's movement in the Manipur valley has been recognized by feminists but curiously not by most environmentalists, for whom the image of women's activism is the more evocative and gentler picture of the Chipko women. Yet, despite their effective role in the Chipko movement to save forest trees, and their lead in the afforestation programmes, the women of the Garhwal and Kumaon hills are a part of a decidedly patriarchal community, even if caste stratification is not as severe as in the plains. The women do not own land; their right to the income from forest produce is restricted; and they have little freedom of movement. Of course, the goals of the Manipur women and those of the Chipko movement are very different. This very difference between their situations suggests that women's collectivity centred around a developmental feature like local markets is perhaps more effective with regard to their own position in the household and community, than when women's organization is geared primarily to conserving the natural environment, however vital and effective this may be. (Krishna 1996b)

Clearly, control of natural resources needs to be taken a stage further to augment the value of resources, by opening up new avenues of employment and income-generation. There is one well-documented case, in West Bengal's Bankura district, which goes some way towards this. The Santals of Bankura had lost control of much of their land, and the once thick forests in the region were severely depleted. The women had to migrate to distant places in search of work. Operation Barga, the West Bengal Government's innovative programme to determine the rights of sharecroppers and to distribute land, had not been particularly beneficial to the women, because homesteads were not being given to them. In 1980, the state government invited a New Delhi-based NGO, the Centre for Women's Development Studies (CWDS) to work with the women of Bankura, who had to migrate seasonally because of impoverishment. The Bankura project started by forming village women's *samitis* for the cooperative greening of wastelands, with species that support the rearing of tussar cocoons. The samitis obtained plots of degraded land donated by individual owners.

The project was supported by the State Tribal Welfare Department and other agencies, and by CWDS (which in turn received funding for its staff from the ILO). Within three years, the first plot of waste land had been afforested with *Terminalia arjuna* and Shorea robusta trees on which tussar silk worms were being reared. A few years later the movement had spread to other villages and the membership of the samitis increased significantly. The women also gained representation on local development co-operatives, and those concerned with trade in forest products. The income from the annual yield of tussar cocoons has helped to finance diverse individual and group enterprises, which 'are not only businesses' but 'an expression of women's self-worth' (Singh 1991). Participating in a business and planning ahead has given the women a sense of security. A significant change is that the women say that now they can '*choose* when to migrate' (Malavika Karlekar personal communication 1993). However, optimism about the Bankura experience has to be tempered as this is a rather unique project. First, it has had continued support from CWDS Secondly it has had an assured high level of international funding —although this is reckoned to be less than the value of the 100 ha. of degraded land which was restored. What remains to be seen is how the Bankura women's movement will evolve if CWDS withdraws, and how effectively the movement spreads to other districts.

As the Bankura project shows, the gender perspective involves much more than a 'women's angle' on environmental issues. This is rarely recognized in both governmental and non-governmental interventions which are designed and implemented to fulfil sectoral and limited goals.

If women acquired greater control over the material basis and the processes of production, and of their own labour, they would be better equipped to cope with the problems of transition under India's new economic policies. Yet, such empowerment has been most elusive. The Shetkari Sanghatana's work in Maharashtra is among the rare instances where political organization is reported to have brought about a change in the gendered ownership of land (Omvedt 1992).

The linkages between environment and gender are complex. But the terms of discourse tend to be simplistic and perhaps deliberately confused. Perceptions remain at a rhetorical level leading to the proliferation of assumptions, idealizations and myths. This obscures the varied experiences of different social groups and classes of women over time. The tendency is to hasten to conclusions based on ad hoc observations and limited anecdotal information. This methodology sometimes leads to sensitive perceptions, but also results in sweeping generalizations. So it is not surprising that our understanding of the gender impact of environmental transformation is inadequate, and that many interventions are flawed.

The question that environmentalists and feminists must now face is how environmental activism and management can be developed to strengthen women's familial and social status. If this does not happen, then the effectiveness of an environmental strategy that emphasises women's nurturing role, or even women's participation in resource management, can only ease women's labour without changing their position. The value of the political education that women may derive from their participation in environmental struggles and activities lies in its being directed towards their wider empowerment.

Professional Women as Natural Resource Managers

Comprehensive and disaggregated data on the number of women in the life science disciplines (micro-biology, botany, zoology, ecology etc) and the applied sciences (agriculture, veterinary science) are not easily available. Earlier, the lack of women's hostels was a major obstacle faced by students in Himachal Pradesh, Orissa, Kerala, Uttar Pradesh, Assam and other states in north-eastern India. During the 1990s, the Indian Council of Agricultural Research (ICAR) provided substantial grants to state universities for residential facilities for women and 14 hostels were set up during the eighth plan period, such as one at the College of Fisheries in the Kerala Agricultural University, Kochi. My own observations in Mizoram indicated that apart from medicine and pharmacy, agriculture is the next professional choice for women in science. In recent years, notably in Kerala but also in other states, veterinary science, once a male bastion, is emerging as an important career choice for young women. A few years ago, at a workshop with which I was associated in Trichur, Kerala, the knowledge and skills of young women veterinarians upset the stereotypical assumptions of everyone else present. Not only were they dealing confidently with bovine cattle and other large animals, supposedly in the male domain, they had also come through their professional education without facing the kind of traumas described by Sagari Ramdas (2000) in an earlier generation at

Hissar in Haryana where sexism in veterinary education was blatant. In many universities across the country, today, girls outnumber boys in life science courses, and they are also doing better than the boys.

Despite the growing number of women graduates and post-graduates in the biological sciences, however, there is no gender balance in the professional institutions for agriculture, forestry and biodiversity management. Data on the ratio of women in professions related to biological diversity is hard to find, whether in government services, international agencies or private corporations. When I first studied this in 1997, I found that apart from the secretarial and support staff, the ratio of women in the Botanical and Zoological Surveys of India is minuscule. Moreover, the women tend to be concentrated in herbaria and museum jobs, and do not undertake field explorations. In certain scientific fields, the membership lists of professional associations are a fair indication of the ratio of women. For example, women constituted just 9.5 per cent of the Indian Society for Seed Technology. This included ordinary and life members taken together. Considering life membership alone, the ratio fell to 8.5 per cent .The women are mainly in government service, in the seed technology departments of agricultural institutions; some are in university departments. Despite the high visibility of a few individual women professionals, the ratio of women is even lower if we consider professional recognition in the biological and agricultural fields. In 1997, the elected fellows, men and women, of the National Academy of Agricultural Sciences since its inception numbered a total of 225. This elite group represented a variety of agricultural disciplines— plant breeding, genetics, soil conservation and so on. Only seven of them were women, mainly nutritionists and social scientists (agricultural economists). This is a ratio of under 3 per cent. Not much has changed since. These facts speak for themselves. (See also Ponnacha and Gopal 2004)

Various gendered pressures hamper the long-term commitment of women scientists to their professions. This may, of course, be so for all professional women. The gender-biased attitudes and systems within scientific institutions and agencies, that are part of the wider social milieu, contribute to these pressures.

Yet, most women who do survive these pressures claim that being women has not been an obstacle in their work situations. Many also feel that the institutions are not gender-biased in their dealings with the public. This is, perhaps, not surprising because the women's professional progress is implicitly linked to their identification with the overall male ethos of their institutions.

The proportional representation of women in NGOs concerned with biodiversity management is much better, particularly at the student-volunteer and junior levels. Volunteer conservation groups involved in activities like conducting bird counts attract as many young women as men, if not more. However, even in these groups the ratio of women falls at the middle and senior levels. This is true of a cross-section of major NGOs and agencies concerned with biodiversity including progressive groups such as the Kerala Sahitya Shastra Parishad (KSSP) and managerial organizations such as the World Wildlife Fund (WWF).

The case of the Indian Forest and Wildlife Service is especially telling. In the pre-Independence era, the service was built on a forest-policing and revenue-collection model. The forest service officer was stereotypically envisioned in the macho male 'hunter' image; his training involved activities such as horse riding, shooting, building physical agility and strength. The forest officer was expected to have the mental toughness to serve in remote areas where the living conditions would be difficult. Independence did not change this mindset. Other civil services, notably the Indian Administrative Service, were opened up to women but there was no place in the forest service for women or indeed for 'weak' men. The arguments advanced against allowing women into the forest service in the 1970s were very similar to the arguments that are now being advanced by the Indian army against women serving in field units such as the infantry. In 1980, when the forest service was eventually opened to women, this was partly in response to pressures from the prevalent Women-in-Development approach (of bringing more women into various developmental fields), and partly as a feeble reaction to the growing public opposition to conventional forestry practice. It was thought that women forest officers would give the service a 'softer' face. Both reasons may have also have played a part in motivating the women officers who joined the service. For some, this was a matter of proving their worth in a hitherto male arena. For others, there was a genuine belief that they could work towards change from within. For the women at the lower rungs of the forest service, rangers and foresters, it was simply another avenue of badly-needed employment. In 1980, there were two women officer entrants; this increased to nine in 1986 and 1987, but since then there has been no great rush of women into the forest service. During the 1990s, four or five women have joined on average, each year. In 1995, when the seniormost women forest officers had completed 15 years of service, there were 72 women in a total cadre strength of 2,576—just 2.8 per cent. The ratio of women rangers and foresters in the mid-1990s was less than 1 per cent. (GoI, 1997). Women IFS officers have been allotted to almost all states, including the less popular umbrella cadre that covers Arunachal Pradesh, Mizoram, the Andaman and Nicobar islands, Goa and the Union Territories. They have also served in fairly difficult field postings in north-eastern India.

The avowed purpose of having women forest officers was to use them as instruments to carry the message of forest protection to village women, and through them to village communities. The assumption was that women officers would have skills of communication and interaction, and succeed where their male colleagues had failed. This was made quite explicit at the first national convention on the role of women forest officers in forestry and sustainable development. Najma Heptulla (1995), then Deputy Chairperson of the Rajya Sabha, told the convention: 'In you, we have the communication channels. If you take up this job, we do not need a separate machinery to popularize these eco-friendly technologies. . . . The target group is the same. Without any bias, it is my belief that women officers have better communications skills and are more compassionate while dealing with those who are not familiar with official processes.' Heptulla's comments are a typical example of what I have called the conventional approach (women as more efficient instruments to deliver development messages) with some traces of the celebratory approach (women's greater compassion). The women officers themselves iterated the theme of being better communicators, but were clearly more interested in using the forum as a means to further careerist ends—parity in status, pay and service conditions with the other all-India services; more jobs at the level of Joint Secretary; and foreign training for women officers. The meeting was held in the month before the 1995 United Nations Conference on Women at Beijing, but the women forest officers' discussions reflected little or no awareness of the gender issues that were being publicly debated at that time. So much for women's compassion and female solidarity!

Indeed, my experience has been that women scientists and foresters, generally, do not show any greater awareness or sensitivity to gender issues, unless these concern their own personal and professional lives. However, although a larger ratio of women in an organization does not guarantee a gendered perspective, there may be a critical level, when the proportion of women professionals becomes sufficiently visible and articulate, so that they could then play a part in altering the level of gender awareness in the service. But that level is not within sight. This is, of course, linked to middle class socialization processes and the nature of scientific training and forestry practice, all of which have been moulded in male terms.

Gender and the Biodiversity Act, 2003: Some Comments

Most environmental legislation and Government Orders since the Forest Act of 1927 have been strongly undemocratic even as they are couched in the rhetoric of democracy. For example, in 1979, at the height of the Chipko movement against commercial tree-felling, the Uttar Pradesh government passed an 'immediate action' order suspending *all* green fellings. This was ostensibly in response to a fast undertaken by one of the Chipko leaders, Sundar Lal Bahuguna. Many liberal supporters of Chipko welcomed the Government Order. They did not realize its implication: commercial felling would be stopped temporarily but forest-dwellers too would not be able to get vital requirements of small timber for house construction or to make agricultural implements. The order curtailed rather than enhanced the people's rights. I fear something similar is happening with the Biological Diversity Act, recently. Like other environmental legislation it is strongly centralizing and anti-people. By increasing bureaucratic authority, it might well lead to corroding the very rights of the communities that a biodiversity legislation should seek to protect. Indeed, the legislation includes provisions that could be termed anti-community and draconian.

Consider the concentration of powers in the National Biodiversity Authority. Apart from an 'eminent' Chairperson, the Authority includes 10 official members appointed by the central government, representing the Ministries of Tribal Affairs, Environment and Forests, and the Director General of Forests, and seven other related central ministries. Only five non-official members are included who will represent scientists, industry and the people. The Act also says that decision-making will be through majority vote. Regardless of inter-Ministry differences it is likely that the three-plus-seven official representatives would promote a consensus of the Central Government's interest on issues. The five non-official members, however, representing diverse sections of the population are unlikely to have common views, and if they did, could be out-voted. So, whose rights are we talking about?

The Constitution of India recognizes the complexity of rights, to some extent. While individual rights are upheld, community rights are also supported in certain cases. This, I believe, is a positive aspect of the Constitution. The same Constitution sanctions the continuation of pre-Constitutional personal laws which evolved in a pre-democratic era which was not marked by gender egalitarianism. The negative impact of this for women in relation to both the Plant Variety Act, 2002, and the Biodiversity Act needs to be more deeply examined.

At the superficial level of gender-neutral grammar, the Biodiversity Act seems to have benefited from the criticisms of the Plant Variety Act. The law-drafters have been careful to use the gender-balanced he/she throughout the text and the neutral term 'Chairperson' (Although towards the end of the Act, we find the Chairperson placing '*his* casting vote'!) At a deeper level, however, the patriarchal mindset of the law-maker is clearly visible. A section exempting local people from the requirement of prior intimation for obtaining biological resources, specifically mentions '*vaids* and *hakims*', indigenous (male) medicine practitioners. What about *dais* (traditional birth attendants) and other women healers? Would we have to take recourse to the 'general law' in India by which legally 'he' includes 'she'? And so argue that male 'vaids and hakims' include female dais? One approach is that the Rules under an Act can compensate for any vagueness in the Act. Yet, we also have the very well-documented evidence of Rules being used to derail major policy initiatives. The working of Joint Forest Management is well-documented and shows how communities in different States have used seemingly simple Rules (such as for quorum at a meeting) to subvert gender-egalitarian functioning.

The Biodiversity Act gives the state government the power to notify 'biodiversity heritage sites' and for 'compensating or rehabilitating' those who are 'economically affected'. Can local people's interests be protected through the local Biodiversity Management Committees set up under the Act? (Incidentally, it should be noted that the size of a panchayat is very varied and may include hundreds of villages in Assam or Orissa. The 'territorial jurisdiction' of such Committees and their relationship to the Panchayats is a grey area.) The Biodiversity Act seeks to regulate the use of biological resources at the national level, but does not address the traditional knowledge of biodiversity, which is currently in the public domain. This is of great significance to the livelihoods of many resource-poor groups. It is this traditional knowledge, and the process of its evolution, that needs to be acknowledged and protected more comprehensively from the people's point of view.

S8

The 'Earth Mother' Rides a Bicycle! The Changing Rhetoric of Folk Art and Craft

> Sarladevi, a frail old woman, her beady eyes sharp as a bird, sits in the open air of the Crafts Museum [in New Delhi]. She has brought her own stock of clay from Goalpara in Assam, and she moulds a figurine, attaching pellets for the eyes, the lips, the breasts, the braided hair. She could not possibly know that she is creating the Earth Mother, identical in proportions and details and the enigmatic bird-face to those excavated from Mohenjodaro, Harappa, Kalibangan—fashioned perhaps four thousand years ago and miraculously preserved.
>
> Once in a while, as a curious piece of anachronism, she might place the Earth Mother riding a bicycle—bringing us back to the twentieth century!
>
> —Shah and Sen (1992: 129)

Changing functions

On a mild winter afternoon in Delhi, a few years ago, I had three hours to spend while waiting to meet a friend. Just down the road was a bazaar of Orissa handlooms and handicrafts. As a frequent visitor to Orissa during the last decade, it held no novelty for me but having time at my disposal I went slowly through the stalls chatting with the craftspersons who were exhibiting and selling their work. Some purposeful young women customers were buying traditional Sambhalpuri saris and dress materials but casual passers-by, like myself, were more interested in low-priced items:

hand-painted greeting cards on thick hand-made paper and palm leaf, decorative bookmarks printed in bright colours on strips of palm, and small dhokra (bronze/ bell metal) animals. Among those animals was a tiny kangaroo, a perfect replica, a pendant with a loop to be hung on a key chain or necklace. The craftsman told me they had seen it on television and someone gave them a picture; so they were able to create the mould. Dhokra sculpture, which is made through the moulded 'lost-wax' process in Bastar and parts of Orissa and West Bengal, is generally regarded as a 'male' craft but is a family occupation with women preparing the beeswax and often suggesting the design, an especially important input. As Laila Tyabjj, Chairperson of the pioneering NGO Dastkar, which supports craftspersons and helps market their work, says: 'The product can only be marketable if it is attractive to the consumer i.e. the traditional skill is adapted and designed to suit contemporary tastes and needs. Design does not mean making pretty patterns. It is matching technique with a function.' (Dastkar website)

Like dhokra sculpture, Orissa's traditional palm leaf painting of mythological themes, done in monochromatic black, is also considered a male skill but women help prepare the materials and are increasingly suggesting new themes. Besides traditional scenes of the ever-popular god Krishna, the palm leaf bookmarks now depict ordinary village/tribal life, women and men collecting fuel or water, breaking stones, carrying loads, hunting deer in the forest, ploughing the land, children playing among dogs and scurrying hens. One of my printed palm leaf bookmarks shows a migration: women, men and children, camels and mules laden with goods walking across sandy dunes. An Oriya family's vision of life in the deserts of Rajasthan or Arabia? With the shift from hand painting to printing, the designers are also using many bright hues with an eye to the mass market, blue for water and the sky, green for trees and plants, yellow for huts and baskets, bright red, blue and green for clothes.

Alerted by kangaroos ready to leap and camels on the move, I examined the hand-painted greeting cards. In Orissa, as also in Bihar, Maharashtra, Tamil Nadu and other states, village women decorate their mud huts with conventional local designs. These traditional ritual paintings are now being reproduced in black or white on pale-yellow, beige, rust-brown or black cards to approximate the colour of their huts. The single-colour paintings convey the rhythm of life through simple lines, dashes and dots, representational outlines, stylized motifs, and the repetition of figures and borders. My cards had elephants, horses, cattle and fowl, no unexpected animals. But two cards did have a surprise. In the corner of one card a boy was holding a bicycle (instead of the usual cattle); in the other, there seemed to be a girl with a bicycle. The craftswoman confirmed this quite matter-of-factly. Not only was a traditional art being used for new purposes, the motifs were changing.

Folk arts—stories, song, music, dance, painting, crafts etc.– do not exist in definitive, unchanging forms. The new items (e.g. bookmarks, greeting cards), motifs (bicycles, buses or aeroplanes), materials and colours (natural or synthetic) clearly reflect expanding worldviews. Also noteworthy is the depiction, in dhokra work, of village women engaged in diverse activities: crafting a basket (Bengal), beating a drum (Bastar), and even reading: a common dhokra figure is of a girl lying on her stomach, feet in the air, engrossed in a book. The Assamese terracotta woman riding a bicycle (in the epigram above) seems to me an especially fine example of craftswomen confronting new horizons and making these their own.

How significant are these recent innovations in the production of folk art and craft and the visual representations of women? To what extent do the urban demand for folk products and the signs of women's visibility, mobility, literacy indicate a positive, empowering trend for the craftswomen themselves? Can this be strengthened through the new and emerging modes of information and communication technology (ICT)?

Visual rhetoric

Since the 1960s, there have been many critiques of 'visualism' or a 'visualist ideology'. The phonetic alphabet is said to have given us 'an eye for an ear', and the linear sequences of the book to have extended and intensified the eye's visual function, trapping spoken words on the printed page (McLuhan 1964, McLuhan and

Fiore 1967). Taking this further, arguments emerging from different disciplinary perspectives have contrasted visualism to the auditory and tactile worlds of pre-modern cultures that are said to evoke knowledge rather than map information onto a Cartesian plane. Yet, even in pre-modern, auditory cultures and oral traditions, the visual too has a significant (and gendered) role in constituting aspects of social life and nature as is evident in folk art.

For many pre-literate and barely-literate social groups pictorial representations are both means of artistic expression and serve to convey information and knowledge of a way of life, often ritually related to natural resources, and to lifecycle and livelihood ceremonies. These representations are context-specific and have a locally-shared lexicon of symbols as in the diverse rice paste/flour paintings on walls or floors, embroidered materials, and hand-shaped or moulded objects of grass, clay, or metal created in different parts of rural and tribal India. The creators may be women and/or men, usually unnamed, often working together in a family group, using natural materials and vegetable colours. Their creations embody particular constructions of the environment, spiritual visions, images of flora, fauna, and humankind, depictions of seasonal and daily activities. The familiar patterns of folk art and craft, and the objects themselves, emerge from lived experience and particular socio-economic structures and processes. These are forms of cultural education, means of socialization and of negotiating or/and affirming gender identities through a rhetoric which is 'deliberately contrived and regulated' and is as powerful a mode of persuasion as speech and writing. As Vidya Deheja (1997: 16) points out in relation to classical Indian art, 'We tend to think of rhetoric as a verbal skill; the importance of visual forms of rhetoric is only just beginning to be appreciated. Its power of persuasion, often insidious as against more direct verbal rhetoric, should not be underestimated.' For instance, women's quilting is historically well known throughout the world as a means of 'voicing' their silence. In India, groups of poor women (like the banjaras of Andhra and Karnataka, and the kutchis of Gujarat) have used embroidery to create their own spaces, resist and perhaps transcend the constraints around them.

Among the most interesting examples of visual rhetoric to

create 'alternative constructs' are women's ritual wall paintings during the festival of Gangaur in Rajasthan. An analysis of the rituals of four Rajasthani festivals shows different levels of empowerment (Gold 2000: see pp. 225-27; also Gold 2003). Holi contrasts 'demonic men' with 'life-giving women'. Dasa mata celebrates women's superior knowledge. Sitala underlines women's economic assertion as assertive women transgress the taboo on ploughing and claim the right to bequeath property. Compared to these Gangaur, an upper caste festival which celebrates the marriage of the goddess Gauri, seems least empowering: 'Beautiful Gauri, the fair one, is enshrined in an elaborate multicoloured wall-painting along with her perfect husband. First the girls, followed by the household's married women, make offerings to and then manipulate the picture, uniting the divine couple with coloured strings. (Gold 2000: 225)' Each worshipper emulates the male brahman priest (who ties together the clothing of bride and groom in a real wedding) and so, through the ritual-painting, the women emphatically contest familial expectations and social pressures. As Gold points out,

> Ritually, Gangaur celebrates couples. As high-caste pageantry, explicitly defined as important only for those groups who forbid widow remarriage or divorce, it is the nearest among the four festivals to taking a view of females as subservient half-bodies. Yet, just as women plough like men on Sitala's Day, on Gangaur a girl acts the part of a groom, and women— officiating through their "interactive" wall are at the divine couple's union —act the parts of male Brahmin priests at weddings. (ibid. 226)

Elsewhere, women use other kinds of visual rhetoric to negotiate with beings in a realm beyond human sight. On the cowdung-smeared threshold of village houses in Tamil Nadu women draw intricate freehand kolams (geometrical designs of rice-powder or lime). These snake-like motifs are ephemeral, smudged by people's feet during the day and renewed ritually each morning. One interpretation (Gell 1998: 84-90) is that the kolam is a 'snare' intended for protection against demons who lose their way in its maze. Boys and men are not permitted to draw kolams and presumably do not share the women's power to entrap demons. This is an example of how some women have used skills of hand-and-eye to take at least limited control of their environment. Can they continue to do this, and not just symbolically, in the fast-changing information and communication milieu?

Mud walls to websites

Folk art and craft are interactive media, embedded in the context of the village community's own lifeworld and increasingly in that of an elite urban world of the conveyors and consumers of ethnic products. Conventionally, the term 'folk' has been related to a peasant society in which an oral tradition is the most prevalent. In India, where there is a marked tribal-peasant continuum, the folk also encompasses tribal (once called 'primitive') arts and crafts. The folk was disdained and ignored for long by scholars and historians but gained 'respectability' after Independence as an expression of 'indigenous' culture and a celebration of the nation's diversity, as in the national Folk Dance festivals linked to the annual Republic Day celebrations. Today, ethnicity is in vogue and the traditional paintings and crafts created in villages have found urban niche markets in India and abroad. The surging demand has resulted in certain distinct trends, clearly visible in the contemporary evolution of 'Madhubani' painting.

In now-famous villages such as Madhubani and Jitwarpur in the Mithila region of northern Bihar, the women's ephemeral painting on mud walls and floors was a traditional, collective ritual activity. For instance, the *kohbar ghar* (nuptial chamber) was ritually decorated with fertility symbols drawn from nature and meant to inspire a couple to consummate their marriage on the fourth night after the wedding. Different caste groups were confined to specific stylistic elements. The Mithila (Madhubani) paintings of the upper caste women concentrated on mythological themes but only the brahmans were permitted to use the full range of colour. The Godhana paintings of the lower castes were restricted to nature as in traditional 'tree of life' designs against a background of pale bistre (the colour of burnt wood soot).

Following the prolonged drought and crop failure during 1966-68, the All India Handicrafts Board, a government organization, encouraged village women to supplement their income by painting on handmade paper for sale. This led to an extraordinary burst of creativity. The sharp caste and style demarcations collapsed. Even as traditional designs were exploited, a new innovative idiom emerged and 'Madhubani' found an urban market. (Warli tribal painting in Maharashtra has gone through a similar evolution). There is also an interesting new trend: the pedagogic use of folk art in developmental interventions. In a set of 'animal husbandry' paintings, the women have used the traditional style to depict women learning about animal health care, treating animals, running a milk dairy and keeping accounts. Here, art and livelihoods have come together, as art and ritual had done in the past.

While the majority of Mithila women continue to ritually decorate their mud walls, many have gained a new source of income by selling their paintings, and the best individual artists have received national and international recognition. Crossing the gender divide, husbands and sons of women artists are also painting, besides managing the marketing (done through government and non-government agencies and private dealers). The artists' range has extended beyond religious themes and the 'tree of life' to diverse village scenes, innovative single-colour paintings and currently popular tattoo designs. Some painters are also relocating from Bihar to Delhi (a few even to Bangalore) to improve their access to the market and to international dealers who display the works of individual artists on their websites. (A few middle class, educated women too have set themselves up in cities as 'Madhubani' painters!) The market is dominated by traditional mythological figures. Compared to the price paid to the craftswomen the dollar markup on works of folk art, which can be viewed and bought on the internet, is astronomical.

The negative aspects of the de-contextualized, de-ritualized, sometimes bureaucratised, commercial production of folk art and craft is unimaginative assembly-line production. A dubious business in imitations of folk products has also grown. The printed bookmarks from Orissa are very close to the original painted works. But the Bhubaneswar 'factories' that cater to the national and international demand for soft-porn palm-leaf paintings are recognizable by their crudeness, which is uncharacteristic of the original sensuous palm leaf work of the traditional painters. Similarly, the bell-metal figures that are now manufactured in Delhi and sold as 'Bastar' dhokra are easily identifiable. The clumsiness of the workers' skills is visible in cruder body shapes and welded joints, an attempt to conceal flaws in the moulded metal figures. For example, the charming dhokra of a young girl engrossed in reading a book has been transformed into a reclining buxom woman posed holding a book but with her eyes focused far above it!

At the other end of the spectrum is the emergence of uniquely talented individuals like Shakila Baghel of Kondagaon, Bastar, who is celebrated not as a dhokra craftswoman but as a self-aware sculptor (e.g. 'Self as an Artist', Adajania 2003). How significant are these diverse (if still limited) changes in the visual representation of women in folk art? Do these novel roles and activities – as readers, animal health healers, self-conscious artists—indicate a trend towards empowerment for the craftswomen themselves? How can the new and emerging modes of information and communication technology (ICT) serve to enhance women's control over their environment?

Today, it is easier to buy a folk painting through the internet than learn about its history, the social relations of the community of producers, the techniques that they have perfected over generations, the political economy of the craft. There are very few examples of ethnographic studies to 'communicate tacit knowledge across cultures' (Smith 2001) or to understand the 'contending art worlds' of craftspersons and elite consumers (Bundgaard 1999). Therefore, the changing 'materiality' of folk cultures in general and the gendering of crafts in particular, needs to be archived through participatory documentation and using multi-media, such as photography, film and video. This has been done by the National Institute for Science, Technology and Development Studies (NISTADS) with a group of dhokra workers from West Bengal. NISTADS introduced a new technology of large community furnaces, changing an age-old process and this led to a spurt of creativity. NISTADS' sensitive and participatory documentation, however, takes no note of the gender aspects at all.

One can tentatively suggest that it is only the collective solidarity of craftswomen's groups beyond family and caste, their ability to upgrade some of the technical features, and encompass a range of modern communication tools, that would have a vital impact on the sustainability of their art and livelihoods. The most urgent need, therefore. is to facilitate the formation of craftswomen's groups and to develop their capacities to use a range of tools so as to record the production process of the crafts and explicitly include their own contribution (often hidden from public gaze). This is especially important because in the future craftswomen may have to assert new intellectual property rights (IPR). It is a moot point whether it would be possible for, say, the Mithila village painters to claim the 'Madhubani' name under IPR legislation such as India's Geographical Indications Act, 2001. Another urgent need is for training to use electronic media (including the internet) to market their products directly to customers without the exploitation of profiteering traders and the 'protective' interventions of the men of their own communities.

If such a vision were realized, craftswomen would gain the strength to protect their intellectual, artistic knowledge, skills and earnings from the unseen 'demons' across the threshold. Their art and craft might then enable women to traverse the rainbow bridge between mud walls and websites, oral traditions and ICT—and an Assamese terracotta Earth Mother riding a bicycle would no longer be a curious anachronism.

S9

The Light Shines Through Gossamer Threads: Inside-Outside Political Spaces

Gender relations in some adivasi (tribal) societies are relatively more egalitarian than among other communities but enormous changes are now taking place in their resource base and livelihoods. How does this affect the women's spaces in the domestic and public spheres? This article explores the process of change as a scattered semi-nomadic group of adivasi foragers come together to form a village settlement. Focusing on one family, and one woman among them, it reflects upon whether and how an indigenous democratic fabric and relative gender egalitarianism may be retained in the face of structural changes in the adivasi life worlds. Using a personal narrative, shaped by different 'dialogical levels', the article traces the dialogical stages through which the 'story' unfolds. It suggests that the narrative as a qualitative research tool may be used to interrogate women's political spaces and to bring the family into development discourse

Introduction

The family was for long the Pandora's box of development discourse, acknowledged to exist as an economic household but left safely untouched in other respects. Consequently, state policies and interventions were also premised on a public-private dichotomy with public institutional structures being distinct and separate from the politics of space and status within the family.

This perspective began to change when the women's movement drew upon lived experiences and social anthropology to open up the family as a primary site of gender-power relations, and to bring the personal into the collective political domain. Even those development interventions, however, which aspire towards gender-neutrality are insensitive to the location-specificity and complex gradations of intra-family relations, and the transformations that are now taking place in families and communities.

Gender relations in many adivasi (tribal) societies are relatively more egalitarian than among other communities. In India, today, some small and very poor adivasi groups are experiencing a transition from semi-nomadism to a settled way of life.[1] They are interacting with several other social groups and institutions, including settled peasants, land-owners, employers, traders, the government, its agencies and non-government organizations (NGOs). What impact do these widening circles of interaction with non-adivasi institutions and agents have on gender relations? How do the enormous changes in their life worlds affect the adivasi women's political spaces in the domestic and public spheres? Such questions have scarcely been dealt with by development researchers and practitioners. Perhaps this is because practitioners are far more comfortable with using conventional social science tools, mass surveys and interviews, for collecting and presenting quantifiable data. The development discourse is strewn with numbers (however suspect these may be)—so many hectares planted, so much savings made—as indicators of achievement, or non-achievement. Even the newer 'participatory' research methods and focus group discussions are being used to generate quantifiable information rather than qualitative understandings of messy and complex social and human problems. Qualitative research skills, which derive from life experiences and sensitive responses to inequities, may seem more difficult to learn and teach. Yet, if we explore ways to do so, this could make research findings more accessible to wider social groups and perhaps help redirect the policies and practices of development.

Among the most effective and affective tools of qualitative research is the articulation of individual and group voices to 'tell a story'. Personal narratives have been widely used by the women's movement and feminist research. If, however, this is to be more than a 'confessional' and provide insights to changes within a community, the researcher needs also to stand aside and reflect. A narrative has the accessibility of a fictional story with an actual setting, characters with whom one can empathize, and actions which evolve towards a crisis which may or may not be resolved. Like other fictional devices it allows one to depict the contingent, transient processes rather than simply capture the stationary junctures in the stream of our lives. But unlike fiction, the narrative as a research tool strives to make the leap from the particular to the generic, to clarify, explain and collate different strands of analysis. The narrative has rarely been used in development studies which have a disciplinary inclination towards the deliberately impersonalised social science 'account', sometimes illustrated by brief thumbnail sketches or 'case studies'.[2] This paper attempts to extend the scope of development research and writing by depicting the gendering of political spaces through a personalised narrative of 'critical moments' in which the boundaries between life, work and research are blurred.[3] This is the story of a small group of very poor and recently settled adivasis in south-eastern India. It is also a story about one family and one woman among them. And it is a story of what one researcher learnt and unlearnt about gendered political spaces. Embedded in the specific context of this narrative are different levels of dialogue, as they take place and are re-presented by the researcher—among sections in the group; among different individual 'actors', the women, men and children in the story; between some of them and the researcher; between the researcher and peer reviewers (who are far removed from the immediate context), and also between persons playing several different roles, like myself: as a professional adviser-consultant, as a participant in the action, and as a researcher-narrator. There are also 'hidden' dialogical levels in the unvoiced and the 'non-conversational' modes of communication between different actors including the researcher. Indeed, the narrative has grown out of these diverse, overlapping levels of dialogues and is unfolded through different dialogical stages.[4] The narrative opens by 'setting the scene for dialogue' with a brief description of the community that touches upon gender roles and relations. It then proceeds through three parts. First, the focus is on the actors and 'one-to-one dialogues' as one woman, tacitly acknowledged as the leader of the group, initiates and facilitates contacts between the adivasi settlement and an NGO working in the area. Next, the narrative moves to the action, 'dialogues in a group', tracing the seemingly democratic process by which the village (actually just a small hamlet) enters into the NGO programme even as conflicts begin to emerge within the community. This is followed by the crisis, the 'disruption of dialogue' with the distressing heightening of the conflict which engulfs the woman, her family and the rest of the community. Finally, the narrator-researcher reflects on the course of the story, her own part in it and the implications for development practice. The story relates to a specific location but the actual setting and the identity of the persons have been deliberately left somewhat vague. This is the only way in which stories such as these can be shared without appropriating the lives of people for academic purposes.[5] It is a story of relatively recent happenings but I will let it unfold slowly in the manner in which many adivasis tell a tale, starting from a more distant beginning with single strands of the narrative and following the course of my own deepening understanding as multiple strands are gathered together.

The Narrative

These adivasis are migrants from an adjacent state where a couple of generations ago they had lived a nomadic and foraging life. Living off wild foods gathered from the forest, small game hunting and occasional wage labour, they were probably not the self-sufficient, 'original affluent society'.[6] Life expectancy was low and their population may even have been declining. Whether from the pressure of coping with degrading habitats, the imagined promise of a better life elsewhere, or for some other reasons, they had migrated to a very different landscape. In the process they acquired a second language, other occupations and skills to cope with the new environment.

For several decades, the adivasis continued to live in the new setting as they had in the past—as a group of semi-nomadic foragers in small scattered family-units, just a few families in one

vicinity. Each family, usually consisting of a couple and their unmarried children, made a temporary camp on local plantations
where they were employed as watch-keepers and labourers. They
also continued to forage for wild foods, tubers, green fruits, leaves
and seeds, keenly aware of the distribution and seasonal variation
of useful resources in their new habitat. Some of the animal life
was also different, so new ways had to be devised using their old
skills of catching game with their bare hands.

None of the adults in this particular group of adivasis was
literate and till recently none of the children had ever been to
school. The families are all equally poor because foraging, the sale
of foraged produce and intermittent wage income are insufficient
to keep them out of indebtedness to the non-adivasi plantation
owners or the tradeswomen in the local market. The adivasi women
are in daily contact with the market women who buy their foraged game or other produce and loan them money for necessities,
illnesses and emergencies. Despite being peripherally linked to
the plantation economy the adivasis have retained much of their
old way of life including the relative autonomy of each family, as
in their independent dealings with employers and market women.
Yet, the adivasis also form a kin group who may come together for
foraging and on ritual occasions, such as marriages and festivals.
Viewed from the outside, gender relations appear to have been
relatively egalitarian. Descent is traced through the male line but
does not seem to affect personal autonomy. Both women and men
may choose their marriage partners or divorce a spouse. A couple
may deal jointly with employers to negotiate the family wage,
and even if a plantation owner paid out the wage to the man, he
would hand it over to his wife and they would jointly take decisions about how to spend the money. Since they have had almost
no tools and no property, except for the few cooking vessels which
the women control, questions about inheriting property do not
arise. The division of labour has been flexible. In the spectrum of
daily and seasonal activities, those surrounding the hearth—cooking and feeding of young children—are women's responsibilities
while the traditional panchayat is all-male. Almost all other activities are undertaken by women and men together or by either
as the situation may demand. Women have a subsidiary role to

men in the adivasi rituals. But since these are still conducted in the first language, which some women have retained to a greater degree than the men, the women are consulted during the process of a ritual, for instance to supply the words of a prescribed chant. In practice, therefore, the women often direct the course of the ritual.

The Actors: Dialogues One-to-One

From what I had read, heard and seen of them, it had seemed to me that many of these adivasi women have all the characteristics of solidity, strength and decisiveness stereotypically associated with masculinity in other communities. If feminism is 'resistance to invisibility and silencing'[7] they are feminists. Like other adivasi and peasant women, who depend on physical labour for a livelihood, they too carry their bodies with grace and pride. For years they have been living in close proximity to a town near a frequented tourist route and have interacted with non-adivasis in the local market. They have witnessed visible signs of development in the nearby villages and in one recent adivasi settlement. Some of the adivasi women envisioned a different future, articulated this and planned to lead their people in alternative directions. One such woman, let us call her Ira, was tacitly acknowledged as the leader of the group. Ira, along with her husband, had taken the initiative to convince each family living in scattered camps among the plantations that the times of semi-nomadic life were past. Settling down all together in one permanent location would be to their advantage. A site was staked out near the first adivasi settlement in the area. As Ira's small family (she, her husband and daughter) and other families began to put up their huts in the new settlement, a hamlet took shape. With an eye to the future it was named after the leader of a major political party. In the past, the adivasis were always disadvantaged in their necessary dealings with plantation owners, tradeswomen and the occasional junior government official (usually from the forest department). Like other adivasi groups elsewhere, they were wary of outsiders. This began to change when a new player, an NGO, entered the local scene a few years ago. Ira had watched the NGO staff (almost all of whom were men) scout the neighbouring adivasi settlement and interact with the people on friendly terms. She had seen activities being started and visible changes in the settlement. Perhaps viewing the NGO as a new 'forage-able' resource in the environment, Ira then took a remarkable step. Maybe it had been in her mind all along while she and her husband were persuading their people to settle down in one place. Ira sought out the NGO staff. She asked them to 'take up' her village too. The NGO was at first reluctant. Ira persisted. She visited them in their office in town. She reasoned and pleaded. They finally agreed and set out some conditions. The NGO was not a charitable organization. It was engaged in the business of restoring and managing degraded environments for conservation and to improve people's livelihoods.

The Action: Dialogues in the Group

The first step was to determine whether the entire village agreed to take on this activity. Discussions were held in the shade of a tree in the sandy ground near the village. Ira's enthusiasm carried the group and, of course, they agreed. The NGO staff then explained that they would help the adivasis with technical inputs and some financial support, but first a village 'development committee' would have to be formed. This would have to be done in a participatory, democratic fashion, with an 'executive' consisting of a president, secretary, treasurer and other members. A bank account would also have to be opened in the town. The discussions continued. The children, including Ira's daughter, were excited by all the activity. They would stop playing catch around the trees and listen to the elders' discussions. Soon the English language words 'committee', 'meeting', 'president', 'bank' became familiar even to the young children.

The recently settled adivasis continued to discuss all this among themselves without coming to a point. They knew that the committee would be given a grant which would be deposited in the bank and that the committee would then pay out wages to the women and men who were engaged in the restoration work. The NGO staff were eager to get on with important decisions, the formation of the committee, opening the bank account, fixing the wage rates for the men and women who would do the labour of digging, carrying, planting and so on. The staff had to fulfil project schedules and other requirements set out by their headquarters and meet commitments made to the foreign donor agency.

The first issue to be decided was the daily wage rate. The adivasis informed the NGO staff that they had all agreed that the men would be paid let us say rupees 'x' and the women half of that amount. They had worked this out keeping in mind a 'fair' familial wage of roughly rupees one and a half 'x' a day. The NGO team leader felt the difference between the male and female wage rate was too much. A meeting of the adivasis with the NGO staff was arranged to reconsider this.

At that time I was visiting the area and went along to the meeting with the staff. It took a long while for the women and men to gather under the tree; there were some older women; then the men came in twos and threes forming separate little groups; it was mentioned that the women were busy cooking the evening meal; some of the young men got bored as nothing seemed to be happening, got up and left. Ira did not come at all. Eventually, there were enough people to start the meeting. The adivasis seemed to feel there was nothing to discuss. An elderly man said this was the prevailing wage rate for men and women in the local contract labour market. One of the staff said to me that the official daily wage rate for unskilled labour in the state was also different for men and women because they did 'different kinds of work'. So, what was the problem? At this stage, I suggested to one of the NGO staff that he might like to initiate a discussion on broader lines—on the differences in the life worlds of the adivasis and the local non-adivasi communities, moving on to the strengths in the adivasi way of life. This discussion led to identifying the relative gender equality among adivasis as one of their strengths. Why did they want to change that in this new matter of daily wages, I asked. The women remained silent through most of the meeting. The men agreed, almost too quickly, that the women should be paid more even if the work they did was different (carrying and transporting rather than digging), but said that their own wage should not be reduced. Someone then pointed out that the funding could not be stretched to pay both women and men rupees 'x' a day. This was a difficult knot to untangle.

The knot was ingeniously untied. One of the men said that

the women should be paid according to the number of hours they would work. Why would the women be working less hours than the men, I asked. Because they would have to cook and bring the meal for them at the work site, the men said. At this point some of the women spoke up to say, yes, this was true, they would be working for fewer hours than the men on the site. By this time it was dusk and the NGO staff did not want to go back to the town without a decision. So, it was agreed by consensus that the principle of equality of wages would be recognized but that women and men would be paid in proportion to the number of hours they spent actually working at the site. This would increase the group's daily expenditure on wages only marginally. Everyone seemed satisfied with this outcome.

I got up, searched for my sandals and bent down to put them on. Suddenly the women were clapping and singing. They had formed a circle around me and were dancing. It took a little while for me to figure out that the song and dance were in some way related to me. I did not understand the words (which seemed to be in their first language), nor could I fathom the emotions being expressed—laughing one moment, sad the next. I did not know how to respond and was embarrassed. When it was over and the circle broke up, they crowded around me; there was a lot of touching, holding hands and hugging but nothing much was said to me. What was it all about I asked one of the women staff and learnt that it was the song sung when a girl gets married and leaves the group. Why had a middle-aged woman, whom they had never met before, been adopted (apparently spontaneously) as one of their own and bid farewell as they would a bride? At that time I thought this was perhaps the women's way of acknowledging my interest in them. On reflection, it seemed possible that they saw me as some kind of 'authority', since I was an older city person who was being treated with respect by the young NGO staff. A few of the adivasi women had asked whether I was the NGO's 'teacher'. I do not know whether the episode signified fellowship or strategy on their part, or both. It is easy to romanticise adivasi emotion; one need not, however, swing with the pendulum to the other extreme and read tactics into every friendly gesture.

The Crisis: Disrupted Dialogues

The following day, we set out again to the adivasi settlement carrying the cheque. For the NGO it was imperative that the formalities of organization be completed, that the president and other important members of the executive committee be chosen that very day. I learnt that the staff had earlier suggested that the adivasis choose Ira as president. They were impressed by her initiative, energy and leadership and her selection to the top post would reflect the NGO's own gender sensitivity. The adivasi women and men were agreeable to this. Ira was well-respected and liked. But the suggestion had caused considerable disquiet because Ira's husband had felt slighted by this public recognition of his wife's informal status as the leader of the group. This was perhaps why he had also vigorously opposed increasing the women's wage rate on the previous evening. Ira's absence from that meeting now seemed ominous.

When the adivasis gathered, once again, Ira was not present. She had sent word that she did not wish to be the president. The women who had sung for me the night before were subdued. I learnt from them that the relations between husband and wife had deteriorated so much that 'the hearths had been separated'. The NGO staff said it was not good that the couple's domestic differences should 'spill over' into official work. Their view was that these spaces should be kept separate.

The staff insisted that Ira be called. She then came with extreme reluctance, almost being dragged by some of the women. She looked frightened and sat among the group only after her husband had nodded permission. There was nothing about her bearing when I saw her that day to suggest the strong woman I had been told about. The discussion began. When it was her turn to speak, without looking at anyone, drawing circles in the ground with her forefinger, she said let him be the president—meaning the husband. Many of the adivasis agreed. The matter seemed to have been nearly decided. But there were some rumblings and a few of the NGO staff were also not satisfied; it was felt the husband would not make a 'good' president.

At that point, one woman began to speak quietly. She was

identified for me as Ira's friend. A little later I learnt that she was also Ira's sister-in-law, the husband's sister. She spoke of her anguish at the separation of the hearths, of how this had divided the village with people taking sides, something unprecedented in the life of this community. She mentioned the eight-year-old daughter, only one child, now with the mother who was separated from the father. She retold the story of how the group had been living in scattered camps, how Ira along with her husband, the two together, had worked so hard to bring all the families to settle at this place. She said, the village owed everything that they had now to this couple. Bringing her fingers and palms together as in a 'namaste', she said, the husband and wife were like this. What had happened now?

The palms together gesture stirred a thought in my mind. I asked the NGO team leader whether there was any rule, of the bank, the NGO or the donor, that the executive should have only one president. Why not joint presidents? Indeed, this was roughly how Ira and her husband had functioned earlier. Why not formalise that instead of pushing the two of them around one chair, a game in which one would have to take a fall? The idea quickly caught on. With the exception of Ira herself everyone was pleased at the seeming resolution. It was formally accepted, recorded and witnessed. Other posts were swiftly filled. The cheque was handed over. The work was soon to begin. There was relief all around.

It was quite dark before we could leave. The women knew that I would not be back. There was warmth in the leave-taking but no dancing and singing. In the darkness, Ira took me aside. She was nearly in tears. Where are you going, she asked. I told her. Take me with you, she said. I misunderstood her, thinking she wanted to visit. I told her that I would be glad to welcome her to my home. In fact, I would soon be moving south and then it might be arranged more easily. She said, she wasn't talking about a visit, she wanted to come away permanently. What about the village, what about your daughter, I asked. Clinging to my hand, she said it would never be the same again. I could make no response.

Soon after that, for unconnected reasons, my own relations with the NGO changed and I had no way of knowing how things had turned out. A year later, I made discreet enquiries and learnt that the work had progressed very well. What about Ira? She, her husband and daughter had moved their hut to the adjacent village because the relations between the husband and the rest of the group had worsened. They didn't like his style of functioning, and Ira did not intervene. The joint-presidentship was only in name. The 'naming' itself had become the problem.

I knew that among some other adivasi groups conflicts are traditionally avoided; when things get really bad they are dealt with simply by one party moving away to ease the tension. There is no elaborate discussion. Perhaps this was the way among these adivasis too. Ira and her husband still belonged to the village that they had dreamt about and set up but they no longer lived in it. That year the NGO's published reports stated that women's empowerment in the project villages had been substantially increased by their greater participation in the executives of the development committees.

Reflections

In life (as in narrative) the task of gathering together single threads into multiple skeins, without getting them entangled, is fraught with difficulties. As another year passed and I reflected on the course of the story—from one-to-one dialogues to dialogues in the group and the crisis of disrupted dialogue—I continued to be troubled by my own part in it, my presumptions, complicity and eventual helplessness as an 'outsider' unable to help the NGO staff or the village beyond circumscribed limits. It is also disturbing that none of the persons involved, with the possible exception of Ira herself, realized how things would unfold. In Ira's life, and in that of this adivasi group, the public and private worlds were closely intertwined. The political spaces both within families and the group were relatively gender egalitarian. This enabled her to act in the new public political spaces opening up for a community in the process of transition from a semi-nomadic to a settled way of life. Yet, her confident assertion of a vision for her people had repercussions that were deeply disrupting for herself, her family and the community.

The well-meaning NGO staff were constrained by the inflex-
ibility of project schedules and formal procedures, and did not
have the imagination, experience, or skills to deal with the cascad-
ing impacts. Yet, the reasons why they were so constrained lie at
the core of many developmental interventions which are instrumentalist in approach and may even undermine women's existing
rights. Furthermore, their (and my) inability to perceive and an-
ticipate the tensions between the prevalent adivasi decision-
making systems (the overtly informal and individualistic and yet
democratic structures and processes) and the attempt to incorporate new activities and institutional mechanisms shaped by our
particular conception of democracy, reflects our collective misun-
derstandings. I do not know whether in such a case a conventional
NGO could set the right pace and direction simply by more sensitive facilitation. The 'feminist' strengths, autonomy and decision-making power, of the adivasi women in this small 'face-to-
face' community seem to have been garnered within a framework
which maintains (or is seen to maintain) men's pride (*izzat*) and
their socially sanctioned role and position (*maryada*) in the political and ritual spheres. In terms of political strategy this has some
resonances with the manner in which middle class women, in
urban milieus of vastly different scale and levels of interaction,
negotiate paths by skirting around the rocks of male izzat and
maryada. The adivasi women, however, are not seeking to establish democratic norms in the family but to prevent the loss of
relative equity and existing democratic strengths. Ira herself was
not blind to the complex linkages between gender-power relationships in the privacy of the family and the quick sands of the
public democratic domain—the spaces between which this impoverished adivasi community was caught. I do not want to ideal-
ize a 'traditional' adivasi way of life imagining the collapse of inner and outer spaces, an open, free-flowing, undifferentiated fluidity. Such a perspective would only be the obverse of the view
that sees no linkages between intra-household dynamics and the
public domain. When a household is marked by just a few palm
fronds in a coconut grove, when there is no door to shut, no yard
to cross, there can be no sharp physical boundary between the

worlds of home and work. Yet, that does not mean that there is no division at all. In an adivasi community, such as this, the swaying threads that separate 'inside' and 'outside' spaces are gossamer thin; there is a certain translucency through which the light shines. When we attempt to wind these threads on a spool, weave a democratic cloth in looms of our making, in patterns set to our conventions, the threads do not hold. Yet, the problem is not only one of the 'master's tools'.[8] The question is 'who wields them and to what purpose?'[9] One can venture to suggest that the narrative is a tool that may be used collaboratively and creatively to bring the family into development discourse. The understanding gleaned from the particularities of this narrative may enhance our comprehension of the impact of modern democratic institutions on the inside-outside political spaces of similarly placed adivasi women elsewhere. Many such adivasi groups have an indigenous conception of democracy, which is relatively gender egalitarian, and processes by which this is realized within the community. This indigenous democratic fabric, however, may be frayed by various forces of change, by the people's own needs and aspirations for wider social integration and by developmental interventions inspired by other conceptions of democracy having different institutional processes. The problem for adivasi women and men, and for those who work with them, is to find innovative ways to accomplish the transformation from semi-nomadic foraging to a settled way of life and new processes of formal collective decision-making, while retaining the autonomy of individuals and families and the relative gender egalitarianism that seems connected to this.

Perhaps this could all have been handled differently. Perhaps if Ira and the other adivasi women and men had been freer to devise their own institutional processes, in the light of their own lived experiences, and at their own pace, then the complexity, fluidity, translucency of the linkages between their private and public political spaces might not have been rent asunder. The gossamer threads might have been unravelled with a gentler, defter touch.

NOTES

[1] The major shifts from nomadism to settlement were completed in the pre-colonial period, as is borne out by Indian sociology and ecological history, however, even today there are some small, semi-nomadic adivasi groups scattered in pockets along the coastal and hill-forest regions of the country. They are gatherers, hunters, animal-trappers, 'non-gear' fishers or any combination of these who did not hitherto practise any form of cultivation. Despite their small numbers, their significance for action-research is that they are now choosing, or being propelled by circumstances, to settle as farmers, fishers or wage labourers.

[2] A very early attempt in this direction was Kusum Nair's (1961) *Blossoms in the Dust: The Human Element in Indian Development* whose content and methodology marked a shift from conventional economic research and writing. When development studies in India grew as a bounded discipline, however, it adopted the more 'objective' and impersonalised approach of orthodox social science. Among the few recent examples of a different kind of writing is 'Becoming a development category', the moving story of the Nepalese-born US academic Nanda Shrestha (1995); and the 'travelogue' by Subhash Mendhapurkar (2004), of the NGO Sutra in Himachal Pradesh, which winds its way with remarkable frankness through the fluid interfaces between the professional, personal, institutional and methodological.

[3] There are many 'messy, unspoken, complex and disturbing moments' in qualitative research which Horsfall, Higgs and Byrne-Armstrong (2001:4) call 'critical moments'. As Mulligan (2001: 141) says 'We can consciously blur the boundaries between life, work and research when we look for overlapping interests, projects and discourses. We can learn to love the creative chaos that this involves. But we will also experience frustration and despair when we are torn apart by competing priorities or overcome by a sense of failure. We might reconceive life and work as artificially constructed conceptual categories, but we all know that they often seem to collide with such force that sparks fly, leading to heated arguments or smouldering tensions. In the chaotic interaction of conflict we may discover the spark of a new idea or we may even find that our lives reemerge in a new form like a Phoenix rising from the ashes.'

[4] The idea of dialogical stages of narrative in this paper was inspired by P Thamizoli who also drew my attention to Mannheim and Van Vleet's (1998) study of the dialogical levels of the oral narratives of the Southern Quechua (Andean Inkas). Their work integrates narrative analysis with ethnography by distinguishing four different (and simultaneous) dialogical levels. An earlier work, The Dialogic Emergence of Culture (1995) edited by Tedlock and Mannheim shows how narrative (from field research to publication) is the product of social interaction. Recognizing the resonances between this approach and the course of my narrative, as it was first presented, I have framed the story through consecutive dialogical stages and briefly drawn attention to its different dialogical levels.

[5] Some have asked why I have refused to identify the main protagonist of the narrative, and said that this may take away from its authenticity. My answer is that if it were a story of an educated middle-class woman (such as myself) I would wish to ensure the privacy of the individual. I believe that the same principle needs to be applied in research with poor illiterate women.

[6] The notion of the 'original affluent society' put forward by Sahlins (1971) has fostered the widespread assumption that the low-energy subsistence lifestyles of gatherer-hunters satisfied their 'basic needs' and was a consciously chosen way of life inspired by ecological wisdom. Many, including myself, have disputed this; as I have written elsewhere (Krishna 1996: 89-92): 'Although nature may be bountiful in the humid tropics, it is simplistic to presume that the population was somehow always in happy equilibrium with the food supply, and that painful and desperate choices were not necessary.'

[7] Feminism is variously defined but the concept of feminism as resistance suggested by Karleen Faith (1995) provides a common denominator to strategise women's political articulation against subordination in different cultural and socio-economic contexts.

[8] Contrary to the feminist Audre Lorde's (1984) precept, 'The master's tools will never dismantle the master's house', I would suggest that we do need the 'master's tools' to dismantle patriarchal epistemologies but feminist and gender studies also need other kinds of tools to build other kinds of houses. Innovative action-researchers could break new methodological ground by fostering dialogues in particular local contexts between different ways of knowledge construction, different institutional practices and forms of representation. (See also note 9)

[9] In the context of the 'unacknowledged tribes' of California, Field (1999: 193) asks 'How do these [anthropological] tools change depending upon who wields them and to what purpose? Are there other kinds of intellectuals who have other tools at their disposal? In the hands of other such intellectuals, might anthropology's tools prove useful for undermining the foundations of the master's house?' Drawing upon Gramsci (1971), he suggests the possibility of collaboration between the leadership of the tribes ('indigenous intellectuals') and 'the academics who wield the master's tools' (traditional intellectuals).

Signposts: Sources

S1   First published in 1975 as 'In Chhatera: Maya, Bhim Kaur and Chalti', *Indian Farming*. November, pp. 43-46.

S2   Compiled from: 'The Ugly Outsider' *The Hindustan Times Magazine* 1981: Feb. 22, and 'From Hatgamaria to Chaibasia: Marketing tusser cocoons', *Environmental Politics*. 1996. pp. 20-23.

S3   First published in 1997 as 'A Patchwork Quilt: The Story of Ecofeminism' in *50th Milestone: A Feminine Critique*, eds. Shanta Serbjeet Singh and Jyoti Sabharwal, pp. 253-61. (My subtitle 'Women and Environmental Activism' was altered by the editors, perhaps with the mistaken belief that all environmental activism involving women is ecofeminist.)

S4 Slightly shortened version of 'Towards a New Reproductive Ecology', *The Book Review*. Special Issue on Women. July 1995. XIX: 7. (A shorter review, *Variations on a Theme*, appeared in 1994 in *The Hindustan Times*: 17 January)

S5 Slightly edited version, first published 1995 in *The Administrator*, Special issue on Gender and Development, Vol XL: 3, July-September, pp. 93-104.

S6 Revised version, based on a section of my chapter 'Gender and Biodiversity Management' in Swaminathan ed. 1998 *Gender Dimensions in Biodiversity Management*.

S7 Slightly edited comments made orally in 2003 at a workshop on 'Farmer's Rights and Biodiversity Act: A Gender and Community Perspective' Chennai: MSSRF, 27-28 February.

S8 Revised version of an essay published in 2003 in *Empowering women through information and knowledge: From oral traditions to ICT*, Conference Proceedings, Vol 1, Mumbai: SNDT, and New Delhi: CWDS. Pp. 197-202.

S9 Reprinted from my article of the same title in the *Economic and Political Weekly*, 26 April 2003.

APPENDIX II
KEYWORDS

Keywords: An Interpretive Glossary

> 'When I use a word,' Humpty Dumpty said, in a rather scornful tone, 'it means just what I chose it to mean—neither more nor less.'
> 'The question is,' said Alice, 'whether you can make words mean different things.'
> 'The question is,' said Humpty Dumpty, 'which is to be master—that's all.'
>
> —Lewis Caroll: *Through the Looking-Glass*

At any given time, the straightforward or 'dictionary' meaning of a word usually remains the same regardless of who uses it, but over a period of time the meaning of a word may change. In the course of its development the English language has been enriched by words drawn from several other languages. Some words may now be used very differently from their original meaning; others may retain a trace of their history even if they have evolved very differently. A word may also acquire a technical meaning within a particular context. It then becomes a 'term'. Different disciplines develop specialized sets of terms, or terminologies that enhance discussion. Sometimes, however, the terms can themselves become an obstacle to understanding (jargon). This interpretive glossary covers a selection of keywords, terms used in specific ways. Any such selection necessarily reflects the interests and concerns of its author and, in that sense, is incomplete. However, I hope that

these hundred and more glosses will further a gendered understanding of how words 'travel' in the process of making meanings
and constructing knowledge. Many of the words form an
interlinked cluster. The words used to explain a keyword may
themselves need a gloss. Such words and word-clusters are indicated here by SMALL CAPITALS. Some keywords may be discussed
more extensively in the book than in the glossary.

ACTION-RESEARCH Action involves meaning and intention. In
action-research, the research component is subsidiary to and related to the action. The objective extends beyond understanding
social conditions to transforming the lives of people. In action-
research, interventions are designed and carried out by the researchers working in partnership with the concerned SOCIAL GROUP.
The level of participation achieved varies greatly in practice. One
of the best-known examples of Participatory Action Research (PAR)
in India, which aimed to organize and empower women through
wasteland development, is in Bankura district West Bengal (initiated by the Centre for Women's Development Studies, New Delhi
in the early 1980s.) During the 1990s, PAR was overtaken by
Participatory Rural Appraisal (PRA) which is now more widely
used. See PARTICIPATORY APPROACHES, PARTICIPATORY TECHNOLOGY DE-
VELOPMENT.

ADIVASI/INDIGENOUS PEOPLES The words *adivasi* and tribe/tribal are
often used interchangeably. Tribe is the term used in the Constitution of India, which recognizes 'Scheduled Tribes' as a category
but does not define it. In the Hindi translation of the Constitution, the term used is *adimjati* (meaning 'primitive race'). The
term tribe has negative connotations related to its conceptualization
in evolutionary anthropology as a primitive stage and its use by
the administration in colonial times. In much of India, tribe has
been replaced by adivasi in the people's own conceptualization of
their identity. In north-eastern India, however, adivasi refers specifically to plantation labourers, who are tribal migrants from north,
south and east India, and the preferred term is indigenous rather
than tribal. The term indigenous was used by the United Nations
in its 'Year of the Indigenous Peoples' (1993). In Australia and

the Americas, indigenous refers to the original (aboriginal) populations as distinguished from later settlers. In the Indian subcontinent, this distinction is of less value. Right-wing political groups
(who claim indigenous status for upper caste Hindus in the Indian subcontinent) have tried to replace adivasi by *vanvasi*, literally forest-dweller, which is inaccurate (because not all adivasis
live in the forest) and perceived by many as being derogatory.
Recently, 'adivasi/indigenous people' has been accepted by activist groups as an alternative for tribal, as in the 'All-India Coordi-
nated Forum for Adivasi/Indigenous Peoples.'

AGEISM Systematic discrimination on the basis of age is ageism
(like systematic discrimination on the basis of sex is sexism). A
society which is dominated by a particular stage of the human
life-cycle, usually middle-aged male adults, may be prejudiced
against other stages, childhood, youth and old age. For instance,
the special needs of children and old people are often neglected in
conservation and development programmes. Ageism and sexism
are mutually reinforcing; so old women, especially widows, are a
particularly subordinated group.

AGENCY Having the power to act and to define the meaning of
things. Agency may be exercised by individuals and groups. Social agents can reinforce or transform SOCIO-CULTURAL SYSTEMS, even
as these systems may enable or constrain the actions of agents.
Disempowered individuals and groups (e.g. DALITS, poor women,
and old people) lack agency. See EMPOWERMENT.

AGRIBUSINESS The term was coined in the 1950s to indicate the
corporate management of agriculture and its integration into a
larger industrial economy. It is now used mainly to indicate the
domination of agriculture by Trans-National Companies TNCs)
which either directly or through subsidiaries gain control over the
production of particular primary commodities and/or the manufacture of food. The term is not simply descriptive; it often has a
negative connotation because trans-national agribusiness is perceived as being detrimental to the interests of local people.

ANDROCENTRICITY The attitude that privileges and defends men's interests and the male view: masculinity, male NORMs, values and practices, as also masculine domination and control of INSTITUTIONS and knowledge. Male bias which excludes or is harmful to women's concerns and interests has serious implications for research and action. Androcentricity may also be associated with anthropocentricity ('man at the centre'), the view that privileges humans vis-à-vis nature. See ETHNOCENTRICITY, PATRIARCHY.

ANDROGYNY Derived from the Greek term for 'man-woman-ness' to describe the occurrence of both male and female qualities in a person. FEMINISTS initially treated androgyny as a solution to male-female difference and inequality but it is now recognized that in PATRIARCHAL systems dominant males have used the androgynous figures of mythology and religion to appropriate aspects of FEMININITY for their own purposes. An Indian example is the *Ardhanareishwara*. See APPROPRIATION, BINARY OPPOSITION, GENDER, INTERGENDER

APPROPRIATION Taking possession of the meanings of other people's actions and language for one's own purposes, such as using terms differently, in a different context or with a different meaning, so as to undermine dissent. For example, the phrase 'women's EMPOWERMENT' has been appropriated by international agencies and national governments and used without its political and FEMINIST content. Appropriation may also take place through co-opting the agents of a SOCIAL MOVEMENT in order to undermine its oppositional power. Thus, appropriation manifests itself through coercion rather than force.

AUTONOMY; AUTONOMOUS WOMEN'S GROUPS Derived from the Greek word for being self-governed, autonomy refers to the ability of an individual or group to act without external control. This is a central value in DALIT and FEMINIST ideas of EMPOWERMENT and AGENCY. Personal autonomy relates to an individual's power to take decisions that pertain to the self. Autonomous women's groups are organizations of women who have come together, independently of the state, trade unions, universities etc. to further women's interests. The autonomous groups in the Indian women's movement have played a significant activist and educational role in high-lighting issues such as violence against women and the struggle for women's political representation, but till recently were less active on LIVELIHOOD issues.

BACONIAN METHOD The English philosopher, Francis Bacon (1561-1626) visualized science as an organized and methodical system of enquiry about nature for the benefit of humanity, rather than a haphazard quest by individuals or a metaphysical speculation into final causes. Bacon mapped the scope of science and categorized its methods, of which induction was one. In common usage, however, the Baconian method is treated as synonymous with the inductive method.

BALANCE OF NATURE Formerly, a significant concept in ecology, the metaphor evoked stability, order and predictability. It harks back to earlier Western beliefs in the 'Great Chain of Being' created by divine intent in which every creature had its pre-ordained place. In population ecology the concept was used to denote states of equilibrium, when removing one element would disturb the entire system, for instance the harmonious inter-relationship of organisms to one another and the environment as in a climax forest. The implication was that 'nature knows best' and should be left undisturbed. Modern ecologists believe that there is no balance of nature and that the seeming equilibrium is being constantly unbalanced by natural events. See CONSERVATION, HOLISM.

BASIC NEEDS The concept of basic needs is culturally and historically variable. It relates to the need to survive with dignity, and encompasses the physical, social and economic well-being of people, that is LIVELIHOOD and EMPOWERMENT. Besides adequate food, fuel, water, shelter, clothing, health etc., basic needs could be extended to include gainful employment and access to information and resources. A narrower concept of basic functional necessities for life gained prominence following the publication of *Limits to Growth*, the report of the 'Club of Rome'. The World Bank uses a functional definition. See FAMILY/ HOUSEHOLD.

BINARY OPPOSITION The structuring of the world into two conventionally opposed categories which seem to be fixed and mutually exclusive, such as male/ female, mind/ body, NATURE/ CULTURE, master/ slave, PRODUCTION/ REPRODUCTION etc. Such dualism overlooks both the inter-relationship between categories and their SOCIAL CONSTRUCTIONs in varied and specific contexts. See DISCOURSE, MARKED/ UNMARKED, OTHER.

BIODIVERSITY The concept of biodiversity (an abbreviation of 'biological diversity') emerged from the attempt to overcome sectoral approaches to CONSERVATION. As defined by the United Nations Environment Programme (UNEP), it relates to the variability of genes, species and ecosystems, and includes biological resources (organisms or their parts, populations and any other biotic components of the ecosystem) of actual or potential use, or value, for humanity. Thus, people are central to biodiversity. The concept of biodiversity has now become a rallying theme for the conservation movement, displacing the symbolic power of environment, ECOLOGY, and even NATURE. The three main features of the UN Convention on Biological Diversity, (which was signed in 1992 by 150 nations at the 'Earth Summit', the UN Conference on Environment and Development, in Rio de Janeiro) are that it affirms national sovereignty over biodiversity; recognizes the role of traditional knowledge of local communities in managing natural resources; and provides for a global financial mechanism to support conservation.

BIOLOGICAL DETERMINISM/ BIOLOGISM See DETERMINISM

BIOPOWER A term used by the French philosopher Michel Foucault (1926-84) to describe the ways in which power works on human bodies: by institutional practices which regulate the BODY through defining and shaping its activities and producing different kinds of knowledge about its capacities. He saw this as a new 'power over life' that evolved between the 17th and the 19th centuries in Europe and produced concepts of sexuality and criminality which positioned individuals in webs of subjugation. The concept of biopower blurs the boundaries between the material body and its SOCIAL CONSTRUCTION, between the individual and the social. This concept has been applied to other forms of social exclusion such as race, colonialism and GENDER. See BODY, GENDER-POWER RELATIONS.

BIOTECHOLOGY There is much confusion over the meaning of biotechnology. In its most benign meaning it simply refers to the use of biological agents in a technological process, for example the age-old practice of adding yeast to make bread ferment. The contemporary use of the term, however, involves the concept of genetic engineering, that is the introduction into living organisms of genes for specific purposes, such as for pest-resistance in cotton and salt tolerance in rice crops, or genes that speed up physiochemical processes as in the manufacture of some vital drugs. Public apprehensions of the environmental and health effects of biotechnology, including genetically engineered or genetically modified (GM) crops, has fuelled protests. Ecofeminists are absolutely against biotechnology; other feminist approaches, however, seem to be more in favour of a vigilant and case-based assessment of the applications of biotechnology. The ethical aspects of the use of biotechnology in assisted reproduction are of concern to all.

BIOVILLAGE The term was first used in western Europe to attract tourists to homely village holidays and organic food. It has been ingeniously appropriated by agricultural scientist M. S. Swaminathan, to denote a particular 'model' in which human development is based on the conservation, equitable utilization and sustainability of natural resources. The biovillage model envisages that poor people (who lack material assets) can improve their economic condition through enhanced skills and knowledge. It seeks to apply sophisticated technologies (including biotechnologies, and information and communication technologies) to local needs in a participatory manner and without harming the ecological and natural resource base. The model has had some successes in identifying relevant technologies and facilitating their local use for asset creation. As with other SUSTAINABLE LIVELIHOOD approaches its sustainability is dependent on the ability of facilitators to address the conflicts in social and gender relations that arise from such asset creation.

BODY, the The human body is a living organism, with an anatomy and a physiology. It is also the focus of social rituals and beliefs, which determine bodily experiences through different stages in the life cycle and also reflect the social status, gender, ethnic, and religious identity of a person. GENDER IDEOLOGY shapes the bodily practices of women and men, how they develop, sit, stand, move, what they wear. The female body is a site of male oppression through force (e.g. rape) or coercive practices that control the sexuality and mobility of women as individuals and as a group (e.g. female circumcision in parts of Africa, feet-binding in China) or even through apparently benign practices of bodily decoration (e.g. wearing heavy anklets that make walking difficult, a practice which is prevalent in many parts of India like Rajasthan). The understanding that a body becomes what it is through the performance of socially prescribed functions overcomes the earlier dualism of sex and gender. See BIOPOWER

BRAHAMANICAL PATRIARCHY A concept put forward by feminist historian Uma Chakravarti that situates PATRIARCHY in the Indian context both historically and in relation to caste. Gender roles and identities are seen as emerging from and being legally sanctioned by the stratified Hindu caste structure. This was maintained through male domination and control over land, ritual purity and women's sexuality. The upper caste woman's compliance was ensured through 'the production of consent', that is the powerful GENDER IDEOLOGY of *pativrata* and *stridharma* (husband worship and wifely virtue), combined with coercion by the men in the family and by the state.

CAPITALISM An economic system organized around the use of capital for profit; a system in which natural resources, machinery and finance, i.e. the means of PRODUCTION, are exclusively under private ownership and control, and in which workers are employed to produce goods and services for wages. Such an organization is the basis for CLASS formation. Capitalism is commonly equated with free enterprise in contrast to the system of public-ownership and control in socialist societies. This is inaccurate because in most contemporary capitalist societies there is some degree of public ownership of goods and decision-making, even as private ownership and trade also exists in socialist societies. See PATRIARCHY, SOCIALISM.

CASTE The stratified organization of society into kinship units marked by birth and status, which has been most elaborated as *jatis* (sub-castes) among Hindus in India. The separation of these units is maintained through status-ranking, rules governing marriage and social contact (ideas of purity and impurity), and the hereditary division of labour and occupations. The hierarchical ordering of castes is not universal and rigid throughout India. There are many local variations related to different agrarian and economic contexts. The influence of caste segregation has endured despite the official ban on 'untouchability' in the Constitution of India. Caste-like elements have also been present in other societies, particularly the former apartheid regime in South Africa and the racial stratification in the southern US, as also in Japan in the seventeenth and eighteenth centuries. Forces such as COLONIALISM have also had an impact on caste relationships. Caste and GENDER relations are closely inter-linked, as caste both shapes GENDER IDEOLOGY and is reinforced by it. Caste affects women's lives in deep ways, determining occupation, food practices, rituals, as also marriage and sexuality. See BRAHAMANICAL PATRIARCHY; CLASS, DALIT.

CAUSE AND EFFECT A causal explanation links a particular phenomenon, an effect, to other phenomena which precede it. This is possible and useful for some kinds of physical, chemical and biological phenomena where the linkage can be verified through observation and experiment or mathematical calculations. But such linkages are much more difficult to establish for ecological and social phenomena (and even for some kinds of physical phenomena) that cannot be reproduced in experimental conditions. See COMPLEXITY, DETERMINISM.

CIVIL SOCIETY The contemporary concept of civil society is a rather amorphous grouping that usually refers to voluntary public associations in contrast to the institutions of government, and business/ market networks. Civil society could be seen as comprising a range of organizations: not-for profit institutions, trade unions, cooperatives, non-government organizations (NGO) and socio-political movements. Increasingly, civil society is used as a substitute for NGOs. Civil society organizations may advocate the interest of citizens/ families vis-à-vis that of government and/or business, or they may advance the interests of government and/or business. The concept masks deep social and political differences and this negates its usefulness as a defined public space in society.

CLASS, Social The stratification of society into divisions by economic position, by power, status, authority and by self-definition. In anthropology, increasing specialization in the division of labour is seen as the basis for the emergence of different social classes. Marxism defines classes more specifically by their differential access to means of production. In this view, the dominant class, which controls the means of production, appropriates the surplus produced by other classes and thus also controls their labour. The polarization of classes and class conflict arises from the fundamental antagonism of classes under CAPITALISM. In India, there is a strong co-relation between class and CASTE stratification. Class, caste and GENDER are inter-related; class and caste generally work together in shaping GENDER IDEOLOGY, but class may also cut across caste independently impinging on GENDER-POWER RELATIONS. Thus, class in its social sense is much more complex than the same word used in biological and chemical nomenclature, to denote a particular group, a class of animals, plants, or chemicals.

COLONIALISM From the Latin word for colony, a settlement of ex-soldiers in a foreign land. During the colonial period, European nations (Britain, France, Spain, Portugal, Belgium) gained control over large parts of Africa, Asia and Latin America (which used to be collectively called the 'Third World') through war, force and coercion. Colonial administrations advanced their own economic and political interests by exploiting the material and human resources of the colonized country and by exporting naturally-occurring resources like minerals and forest timber, and cultivated plantation crops like cotton and tea. Under colonialism, economic relations are exclusive and binding, i.e. the colonized country has to sell its raw materials to the colonizer and buy finished goods from it and not from any other country. Colonialism was crucial to the advance of CAPITALISM in Europe. Associated with imperialism, it set in motion complex ideological, cultural and technical modes of domination in the colonies. The impact of colonial and imperial power included attempts to control the minds and bodies of the colonized through the introduction and spread of European languages, western medicine and approaches to knowledge. Colonialism is associated with the emergence and growth of disciplines like anthropology which provided colonizers with the information to manage colonized peoples. See ANDROCENTRICITY, FEMINIST ANTHROPOLOGY, NEOCOLONIALISM, GLOBALIZATION.

COMMUNITY A difficult and variously interpreted concept. In the science of ECOLOGY, this refers to an association or group whose members share certain characteristics and are assumed to live together, although in nature communities cannot be so neatly isolated. In sociology, a community is a network of relationships in a particular locality, and can also refer to a kind of relationship: e.g. community participation, community CONSERVATION. Communities may be bounded by physical territory (village community), and administrative criteria (Scheduled CASTE/ Scheduled TRIBE) or by a shared perception of belonging (FEMINIST community). A 'local community' usually refers to a geographically proximate group of people who dwell within a certain natural resource area, sharing some interdependency, even if socio-culturally heterogeneous. The noun 'community' in all of these senses has a positive connotation, which should not be confused with its adjectival form, 'communal', used negatively in India to denote religious sectarianism.

COMPLEXITY This refers both to the complex composition of a particular entity, a concept, element or variable, and the multiple ways in which a number of different entities are related to and interact with one another in specific contexts. For example, GENDER, CLASS, CASTE are complex in themselves and they interact in complex ways. Complexity involves both diversity and dynamism: a multiplicity of local conditions, each of which is the outcome of historical, socio-economic and political factors that change over time. Different kinds of knowledge (rational, experiential, imaginative etc.), different approaches and methods may be required to understand complex situations. This makes explanations of CAUSE AND EFFECT difficult. See CONTEXT-SPECIFICITY.

CONSERVATION The science of CONSERVATION relates to the use and maintenance of natural resources and life support systems in a sustainable manner, i.e. without being wasteful or destructive in the long-term. The principles of scientific conservation may be applied at different levels, that of landscapes, ecosystems, habitats, species, or genes. Conservation does not mean simply preserving the status quo, although it is often interpreted in this way. Both scientific understanding of the functioning of ecosystems and public concern for maintaining the BALANCE OF NATURE are increasingly drawing upon traditional knowledge and COMMUNITY conservation practices which emphasize social equity and environmental issues. However, the conceptual and policy shifts from conventional scientific conservation to PARTICIPATORY APPROACHES and community-based management of natural environments have yet to make a significant difference in conservation practice, and have been largely unable to incorporate GENDER concerns.

CONSERVATISM Political conservatism favours the status quo and what is seen as the slow 'natural' order of change as against revolutionary transformations. It tends to hark back to 'tradition' and accept social inequality as inevitable in the 'natural' order of things. See LIBERALISM.

CONTEXT-SPECIFICITY The word 'context' comes from the Latin for 'weaving together'. The specificity of a context may be taken as the weaving together of a particular set of ecological, socio-cultural, and historical factors. The concept of context-specificity is crucial to the SOCIAL CONSTRUCTION approach.. Gender roles and GENDER IDEOLOGIES are context-specific, varying over space and time. Knowledge systems, theories about how the world works, are also context-specific. See COMPLEXITY, PLACE.

CULTURE Culture involves so many layers of meaning and value judgements both in popular usage and in different academic disciplines that it is one of the most disputed terms. It may refer to the accumulated store of material artefacts of a particular place or period (e.g. stone-age culture); or the symbols, ideas, values and belief systems of a group of people. Sociologists treat culture, SOCIAL STRUCTURE and population as the main elements of social organization. Cultures are not necessarily homogenous and neatly bounded; there may be sub-cultures and counter-cultures (say, of DALIT women.) Culture and NATURE are commonly perceived as binary opposites with culture being equated with 'nurture' (e.g. Sherry Ortner in 'Is Sex is to Gender as Nature is to Culture?'). Adding to confusion, British social science distinguishes between culture and society, whereas American social science does not. In science, the term retains the sense of its Latin origin 'to cultivate' as living cells are cultured in an external medium, e.g. tissue culture. See BINARY OPPOSITION.

CUSTOMARY LAW Habitual actions and patterns of behaviour lead to the development of 'customary NORMS', which may become rigidified as 'customary law' in a COMMUNITY. The movement for the recognition and codification of customary law, as in some of the tribal societies of north-eastern India, is seen as political decentralization. But this is a matter of concern for women because customary laws are often gender-biased, for instance they could exclude women from owning property.

DALIT From the Indo-European root *dal*, meaning to cut. (The English word 'dale' for valley has its root in dal, meaning a cut in the ground.) In Sanskrit *dal* is to crack or split open. The term Dalit was probably first used in the 19th century by the Marathi social reformer and revolutionary leader Jyotirao Phule (1826) to describe groups oppressed by the Hindu caste structure. The term was also used by the British administration to describe 'depressed classes' and gained political currency under the Neo-Buddhist Dalit leader B.R. Ambedkar (1891-1956). It was revived in the 1970s by the Dalit Panther Movement in Maharashtra to encompass not only the Neo-Buddhists but all people who are politically and economically exploited because of their religion, including Scheduled Tribes, working people, landless and poor peasant women. Dalit is, therefore, not a caste but a self-constructed identity of oppressed people. Since the 1980s, with greater political organization of Dalits, the term has also come to be seen more positively as an expression of self-identity and political strength. Although it does not mean 'low caste', Dalit is commonly used as a synonym for Scheduled Caste, replacing 'Harijan'. During the Indian movement for Independence, the national leader Mahatma Gandhi (1869-1948) had coined the euphemistic term Harijan (meaning 'children of god') for the lowest social and ritual castes in the Hindu caste order. The term was widely adopted as a self definition instead of Scheduled Caste and commonly used till the 1990s.

DEEP ECOLOGY A radical strand of the environmental movement characterized by a philosophical approach that combines deep spiritual experience of nature, deep questioning of western society and deep commitment to an alternative holistic ecological worldview. The ecosystem is experienced as valuable in itself and not for its use to humans. The approach is somewhat ambivalent towards scientific progress and is against GLOBALIZATION and free trade which are seen as destroying humans, their culture and the natural world. Deep ecology seeks to establish ecological lifestyles through Gandhian non-violence. It is pluralistic in embracing some ecological philosophies, such as ECOFEMINISM and certain strands of nature CONSERVATION, but is opposed to approaches which are seen as anthropocentric, such as SOCIAL ECOLOGY. See BALANCE OF NATURE, HOLISM.

DETERMINISM Derived from an old French word meaning 'to fix,' determinism referred to the belief that behaviour and actions are governed by forces and SOCIAL STRUCTURES/ SYSTEMS that are beyond the control of human agents. For example, the particular view of the universe based on Newtonian laws of CAUSE AND EFFECT in which both the present and the future are seen as fixed by 'natural law'. Determinism is now used, usually negatively, to describe a variety of approaches that seek predictability based on a small range of factors. Biological determinism or 'biologism' gives primacy to biological factors (such as genetics, physiology, population) to explain the organization of societies and the constraints on AGENCY, on exercising choice and decision-making. (In *The Selfish Gene*, Richard Dawkins says 'we are survival machines—robot vehicles blindly programmed to preserve the selfish molecules known as genes.') Dawkins also coined the term 'meme' as a 'unit of cultural inheritance' analogous to the gene. Social determinism sees social life as being dependent on systems that are free from biological influences. Similarly, cultural, ecological, economic, or TECHNOLOGICAL DETERMINISM see one or the other of these factors as determining social action. Deterministic arguments are often used to justify women's subordination. See SOCIAL DARWINISM.

DISCOURSE Derived from the Latin word *discursus* meaning running from one place to another, discourse refers to a formal CONTEXT-SPECIFIC system of organizing communications among a group of people. Discourse may cover a range of modes: verbal exchanges, written texts, various forms of representation, and institutionalized interaction. e.g. 'development discourse'; 'environmental discourse'. Our discourses, the flow of thought in speech, conversation, argument, narrative, also shape our behaviour. How we talk and think about the world helps to create the world. Discourse analysis is an effective tool to understand the construction of social life and uncover prejudices (including gender-bias). Discourses are often characterized by their own META-NARRATIVES and BINARY OPPOSITIONs. See SOCIAL CONSTRUCTION.

DIVISION OF LABOUR A straightforward use of the term is the mechanical sub-division of work into component tasks as in an assembly line (where everyone does the same work). More complicated is the division of labour where people do different tasks: the economic specialization of work by activity and the social division of roles and responsibilities, based on a cluster of factors: sex, caste, wealth, prestige, power etc. The international division of labour reflects the power of trans-national corporations to increase their profits by splitting tasks of manufacturing and assembling (like computer parts which are manufactured in the US and assembled in Asia). The division of labour within a particular society may appear to contribute to its cohesion and efficiency but may mask deep conflicts. For instance, the sexual division of labour is broadly associated with male domination, and in some societies with women being confined to 'private' family spaces.

DOMINANT IDEOLOGY Broadly understood as a pattern of ideas that serve the interests of a powerful group, usually that of the dominant or ruling classes. In all societies, subordinate groups also have their own cultures and ideas about the world but they do not have the power to impose these ideas on others. Dominant groups, however, have the power to impose their ideologies on society, shaping and controlling the SOCIO-CULTURAL SYSTEM and relations between people. See GENDER IDEOLOGY

ECOFEMINISM An idealistic and holistic approach to life that combines many of the beliefs of radical feminism and DEEP ECOLOGY. Ecofeminists recognize a 'feminine principle' in NATURE and see all women as essentially nurturant. This has resonances with the idea of the Greek philosopher Aristotle that every thing has the principle within it to become what is in its nature to be. Some strands of ecofeminism (Mary Daly: GynlEcology; J. Plant: The Promise of Ecofeminism) seem to advocate an inverted sexism. In the ecofeminist approach of the German sociologist Maria Mies and Indian environmentalist Vandana Shiva three phenomena are interlinked: the European colonization of other lands, the scientific 'colonization' of nature and male 'colonization' of women's bodies. Because of differences in approach, it is more appropriate to speak of ecofeminisms in the plural. In common usage the term ecofeminism is used loosely and inaccurately to denote any or all activities that involve women and the environment. See DEEP ECOLOGY, FEMINISM, HOLISM.

ECOLOGY The Greek word oikos, meaning house or home, is the root of three significant English words: ecology, economics and ecumenism (the movement that seeks worldwide Christian unity). The common 'dictionary' definition of ecology is simply 'the branch of science dealing with the relationship of organisms to one another and to their surroundings'. The science of ecology is specifically concerned with the natural cycles that transfer elements between the environment and organisms, and the structuring of these relationships through space and time in ecosystems. In the hierarchical classification of the life sciences, ecology is at the top incorporating zoology, botany and micro-biology. This gives ecology a vast and complex empirical content and, perhaps in consequence, its appeal to holistic philosophies and those strands of the environmental movement (DEEP ECOLOGY, ECOFEMINISM) which see themselves as furthering a specifically ecological philosophy. Yet, in practice, ecological science and the philosophy of ecology may follow divergent paths. See ECOSYSTEM APPROACH, FEMINIST POLITICAL ECOLOGY, SOCIAL ECOLOGY.

ECOSYSTEM APPROACH An ecosystem is a relatively straightforward concept to denote an interdependent community of living organisms in an environment, such as a pond. The ecosystem approach is a useful tool to understand a set of relationships but in nature, an ecosystem is rarely self-contained and separate from the surrounding ecological conditions. From a LIVELIHOOD perspective, it may be more useful to look at the network of ecosystems over a broader expanse, such as a landscape.

EMPIRICISM In science, an approach that assumes the independent existence of things (data) that can be known and collected experimentally to establish positive, unambiguous, scientific facts. Empiricists tend to separate observation from theory; and facts or observational 'truths' from values. The approach gives importance to experience but does not recognize the historical and ideological construction of 'truths' in different contexts, such as through the use of language or other means of representation, which have been highlighted by FEMINISTs.

EMPOWERMENT The term is a fairly recent entrant into the development DISCOURSE to denote a process by which the less powerful groups of a COMMUNITY are enabled to put forward their perspectives and determine their own priorities. In one view, this involves a process of 'levelling the playing field' through equitable entitlements, regardless of class, ethnicity or gender. Another view is that power cannot simply be given or authorized but must be taken. The term is now widely used devoid of its radical, political de-stabilizing connotations. See AGENCY, APPROPRIATION, GENDERPOWER RELATIONS.

ENLIGHTENMENT This refers to the intellectual movement of 18th century Europe that built upon the earlier RENAISSANCE spirit of individualism, humanism and enquiry to lay the foundations of the modern Western world. In 1784, the German philosopher Immanuel Kant (1724-1804) captured the philosophy of the movement in a phrase, 'Dare to Know', i.e. dare to take the risk of discovery and the freedom of taking autonomous decisions. The movement emphasized rationality and scientific progress (rather than religious and supernatural traditions) in the quest for moral and social uplift of society. The Enlightenment is associated with the rise of European modernity in various spheres—the decline of Church power and feudalism, the rise of a middle class, and the advent of the technology of printing. It has been critiqued by FEMINISTs for excluding and devaluing women's knowledge and concerns. However, contemporary feminist ideas of SOCIAL CONSTRUCTION do have some resonances with Kant's belief that perceptions and experience are actively generated by the mind, that the mind could produce the world. See MODERNIZATION

ENTITLEMENTS A concept advanced by the economist Amartya Sen. In *Poverty and Famines* (1981), Sen argued that starvation did not reflect an overall shortage of food but rather that poor people lacked the power to claim their rightful share, their entitlements. Within the FAMILY/HOUSEHOLD, women and the aged are more likely to lack entitlements. The entitlement approach has been influential in understanding how policies for public action can be changed to address inequality and inequity. See EQUALITY/EQUITY, RIGHT TO LIVELIHOOD.

ENVIRONMENTALISM An example of the APPROPRIATION of an existing term for new purposes. Before the 1970s envrionmentalism (from the French word meaning 'to surround') was used to identify the approach in psychology that held that the social and cultural environment (nurture) was more significant than nature in shaping human personality and behaviour. Since the 1970s, environmentalism has been used as an umbrella term that describes the spectrum of pro-nature approaches advocated by the environmental movement and more specifically to denote the politics of the environment. See ECOLOGY, FEMINIST ENVIRONMENTALISM, FEMINIST POLITICAL ECOLOGY, NATURE/NURTURE.

EQUALITY, EQUITY The distinction between equality, i.e. the condition of being equal, and equity, i.e. fairness particularly in justice and law, is of relevance to programmes of women's EMPOWERMENT. Approaches that emphasize equality seek parity for women and men, such as the demand for equal wages for equal work. Approaches that emphasize equity seek to establish the principle of gender justice at the level of GENDER-POWER RELATIONS, ENTITLEMENTS.

ESSENTIALISM An approach that emphasizes traits that are seen as intrinsic and essential to the natures of men (e.g. aggression and violence) and women (e.g. nurturing and caring) and distinguishes such traits from accidental social differences. See DETERMINISM, ECOFEMINISM.

ETHNICITY The term ethnicity is used to denote a shared identity which may be either objective or subjective or both. This could mean a composite collection of traits such as physical features and language, and a sense of belonging together. Ethnic groups are endogamous, i.e. their members marry within the group, and have a real or imagined common ancestry. Broad ethnic identities may be the basis for nation-formation, or of regions or states within a nation. Ethnicity is now preferred to 'race', which has been shown to have been based on invalid generalizations. Even in current usage, however, ethnicity still implies a certain degree of marginalisation from the 'mainstream'. See ETHNOCENTRICITY.

ETHNOCENTRICITY 'Ethnos' is the Greek word for nation. The sociological term ethnocentricity was coined in the early 20th century to describe the attitude that privileges one's own cultural

NORMs, values and practices. This may be reflected in not being able to perceive cultural differences or by distorted perceptions of such differences. The domination of institutions and knowledges that are controlled by one's ethnic interests, excluding or detrimental to the concerns and interests of others, and leads to social oppression. It is often closely allied to ANDROCENTRICITY, and several science and social science disciplines that evolved during the ENLIGHTENMENT have been critiqued on both counts. This has led some disciplines, notably anthropology, to re-examine their own early premises. For example, anthropology has attempted to shed its colonial approach of locating societies on an evolutionary scale from 'primitive' to 'civilized'.

ETHNOGRAPHY This may refer either to a method of field research or the qualitative reconstruction of it in writing as in a monograph. The method of ethnographic research is widely used in socio-cultural anthropology and development studies to gather information from a COMMUNITY through empathetic participant-observation and intensive interaction over an extended period. Conventional ethnography tends to be ahistoric, concentrating on single, small socio-cultural groups, often artificially isolated as a hunting-gathering band, tribe or peasant community, and without considering the impact of wider social, economic and political forces of change. Contemporary ethnography recognizes that the attempt to analyse and convey experience is limited by the researcher's own world-view and perspectives. Alternative ethnographic approaches are now striving to find more participatory ways for a group to articulate and analyse their own experiences. Such participatory ethnography has been particularly significant in some areas of FEMINIST thought and action, such as women's health. See PARTICIPAOTRY APPROACHES.

EXPLOITATION A word that simply meant the use and development of resources as in the exploitation of mineral ores in mining. The term has acquired a more complex and negative meaning to denote the unfair taking of what belongs to or is produced by another. In this sense, exploitation characterizes social relations that are structured by CAPITALISM or/and PATRIARCHY. The exploitation of women's sexuality and labour is a central concern of gendered approaches.

FAMILY, HOUSEHOLD The origin of the word 'family' can be traced from the Latin *femina* (woman or wife) through *famula* (female slave) and reflects its function as a social institution for reproducing and socializing the young, providing emotional support for adults, being a centre of productive work and reinforcing status. In anthropology and sociology, the term family refers to a group linked together by kinship relations who may or may not reside in the same place. In economics, the term household is a common dwelling unit with shared domestic activities usually but not necessarily having a single common hearth. Families/households may vary greatly in structure and function. Currently, most households are formed by one family but a household may also include more than one family with a common or separate hearths. There are also single-parent families and women-headed households. Challenging the conventional perception of families and households as composite and altruistic units, the women's movement and gender studies 'opened' them up to reveal disjunctions and GENDER-POWER RELATIONS that operate within them. In modern industrial societies, the family as a unit of social organization is declining and the household has become more important. The concept of family carries a great ideological and patriarchal load. One example of this was the attempt in 2003-04 by the then Government of India (of the National Democratic Alliance led by the Bharatiya Janata Party) to rename the Women's Studies Centres in Indian universities as Family Studies Centres. Feminists objected that women and family were not synonymous. They argued that family studies, already a conventional part of the discipline of sociology, was treated quite differently from the approach of women's studies that critiqued the patriarchal family and its impact on women.

FEMININE, FEMININITY/MASCULINTY The literal meaning of feminine in Latin (like *dhyati* in Sanskrit) is the one who suckles her offspring, referring to woman's capacity to breast-feed. In common English usage the term extends to traits that are considered 'womanly', daintiness, coyness, gentleness. In ecofeminist usage, femininity lies in woman's procreative power and instinctive linkage with nature. Femininity is contrasted to masculinity, which is similarly considered to be made up of traits that are considered 'manly', virility, aggressiveness and so on. FEMINISTS have been deeply concerned with the socialization processes by which the stereotypes of masculinity and femininity are perpetuated in society.

FEMINIZATION OF POVERTY An outcome of gender inequality in specific rural and urban contexts, the term feminization of poverty, attempts to express the greater impact of poverty and deprivation on women as compared to men. It is often associated with single parent, female-headed households.

FEMINISM/FEMINIST Feminism refers to the modern socio-political movement for the rights of women and their 'resistance to invisibility and silencing'. The political ideology of feminism has also resulted in new theories of knowledge and research methodologies that have changed the way in which the construction of gender is analysed and understood. Feminism is a broad term which involves many different strands all of which are opposed to male domination but draw upon different socio-political theories about how such domination arose and has been sustained, and how it may be overcome. Western feminism distinguishes between liberal, radical and socialist (and Marxist) feminists. According to this typology, liberal feminists are concerned with gaining equal rights through economic independence, political representation and legal measures that further the struggle against customs and attitudes that are biased against women; radical feminists (including ecofeminists) celebrate femininity and oppose militarism; socialist/Marxist feminists are concerned with the construction of gender, with unpacking the 'natural' and with the struggle against PATRIARCHY. Most feminists emphasize women's own experience in raising their consciousness, aptly summarized in the slogan: 'the personal is the political'. Most feminists are also concerned with the ways in which women are subordinated by social institutions and in the pattern of their daily lives. Feminists differ on some fundamental issues such as on the linkages between capitalism and patriarchy, and questions related to male violence against women but have often come together to further the women's movement. Feminists have also drawn male support. There is some controversy over whether men may be called feminist; currently, the most acceptable term for men who subscribe to feminist views is 'pro-feminist men'.

FEMINIST ANTHROPOLOGY The discipline of anthropology developed in the 19th century during the period when the colonial powers were establishing their HEGEMONY in Africa, Asia and Latin America. Notoriously defined by the Polish anthropologist B.K. Malinowski (1884-1942) as the 'study of Man embracing women', anthropology subsequently provided strong evidences to counter its own early androcentric and ethnocentric phase. By documenting the diversity of women's situations, and the cross-cultural variability of gendered divisions of labour in different contexts, since the 1970s feminist anthropology has served to undermine belief in the naturalness of women's roles. This has opened up the question of whether women as a group have been universally subordinated due to their biological nature or through SOCIAL CONSTRUCTION and male domination of social INSTITUTIONS. See ANDROCENTRICITY, ETHNOCENTRICITY, FEMINIST EPISTEMOLOGY, GENDER, PATRIARCHY.

FEMINIST EPISTEMOLOGY Epistemology is the science or theory of knowledge, the nature of knowledge and what can be known. Epistemology may be contrasted with ontology or the theory of 'reality'. Feminist epistemology holds that the knowledge systems and DISCOURSEs that shape our constructions of the world are themselves socially-constructed and reflect a partial vision. Feminist epistemology has forced a rethinking in science and social science by showing how major disciplines like biology, psychology, sociology and anthropology have been gender-biased by men's values and interests. See SOCIAL CONSTRUCTION, FEMINIST ANTHROPOLOGY, FEMINIST POLITICAL ECOLOGY.

FEMINIST ENVIRONMENTALISM The term was first used to denote linkages between the feminist and environmental movements. Various approaches including ECOFEMINISM were subsumed under the umbrella of feminist environmentalism. As the popularity of ecofeminism overtook feminist environmentalism, the latter term re-emerged in the early 1990s as a counterpoint to ecofeminism. Indian feminist economist Bina Agarwal sees the linkage between women and the environment as being 'structured by a given organization of production, reproduction and distribution'. Ideological constructions of GENDER, NATURE and the relation between them may be a part but not the whole of such structuring. Although this more defined meaning of feminist environmentalism has entered the academic gender DISCOURSE, in common usage the term continues to carry its earlier and broader sense and, adding to confusion, it is also sometimes used as a synonym for ecofeminism.

FEMINIST POLITICAL ECOLOGY This approach attempts to integrate a gendered perspective into political ecology studies. Political ecology is at the interface of two distinct disciplines, cultural ecology and political economy. While cultural ecology studies the relationship between human society and the natural environment that supports particular ways of life, political economy studies the political and economic processes around which social life is organized. Political ecology is also concerned with the manner in which different nation-states and societies interact globally and how this affects development. From this inter-disciplinary origin, feminist political ecology has emerged as an especially fruitful mode of analysis to understand complex, context-specific situations and has led to rich and nuanced insights.

GENDER The word gender is derived from the Latin *genus* for birth, via the French *gendre* meaning kin or kind and in English it came to mean type. In linguistics gender defines grammatical categories, the masculine, feminine and neuter genders. In common usage gender is a synonym for sex, referring to biological types, based on anatomical sex. US anthropologist Margaret Mead (1901-1978) is credited with first distinguishing between sex and gender in her book, *Sex and Temperament in Three Primitive Societies* (1935). But it was the French feminist writer Simone de Beauvoir's *The Second Sex* (translated in 1953 from the original French publication 1949) who laid the groundwork for understanding gender as being socially-constructed. The social science use of gender refers to the socio-cultural construction of notions of FEMININITY and MASCULIN-ITY and is opposed to the idea that female and male traits, behaviour and roles are exclusively determined by anatomical or physiological factors and reproductive functions (e.g. that the sex hormone testosterone is responsible for male violence). While some see gender as an analytical category or variable, others see gender as a more complex and dynamic process. Gender socialization begins at birth. How women, men and 'in-between' genders are 'constructed' is a matter of much dispute. The understanding of gender has given rise to new observations, terms and frameworks of analysis, a reassessment of conventional disciplines and the politics of environment and development, See GENDER ANALYSIS, GENDER DIMENSIONS, GENDER IDEOLOGY, GENDER PERSPECTIVE, GENDER-POWER RELATIONS, INTERGENDER, SOCIAL CONSTRUCTION

GENDER ANALYSIS Various gender analysis frameworks have been developed by particular development agencies to meet specific needs. These frameworks are tools that help reveal the gendered SOCIO-CULTURAL SYSTEM behind the surface of societies. When the frameworks and tools of gender analysis are, however used mechanically as a check list, in such cases the transformatory power of a GENDER PERSPECTIVE is undermined.

GENDER-BUDGETING Gender-budgeting or gender-just budgeting refers to analyses that ensure the gender impact of budget allocations, usually government budgets, does justice to women's needs and concerns, i.e. that it is gender-equitable. There are two schools of thought: one favours separate allocations for women while the other wants all sectors of a budget to be gender-sensitive, incorporating just allocations to women and men, and to particular sections among them.

GENDER DIMENSIONS The word dimension comes from the Latin word for 'measuring across', a geometrical concept that incorporates the idea of the different linear coordinates of a space, i.e. length, breadth and depth. The term gender dimensions extends the quantitative and literal meaning of dimension to include the qualitative aspects of gender in the evaluation or review of a particular theme. e.g. the 'Gender dimensions of biodiversity management'.

GENDER DEVELOPMENT INDEX (GDI) The Human Development Index (HDI) was evolved by the United Nations Development Programme to provide a measure of social and economic progress of nations based on a variety of indicators, demographic, educational, standard of living etc. GDI is a gender-related development index that specifically considers measurable GENDER GAPs. Nations which are low on the HDI may do well on the GDI and vice versa.

GENDER GAP The disparity between men and women. These may be quantifiable disparities such as the difference in literacy rates or life expectancy, or qualitative disparities, for example differences in values and attitudes. See GENDER DEVELOPMENT INDEX

GENDER IDEOLOGY An ideology is a mental picture, which provides a consistent and systematic explanation that underpins a COMMUNITY. A gender ideology brings various beliefs, values and ways of thought into a socio-political unity. It shapes the knowledge, attitudes and practice of individual women and men, and their institutions, determining the roles and relations in the household, community and wider society. Some speak of various gender ideologies of which PATRIARCHY is the most widely prevalent. Others prefer to distinguish between various different forms of patriarchy.

GENDER-MAINSTREAMING See MAINSTREAMING.

GENDER PERSPECTIVE An attempt to reflect gendered viewpoints. Perspective is literally a visualization technique developed in the RENAISSANCE by Italian artists of the mid-15th century, who used geometrical knowledge to create a realistic impression of the solidity and relative proportion of objects within a drawing, i.e. the illusion of three dimensions on a two-dimensional space. Perspective is associated with scientific rationalism and the view-point of a single, unmoving spectator, and only partially embodies the COMPLEXITY of GENDER-POWER RELATIONS.

GENDER-POWER RELATIONS In common use, power retains its original Latin meaning, 'to be able', i.e. the ability to bring about an effect either through persuasion or force and despite resistance. However, the concept of power has been variously approached by philosophers and thinkers. The German sociologist Max Weber (1864-1920) defined power as the ability to control other people, events and resources, to make things happen despite obstacles, resistance and opposition. FEMINISTs call this 'power-over' in contrast to power that exists and is used in more subtle and indirect ways, e.g. the power to influence people's lives by simply not taking action, or by controlling educational institutions and mass media. For revolutionary thinker Karl Marx (1818-1883), personal power was not as important as the power that rested in the position that a social CLASS occupied in the relations of production, e.g. capitalist ownership of the means of production. He saw such power as significant in structuring the dominant and subordinate positions of different classes. Following Marx, socialist/Marxist feminists see power as inherent in class and gender relations. Many feminists also see power as the individual and collective capacity to do things, to make autonomous choices. The French philosopher-historian Michel Foucault (1926-1984) saw power as simply existing, being present invisibly in all kinds of human relationships. In a relation of power one person tries to control the way another behaves and this can happen in many overt and subtle ways, even silently. Following Foucault, gender-power relations may be seen as a form of control, active and mobile, resisted and negotiated, involving bargaining between the less powerful and the more powerful. The power of PATRIARCHY lies in the power appropriated by men in a particular structure of GENDER relations. For instance, women may be beneficiaries of development programmes without being able to exercise power, without having AGENCY and AUTONOMY.

GENDERSCAPE(S) The term was originally used in art, film studies and landscape architecture. It is redefined in this book and used together with 'wordscapes', 'workscapes' and 'actionscapes' to understand and represent the ideological and material features that make up the entirety of women's life-worlds. The postfix 'scapes' is used to reflect the many-layered spread and dynamic complexity of concepts and terms of discourse (that is, *words*), ethnographic accounts of women's day-to-day life (their *work*), and research, policy and programme interventions (*actions*) that elucidate or have an impact upon women's LIVELIHOODS. While focusing on particular aspects of women's selves, their lives and livelihoods in specific familial and community situations, natural environments and developmental contexts, genderscapes incorporate greater complexity than ecosystem approaches and are more layered and nuanced than gender analysis frameworks. A genderscape encompasses the physical-spatial, socio-economic and socio-political; it seeks to draw out gender-power relations, conflicts, resistances and negotiations in the process of empowerment. Genderscapes resonate with the concept of 'taskscapes' developed by the anthropologist T. Ingold (1993) and deepen it by building upon the feminist perspective of 'outsider-within'.

GENDERED SPACE A notion of space where the division between inside and outside, domestic and public, is not marked by a physical boundary but by people's perceptions. Gendered space is contrasted to 'Cartesian space', a concept derived from the mathematical ideas of seventeenth Century European philosopher Rene Descartes who tried to understand nature rationally, summed up in his famous phrase: 'I think, therefore I am'. Gendered space is non-Cartesian in that it is not a physical entity that can be mechanically measured and mapped. 'Outside' spaces are those places where women feel, or are made to feel, uncomfortable, unsafe, unwanted; 'out of bounds' locations or activities perceived to be beyond the 'women's domain'. See PLACE.

GLOBALIZATION, Economic Contemporary economic globalization is characterized by openness to international trade, investment and finance, which has been made possible by vastly improved telecommunications. Economic liberalization, as advocated by the World Bank and the International Monetary Fund, also involves the flow of technology, information and services across national borders. Integration into the international foreign exchange and capital market exposes poor countries to unregulated speculative flows of capital. While globalization offers opportunities for advancement to some sections of people, it has aggravated socio-economic polarization and intensified the contradictions between private and social benefits. See CAPITALISM, MODERNITY.

GRAND NARRATIVE See META-NARRATIVE.

HARIJAN See Dalit

HEGEMONY The term originally meant leadership. It was used by Italian social theorist Antonio Gramsci (1891-1937) to denote domination and control by the state and the dominant elite through building alliances and using coercion (rather than force) to gain acceptance of institutions and ideas. Counter-hegemony works against the dominant powers in society by asserting alternative meanings. The tension between the hegemonic and counter-hegemonic forces keeps society in constant flux. The concepts of hegemony and counter-hegemony are useful to understand the interplay of force and coercion in maintaining GENDER IDEOLOGIES. See APPROPRIATION, DOMINANT IDEOLOGY, GENDER-POWER RELATIONS.

HOLISM The term holism is popularly used in opposition to reductionism. The concept of holism is that the whole is more than the sum of its parts because it encompasses the functional relationships among the parts, as in the model 'Gaia' that has been put forward to visualize the planet Earth and all its systems as a single self-regulating organism. Holism has a powerful appeal. An associated concept is that of a supposed BALANCE OF NATURE. According to some sections of the environmental movement, people living subsistence lifestyles and more directly dependant on NATURE (such as forest-dwellers and tribal peoples in Africa and Asia) have holistic world views. Similarly, some sections of the women's movement have ascribed holistic worldviews to women because of their supposedly intuitive understanding of nature. (The word holism has a curious origin. It was coined in the 1920s in a different context by J.C. Smuts the prime minister of South Africa during the period of apartheid and first appeared in the title of his book, *Holism and Evolution*.)

HOUSEHOLD See FAMILY.

HUMANISM European social movement, in the 14th-15th centuries, that emphasized the role of human intellectual and cultural endeavour and achievement in contrast to divine interventions. Associated with the RENAISSANCE, the rediscovery of the pre-Christian 'classics' of Greece and Rome, and the spirit of individualism and exploration in art, literature, navigation and other fields. Also associated with the ENLIGHTENMENT of the 18th century, rational attempts to understand the world and to free intellectual activity from the shackles of religion. Both these celebrated periods of European history have been critiqued by feminists who have argued that the Renaissance and the Enlightenment were marked by ANDROCENTRICITY.

HYSTERIA In the English language the word 'hysteria' denotes wild uncontrollable emotion or excitement. It is derived from the Greek *hysterikos* (of the womb) because it is said to occur more frequently in women than in men. This is an instance of how the meaning of a word reflects GENDER-POWER RELATIONS. 'Unpacking' the word helps us to see how it has been defined in men's interest.

INDIGENOUS PEOPLE See ADIVASI

INSIDE/OUTSIDE See GENDERED SPACE

INSTITUTION A widely used and variously interpreted term. The FAMILY/ HOUSEHOLD, MARKET, parliament, school, prison are all institutions. Institutions may serve socio-cultural, economic or political functions. One interpretation of social institutions is that they are seen as the formal and informal rules, the NORMS that shape interactions among people and between them and the environment. In common usage institutions are sometime confused with ORGANIZATIONS.

INTERGENDER Currently, people who 'gender' themselves in various different ways have adopted specific terms to express their self-perceived identity, such as 'gender continuum' to encompass gender variations from woman to man. Others reject the binary 'bounded-ness' of 'man' and 'woman' and prefer the term 'intergender' to describe a more fluid identity. An imaginative and powerful expression of this is in the feminist science fiction of Ursula le Guin; in the *Left Hand of Darkness* (1969), le Guin visualizes a humanity in which all have a cyclical potential for developing physiologically as mothers and fathers, but where there is no concept of Man or Woman, or division of humanity into binary opposites, strong/weak, protective/protected and so on. See ANDROGYNY, BINARY OPPOSITION, GENDER.

INTERPRETIVE APPROACH In philosophy, anthropology and gender studies an interpretive (or interpretative) approach emphasizes the significance of people's own explanation of their philosophy, culture and social systems rather than imposing meanings from outside. The challenging role of the observer/ researcher is to 'give voice' to different local points of view, using people's own description and terms without misrepresentation and homogenization. Interpretative approaches help to articulate women's 'silence'.

LIFEWORLD(S) The everyday world in which people live and work as contrasted to larger political and economic world systems. The concept of life-worlds is especially significant in developing a gendered understanding of human activities, such as those of poor women, children and the aged, that are marginalised by the larger systems.

LIBERALISM Historically, liberalism, the commitment to individual liberty, is distinguished from CONSERVATISM but in India this distinction is less clear. Both the environmental and women's movements have been greatly influenced by liberal attitudes. Liberalism is critiqued for its reliance on the state to protect individual rights against CAPITALIST exploitation. By buffering society from the excesses of CAPITALISM its critics say that liberalism also contributes to the continuance of capitalist exploitation.

LIVELIHOOD(S), SUSTAINABLE LIVELIHOODS APPROACH Till the 1990s, livelihood had a straightforward 'dictionary' meaning: the means of gaining a living. However, since then it has been adopted in the development DISCOURSE to form the core of a new cluster of strategies, loosely called the Sustainable Livelihoods Approach (SLA). This strives to be more people-centred and go beyond earlier income-generation strategies for poverty reduction. The broader focus on sustainable livelihoods rather than incomes gained prominence in Agenda 21, the non-binding preamble to the 1992 UN Convention on Environment. An influential definition of livelihood (put forward by Robert Chambers, 1995) is the 'means of gaining a living, including tangible assets (resources and stores), intangible assets (claims and access), and livelihood capabilities' that includes coping abilities, opportunities and various freedoms. The United Nations Development Programme (UNDP) emphasizes sustainability, 'the capability of people to make a living and improve their quality of life without jeopardizing the livelihood options of others, either now or in the future'. This has resonances with the earlier concept of SUSTAINABLE DEVELOPMENT. As with other HOLISTIC approaches, SLA is open to many different interpretations. It is treated as an objective, a framework for analysis, and a method, or all of these; this makes it difficult to put into practice in specific contexts. See BIOVILLAGE, RIGHT TO LIVELIHOOD.

MAINSTREAMING, GENDER-MAINSTREAMING The term was originally used in the field of education for the process of bringing children who were specially challenged, either physically or with learning disabilities, into the main educational stream instead of being enrolled in separate, special educational institutions. Experience shows that such 'mainstreaming', say of blind children in regular schools, is beneficial both to the specially challenged children and to the others. Its use in the context of 'gender-mainstreaming' is more recent and generally refers to the explicit inclusion of women, who have been excluded for various reasons into, say, development programmes. It has gained currency through its adoption, both as a strategy and as a goal, by various international agencies. Some agencies are clear that gender-mainstreaming should reflect integration at all levels from planning to implementation and outcomes. However, in practice in the Indian subcontinent it has usually meant just adding a 'woman component' into existing programmes. In Europe, gender-mainstreaming has been critiqued by women's groups who say that funding for specific women's programmes has been withdrawn because these have supposedly been incorporated into general programmes for all citizens.

MARKETS These may be informal or formal means of exchanging goods and services, including labour. Unregulated markets tend to privilege those who already enjoy positions of power and wealth, and therefore have greater bargaining power. As an economic IN-STITUTION, markets are extremely diverse existing at different levels from the local village *haat* that caters to a few villages to international markets that have a global reach. At every level, markets are shaped by the structure of social relations and in turn help maintain these structures. The values assigned by the market to different kinds of products or work reflect the inequalities in a society. Both rural and urban markets privilege men in many ways, by deeming certain market spaces beyond women's physical and social domain, by limiting women's access to various occupations, and by controlling how much women are paid in exchange for their labour or produce.

MARKED/UNMARKED In BINARY OPPOSITIONs like male/ female, the first category (male) is taken as the unmarked NORM, while the second (female) is marked as the OTHER which deviates from the NORM. e.g. doctor/ lady doctor; farmer/ woman farmer. The marked category may also be male, as in nurse/ male nurse..

MATRIARCHY A much misused word commonly understood as 'mother-rule' (from its literal Greek origin) as the mirror-image of PATRIARCHY (father-rule). In such a view, matriarchy is female dominance of INSTITUTIONS and the privileging of female values and interests, which may be associated also with matrilineal descent traced through the female line and matrilocality, i.e. the husband moving to the wife's or her parent's natal home. One view is that matriarchal societies with women-centred religions, which deified a female principle in the form of 'mother goddesses', preceded the emergence of the patriarchal religions such as Christianity, Hinudism and Islam whose central deities are male. There is little historical evidence, however, of functioning matriarchies in past societies even among those which worshipped mother goddesses, or in contemporary societies which practise MATRILINY and matrilocality.

MATRILINY A term which is commonly confused with MATRIARCHY. Matriliny, the principle of descent through the female line, is characteristic of a few communities in South Asia, including the Khasis and Garos of Meghalaya and the Nairs of Kerala. Matrilineal societies may be male-dominated, as for example the Muslim matrilineal society of Lakshadweep. See PATRIARCHY.

META-NARRATIVE A 'master' story of the world, that tries to comprehensively explain all aspects of social relations and define the human condition in a single universal framework, whether it be a religious belief system, a scientific, political, psychoanalytical or other theory. These meta or 'grand narratives' were famously critiqued by the French philosopher and literary theorist Jean-Francois Lyotard (1924-1998) for their totalizing visions which failed to grasp the COMPLEXITY of local situations. Lyotard's critique has considerable appeal to a wide range of feminists, although some strands, notably ECOFEMINISM, also have their own meta-narratives. See CONTEXT-SPECIFICITY.

MODERNIZATION Derived from the Latin *modo* (just now), the word was at first used to identify the economic and socio-cultural impact of factory production (industrialization) as reflected in Charlie Chaplin's famous film *Modern Times* (1936). In the early 20th century, German sociologist Max Weber (1864-1920) associated modernization with the spread of commerce and the ethic of work in Christian (specifically Protestant) nations such as Britain and Germany that favoured individual effort and enterprise. Modernization has, however, taken place in other kinds of societies such as Catholic France and Buddhist Japan. In India it is often equated with technological development, following Western models. The impact on natural resource systems, LIVELIHOODS, life styles and gender equity is a matter of considerable debate. The DISCOURSE on modernization has now been overtaken by GLOBALIZATION. See TECH-NOLOGICAL DETERMINISM.

NATURE/CULTURE One of the most enduring of BINARY OPPOSITIONs, encompassing many other polarities, e.g.: animal nature/human culture; 'primitive' humans, supposedly nearer 'wild' nature/civilized humans, who supposedly have culture; women, presumed to be 'naturally' closer to nature because of their procreative capacity/men who make the artefacts of culture and organize civilized societies. Given that Nature itself may be variously interpreted, such polarities are open to be critiqued for their ETHNO-CENTRICITY and culturally constructed premises. Some approaches reverse the qualities or values associated with each pole. This is reflected in German ecofeminist Maria Mies' assertion that 'to create a child is quite different from constructing a car or other machine', where creating (i.e. the natural function of birthing) a child is valorized and opposed to the cultural function of making a machine. See ECOFEMINISM, DEEP ECOLOGY.

NEOCOLONIALISM This refers to the former colonial powers (or new industrial powers) adopting strategies that perpetuate the political and economic independence and political subordination of former colonies, such as through unequal trade treaties and interference in their political affairs. See COLONIALISM.

NORMS Guidelines for normal behaviour in different social contexts based on rules of conduct prescribed and enforced by a group of people. Such norms often reflect the interests of the more powerful sections and their perceptions of what is normal and appropriate. See ANDROCENTRICITY, ETHNOCENTRICITY, INSTITUTIONS, NORMALITY.

NORMALITY The concept of normality is derived from the Latin word for 'normal' or 'square'. It originally meant standing at right angles to the ground. It was only in the mid-19th century that normal in English came to mean normal conditions or states and normality was used to discriminate against those who do not conform. Arguments of normality are a potent tool to make women follow prescribed behaviours. In women's history the denunciation and persecution of non-conforming women as 'witches' is now well-documented. Some women's groups use the term 'heteronormality' to emphasize the domination of heterosexually oriented people in society and to challenge the entire range of BINARY OPPOSITIONs, which are centred around the duality of female and male. See INTERGENDER, NORMS, OTHER.

ORGANIZATION In common usage often confused with INSTITUTION, an organization is a formal unit set up to achieve a particular purpose. Organizations may comprise of a very large number of sub-units and individuals in several nations (e.g. the International Labour Organization), or may be quite small, located in a few centres (e.g. Kerala Sastra Sahitya Parishad). Larger organizations such as government bureaucracies are bound together by hierarchical authority structures. Smaller non-governmental organizations (NGOs) may have more flexible network-like structures and non-authoritarian relations, as in some of the AUTONOMOUS WOMEN'S GROUPS.

OTHER, the The opposite of the normative category in a BINARY OPPOSITION, i.e. the 'marked' category, e.g. woman, in man/woman). In social relations, the disempowered 'Other' serves to define and underscore the power of the dominant category. For example, in the binary *malik* (employer)/*mazdoor* (worker), the mazdoor is the other. See MARKED/UNMARKED.

PARADIGM SHIFT A paradigm is a world view, a mental model or a pattern of thought that provides a coherent explanation for a body of information. A paradigm shift is a revolutionary change in perceptions, for which the impetus may be new information or new ways of interpreting existing information. The term was originally applied in the field of science and popularized by Thomas Kuhn's *The Structure of Scientific Revolutions* (1962). An example of a paradigm shift in science would be the displacement of the Lamarckian concept of evolution by the inheritance of acquired characteristics by the Darwinian concept of evolution by natural selection.

PARTICIPATORY APPROACHES This is a very fluid umbrella concept with a varied history. During the 1960s, many non-formal education programmes began experimenting with people's own modes of communication, such as folk music, drama, puppetry etc., to involve people in their own development. This was given an entirely different direction by the revolutionary Brazilian educationalist Paulo Freire (1921-1997) whose work *Pedagogy of the Oppressed* (1970) had a profound influence in all of Latin America. Freire emphasized dialogue, working *with* oppressed people, and education for liberation from oppression through conscientisation, i.e learning to perceive social, political and economic contradictions and acting against oppression. As the participatory approach spread around the world, a range of different methodologies emerged, although often devoid of the revolutionary content. Participatory ACTION RESEARCH is one such method used to raise individual and collective consciousness and is perceived as liberatory. It has now been replaced in development programmes by Participatory Rural Appraisal (PRA) and Participatory Learning and Action (PLA), which combine elements of a participatory approach with the objectives of conventional rural appraisals. PRA is based on the belief that people have the capacity to analyse their own 'realities' and that given the opportunity they can act on the basis of their own analysis, which is a form of EMPOWERMENT. It uses visual tools such as mapping and local materials (sticks and stones) to enable communities to develop their own knowledge, skills and understanding. PRA has been critiqued for its seeming inability to deal with wider social relations, including GENDER-POWER RELATIONS. See PARTICIPATORY TECHNOLOGY DEVELOPMENT.

PARTICIPATORY TECHNOLOGY DEVELOPMENT The systematic blending of local knowledges and modern science through interactions between rural people and outside facilitators. The aim is to enhance the understanding of local farming systems, define problems and select the best technological options for immediate interventions and long-term sustainability. The PTD process builds upon the tools of participatory rural appraisal (PRA). See ACTION RESEARCH, PARTICIPATORY APPROACHES.

PATRIARCHY Patriarchy is a gender ideology characterized by systemic male dominance of the INSTITUTIONS of society, and the privileging of male values and beliefs. In a patriarchal society, kinship is usually though not necessarily patrilineal (a system in which descent, inheritance and succession is traced through the male line) and patrilocal (where a woman moves to the husband's home or his paternal home, and authority is vested with patrilineal kin). As the forms of systemic domination vary, some prefer to speak of patriarchies in the plural (e.g. BRAHMANICAL PATRIARCHY, tribal patriarchies), or of different forms of GENDER IDEOLOGY of which patriarchy is one. Patriarchal power pervades social INSTITUTIONS and both traditional and modern knowledge systems. The participation of some women in patriarchal institutions may only be 'tokenism' if the masculine NORMS of the institution do not change. Women's movements have developed different strategies to counter patriarchy by identifying its mechanisms and revealing fundamental falsehoods (such as the projection of patriarchy as a natural phenomenon), by devising new vocabularies and methods of analysis, and by supporting women's individual and group actions towards EMPOWERMENT.

PLACE A commonly used word with a special meaning in geography. The character of a place is shaped by environmental and human actions over time. Places reflect a particular socio-political and economic history. People relate to and identify with places on a varied scale (e.g. villages, neighbourhoods, areas, localities) according to their perceptions, experience, mobility and work. Places are subject to disputes over how they are used and to territorial conflict between peoples. Gender is a neglected dimension in the DISCOURSE on place. See GENDERED SPACE.

POSITIVISM The approach in science that confines itself to what can be directly observed and experienced. Positivists seek to separate theory from tangible perceptions, values from 'facts', and to establish universal natural laws that explain the relations between observed phenomena through inductive methods. Positivist social science seeks to explain human behaviour using the same methods developed by natural science for material phenomena. This has been critiqued because the meanings that people attach to behaviour (their awareness and purpose) cannot be ignored. However, systematic methods and analysis can be used without being positivist. See interpretive approaches.

PRA, PARTICIPATORY RURAL APPRAISAL See PARTICIPATORY APPROACHES.

PRODUCTION The concepts of production and REPRODUCTION are central to Marxist theory and newer approaches that have built upon this. According to Marx, the production of goods also involves production of specific social relations including the ownership of the mean of production. The mode of production is constituted by the relationship between the means of production and the social relations in the production process, which are constantly evolving. Different modes of production may exist in the same context.

RADICAL FEMINISM See FEMINISM

RENAISSANCE Literally re-birth, a term used in 19th century France to describe a period of European history extending from the early 14th to the late 16th century. It was characterized by a spirit of enquiry, HUMANISM and individualism which led to a renewed interest in the forgotten arts of Greece and Rome and a great burst of creative exploration in many fields including painting, sculpture, literature and the sciences. The Renaisance man, exemplified by the Italian Leonardo da Vinci, stands for the fusion of art and science. Some feminist historians have critiqued the glorification of the period, arguing that the Renaisance excluded women and objectified them. See ENLIGHTENMENT.

REPRODUCTION Feminists use the term reproduction at many different levels, from the straightforward biological and physical reproduction of the population to the more layered Marxian concept of social reproduction, which includes the reproduction of labour, technology, tools and knowledge. In the latter sense, social reproduction involves reproducing both the social relations and the ideologies that maintain the SOCIO-CULTURAL SYSTEM. See PRODUCTION.

RIGHT TO LIVELIHOOD The right to livelihood has been an enforce-able right under the Constitution of India since the 1985 judge-ment of the Supreme Court on the eviction of impoverished pave-ment-dwellers from the streets of Mumbai (*Olga Tellis and others versus the Bombay Municipal Corporation*). The landmark judge-ment extended Article 21 of the Constitution to include the right to livelihood. Since then, the active jurisprudence of the Supreme Court has led to the enunciation of several new basic rights, in-cluding rights to: dignity; gender equality; health; education; environment; and information. See LIVELIHOODS.

SCHEDULED CASTE See DALIT

SHG The acronym SHG stands for Self-Help Group, usually an association of about 20 women and/or men who form a group primarily for savings and credit. The members of an SHG deter-mine their own rules and procedures for depositing and lending money, and manage their own funds. The inspiration (largely unacknowledged) for SHGs came from the success of the Mahila Samakhya programme, an unusual government intervention in several states in the 1980s based on the political principle of edu-cation as empowerment; micro-credit was only one element in a much broader transformatory agenda for collective action to change rural women's lives. In the early 1990s, however, the model was appropriated and divested of its political content by the govern-ment and the banking sector, flush with funds to disperse and confident about the proven ability of women's groups to return loans. Within a short span, with the active facilitation of non-government ORGANIZATIONS, hundreds of thousands of SHGs were formed (now said to be well over a million). The immediate finan-cial objectives were cast in the theoretical framework of consoli-dating SOCIAL CAPITAL. Even as corporate interests have sought to enter the rural Indian market through SHGs, some of these groups have been able to start small enterprises and many women have strategically used the strength of the group in individual and col-lective political action. See EMPOWERMENT

SOCIAL CAPITAL A politically contentious term that locates mutu-ally supportive social relations and institutional networks in an economic framework as 'capital', by implication a resource or asset that can be utilized for profit. The idea that customary networks of trust and reciprocity were social capital that could be encashed emerged in the development DISCOURSE in the 1980s, although the concept had been sporadically advanced throughout the 20th century. Its swift adoption by the World Bank as the 'missing link' in development has been critiqued as a systematic attempt to obscure CLASS conflicts and deflect political action into social ORGANIZATION (John Hariss 2002. *Depoliticising Development: The World Bank and Social Capital*). See INSTITUTION, SHG.

SOCIAL CONSTRUCTION The theory that holds that ideology and language as well as economic relations have shaped the meanings that are attached to most things in the world including the 'facts' of science. Since the 1980s, the interpretive approach of social construction has undermined the POSITIVIST approach in many disciplines.

SOCIAL DARWINISM, SOCIOBIOLOGY Darwinism is the revolution in biology stimulated by Charles Darwin's ground-breaking thesis *On the Origin of Species* (1859) containing his ideas on adaptation, natural selection and fitness in the evolutionary process. Neo-Darwinism retains the principles of Darwinian evolution but is based on a genetic explanation for the process of evolution. Social Darwinism is an approach, with roots in animal ecology that attempts to apply neo-Darwinian concepts to human socio-cultural evolution, claiming that human social behaviour is genetically programmed. This forms the basis of sociobiology propounded by the US ecologist E. O. Wilson (*Sociobiology: The New Synthesis* 1975 and *On Human Nature* 1978). The approach has been strongly contested first by the philosopher Philip Kitchner, geneticist RC Lewontin, palaeontologist Stephen Jay Gould, and by many feminists. Among the best known refutations of sociobiology and genetic determinism are *Not in our Genes* (1984) by RC Lewontin, Steven Rose and LJ Kamin and Lewontin's *Biology as Ideology* (1991). See DETERMINISM.

SOCIAL ECOLOGY This is a clearly defined approach that sees the contradiction between economic growth and the degradation of the natural environment as the direct result of CAPITALISM, but believes that the anti-capitalist ideologies of the past, including Marxism, are not relevant to the current forms of capitalism and technological advancement. It envisages a progressive, ecologically-oriented society that uses technology and science for material well-being and human happiness. It emphasises rational levels of consumption and democratic processes of management. Social ecology has appealed to a cross-section of environmentalists and scientists but in comparison to political ecology has not been influenced by a gendered perspective. See FEMINIST POLITICAL ECOLOGY.

SOCIALISM In theory, the term refers to a social system in which the major means of production and distribution are owned and controlled by government, the community, or workers' associations. In practice many variations of socialist systems of organization exist. All strands of socialism favour some form of economic planning and distribution based on cooperation rather than on competition. The Premable to the Constitution of India includes the term socialist in its definition of the country. In India, the combination of socialist/Marxist approaches and FEMINISM has led to politically alert and gender-sensitive approaches to issues of concern to women.

SOCIALIST/ MARXIST FEMINISM See FEMINISM.

SOCIO-CULTURAL SYSTEM, SOCIAL STRUCTURE, SOCIAL SYSTEM, Social structure is a widely used anthropological term that is not easily defined. It usually refers to the elements (such as institutions, roles, status) around which a society is organized, and the inter-linkages between these elements. It has been critiqued because of the implication that structures are coherent, unchanging and deterministic. An alternative term is social system, which is like a social structure in that it denotes the elements in a social organization and their relations. It differs in the implication that it is more coherent, orderly and dynamic, changing and reproducing itself over time. The boundaries of a social structure or system are difficult to demarcate. Currently, the preferred term is socio-cultural system as this seems to avoid the implication of DETERMINISM while giving equal emphasis to both the social and the cultural, as also their inter-linkage in the organization of societies over time.

STAKEHOLDER Any person or group having a stake (i.e. with an interest) in a particular issue such as the management of a resource. Stakeholders may have formal and/ or informal stakes and may be at different levels: international, national, local. There may be a number of different stakeholders in a village or household with varied realtionships to one another and to the resource. Stakeholder and gender analysis help to uncover these relationships.

SUSTAINABLE DEVELOPMENT The umbrella concept of sustainable development was advanced by the World Commission on Environment and Development (*Our Common Future* 1987) and defined as that which 'meets the needs of the present without compromising the ability of future generations to meet their own needs.' It recognized three inter-linked elements, the need to: conserve ecological systems and resources, maintain the sustainability of economic growth, and ensure the equitable sharing of benefits. This allowed for almost any kind of interpretation and in the 1990s the concept grew to encompass a future in which historical conflicts, both between humankind and nature and between different sections of people, would be peaceably reconciled. The concept has been critiqued for its broad expanse and its avoidance of issues related to resource conflicts, power relations and GENDER. See LIVELIHOOD(S).

SUSTAINABLE LIVELIHOODS APPROACH See. LIVELIHOOD(S)

TECHNOLOGICAL DETERMINISM An approach that sees technology as the determining factor in social change, independent of social and cultural factors and processes. The approach has been discredited, however, because of the failure of technologically deterministic interventions in development.

Bibliography

Adjania, Nancy. 2003. 'Dialogues on Representation', *The Hindu Magazine,* 16 February.

Agarwal, Bina. 1992. 'The Gender and Environment Debate: Lessons from India.' *Feminist Studies* 18 (2): 119–53.

———1994. *A Field of One's Own: Gender and Land Rights in South Asia.* New Delhi: Cambridge University Press.

———1997. 'Environmental Action, Gender Equity and Women's Participation,' *Development and Change,* 28 (1): 1-44.

———2003. 'Gender and Land Rights Revisited: Exploring New Prospects via The State, Family and Market', in Shahara Razavi (ed.). *Agrarian Change, Gender and Land Rights.* pp. 184-224. Oxford: Blackwell.

Agnihotri, Anita. 2001. *Forest Interludes.* New Delhi: Kali for women.

Agnihotri, Satish B. 2000. *Sex Ratio Patterns in the Indian Population.* New Delhi: Sage Publishers.

Ahmed, Sara and Hari Krishna. 1998. 'Changing Gender Roles in Irrigation Management: The Case of Sadguru's Lift-Irrigation Co-operatives,' Working Paper 120. Anand, Gujarat: Institute of Rural Management, June.

Aier, Anungla. 1998. 'Women in Ao Society', in Lucy Zehol (ed.), *Women in Naga Society,* pp. 92-103. New Delhi: Regency Publishers.

Aier, Anungla and Sapu Changkija. 2003. 'Indigenous Knowledge and Management of Natural Resources,' in T.R. Subba and G.C. Ghosh (eds.) pp. 333-378.

AMFU. 1995. *New Mizo Method of Permanent Farming.* Aizawl: All Mizoram Farmer's Union.

Anand, Manoj. 2005. 'Mizos Want New Marriage Law'. *The Asian Age*: 20 June

Anderson, C. 1992. 'Practical Guidelines', in L. Ostergaard (ed.) *Gender and Development: A Practical Guide.* London: Routledge.

Anderson, M.B. and P.J. Woodrow 1989. *Rising from the Ashes: Development Strategies in Times of Disaster,* Paris: UNESCO and Westview Press. (Second edition 1998, Lynne Rienner Publications.)

Anon. n.d. *Nagaland.* Kohima: Directorate of Tourism, Government of Nagaland.

Appadurai, Arjun. 1990. 'Disjuncture and Difference in the Global Political Economy.' *Public Culture* 2 (2): 1-24.

———1996. *Modernity at Large: Cultural Dimensions of Globalization* (Public Worlds vol.1) Minneapolis: University of Minnesota Press.

Ariyanamdu, Madhavi Malalgoda and Maithree Wickramasinghe 2005. *Gender Dimensions in Disaster Management: A Guide for South Asia.* New Delhi: Zubaan

Arora, R.K. and Anjula Pandey. 1996. *Wild Edible Plants of India: Diversity, Conservation and Use.* New Delhi: National Bureau of Plant Genetic Resources, Indian Council for Agricultural Research.

Bandhyopadhyay, J. 1993. Reported in *Policy Action for Biological Diversity, Proceedings No. 5.* (Report on Policy Makers Workshops on Conservation and Sustainable Management of Biological Diversity, 19-20 December, 1992) Madras: M.S. Swaminathan Research Foundation.

Banerjee, Narayan K. 2004. 'Organising Women through Wasteland Development: Bankura District, West Bengal', in Sumi Krishna (ed.) pp. 109-124. Op. cit.

Barkataki, S. 1967. *Tribes of Assam.* New Delhi: National Book Trust.

Barnard, Alan. 2002. 'Hunting and gathering society: an eighteenth-century Scottish invention,' Paper presented at Ninth International Conference on Hunting and Gathering Societies (CHAGS 9): Hunter-Gatherer Societies and the Reshaping of Anthropology. Edinburgh. 9-13 Sept.

Barthakur, J.K. 1995. 'Shifting Cultivation and Economic Change in the North-Eastern Himalaya', in J.S. Lall (ed.) *The Aspects of the Himalaya: A Selection.* New Delhi: Oxford University Press.

Baruah, Apurba K. and Manorama Sharma. 1999. 'Matriliny, Land Rights and Political Power in Khasi Society', *Indian Journal of Human Rights.* Special volume: Women and Violence. 3 (1,2): 210-228.

Baruah, T.K. 1976. 'The Effect of Bride-price on a Mishmi', in Anon. *Resarun 1975,* pp. 110-13. Shillong: Department of Information and Public Relations, Government of Arunachal Pradesh.

Beauvoir, Simone de 1949. *Le Deuxieme Sexe* (translated from the French as *The Second Sex.* 1953 Jonathan Cape; translated and edited H.M. Parshley 1972. Harmondsworth UK: Penguin Books.)

Bhagabati, A.C. 1988. 'Tribal Transformation in Assam and North-East India: An Appraisal of Emerging Ideological Dimensions'. Presidential Address to Anthropology and Archaeology Group, 75th Indian Science Congress, Pune.

Bhargava, Meena. 1999. *State, Society and Ecology: Gorakhpur in Transition 1750-1830.* New Delhi: Manohar.

Bhattacharjee, Tarun Kumar. 1983. *The Idus of Mithun and Dri Valley.* Directorate of Research, Government of Arunachal Pradesh.

Birke, Linda 1992. 'In pursuit of difference: scientific studies of women and men', in. Gill Kirkup and Laurie Smith Keller eds. *Inventing Women: Science, Technology and Gender,* pp. 81-102. Cambridge, UK: Polity Press.

——1999. *Feminism and the Biological Body.* Edinburgh: University Press.

Bleier, Ruth. 1984. *Science and Gender: A critique of biology and its theories on women.* New York and Oxford: Pergamonn Press.

——1986 'Sex Difference Research: Science or Belief', in R. Bleier (ed.) *Feminist Approaches to Science,* pp. 147-164. New York: Pergamon Press.

Boserup, Ester 1970. *Women's Role in Economic Development.* London: George Allen.

Braidotti, Rosi, Ewa Charkiewiwcz, Sabie Hausler and Saskia Wieringa. 1994. *Women, the Environment and Sustainable Development. Towards a Theoretical Synthesis.* London: Zed books.

Burling. 1963. cited in Agarwal 1994. Op.cit.

Bundgaard, Helle. 1999. 'Contending Indian Art Worlds' *Journal of Material Culture.* 4 (3): 321-337.

Burman, B.K. Roy 1966. 'Structure of bridge and buffer communities in the border areas. *Man in India.* 46(2).

——2002. 'Demographic Profile of the Hill Areas of North East India,' in Sarthak Sengupta (ed.) pp. 1-19. Op. cit.

Chaki-Sircar, Manjusri. 1984. *Feminism in a Traditional Society-Women of the Manipur Valley.* New Delhi: Shakti Books.

Chakma, Kabita. 1994. 'Development, Environment and Indigenous Women in the Chttagong Hill Tracts of Bangladesh', in Krattiger, Anatole F. et. al. (eds.) *Widening Perspectives on Biodiversity,* pp. 233-241. Gland, Switzerland and Cambridge, UK: IUCN, The World Conservation Union.

Chakrabarti, S.B. 'Agrarian Relations in the Tribal Milieu', in T.B. Subba and G.C. Ghosh (eds.), pp. 242-257. Op.cit.

Chakravarti, Tapati. 1991. 'The Riang Women of Rural Tripura: Their Participation in Economic Activities and Social Status', in R.K. Samanta (ed.) *Rural Development in North-East India: Perspectives, Issues and Experience.* New Delhi: Uppal Publishing House.

Chakravarty, Sukhamoy. 1992. 'Sustainability: The Concept and its Economic Application in the Context of India.', Keynote Address, in Anil Agarwal (ed.), *The Price of Forests,* Proceedings of a Seminar on the Sustainable Use of Forest Resources, pp. 7-10. New Delhi: Centre for Science and Environment.

Chakravarti, Uma. 1993. 'Conceptualising Brahminical Patriarchy in Early India: Gender, Class, Caste and State'. *Economic and Political Weekly.* 3 April

——1999. 'The World of the Bhaktin in South Indian Traditions—The Body and Beyond', in Kumkum Roy (ed.) *Women in Early Indian Societies,* pp. 289-321.

——2003. *Gendering Caste Through a Feminist Lens.* Calcutta: Stree.

Chakravarty, Radha, Anju Chawla and Geeta Mehta 1984. *The Status of Women Scientists in India.* New Delhi: National Institute of Science, Technology and Development Studies.

Chambers, Robert. 1995. 'Poverty and Livelihood: Whose Reality Counts', *Environment and Urbanization.* 7 (1): 173-204.

Chambers, Robert, A. Pacey, L. A. Thrupp eds. 1989. *Farmer First: Farmer Innovation and Agricultural Research.* London: International Technology Publications.

Champion, H.G. and S.K. Seth. 1968. *General Silviculture for India*. Delhi: Government of India, Manager of Publications.

Chatterjee, Piya. 2003. *A Time for Tea: Women, Labour and Post-Colonial Politics in an Indian Plantation*. New Delhi: Zubaan an imprint of Kali for Women.

Chauhan, Sumi Krishna. (see also Krishna, Sumi) 1979. *A Village in a Million: An Energy Portrait of Akbarpur-Barota, India*. London: Earthscan, International Institue for Environment and Development.

———1980. 'Dongri Women Dare', *The Hindustan Times*. New Delhi, Aug 1.

Chauan, Sumi Krishna and K. Gopalakrishnan 1983. *A Million Villages, A Million Decades: The World Water and Sanitation Decade from two South Indian villages*. London: Earthscan, International Institute for Environment and Development.

Chauhan, Sumi Krishna with Zhang Bihua, K. Gopalakrishnan, Lala Rukh Hussain, Ajoa Yeboah Afari and Francisco Leal. 1983. *Who puts the water in the taps? Community participation in Third World drinking water, sanitation and health*. London: Earthscan, International Institute for Environment and Development.

Chen, Martha Alter. 1991. *Coping with Seasonality and Drought*. New Delhi: Sage Publishers.

Chodorow, Nancy. 1978. *The Reproduction of Mothering*. University of California Press: Berkeley and Los Angeles.

Choudhury, Arundhuti Roy. 2001. *Common Property, Resource Management: Gender, Equity and Participation—A case study of the fish workers of Kerala*. New Delhi: Indian Social Institute.

———2004. 'Community Institutions and Gender: Fishworkers in Kasargode, Koshikode and Thiruvanthapuram Districts, Kerala', in Sumi Krishna (ed.) pp. 375-394. Op. cit.

Choudhury, Pratap. 1993. 'Status of Women in the Tribal Societies of Tripura,' in Malabika Das Gupta (ed.) *Status of Tribal Women in Tripura*, pp. 23-24. New Delhi: Vikas Publishing House Pvt. Ltd.

Chowdhury, J. N. 1976. 'Evidence of Some Caste-like Features in Some Arunachal Tribes', *Resarun 1975*. Itanagar: Department of Information and Public Relations, Government of Arunachal Pradesh.

———1990. *The Tribal Culture and History of Arunachal Pradesh*. New Delhi: Daya Publishers.

Cockburn, Cynthia. 1983. *Brothers: Male Dominance and Technical Change*. London: Pluto Press.

———1992. 'Technology, Production and Power', in Gill Kirkup and Laurie Smith Keller (eds.) *Inventing Women: Science Technology and Gender*, pp. 196-211. Cambridge: Polity Press. (extracted from Cockburn 1985. *Machinery of Dominance: women, men and technical know-how*. London: Polity Press pp. 15-43.)

———1999. 'The material of male power', in Donald MacKenzie and Judy Wajcman (eds.) *The Social Shaping of Technology*. Buckingham UK and Philadepphia, US: Open University Press. (Reprinted from *Feminist Review* 1981: 41-58.)

Collins, Patricia Hill. 1986. 'Learning from the Outsider Within: The Sociological Significance of Black feminist Thought,' *Social Problems*. 33 (6): 14-32.

——1990. *Black Feminist Thought.* Cambridge, UK: Cambridge University Press.

Correa, Mariette. 1999. 'The Need for Participatory Research Experiences', in Roger Jeffrey and Nandini Sundar (eds.) pp. 216-235. Op. cit.

Crawley, Heaven. 1999. 'Living Up to the Empowerment Claim? The potential of PRA,' in Irene Gujit and Meera Kaul Shah (eds.), *The Myth of Community: Gender Issues in Participatory Development,* pp. 24-34. New Delhi: Vistaar Publications.

Crowell, Daniel W. 2003. *The SEWA Movement and Rural Development: The Banaskantha and Kutch Experience.* New Delhi: Sage Publications.

CSE 1985. Agarwal A and Sunita Narain (eds) *The State of India's Environment, 1984-85: A Citizen's Report.* New Delhi: Centre for Science and Environment.

D'Andrade, Roy G. 1970. 'Sex Differences and Cultural Institutions', in Liam Hudson (ed.) *The Ecology of Human Intelligence.* pp. 15-49. London: Penguin Books.

D'Souza, Alphonsus. 2001 a. 'The Traditional Angami Naga Forest and Water Management: Implications for Climate Change and Sustainable Tribal Living', in Walter Fernandes and Nafisa Goga D'Souza (eds.) *Climate Change and Tribal Sustainable Living: Responses from the Northeast,* pp. 88-113 Guwahati: North Eastern Social Research Centre and Indian Network of Ethics and Climate Change.

——2001b. *Traditional Systems of Forest Conservation in North East India: The Angami Tribe of Nagaland.* Guwahati: North-East Social Research Centre.

Dalwai, A. 1997. 'Can women do participatory irrigation management (PIM)?' *INPIM Newsletter 5.* Washington D.C.: The World Bank.

Daly, Mary. 1973. *Beyond God the Father: Towards a Philosophy of Women's Liberation.* Boston: Beacon Press.

Deheja, Vidya. 1997. 'Issues of Spectatorship and Representation', in Vidya Deheja (ed.) *Representing the Body: Gender Issues in Indian Art,* pp. 1-21. New Delhi: Kali for Women.

Danda, Dipali G. n.d. presumed 1998. 'Gender Inequalities in Arunachal Pradesh: Some Observations', in Manis Kumar Raha and Aloke Kumar Ghose (eds.) *North-East India: The Human Interface,* pp. 265-78. New Delhi: Gyan Publishing House.

Darwin, Charles. 1871. *The Descent of Man and Selection in Relation to Sex.* (Republished 1936.) New York: Modern Library.

Dastkar website. http://www.dastkar.org/

Datar, Chhaya and Aseem Prakash. n.d. presumed 2000. *Women Demand Land and Water.* Mumbai: Tata Institute of Social Sciences (booklet)

——2004. 'Engendering Community Rights: Women's Access to Water and Wasteland in Gujarat, Maharashtra, Madhya Pradesh, Andhra Pradesh and Karnataka', in Sumi Krishna (ed.) pp. 137-170. Op.cit.

Das, Vidhya. 2000. 'The Agragamee Experience'. Presentation at a Panel Discussion on 'Rural Women and Grassroots Organisations: Expectations and Outcomes', 23 September. New Delhi: Centre for Women's Development Studies.

Davis, Elizabeth Gould. 1971. *The First Sex*. New York: Putnam.

Dawkins, Richard. 1976. *The Selfish Gene*, London: Oxford University Press.

————1997. *Climbing Mount Improbable*. London: Penguin Books.

DDS. 2005. Deccan Development Society: http://www.ddsindia.com/ (See Rao, Rukmini)

Derekar, Jayanand. H. 2001. *Baseline Data on Villages in Joida Taluk with a Concentration of Kunbi Population*. Mysore: CIDA-Shastri Partnership Project Publication.

Devadas, Rajamal. P. 1994. *Role of Rural Women in Biodiversity and Seed Technology.* Background Paper, 'Workshop on Women, Biodiversity and Seed Industries'. Chennai: M.S. Swaminathan Research Foundation.

Dietriche, Gabrielle. 2003. 'Dalit Movements and Women's Movements', in Rao (ed.), pp. 57-79. Op. cit. (from 1992. *Reflections on the Women's Movement: Religion, Ecology, Development*. New Delhi: Horizon India.)

Dobhansky, Theodosius. 1937. *Genetics and the Origin of Species.* New York: Columbia University Press.

————1944. 'On species and races of living and fossil man'. *American Journal of Physical Anthropology.* 2: 251-65.

Douma, Willy, Chulani Kodikara, Hanny Maas. 2004. 'Analysing the Rice Chain: Towards a sustainable (p)rice'. Report of a workshop. Polonnaruwa, Sri Lanka: Hivos. (India case study by Virendra Khatana, K. Ravi and V. Gandhimathi.): http://www.hivos.org/

Down to Earth. 2003: December.

Dube, Leela. 1986. 'Seed and Earth: The Symbolism of Biological Reproduction and Sexual Relations of Production', in Leela Dube, Eleanor Leacock, Shirley Ardener (eds.), *Visibility and Power: Essays on Women in Society and Development*, pp. 22-53. New Delhi: Oxford University Press.

Dubiansky, Alexander M. 1998. 'Mountain Forests in Tamil Culture', in Roger Jeffery (ed.) *The Social Construction of Indian Forests*, pp. 17-24. New Delhi: Manohar.

Dutta, P.C. and D.K. Baruah (eds.) 1997. *Aspects of Customary Laws of Arunachal Pradesh*. Itanagar: Directorate of Research, Government of Arunachal Pradesh. (Revised edition of 1990. *Customary Laws of Arunachal Pradesh: A Profile*.)

Dutta, Parul 1976. 'Women in Arunachal and their Status in the Socio-Cultural Life.' *Resarun 1975*. Itanagar: Department of Information and Public Relations, Government of Arunachal Pradesh.

Dwivedi, J. L. 1996. 'Conserving Genetic Resources and Using Diversity in Flood-Prone Ecosystems in Eastern India', in Louise Sperling and Michael Leevisohn (eds.) *Using Diversity: Enhancing and Maintaining Genetic Resources on Farm*. Proceedings of a Workshop held on 19-21 June 1995. New Delhi: IDRC.

Ecologist, The (Asia). 2003. 'Large dams in Northeast India" rivers, forests, people and power'. 11(1).

Eckholm, Erik. P. 1976. *Losing Ground: Environmental Stress and World Food Prospects.* New York: W.W. Norton.

Elwin, Verrier. 1958 (reprinted 1993). *Myths of the North-East Frontier of India.* Itanagar: Department of Information and Public Relations, Government of Arunachal Pradesh.

———1970 (reprinted 1991) *A New Book of Tribal Fiction.* Itanagar: Government of Arunachal Pradesh.

Enarson, Elaine. 2001. 'Promoting Social Justice in Disaster Reconstruction: Guidelines for Gender Sensitive and Community Based Planning', Draft Report, Ahmedabad: Disaster Mitigation Institute.

Engels, F. 1884. *The Origin of the Family, Private Property and the State: In the Light of the Researches of Lewis H. Morgan.* Moscow: Progress Publishers. 1972

Faith, Karleen. 1995. 'Resistance: Lessons from Foucault and Feminism', in H Lorraine Radtke and Hendrikus J Stam (eds) *Power/Gender: Social Relations in Theory and Practice,* New Delhi: Sage Publications.

Fals-Borda, Orlando and Muhammad Anisur Rahman. 1991. *Action and Knowledge: Breaking the Monopoly with Participatory Action-Research.* London: Intermediate Technology Publications. New York: Apex Press.

Fausto-Sterling, Anne. 1985. *Myths of Gender: Biological Theories about Women and Men.* (Revised ed. 1992) New York: Basic Books.

———2000. *Sexing the Body: Gender Politics and the Construction of Sexuality.* New York: Basic Books.

Fedigan, Linda Marie. 1986. 'The Changing Role of Women in Models of Human Evolution'. *Annual Review of Anthropology.* 15: 25-66. (also reprinted in Gill Kirkup and Laurie Smith Keller eds. *Inventing Women: Science, Technology and Gender.* Cambridge, UK: Polity Press.)

Ferguson, Anne. 1994. 'Gendered Science: A Critique of Agricultural Development. *American Anthropologist.* 96: 540-52.

Fernandes, Walter. 2002. 'The Indigenous Issue and Women's Status in North East India.' Paper submitted to Indigenous Rights in the Commonwealth project. South and South East Asia Regional Expert Meeting, Indian Confederaton of Indigenous and Tribal Peoples. New Delhi: 11-13 March. http://www.cpsu.org.uk/download/Walter_F.pdf

Fernandes, Walter and Sanjay Barbora 2002. *Modernisation and Women's Status in North-Eastern India.* Guwahati: North Eastern Social Research Centre.

Fernandes, Walter and Geetha Menon. 1987. *Tribal Women and Forest Economy: Deforestation, Exploitation and Social Change.* New Delhi: Indian Social Institute.

Field, Les W. 1999. 'Complicities and Collaborations', Current Anthropology, 40 (2): 193-209.

Field, Joanna: 2nd ed. 1981, *A Life of One's Own,* London, Chatto and Windus 1936, reprinted New York.

Foucault, Michel 1984. *The Foucault Reader* Paul Rabinow (ed.). New York: Pantheon Books.

Freire, Paulo. 1970. *The Pedagogy of the Oppressed.* New York: Herder and Herder.

Furer-Haimendorf, C. Von. 1982. *The Tribes of India: The Struggle for Survival.* New Delhi: Oxford University Press.

———1983. *Himalayan Adventure: Early Travels in North-East India*, New Delhi: Sterling. (Reprint of *Himalayan Barbary.)*

Gadgil, Madhav. 1993. 'In love with life'. *Seminar* (Issue on 'Our Scientists') 409: 25-30.

Gadgil, Madhav and Ramachandra Guha. 1992. *This Fissured Land: An Ecological History of India.* New Delhi: Oxford University Press.

Gadgil, Madhav and M.D. Subash Chandaran. 1992. 'Sacred Groves', in Geeti Sen (ed.) *Indigenous Vision,* pp. 183-187. *Peoples of India: Attitudes to the Environment.* New Delhi: Sage Publications and India International Centre.

Ganesh, Kamala. 1999. 'Patrilineal Structure and Agency of Women: Issues in Gendered Socialization', in T.S. Saraaswati (ed.) *Culture, Socialization and Human Development: Theory, Research and Applications in India,* pp. 235-253. New Delhi: Sage Publications.

Ganguly, J.B. 1993a. 'The Status of Tribal Women in the Post Jhuming Stage of Tribal Economy in Tripura', in Malabika Das Gupta (ed.) *Status of Tribal Women in Tripura,* pp. 72-79. New Delhi: Vikas Publishing House.

———1993b. 'Development of Peasant Farming in the North-East Tribal Region: A Study in Tribal Communities', in Mrinal Miri (ed.) *Continuity and Change in Tribal Society,* pp. 298-313. Shimla: Indian Institute of Advanced Study.

Gangwar, A.K. and P.S. Ramakrishnan. 1990. 'Ethnobiographical Notes on Some Tribes of North-Eastern India.' *Economic Botany* 44: 94-95.

———1992. 'Agriculture and Animal Husbandry among the Sulungs and Nishis of Arunachal Pradesh. In Walter Fernandez (ed.) *National Development and Tribal Deprivation,* pp. 100-128. New Delhi: Indian Social Institute.

Geetha, V. 2002. *Gender.* (Theorising Feminism series) Calcutta: Stree.

Geetha, V. and S.V. Rajadurai. 1998. *Towards a Non-Brahmin Millennium. From Iyothee Thass to Periyar.* Calcutta: Samya.

Gell, Alfred 1998. *Art and Agency: An Anthropological Theory.* New York: Oxford University Press.

Gill, Rosalind and Keith Grint. 1995. 'Introduction'. In Keith Grint and Rosalind Gill (eds.) *The Gender Technology Relation: Contemporary Theory and Research.* Taylor and Francis.

Glazmann J.C., P. Benyayer and M. Arnaud. 'Genetic divergences among rices from Northeast India'. http://www.gramene.org/newsletters/rice_genetics/rgn6/v6p63.html

Gold, Ann Grodzins. 2000. 'From demon aunt to gorgeous bride: women portray female power in a North Indian Festival Cycle,' in Julia Leslie and Mary McGee Eds. *Invented Identities: The Interplay of Gender, Religion and Politics in India.* pp. 203-230. New Delhi: Oxford University Press.

———2003. 'Outspoken Women: Representations of Female Voices in a Rajasthani Folklore Community', in G.G. Raheja (ed.) pp. 103-133. Op. cit.

Goswami, M.C. 1983. 'Peasants and Neo-peasants in Northeast India and their New Dimension.' In Joan P. Mencher (ed.) *Social Anthropology of Peasantry,* pp. 266-275. Mumbai: Somaiya Publications.

Gould, Stephen J. 1980. *The Panda's Thumb: More Reflections in Natural History.* London: Penguin Books.

——1983. *The Mismeasure of Man.* Penguin Books. (New York 1996: W.W. Norton.)

Government of Arunachal Pradesh. 1994. 'The Arunachal Pradesh Protection of Customary Laws and Social Practices Act. 1994.'

Government of India. 1993. 'National Nutrition Policy'. New Delhi: Department of Women and Child Development, Ministry of Human Resource Development, Government of India.

——The 'Panchayats (Extension to Scheduled Areas) Act, 1996'.

——1997. *The Indian Forest Service Civil List* (as on 1st January 1996). New Delhi: Ministry of Environment and Forests.

——'Approach to the Mid-Term Appraisal of the Tenth Plan (2002-07). Planning Commission. http://planningcommission.nic.in/plans/planrel/fiveyr/welcome.html

——2002. 'National Water Policy'. New Delhi: Ministry of Water Resources.

Government of Tamil Nadu. 2005. 'Policy Note 2005-06', Environment and Forest Department. http://www.tn.gov.in/policynotes/environment_forest.htm

Gramsci, Antonio. 1971. *Prison Notebooks.* New York: International Publishers.

Griffin, Susan. 1978. *Woman and Nature: The Roaring Inside Her.* New York: Harper and Row.

Guha, Ramachandra. 1989. *The Unquiet Wood: Ecological Change and Peasant Resistance in the Himalaya.* New Delhi: Oxford University Press.

Haldipur, Krishna 1985. *Around the Hills and Dales of Arunachal Pradesh.* Shillong: North-Eastern Hill University.

Haraway, Donna. 1992. *Primate Visions: Gender, Race and Nature in the World of Modern Science.* London and New York: Verso.

Harding, Sandra. 1986. *The Science Question in Feminism.* Ithaca, NY: Cornell University Press.

——1987. 'Introduction: Is There a Feminist Method?' in Sandra Harding (ed.) *Feminism & Methodology,* pp. 1-14. Bloomington: Indiana University Press.

——1991. *Whose Science, Whose Knowledge? Thinking from Women's Lives.* Ithaca, NY: Cornell University Press.

——2000. 'Democratising Philosophy of Science for Local Knowledge Movements: Issues and Challenges'. *Gender, Technology and Development* 4 (1): 1-23.

——2001. 'Just add women and stir?' in Gender Working Group, U.N. Commission on Science and Technology for Development (ed.) *Missing Links: Gender Equity in Science and Technology for Development,* pp. 295-307. Ottawa: IDRC, London: IT Publications and New York: UNIFEM.

Haq., Mahbubul. 1997. *Human Development in South Asia.* Karachi: Oxford University Press.

Heptullah, Najma 1995. Address in 'Proceedings of National Convention on Forestry, Sustainable Development and the Role of Women Forest Officers.' New Delhi: Government of India, Ministry of Environment and Forests.

Hirsh, Elizabeth and Gary A Olson. 1995. 'Starting from Marginalized Lives: A

Conversation with Sandra Harding' *A Journal of Composition Theory* 15.2 http://jac.gsu.edu/jac/15.2/Articles/1.htm

Hoon, Vineeta. 1998. 'Lakshadweep Islands,' in M.S. Swaminthan (ed.) pp. 80-95. Op. cit.

Hore, D.K. 1999. cited. in B.D. Sharma 2002. Op. cit.

Horsfall, Debbie, Hillary Bryne-Armstrong and Joy Higgs. 2001. 'Researching Critical Moments', in Hilary Bryne-Armstrong, Joy Higgs and Debbie Horsfall (eds), *Critical Moments in Qualitative Research*, pp. 3-13, Oxford: UK Butterworth-Heinemann.

Huxley, Julian. 1923. *Essays of a Biologist*. London: Chatto and Windus.

———1931. *What Dare I Think? The Challenge of Modern Science to Human Action and Belief.* London: Chatto and Windus.

ICSSR 1974. *Towards Equality.* Report of the Committee on the Status of Women in India. New Delhi: Indian Council for Social Science Research.

Illich, Ivan 1997. *Disabling Professions.* London; Salem, US: Marion Boyars.

Indira, M. 2005. 'Do Property Rights in Land Ensure Greater Participation of Women in Resource Management? A Study in Rural Karnataka.' Paper presented at the Indian Association for Women's Studies Conference (sub-theme: Citizenship, Livelihoods, Work and Natural Resource Rights) Dona Paula, Goa: 3-6 May.

Indira. R. 2002. *Gender and Forest Management: The Joida Experiences.* Mysore: CIDA-Shastri Partnership Project. (booklet)

Ingold, T. 1993. 'The Temporality of the Landscape', *World Archaeology,* 25 (2): 152-74.

Inhorn, Marcia C. and K. Lisa Whittle 2001. 'Feminism meets the "new" epidemiologies: toward an appraisal of anti-feminist biases in epidemiological research on women's health.' *Social Science & Medicine.* 53: 553-567.

IWSA. 1978. *Down the Memory Lane: Trials and Tribulations of India's Women in Science.* New Delhi: Indian Women Scientists' Association, Bombay.

Jackson, Cecile. 1993. 'Doing What Comes Naturally?' Women and Environment in Development', *World Development.* 21(12): 1947-1963.

———1998. 'Rescuing Gender from the Poverty Trap', in *Feminist Visions of Development: Gender Analysis and Policy.* London and New York: Routledge.

Jagger, Alison. 1992. 'Human Biology in Feminist Theory: Sexual Equality Reconsidered', Article 2.2, in Helen Crowley and Susan Himmelneit (eds.) *Knowing Women: Feminism and Knowledge.* UK: Polity Press.

Jain, Devaki with Nalini Singh and Malini Chand. 1980. *Women's Quest for Power: Five Indian Case Studies.* Ghaziabad, India: Vikas Publishing House Pvt. Ltd.

Jairath, Jasveen 2000. 'By-passing the Women: The Case of Participatory Irrigation Management Reforms in Andhra Pradesh,' Paper presented at the Indian Association for Women's Studies Conference, Hyderabad: 8-11 January.

Jeffrey, Roger. 1998. 'Introduction' in Roger Jeffery (ed.) *The Social Construction of Indian Forests*, pp. 1-16. New Delhi: Manohar.

Jeffrey, Roger and Nalini Sundar 199. (eds.) *A New Moral Economy for India's Forests? Discourses of Community and Participation*, New Delhi: Sage Publications.

Jewitt, Sarah. 2000. 'Unequal Knowledges in Jharkhand, India: De-Romanticizing Women's Agroecological Expertise.' *Development and Change*. 31: 961-985.

Jodha, N.S. 1986. 'Common Property Resources and Rural Poor in Dry Regions of India'. *Economic and Political Weekly*, 23 (special number): 45-7.

——1990. 'Rural Common Property Resources: Contribution and Crises.' Foundation Day Lecture. New Delhi: Society for Wasteland Development.

Joekes, Susan, Mellissa Leach and Cathy Green (eds.) 1995. 'Gender Relations and Environmental Change' *IDS Bulletin*. 26(1).

Kabeer, Naila 1994. *Reversed Realities: Gender Hierarchies in Development Thought*. New Delhi: Kali for Women.

Kanvinde, Hemal. 1998. 'Bhitarkanika, Orissa,' Case Study in M.S. Swaminathan (ed.), pp. 139-147. Op. cit.

Kaplan, Gisela T. and Lesley J. Rodgers. 1990. 'The Definition of Male and Female: Biological reductionism and the sanctions of normality', in Suneja Gunew (ed.) *Feminist Knowledge, Critique and Construction*. Routledge.

Kapur, Ratna. 1993. 'The Gender of Progressive Social Movements', *The Hindu:* 13 June.

Karlekar, Malavika. 2000. 'Women's Health—A View from the Household.', in CWDS (eds.) *Shifting Sands: Women's Lives and Globalization*, pp. 87-139. Calcutta: Stree.

Kelhou. 1998. 'Women in Angami Society,' in Lucy Zehol (ed.), *Women in Naga Society*, pp. 55-61. New Delhi: Regency Publishers.

Kelkar, Govind. 1981. 'The impact of Green Revolution on Women's Work Participation and Sex Roles', Paper prepared for the I.L.O. Tripartite Asian Regional Seminar on 'Rural Development Women', Mahabaleswar. Maharashtra.

Kelkar, Govind and Dev Nathan. 1991. *Gender and Tribe: Women, Land and Forests in Jharkhand*. New Delhi: Kali for Women.

Kelkar, Govind, Dev Nathan and Rownak Jahan. 2003. 'We were in Fire, Now we are in Water: Micro-Credit and Gender Relations in Rural Bangladesh.' New Delhi: Institute for Human Development. (booklet)

Keller, Evelyn Fox. 1983. *A Feeling for the Organism: The Life and Work of Barbara McClintock*. San Francisco: W. H. Freeman.

——1995. *Reflections on Gender and Science*. 10th Anniversary Edition. New Haven and London: Yale University Press.

——2004. 'What impact, if any, has feminism had on science?' Public Lecture, Bangalore: National Centre for Biological Sciences and Indian Academy of Sciences, 19 Feb. (based on a talk given in Valencia, June 2003, and previously published writings.)

Keller, Evelyn Fox and Helen E. Longino. (eds.) 1996. *Feminism and Science*. Oxford and New York: Oxford University Press.

King, Ynestra. 1983. 'Toward an Ecological Feminism and a Feminist Ecology', in J. Rothschild ed. *Machina ex Dea: Feminist Perspectives on Technology*. pp. 118-28. New York: Pergamon Press.

Kishor, Sunita and Kamal Gupta, 2004, 'Women's Empowerment in India and its States,' *Economic and Political Weekly*, Vol. XXXIX, No. 7.

Kitcher, Philip 1985. *Vaulting Ambition: Sociobiology and the Quest for Human Nature.* Cambridge, M.A.: MIT Press.

Klein, Viola. 1945. *The Feminine Character: History of an ideology.* (Republished 1971. University of Illinois Press.)

Kochar, Rajesh. 1999. 'The Truth Behind the Legend: European doctors in precolonial India' *Journal of Biosciences.* 24 (3): 259-268.

Kochar, S. and K.P.S. Chandel. 1996. cited in B.D. Sharma. 2002. op. cit.

Kosambi, D.D. 1965. *The Culture and Civilization of Indian Historical Outline.* London: Routledge and Kegan Paul.

Krishna, Sumi (see also Sridharan, Sumi; Chauhan, Sumi Krishna) 1991. *India's Living Languages: The Critical Issues.* New Delhi: Allied Publishers.

——1994. 'The Impact of Structural Adjustment Policy on Gender and Environment in India', Paper presented at a workshop on 'The Gender Impact of Structural Adjustment: Perspectives from India and Canada'. New Delhi: Centre for Women's Development Studies. (See Krishna 2000)

——1995a. 'It's Time to Clear the Cobwebs: The Gender Impact of Environmentalism', *The Administrator*, (Mussoorie: Lal Bahadur Shastri Academy of Administration), August: 93-104.

——1995b. 'Towards a new reproductive ecology', *Bookreview*

——1996a. *Environmental Politics: People's Lives and Development Choices*, New Delhi: Sage Publications.

——1996b. 'The Appropriation of Dissent: The State *vis a vis* People's Movements,' in T.V. Sathymurthi (ed.) *Class Formation and Political Transformation in Post-Colonial India*, (Vol. 4 of series on *Social Change and Political Discourse in India: Structures of Power, Movements of Resistance*), pp. 238-257. New Delhi: Oxford University Press.

——1996c. *Restoring Childhood: Learning Labour and Gender in South Asia.* New Delhi: Konark.

——1997. 'Integrating a Gender Perspective into Environmental Projects', Paper presented at a Panel Discussion, 'Gender and Development: The Research-Action Interface', Uttara Devi Resource Centre for Gender and Development, M. S. Swaminathan Research Foundation, Chennai. 22 September.

——1998a. 'Gender and Biodiversity Management', in M. S. Swaminathan (ed.). *Gender Dimensions in Biodiversity Management*, pp. 23-61. New Delhi: Konark.

——1998b. 'Arunachal Pradesh,' Case Study in M.S. Swaminathan (ed.) pp. 148-181. Op. cit.

——1998c. 'Mizoram,' Case Study in M.S. Swaminathan (ed.) pp. 182-210. Op. cit.

—— 1998d. 'A Patchwork Quilt', in Shanta Serbjeet Singh and Jyoti Sabherwal (eds.) *The Fiftieth Milestone: A Feminine Critique.* pp. 253-261. New Delhi: Sterling.

——1999. 'Involving Women, Ignoring Gender', Paper presented at 'Gender Dimensions in Biodiversity Management and Food Security,' FAO Technical Consultation. Chennai: M.S. Swaminathan Research Foundation. 2-5 November.

——2000. 'The Impact of the Structural Adjustment Programme on Gender and Environment in India,.' in CWDS (eds.) *Shifting Sands: Women's Lives and Globalization.* pp. 173-234. Calcutta: Stree.

——2002. 'Introduction: Towards a "Genderscape" of Community Rights in Natural Resource Management', *Indian Journal of Gender Studies.* (Special Issue: Gender and Community Rights in Natural Resource Management. ed. Sumi Krishna). 8(2): 151-176.

——2004a. 'A "Genderscape" of Community Rights in Natural Resource Management: Overview.' In Sumi Krishna (ed.) *Livelihood and Gender: Equity in Community Resource Management.* New Delhi: Sage.

——2004b. 'Gender, Tribe and Political Participation: Control of Natural Resources in North-eastern India,' in Sumi Krishna (ed.) pp. 375-394. Op. cit.

——2004c. 'Knowledge Systems, Equity and Rights: A Dialogue with Vina Mazumdar,' in Sumi Krishna (ed.) pp. 425-431. Op. cit.

——2004d. (ed.) *Livelihood and Gender: Equity in Community Resource Management,* New Delhi: Sage Publications.

——2005a. 'About the Study' in M.K. Ratheesh Narayanan et. al. Op. cit.

——2004b. 'Gendered Price of Rice', *Economic and Political Weekly.* (Special issue on 'Gender and Food Security') Vol. XL. No. 25: 2555-2562.

——2007 (ed.) *Women's Livelihood Rights: Recasting Citizenship for Development.* New Delhi: Sage.

Krishnaraj, Maitreyi 1991. *Women and Science.* Bombay: Himalaya Publishing House.

Kyndiah, P.R. 2004. Interview (p. 63) in 'Hymns of Resurgence', *Outlook*: 25. October: pp. 61-65.

Lahiri, Tarun Bikas 2004. 'Rural Development in North East: An Overview', in B. Datta Ray and G. Das (eds.) *Dimensions of Rural Development in North-East India*, pp. 13-27. New Delhi: Akansha Publications.

Lalnithanga, P. 1997. *Mizoram,* New Delhi: Publications Division, Ministry of Information and Broadcasting, Government of India.

Lama, Anupama and Marlene Buchy. 2004. 'Gender, Class, Caste and participation: Community Forestry in Central Nepal,' in Sumi Krishna (ed.), pp. 285-305. Op. cit.

Landau, Misia. 1984. 'Human evolution as narrative'. *American Scientist.* 72: 262-268.

Leach, Mellisa. 1994. *Rainforest relations: gender and resource use among the Mende of Gola, Sierra Leone.* Edinburgh: University Press.

Leacock, Eleanor. 1977. 'Women in Egalitarian Society', in R. Bridenthal and C. Koontz (eds.) *Becoming Visible: Women in European History,* pp. 11-35. Boston: Houghton Mifflin.

——1981. 'Women's Status in Egalitarian Societies: Implications for Social Evolution,' in *Myths of Male Dominance.* New York.

Lee, Richard and Irven DeVore (eds.) 1968. *Man the Hunter.* Chicago: Aldine.

Lefebvre, Henri. 1991. (English translation by Donald Nicholson-Smith of Lefebvre 1974). *The Production of Space.* Oxford: Blackwell.

Lerner, Gerder. 1979. *The Creation of Patriarchy.* New York: Oxford University Press.

Levi-Staruass, Claude. 1956 (1971). 'The Family'. In Harry L. Shapiro ed. *Man, Culture and Society.* New York: Oxford University Press.

Lewontin, R.C. 1978. 'Adaptation'. *Scientific American.* 239: 212-30.

——1979. 'Sociobiology as an adaptationist program.' *Behavioural Science.* 24: 5-14.

Liebowitz, Linda. 1983. 'Origins of the sexual division of labour', in R. Hubbard and M. Lowe eds. *Women's Nature: Rationalization of Inequality,* pp. 123-47. New York: Pergamonn Press.

Linton, Sally. 1971. 'Woman the gatherer: Male bias in anthropology,' in Sue-Ellen Jacobs ed. *Women in Perspective: A guide for Cross-Cultural Studies.* Urbana: University of Illinois Press. 9-21 (republished as Sally Slocum 1975. In Rayana R. Rewiter ed. *Toward an Anthropology of Women.* New York: Monthly Review Press. 9-21.)

Locke, Catherine. 1999. 'Women's Representation and Roles in "Gender" Policy in Joint Forest Management', in Roger Jeffrey and Nalini Sundar (eds.), pp. 235-53. Op. cit.

Lorde, Audre. 1984. *Sister Outsider.* Freedom, California US: Crossing Press.

Lovejoy, Owen. 1981. 'The Origin of Man' *Science* 211 (4480): 341-50.

Lowenthal, David. 1991. 'Heritage and the English landscape', *History Today,* 41: 7-10.

Mair, Lucy 1965 (2nd edition 1972) *An Introduction to Social Anthropology.* New Delhi: Oxford University Press.

Majumdar, D.N. 1992. 'Household in the Matrilineal Societies of North East India', in K. Sardamoni (ed.) *Finding the Household: Conceptual and Methodological Issues,* pp. 117-131 New Delhi: Sage Publications.

Mann, K. 'Bride-Price in Tribal North-East India.' in J.P. Singh. N.N. Vyas and R.S. Mann (eds.) *Tribal Women and Development,* pp. 170-78. Jaipur: Rawat Publications.

Mannheim, Bruce and Krista Van Vleet 1998: 'The Dialogics of Southern Quechua Narrative' *American Anthropologist* 100(2): 326-346.

Marathe, Kanta. 2004. 'People's Land Reform Initiatives: A Note on the Bundelkhand-Baghelkhand Area, Madhya Pradesh.', in Sumi Krishna (ed.) pp. 275-281. Op.cit.

March, Candida, Ines Smith and Maitrayee Mukhopadhyay. 1999. *A Guide to Gender Analysis Frameworks.* Oxford: OxfamGB.

Martin, Emily. 1996. 'The Egg and the Sperm: How Science has constructed a Romance based on Stereotypical Male-Female Roles,' in Evelyn Fox Keler and Helen Longino (eds). pp. 103-117. Op. cit.

Marx, Karl and Frederick Engels. *The German Ideology,* in *Collected Works,* Vol. 5., Moscow. (Reprinted 1976.) Progress Publishers.

Mazumdar, Vina 1975. 'Women in Agriculture'. *Indian Farming,* Special issue on Women in Agriculture: 25 (8): 5-10.

——1998. 'Women: From Equality to Empowerment', in Hiranmay Karlekar ed. *Independent India: The First Fifty Years,* pp. 254-279. New Delhi: Oxford University Press.

Mazumdar, Vina and Kumud Sharma. 1990. 'Sexual Division of Labour and the Subordination of Women: A Reappraisal from India' in Irene Tinker (ed.) *Persistent Inequalities: Women and World Development*, New York: Oxford University Press.

McLuhan, Marshall 1964. *Understanding Media: The Extensions of Man*. London: Routledge and Kegan Paul.

Mcluhan, Marshall and Quentin Fiore 1967. *The Medium is the Massage*. Hammondsworth UK: Penguin Books.

Mead, Margaret. 1935. (1980) *Sex and Temperament in three primitive societies*. London: Routledge and Kegan Paul.

——1949. *Male and Female: A Study of the Sexes in a Changing World*. New York: W. Morrow (new edition 1975).

Mehrotra, Nikita. 1992. 'Angami Naga Women: Reflections on their Status' cited in D'Souza 2001a. Op.cit.

Meillasoux, Claude 1981. *Maidens, Meals and Money: Capitalism and Domestic Community*. Cambridge: Cambridge University Press.

Meinzen-Dick, Ruth and Margaret Zwarteveen. 1998. 'Gendered Participation in Water Management: Issues and Illustrations from Water User Association in South Asia. in Douglas Merrey and Shirish Baviskar eds. *Gender Analysis and Reform of Irrigation Management: Concepts, Cases and Gaps in Knowledge*. Proceedings of the Workshop on Gender and Water, Habarana Sri Lanka, 15-19 Sept. pp. 173-192. Colombo: International Water Management Institute.

Mellor, Mary. 1992. *Breaking the Boundaries: Towards a Feminist Green Socialism*. London: Virago.

——1997. *Feminism and Ecology*. Cambridge UK: Polity Press.

Mencher, Joan P. 1993. 'Women, Agriculture and the Sexual Division of Labour: A Three State Comparison', in Saraswati Raju and Deipika Bagchi (eds.) *Women and Work in South Asia. Regional Patterns and Perspectives. pp 99-117*. London and New York: Routledge.

Mendhapurkar, Subhash. 2004. 'From Subjects of Change to Agents of Change: A Travelogue in Himachal Pradesh', in Sumi Krishna (ed.) pp. 397-411. Op. cit.

Merchant, Carolyn. 1983. *The Death of Nature: Women, Ecology and the Scientific Revolution*.. San Francisco: Harper and Row.

——1990. *Reinventing Eden: The Fate of Nature in Western Culture*. New York and London: Routledge.

Mies, Maria 1998. 'Social Origins of the Sexual Division of Labour', in Maria Mies, Veronika Benholdt-Thomsen and Claudia Von Werholf *Women the Last Colony*. London: Zed Books.

Mies, Maria and Vandana Shiva. 1993. *Ecofeminism*. New Delhi: Kali for Women.

Mishra, Kiran. 1991. *Women in a Tribal Community*. New Delhi: Vikas Publishing House Pvt. Ltd.

——1992. 'Nishing Longhouse as a household,' in K. Sardamoni (ed.) *Finding the Household: Conceptual and Methodological Issues*. New Delhi: Sage Publications.

Mishra, Prafulla K., Shaheen Nilofer and Sumananjali Mohanty. 'Gender and

Disasters: Coping with Drought and Floods in Orissa.', in Sumi Krishna (ed.), pp. 226-247. Op. cit.

Mitchell, Juliet 1974. *Psychoanlaysis and Feminism.*

——1966. 'Women: The Longest Revolution' in *New Left Review*, No. 40. pp. 11-37.

—— 1971. *The Women's Estate*, London: Allen Lane.

Mitter, Swasti. 1997. *Women Encounter Technology.* UK: Routledge.

MoEF. 1988. *National Forest Policy.* New Delhi: Ministry of Environment and Forests, Government of India.

Molyneaux, Maxine. 1985. 'Mobilisation without emancipation? Women's Interests, State and Revolution in Nicaragua', *Feminist Studies* 11(2) : 227-54.

Montagu, Ashley. 1953. (Fifth edition 1999.) *The Natural Superiority of Women.* (Foreword by Susan Sperling). Walnut Creek, California: Altamaria Press.

Moore, Henrietta L. 1988. *Feminism and Anthropology.* Cambridge: Polity Press.

Morgan, Elaine. 1972. *The Descent of Woman.* New York: Stein and Day.

Moser, Caroline. 1993. *Gender Planning and Development: Theory, Practice and Training.* London and New York: Routledge.

Mosse, David. 1995. 'Local Institutions and Power: The History and Practice of Community Management of Tank Irrigation Systems in South India', in Nici Nelson and Susan Wright (ed.) *Power and Participatory Development: Theory and Practice.* London: Intermediate Technology Development Group.

MSSRF. 2005. website: http://www.mssrf.org/ and *Annual Reports* 1991-92; 1995-96; 1996-97; 1997-98. Chennai: M.S. Swaminathan Research Foundation.

——2004. *Atlas of the Sustainability of Food Security.* Chennai: M.S. Swaminathan Research Foundation.

Mukhopadhaya, Carol. C. and Susan Seymour (eds) 1994. *Women, Education and family Structure in India* San Francisco: Westview Press.

Mulligan, Martin. 2001. 'Sparks Fly When Life, Work and Research Collide' in Hilary Bryne-Armstrong, Joy Higgs and Debbie Horsfall (eds.) *Critical Moments in Qualitative Research*, pp. 136-143. Oxford, UK: Butterworth-Heinemann.

Murthy, Ranjani K. with Vasanth, Bimla, Renuka, Krishan, Gandhimathi 2005. Report on Gender and Tsunami Relief and Rehabilitation: Issues and Recommendations. Womankind Worldwide: March.

Nadkarni, M.V. with Syed Ajmal Pasha and L.S. Prabhakar. 1989. *The Political Economy of Forest Use and Management.* New Delhi: Sage Publications.

Nair, Kusum. 1961. *Blossoms in the Dust: The Human Element in Indian Development*, (Indian ed 1971), New Delhi: Allied Publishers.

Narayanan, M.K. Ratheesh, M.P. Swapna and N. Anil Kumar. 2005. *Gender Dimensions of Wild Food Management in Wyanad, Kerala.* Kalpetta, Wyanad: M.S. Swaminathan Research Foundation—Community Agrobiodiversity Centre.

Nathan, Dev. 1997. 'Gender Transformations in Tribes', in Dev Nathan (ed.) *From Tribe to Caste*, pp. 247-286. Shimla: Indian Institute for Advanced Studies.

Nath, Alokananda and D. N. Majumdar. 1988. 'Tribal Women of North-East India in the Perspective of Change and Continuity.', in J.P. Singh. N.N. Vyas and R.S. Mann (eds.) *Tribal Women and Development.*, pp. 149-167. Jaipur: Rawat Publications.

Nath, Jahanabi Gogoi 2004. 'Rice Trade in Assam in the 17th and 18th Century'. *Proceedings of North East India History Association.* (22nd Session). Shillong: NEHU and NEIHA.

Nayar, M.P. 1996. *Hot Spots of Endemic Plants of India, Nepal and Bhutan.* Thiruvanthapuram: Tropical Botanic Garden and Research Institute.

Nelkin, Dorothy. 1996. 'The Politics of Predisposition. The Social Meaning of Predictive Biology,' in Agnes Heller and Sonja Puntscher (eds.) *Biopolitics: The Politics of Body, Race and Nature.* Avebury Aldershot.

Nelson, Nici. 1979. *Why has Development Neglected Rural Women: A Review of South Asian Literature.* Oxford: Pergamon Press.

Nieuwenhuys, Olga, 1999. *Childern's Life Worlds: Gender, Welfare and Labour in the Developing World* Indian Edition, New Delhi: Social Science Press.

Nongbri, Tiplut. 1994. 'Gender Relations in Matrilineal Societies', *Lokayan Bulletin,* 10 (5/6): 79-90.

——1998. 'Gender Issues and Tribal Development', in Bhupinder Singh (ed.) *Antiquity to Modernity in Tribal India.* (Vol. II Tribal Self Management in North Eastern India) pp. 221-43. New Delhi: Inter-India Publications.

——2003. *Development, Ethnicity and Gender.* Jaipur: Rawat Publications.

North East India Regional Databank. 2004. NER Databank. Arunachal Pradesh, Assam, Manipur, Mizoram, Meghalaya, Nagaland, Tripura, Sikkim. http://databank.nedfi.com/content.php?menu

Omvedt, Gail. 1990. *Violence Against Women: New Movements and New Theories in India.* New Delhi: Kali for Women. (booklet)

——1992. 'Green Earth, Women's Place, Human Liberation', *Development Dialogue* (Issue on 'Women, Ecology and Health: Rebuilding Connections'.)

——2000. 'Towards a Theory of Brahaminic Patriarchy' Review. *Economic and Political Weekly.* 22. Jan.

OSMDA 2002. *Voicing Silence: Experience of Women with Disasters in Orissa,* compiled by Aurobindo Behera, Prafulla Mishra and Sneha Mishra. Bhubaneswar: Orissa State Disaster Mitigation Authority (booklet).

Panchani, Chander Shekher. 1987. *Manipur: Religion, Culture and Society.* New Delhi: Konark.

Parker, A Rani. 1993. *Another Point of View: A Manual for Gender Analysis Training for Grassroots Workers.* UNIFEM. Reprinted 1998. New York: Women Ink.

Pathak, P.K. 2001. 'Major Cereal Crops of Assam,' in A.C. Thakur et. Al. (eds.) Op. cit. pp. 53-74.

Patkar, Medha. 2004. 'Commitment to ideology is in my DNA' as told to Sudeshna Chatterji. *Sunday Times of India.* 15. Feb.

Patnaik, Utsa. 1987. *Peasant Class Differentiation: A Study in Method with Reference to Haryana.* New Delhi: Oxford University Press.

Pauly, Philip J. 1990. *Controlling Life: Jaques Loeb and the Engineering Ideal in Biology.* Berkley and Los Angeles: University of California Press.

Poonacha, Veena and Meena Gopal. 2004. 'Women's Science: An Examination of Women's Access to and Retention in Scientific Careers', Mumbai: Research Centre for Women's Studies, SNDT University.

Potts. Richard. 1984. 'Home bases and early hominids.' *American Scientist.* 72: 338-47.

Plumwood, Val. 1986. 'Ecofeminism: An Overview and Discussion of Positions', *Australian Journal of Philosophy,* Vol. 64, pp. 120-138.

——1993. *Feminism and the Mastery of Nature.* London and New York: Routledge.

——1994. 'The Ecopolitics Debate and the Politics of Nature." in Karen J. Warren (ed.) pp. 64-87. Op. cit.

Raheja, Gloria Goodwin (ed.) 2003. *Songs, Stories, Lives: Gendered Dialogues and Cultural Critique.* New Delhi: Kali for Women.

Raju, Saraswati. 2005. 'Limited Options—Rethinking Women's Empowerment "Projects" in Development Discourses: A Case from Rural India', in *Gender, Technology and Development* 9 (2) 253-271.

Ramakrishnan, P.S. 1993. *Shifting Agriculture and Sustainable Development.: An Inter-disciplinary Study from North-Eastern India.* New Delhi and UNESCO, Paris: Oxford University Press.

Ramaswamy, Vijaya 1997a. *Walking naked: women, society, spirituality in South India.* Shimla: Indian Institute of Advanced Study.

——1997b. 'The Kudi in Early Tamilham and the Tamil Women from Tribe to Caste', in Dev Nathan (ed.) *From Tribe to Caste,* pp. 223-246. Shimla: Indian Institute for Advanced Studies.

Ramdas, Sagari. R. 2000. 'The How of Engendering the Veterinary Curriculum . . . Some Reflections,' in Sunita Rabindranathan (ed.) *Engendering Undergraduate Agricultural Education: A Resource Guide,* pp 31-33. Proceedings of Brainstorming Workshop, Chennai, 16-17 December 1999. Chennai: M. S. Swaminathan Research Foundation.

Ramdas, Sagari R., Nitya S. Ghotge et. al. 2004. 'Overcoming Gender Barriers: Local Knowledge Systems and Animal Health Healing in Andhra Pradesh and Maharashtra,' in Sumi Krishna (ed.) pp. 67-91. Op. cit.

Ranadive-Deshmukh, Joy 1994. 'Gender Implications of Adjustment Policy Programmes in India: of the Household'. *Economic and Political Weekly.* 20 April.

Rangan, Haripriya. 2000. *Of Myths and Movements: Rewriting Chipko into Himalayan History,* London: Verso Press.

Rani, Geetha and M.S. Swaminathan. 1998. 'Biodiversity in India: Heritage and Management' in M.S. Swaminathan (ed.) *Gender Dimensions in Biodiversity Management,* pp. 4-22. New Delhi: Konark.

Rao, Anupama. 2003. ed. *Gender and Caste.* New Delhi: Kali for Women.

Rao, Nitya. 2004. 'Enhancing Women's Mobility:Transport and Gender Relations in the Santal Parganas, Jharkhand.', in Sumi Krishna (ed.) pp. 248-274. Op. cit.

——2005. 'Gender, Equality, Land Rights and Household Food : Discussion of Rice Farming Systems', *Economic and Political Weekly.* Vol. XL. No. 25: 2509-2513.

Rao, Rukmini. 'Backlash Against Dalit Women Creating Food Security In Rural India: Myopia Or Another Chapter Of Caste And Gender Discrimination?' http://home.vicnet.net.au/~globalsn/raoart.htm

Ravishankar T. 1994. 'Tribal Women and their Contribution for Biodiversity Conservation.' Background paper, Workshop on 'Women Biodiversity and Seed Industries.' Chennai: M.S. Swaminathan Research Foundation.

Reed, Evelyn. 1975. *Women's Evolution: From Matriarchal Clan to Patriarchal Family.* New York: Pathfinder Press.

———1978. *Sexism and Science.* New York: Pathfinder Press.

Reid, Roddey and Sharon Traweek (eds.) 2000. *Doing Science + Culture.* New York and London: Routledge.

Rich, Adrienne. 1976. *Of Woman Born: Motherhood as Experience and Institution.* London: Virago.

Richaria, R.H. and S. Govindaswami 1990. *Rices of India.* Kashell, Maharashtra: Academy of Development Science. (First edition 1966.)

Rocheleau, Diane, Esther Wangari, Barbara Thomas-Slayeter (eds.) 1996. *Feminist Political Ecology: Global Issues and Local Experiences.* London: Routledge.

Rogers, Barbara. 1980. *The Domestication of Women: Discrimination in Developing Societies.* London: Tavistock Publications.

Rose, Steven, R.C. Lewontin and Leo Kamin. 1984/ 1990. *Not in Our Genes: Biology, Ideology and Human Nature.* London: Penguin Books. (First published as Leowntin, Rose and Kamin 1984. New York: Pantheon.)

Roy, Kumkum. 1987. 'Perceptions of Prehistory: Gatherers, Hunters and Painters of the Deccan' (Typescript). New Delhi. Cited in Nathan Dev. 1997. Op. cit.

Roy, Shibani and S.H.M. Rizvi. 1990. *Tribal Customary Laws of North-East India.* New Delhi: B.R. Publishers.

Runte, Alfred. 1979. *National Parks: The American Experience.* Lincoln and London: University of Nebraska Press.

Rustagi, Preet. 1998. *Ranking of Districts in Terms of Indicators of Women's Status.* New Delhi: Central Social Welfare Board.

———2002. *Gender Development Indicators: District Level Analysis for the Eastern Region.* Occasional Paper No. 36. New Delhi: Centre for Women's Development Studies.

———2003. *Gender Biases and Discrimination Against Women: What do different indicators say?* New Delhi: CWDS and UNIFEM.

Sahlins, Marshall. 1971. *Stone Age Economics,* Chicago: Aldine Artherton

Saikia, Anuva. 2000. 'Employment Patterns of Rural Women and Their Involvement in Decision-Making: A Study in Jorhat district of Assam', in *Women in Agriculture and Rural Development.* Proceedings of the Workshop, pp. 44-53. New Delhi: Indian Society of Agricultural Economics. 9-10 November.

Sainath. P. 1996. *Everybody Loves a Good Drought: Stories from India's Poorest Districts.* Penguin.

Saloi, B. and K. A. Singh. 2002. 'Food habits, cultural heritage and agriculture in Arunachal Pradesh,' pp. 216-233. in K.A. Singh. (ed.). Op. cit.

Sardamoni, K. 1988. *Filling the Rice Bowl.* Hyderabad: Sangam Books.

Sarin, Madhu. 1993. 'Wasteland Development and the Empowerment of Women: The SARTHI Experience' *SEEDS*. No. 16.

Sarin, Madhu with Lipika Ray, Manju S. Raju, Mitali Chatterjee, Narayan Banerjee and Shyamala Hiremath. 1998. *Who is Gaining? Who is Losing? Gender and Equity Concerns in Joint Forest Management*. New Delhi: Society for the Promotion of Wastelands Development. (booklet)

Sarkar, Jayanta 2002. 'Ecological Adaptation among the Tribes of Arunachal Pradesh,' in Sarthak Sengupta (ed.) pp. 109-115. New Delhi: Mittal Publications.

Sarkar, Niranjan. 1980. *Buddhism among the Monpas and Sherdukpens*. Shillong: Directorate of Information and Public Relations, Arunachal Pradesh.

Sathyamurthy, T.V. 1996. 'Introduction', in T. V. Sathymurthy (ed.) *Class Formation and Political Transformation in Post-Colonial India*, (series on *Social Change and Political Discourse in India: Structures of Power, Movements of Resistance*. (vol. 4) New Delhi: Oxford University Press.

Saxena, N.C. 1995. 'Gender and Forestry', *The Administrator*, Missouri: Lal Bahadur Shastri National Academy of Administration, August. pp. 71-92

——1997. *The Saga of Participatory Management in India*. Jakarta: Centre for International Forestry Research in India.

Saxena, N.C. and Madhu Sarin. 1999. 'The Western Ghats Forestry and Environment Project in Karnataka: A Preliminary Assessment,' in Roger Jeffrey and Nandini Sundar (eds.) pp. 181-215. Op.cit.

Schatten, Gerald and Helen Schatten. 1984. 'The Energetic Egg'. *Medical World News* 23 51-53. (cited by Martin 1996.)

Scheibinger, Londa. 1991. 'The Private Life of Plants: Sexual Politics in Carl Linnaeus and Erasmus Darwin.' in Marina Benjamin ed. *Science and Sensibility: Gender and Scientific Enquiry.* 1780-1945. Oxford: Basil Blackwell.

——1999. *Has Feminism Changed Science?* Harvard: Harvard University Press.

Seely, Janet, Meenakshi Batra and Madhu Sarin 2000. *Women's Participation in Watershed Development in India*. Gatekeeper Series no. 92. London: IIED.

Sehgal, Rashme. 2005. 'Delhi's skewed sex ratio: "24,000 girls go missing every year" ' http://www.infochangeindia.org/features290.jsp

Sen, Amartya K. 1990. 'Gender and Cooperative Conflicts', in I. Tinker (ed.) *Persistent Inequalities: Women and World Development*. New York: Oxford University Press.

——1992. *Inequality Reexamined*. Delhi: Oxford University Press.

Sen, Gita. 1985. 'Paddy production, processing and women workers in India: The South versus the Northeast', in *Women in Rice Farming*. Proceedings of a Conference. Manila: International Rice Research Institute.

Sen, Gita and Caren Grown 1987. *Development, Crises and Alternate Visions: Third World Women's Perspectives.2nd ed.* New York: Monthly Review Press. (First edition without author's names published by DAWN 1985)

SEWA. 2005. Self Employed Women's Association. http://www.sewa.org

Seymour, Susanne. 2000. 'Historical geographies of landscape', in Brian Graham and Catherine Nash (eds.) *Modern Historical Geographies*. pp. 193-217. Harlow, UK: Pearson Education Ltd.

Shah, Amita. 2000. 'Natural Resource Management and Gender: Reflections from Watershed Programmes in India.' *Indian Journal of Gender Studies*, 7 (1): 86-90.

Shah, Haku and Geeti Sen 1992. 'Maati: Born from the Earth' in Geeti Sen ed. *Indigenous Vision: Peoples of India, Attitudes to the Environment.* pp. 129-144. New Delhi: India International Centre.

Sharma, B.D. 2002. 'Crop Genetic Resources of Arunachal Pradesh', in. K. A. Singh (ed.) pp. 1-8. Op. cit.

Sharma, Kumud. 2000. 'Perspectives on Gender, Poverty and Environmental Connections under Economic Reforms in India' in CWDS (eds.) *Shifting Sands: Women's Lives and Globalization,* pp. 141-172. Calcutta: Stree.

Sharma, Manorama. 2004. 'Women in the Ahom Economy: Some Texts Re-examined', *Proceedings of North East India History Association (*22nd Session). Shillong: NEHU and NEIHA.

Sharma, R. R. P. 1961. *The Sherdukpens.* Shillong: Directorate of Information and Public Relations, Arunachal Pradesh.

Sharma, S.D., Smita Tripathy and Pratima Gurung. 1998. 'Jeypore Tract, Orissa,' in M.S. Swaminathan (ed.) pp. 108-122. Op. cit.

Shimray, R.R.. 1985. *Origin and Culture of Nagas.* New Delhi: Pamleiphi Shimray.

Shimray, U.A. 2004. 'Women's Work in Naga Society: Household Work, Workforce Participation and Division of Labour.' *Economic and Political Weekly.* 24 April: 1698-1710.

Shiva, Vandana. 1988. *Staying Alive in India: Women, ecology and survival in India.* London: Kali for Women.

Shrestha, Nanda. 1995. 'Becoming a Development Category' in Jonathan Crush (ed). *Power of Development.* London and New York: Routledge.

Smith, David. 2001. 'Communicating Tacit Knowledge across cultures: a multimedia archive of the Bankura Dhokra craft industry of West Bengal as a case of the artificial'. Working Paper Series No: WP/EU-IN/2001/15.

Simpson, G.G. 1958. 'The study of evolution: Methods and present status of theory' and 'Behaviour and evolution' in Anne Roe and G.G. Simpson eds. *Behaviour and Evolution.* New Haven: Yale University Press.

Singh, B.N., S.K. Rautray, K. Pande and P.C. Rath 'Towards Rice Self-Sufficiency in North Eastern India.' http://www.icar.org.in/ncap/publications/workshopprocedd/wsp10/pdf/

Singh, Neera M. 2004. 'Women and Community Forests in Orissa: Rights and Management', in Sumi Krishna (ed.), pp. 306-324. Op.cit.

Singh, K.A. (ed.) 2002. *Resource Management Perspective of Arunachal Pradesh.* Basar: ICAR Research Complex for NEH Region, Arunachal Pradesh Centre.

Singh, K.A. and T.K. Bag. 2002. 'Indigenous technical know how relevant to farming systems of Arunachal Pradesh', in K.A. Singh (ed.) pp. 234-267. Op. cit.

Singh, K.S. 2001. 'Gender Roles in History: Women as Hunters.' *Gender, Technology and Development.* 5 (1) : 113-124.

Singh. K. S. (ed.). 1995. *Peoples of India* (Vol. XXIII: People of Mizoram), Calcutta: Anthropological Survey of India and Seagull Publications.

———2003. *Peoples of India* (Vol. XV. Parts One and Two: People of Assam), Calcutta: Anthropological Survey of India and Seagull Publications.

Sinha, A.C. 1998. 'Social Stratification among the Tribes of North-East India,' in Bhupinder Singh (ed.) *Antiquity to Modernity in Tribal India: Vol. II- Tribal Self Management in North Eastern India,* pp. 198-200. New Delhi: Inter-India Publications.

Sinha, Raghuvir 1962. *The Akas.* Shillong: Directorate of Information and Public Relations, Arunachal Pradesh.

Snow, Rachel. 2002. 'Reorienting Public Health: Exploring Differentials in Hip Fracture' in Gita Sen, Asha George and Piroska Ostlin eds. *Engendering International Health,* pp. 167-194. Cambridge, Mass. : The MIT Press.

Sperling, Susan 1991. 'Baboons with Briefcases: Feminism, Functionalism, and Sociobiology in the Evolution of Primate Gender.' *Signs: Journal of Women in Culture and Society.* 17: 1 (reprinted 1996 in Laslett, Barbara, Sally Gregory Kohlstedt, Helen Longino, and Evelynn Hammonds (ed.) *Gender and Scientific Authority.* Chicago: University of Chicago press.)

———1999. 'Foreword' to Ashley Montagu. pp. 12-40. Op. cit.

Spretnak, Charlene. 1990. in Karen J Warren (ed.) Op. cit.

Sridharan, Sumi. 1975. (see also Krishna, Sumi.) 'In Chhatera, Maya, Bhim Kaur and Chalti', *Indian Farming,* 25(8): 43-46.

Srivastava, L.R.N. 1988. *The Gallongs.* Itanagar: Directorate of Research, Government of Arunachal Pradesh.

———1973. *Among the Wanchos of Arunachal Pradesh.* Itanagar: Directorate of Research, Government of Arunachal Pradesh.

Subba, T.R. and G.C. Ghosh (eds.) *The Anthropology of North East India.* Hyderabad: Orient Longman.

Subrahmanyan, Lalita. 1998. *Women Scientists in the Third World: The Indian Experience,* New Delhi: Sage Publications.

Sujaya, C.P. 1995. 'Women's Rights and Development Policies in India', *The Administrator,* (Mussoorie: Lal Bahadur Shastri Academy of Administration). 13-26. August.

Sur, Abha. 2001. 'Dispersed Radiance: Women Scientists in C.V. Raman's Laboratory.' in *Meridians: feminism, race, transnationalism.* 1 (2): 95-127.

Swaminathan, M.S. 1975. Foreword to *Indian Farming* (Special issue on Women in Farming).

———2001a. 'Biovillages: A Blue print for the future?' *Unesco Courier.* January

———2001b. 'Antyodaya Approach to Bridging the Genetic, Gender and Digital Divides', Address to Discussion on 'Ideas that have worked'. New Delhi: Government of India, Ministry of Personnel. 21 March.

Swaminathan, M.S. (ed.) 1998. *Gender Dimensions in Biodiversity Management.* New Delhi: Konark.

Tamil Nadu State Environment and Forest Department website: www.forests.tn.nic.in

Tedlock, Dennis and Bruce Mannheim eds. 1995. *The Dialogic Emergence of Culture,* Urbana, US: University of Illinois Press.

Tewari-Jassal, Smita 2004. 'Limits of Empowerment: Mallahin Fishponds in Madhubani, Bihar', in Sumi Krishna (ed.) pp. 412-424. Op. cit.

Thakur, A.C., Ashok Bhattacharyya and D.K. Sarma. 2001. *Agriculture in Assam*. Jorhat: Assam Agriculture University, Directorate of Extension Education.

Thamizoli, P. 1997. 'Gender Inequality, Tribal and Caste Women: Past and Present: A Case Study of the Nilgiris, Tamil Nadu', *Man in India*, 77 (1): 51-62.

Thamizoli, P. and the MSSRF Team. 2004. 'Mainstreaming Gender Concerns in Mangrove Conservation and Management: The Pichavaram Coast, Tamil Nadu', in Sumi Krishna (ed.) pp. 92-108. Op. cit.

Thamizoli, P. and V. Sudarsen. 1998. *Ethnographic Profile of the Irula of Pichavaram, Cuddalore District, Tamil Nadu: A Tool to Find Out Tribal Identity.* Chidambaram: M.S.S.R.F. (mimeo)

Thansanga, R. 1997. *New Contour Farming System*. Aizawl: Directorate of Agriculture and Minor Irrigation, Government of Mizoram.

Tiger, Lionel. 1969. *Men in Groups*. New York: Random House Inc. (Republished 1984 New York: Marion Boyars Publications Inc.

——1970. 'Male Dominance? Yes. Alas. A Sexist Plot? No.' *New York Times Magazine*. 25 October.

UNDP 1980. *Rural Women's Participation in Development*. New York: United Nations Development Programme.

UNESCO 1952. *The Race Concept: Results of an Inquiry.* Paris: United Nations Educational, Scientific and Cultural Organization.

Unger, Rhoda K. 1990. *Resisting Gender: Twenty-five Years of Feminist Psychology.* London, Thousand Oaks California, New Delhi: Sage Publications.

United Nations. 1985. *The Nairobi Forward Looking Strategies for the Advancement of Women, Nairobi.* http://www.un-documents.net/nflsaw.htm

—— 1995. *Platform for Action and the Beijing Declaration.* Fourth World Conference on Women, Beijing, China 14-15 September. New York. UN Department of Public Information.

United Nations Environment Programme. 1992. *Agenda 21.* United Nations Conference on Environment and Development, 'Earth Summit'. Rio de Janeiro. Brazil. http://www.unep.org/Documents.multilingual/Default.asp?DocumentID=52

——1992. *International Convention on Biological Diversity* 1992. United Nations Conference on Environment and Development, 'Earth Summit'. Rio de Janeiro. Brazil.

Vagholikar, Neeraj and M. Firoz Ahmed. 2003. 'Tracking a Hydel Project: the Story of Lower Subansiri' *The Ecologist Asia.* 11(1): 25-32.

Vedavalli, L. 1998. 'Kolli hills, Tamil Nadu', Case Study in Swaminathan (ed.), pp. 107-122. Op. cit.

Vedavalli, L and Arun Kumar. 1998. 'Wayanad, Kerala', Case Study in Swaminathan (ed.) pp. 96-106. Op. cit.

Vijayalakshmi, B. and R.S.S. Hopper. 2000. 'Hybrid rice—a biovillage experience' in 'International Rice Research Notes'. Manila: International Rice Research

Institute http://www.irri.org/publications/irrn/pdfs/vol25no3/IRRN25-3Socioeco.pdf.

Visanathan, Shiv. 1993. 'Autobiography as the Experiment' 1993. ('Our Scientists') *Seminar.* 409: 12-15.

Visvanath, Ramya. 2003. Sacred Groves in *Down to Earth.* December.

Wajcman, Judy. 1991. *Feminism Confronts Technology.* University Park: Pennyslyvania State University.

Warren, Karen J. (ed.) 1994. *Ecological Feminism.* London: Routledge

Washburn, Sherwood L. and C.S. Lancaster 1968. 'The evolution of hunting'. in Lee and DeVore (ed.) *Man the Hunter,* pp. 229-303. New York: Aldine.

WCED. 1990. *Our Common Future,* Report of the World Commission on environment and Development. New Delhi: Oxford University Press.

Webster, Juliet. 1996. *Shaping Women's Work: Gender, Employment and Information Technology.* London: Longman.

Whitehead, Judy. 2003. 'Space, place and primitive accumulation in the Narmada Valley and beyond'. *Economic and Political Weekly.* Perspectives: 4 October.

Wickramasinghe, Anoja. 2004. 'Gender and Ecological Sustainability: The Traditions and Wisdom of the Local Communities in a Dry Zone, Sri Lanka', in Sumi Krishna (ed.), pp. 171-192. Op. cit.

Williams, George C. 1975. *Sex and Evolution.* Princeton: Princeton University Press.

Wilson, E.O 1975a. *Sociobiology: The New Synthesis.* Cambridge, Mass: Harvard University Press.

——1975 b. 'Human Decency is Animal' *New York Times Magazine.* 12 October.

——1978. *On Human Nature.* Cambridge, Mass: Harvard University Press.

Woolf, Virginia 1928. (republished) 1945. *A Room of One's Own.* Hammondsworth, UK: Penguin Books.

Zehol, Lucy V. (ed.) 1998. *Women in Naga Society.* New Delhi: Regency Publications.

——2003. 'Status of Tribal Women', pp. 293-306 in T.R. Subba and G.C. Ghosh (eds.) (op. cit.) *The Anthropology of North East India.* Hyderabad: Orient Longman.

Zilhman, Adrienne and Nancy Tanner. 1978. 'Gathering and the hominid adaptation', in Lionel Tiger and Heather Fowler (eds.) *Female Hierarchies,* pp. 163-194. Chicago: Beresford Books.

Index

409, 411, 413, 414
biodiversity. *See* biological diversity
Biodiversity Act (2003), 158
    gender and, 348*ff*
Biodiversity Management Committees,
    350
biological determinism/biologism, 48,
    384–85, 392–93
biological diversity (biodiversity), 11, 56,
    105, 140, 208, 214, 254, 334, 384
    conservation, gendered approach,
        10, 18, 140*ff*
    heritage sites, 350
    management, 278, 296, 404;
        women in, 344–5
biological
    capacity for reproduction, 46, 102–
        03
    characteristics, 40
    explanations for sex differences, 44
    factors, 70
    heritage of women, 328
    sex differences, 23, 40–41, 333
biology, 89, 98–9, 100, 102, 327
    and culture, 86
    of women, 72, 81, 102, 277
bio-pesticides, 225, 226, 227
biophysics of egg and sperm, 90–91
biopower, 386
biotechnology, 99, 224, 385
biovillages, 208, 224–26, 385, 410
Birhor tribe, 37
Birke, Lynda, 41
birth control, 313
birthing, 69
Bishnois, 155
Bleir, Ruth, 46, 106
body, 40-41, 385–86
Bolangir district, Orissa, 217
Borbaruah village, Assam, 175
Boserup, Esther (*Women's Role in Eco-
    nomic Development)* 60
botanical
    nomenclature, 92
    taxonomy, 92

and zoological taxonomy, 89
Botanical Survey of India, 141, 344
Brahmanical
    Hinduism, 35, 49
    patriarchy. *See* patriarchy
Brahmaputra, river and valley, 167, 170,
    180, 186, 187
Braidotti, Rosi, 71
Brandis, Dietrich, 243
bride price, 116, 178
British administration
    colonial system of revenue collec-
        tion, 244
    Meitei tradeswomen's war against,
        320, 339–40
Bruegel, Pieter Paul, 300
Brundtland Commission. *See* World
    Commission on Environment and
    Development
Buddhism, Buddhist, 29, 177, 189
    Neo-Buddhist, 392
Bundgaard, Helle, 358
bureaucracy, 216, 291

C
Canadian International Development
    Agency (CIDA), 215, 263
capitalism, 31, 33, 248, 386, 389, 407,
    409, 420
capitalist exploitation, 409
caring and nurturing, ideologies of, 253
cash crop cultivation, 219
caste, 40, 50, 103, 240, 301, 339, 391–
    2
    and community, gendered role, 15,
        23
    and kin networks, 244
    boundaries, 282
    domination, 38, 333
    hierarchy, 27–8, 283
    oppression, 263
    panchayat mafias, 229
    structure and gender, 386, 387,
        388. *See also* class. Dalit
cause and effect, 387, 392

gender concerns, 105
gender continuum, 409
gender development index (GDI), 404
gender differentiation, 30, 93, 262, 298
gender dimension of disasters, 52
gender dimensions of resource usage, 247
gender dimensions, 403–4
gender discourse, 402
gender discrimination, 304
gender disparities and dimensions of development in North-eastern India, 180–85
gender disparity, 163, 188
gender division of domestic labour, 53
gender egalitarianism, 8, 179
gender equality/equity, 7, 79, 241, 242, 247, 262, 332, 413, 418
constitutional commitment, 5
implications, 61–5
and political participation, 12
in tribal communities, 184
gender gap, 404
gender hierarchies, 87, 92, 93, 283, 293
gender ideologies, 28–40, 45, 53, 58, 75, 88, 163, 240, 275–6, 277, 280–95, 386, 394, 403, 404, 407, 416
implication, 48–54
in rice farming groups of North-eastern India, 164–80
gender impact assessment, 267–8
gender inequality/inequity, 14, 35, 276, 382
in tribal societies, 177
gender justice, 76, 77, 289
gender mainstreaming *See* mainstreaming
gender needs, 263
gender oppression, 263
gender perspective and approaches, 55*ff,* 300, 403, 404–5
gender planning, 71
Gender and Tribe, 8
Gender Planning and Development: Theory, Practice and Training, 71

gender power relations, 39, 240, 252, 264, 280, 283, 284, 287, 289, 300, 303, 305, 405, 406, 407, 408, 415
in natural resource management, 8–15, 16–19, 56, 253–4, 275–6, 294–5
gender relations, 26–27, 58, 59, 63, 64, 70, 76–77, 80, 188, 228, 264, 276, 277, 285, 301–02, 362, 405
changing through lift-irrigation, 235–6
in tribal societies, 360–61, 364–75
women's collectivity and, 290–5
gender responsiveness, 76
gender role
and behaviour, 252
differentiation and gender relations, implications, 48, 262
and identities, 386, 390
and labour, 169–75
and resource, 48–9
responsibilities and resource usage, 302
stereotyped, 12, 25, 298
gender sensitivity, 233, 369'
gender socialization, 34
gendered sources of information and decision-making, 50–4
on disasters, 50
gender structures natural science, 90
gender studies, 4, 90, 102, 409
gender training, 71
gendered bargaining, 264
gendered behaviour, 265
gendered knowledge
in science and social science, 100
and skills, 166–69
gendered life worlds, 135
gendered natural science, 103
gendered space, 259, 406, 416
gendering of life experiences, perceptions and behaviour, 47
genderscapes, 276, 302 *ff,* 406
genes and the new hero stories, 98–102